AUTISM SPECTRUM DISORDER *in the* CANADIAN CONTEXT

AUTISM SPECTRUM DISORDER *in the* CANADIAN CONTEXT

An Introduction

Kimberly Maich, Sharon C. Penney,
Kelly Alves, and Carmen Hall

CANADIAN SCHOLARS
Toronto | Vancouver

Autism Spectrum Disorder in the Canadian Context: An Introduction
Kimberly Maich, Sharon C. Penney, Kelly Alves, and Carmen Hall

First published in 2020 by

Canadian Scholars, an imprint of CSP Books Inc.
425 Adelaide Street West, Suite 200
Toronto, Ontario
M5V 3C1

www.canadianscholars.ca

Library and Archives Canada Cataloguing in Publication

Title: Autism spectrum disorder in the Canadian context : an introduction / Kimberly Maich, Sharon C. Penney, Kelly Alves, and Carmen Hall.
Names: Maich, Kimberly, 1969- author. | Penney, Sharon C., 1959- author. | Alves, Kelly, 1977- author. | Hall, Carmen, author.
Description: Includes bibliographical references and index.
Identifiers: Canadiana (print) 20200259725 | Canadiana (ebook) 2020025989X | ISBN 9781773382012 (softcover) | ISBN 9781773382029 (PDF) | ISBN 9781773382036 (EPUB)
Subjects: LCSH: Autism spectrum disorders. | LCSH: Autism spectrum disorders—Canada. | LCSH: Autism spectrum disorders—Treatment—Canada.
Classification: LCC RC553.A88 M35 2020 | DDC 616.85/882—dc23

Cover art by Grace Culliton, *Dandelion Seeds*. Grace was diagnosed with autism at the age of five. Her artwork is characterized by an exuberant use of colour. *Dandelion Seeds* is an original monoprint.
Cover design by Rafael Chimicatti
Page layout by S4Carlisle Publishing Services

20 21 22 23 24 5 4 3 2 1

Printed and bound in Ontario, Canada

Contents

Preface

The publication of this book was supported by a grant from Memorial University's Publication Subvention Program.

Autism spectrum disorder (ASD) has a remarkably complex history, from being misunderstood as a form of schizophrenia to its current recognition as a complex spectrum disorder, allowing for multiple levels of functioning and individuality. However, these issues present themselves as heterogeneous—they are widely variable from person to person. ASD can be described as "characterized by impairments in social communication and the presence of restricted and repetitive behaviours" (Veatch, Veenstra-VanderWheele, Potter, Pericak-Vance, & Haines, 2014, p. 276). Throughout its ever-changing history, we, the authors (Kimberly Maich, Sharon C. Penney, Kelly Alves, and Carmen Hall), have noted not only that ASD is recognized for its clinical and educational implications but also that it has become a common topic in the popular media. We often see ASD highlighted in local newspapers, nightly news, and new television shows. When we ask someone about ASD, most people *now* have a somewhat personal connection with the disorder or a son, daughter, other relative, friend, or acquaintance with ASD. Indeed, both Kimberly Maich and Sharon C. Penney themselves have adult sons with ASD. This increased cultural consciousness, while helpful for raising awareness, can lead to misconceptions and stereotypes about causes, behaviour, interventions, services, and more. In our professional lives and our personal experiences, we see this more often than not, and we find that the wide diversity of Canadian families, educators, and clinicians are often seeking not only information but the right *kind* of information applicable to their individual settings and situations.

Autism Spectrum Disorder in the Canadian Context was written to provide a wide perspective of ASD across our broad, diverse nation, including its historical roots and an explanation of the current diagnostic criteria, which we believe is critical to understanding its nature. By highlighting this information, we hope that the many misconceptions can be dispelled and the true picture of ASD across Canada can be understood. The varied snapshots within the Canadian context provide local understandings of how the development of knowledge about the disorder has influenced Canadian government policies, procedures, and services. Section I examines this historical context of ASD, both in general and specifically to Canada, while examining some common misconceptions and pseudoscience that has been highlighted with false claims to "cure autism," among other things. We have also built this book on the foundation of evidence-based practice and evidence-based interventions (EBIs), terms commonly used in the field to demonstrate that interventions and their claims are founded on empirical, controlled research. This foundation is essential for protecting those in the ASD community, whether we are intervening, teaching, parenting, or simply living in the world. Section II, then, focuses on a summary of effective interventions. These interventions are separated into three areas: social communication–based interventions, behaviour-based interventions, and the sensory profile and interventions (the latter being an emerging area of research included in diagnostic exemplars only since 2013). An overview of EBIs is provided, along with how they have been classified in various evidence-based intervention summary projects for persons with ASD, as well as common strategies in the research literature that support these individuals in these three main areas. Locating all this information in one place is essential for anyone working with individuals with ASD; therefore, we have been careful to feature multiple Canadian examples, research, policy, practice, interventions, and more whenever possible throughout the book.

Section III examines ASD across the lifespan. In focusing this section on the lifespan from childhood to adulthood and on services from childcare centres to supports for adults with ASD, we have underscored the different needs of individuals with ASD at every age. In addition, we have highlighted services and funding models for each age group and area of interest. Although these will differ provincially (and even intraprovincially) throughout Canada, we have included major services and funding sources mandated consistently by the provincial governments. Where there are still gaps in services, we have presented creative ideas and unique models from regional centres, as well as models of support and services to assist families of individuals with ASD. We hope this approach will provide a sense of the continuity of services and experiences—both helpful and challenging—that individuals with ASD and their families, and those who support them, face across the lifespan. Finally, it is important to realize that publicly available policy, practice, and other documentation—even peer-reviewed research studies—may contrast what is happening on the front lines of the ASD field with students, clients, families, educators, and clinicians.

Given the diversity in the ASD population and the rocky history of diagnosis, acceptance, and accurate portrayal of effective interventions, many critical issues, debates, and gaps in services remain. Section IV examines 10 critical issues in ASD in the Canadian context from recent court cases, media coverage, and programs, research, and perspectives from leaders in the field. The goal of this section is to highlight the current debates and issues that remain and provide the reader with an opportunity to critically reflect on their perspective on these issues.

Lastly, but just as importantly, we recognize that many adults in the ASD community prefer identity-first language around ASD (i.e., *autistic*). This book is written with person-first language (e.g., child with autism), reflecting what is commonly understood as best practice in the fields where beginning educators and clinicians reside; yet we acknowledge the important, growing, and essential trend toward honouring and utilizing identity-first language. Our chapter focused on the adult years is written in identity-first language whenever possible (Dunn & Andrews, 2015).

Throughout the book, three main themes are emphasized: the emerging nature of the field of ASD; the importance of using evidence-based interventions in clinical, school, and community-based interventions; and the importance of supporting individuals with ASD across the lifespan.

Additionally, it highlights various Canadian-based practices, resources, and research with featured examples from Canada's 3 territories and 10 provinces (Alberta, British Columbia, Manitoba, New Brunswick, Newfoundland and Labrador, Northwest Territories, Nova Scotia, Nunavut, Ontario, Prince Edward Island, Quebec, Saskatchewan, and Yukon) when possible, available, and relevant. For example, although Chapter 3 relies on definitions of—and a framework for—EBIs from a broader North American base of research, it is supplemented with provincial examples of practices, resources, and research related to the use of EBIs in the Canadian context.

Each chapter features a range of figures, tables, definitions, and questions designed to deepen understanding and elicit reflection on the topics presented through supporting literature in the ASD field. In addition, most chapters include multiple feature boxes, with detailed perspectives provided by members of Canada's ASD community.

ABOUT THE AUTHORS

Dr. Kimberly Maich, PhD, OCT, BCBA-D, is a professor at Memorial University in the Faculty of Education, in St. John's, Newfoundland and Labrador. She is also a registered psychologist (provisional; master's level). Her teaching, research, and writing are typically focused around school-based special/inclusive education, specifically related to students with ASD. She has worked in the field of ASD as a teacher, professor, clinician, and parent since 1998.

Dr. Sharon C. Penney, PhD, R Psych, is an associate professor at Memorial University in the Faculty of Education, in St. John's, Newfoundland and Labrador, and a registered psychologist. She focuses her research and writing on mental health and exceptionalities.

Kelly Alves, MEd, BCBA, is a professor of behavioural science at Seneca College in King City, Ontario, and a PhD student in leadership and higher education at the Ontario Institute for Studies in Education (OISE) at the University of Toronto. She has extensive experience delivering and supervising behavioural services for children and teenagers with ASD. She strongly believes in the positive outcomes associated with group-based education for parents and enjoys educating parents, students, and professionals on applied behaviour analysis (ABA) and its many benefits.

Dr. Carmen Hall, PhD, BCBA-D, is the coordinator and a professor in the Autism & Behavioural Science Graduate Certificate Program at Fanshawe College in London, Ontario. She has worked with children with ASD in a number of different environments, including the school setting and intensive behavioural intervention (IBI). She has also been involved in consulting roles at schools and in clinical environments.

Her research has focused on social skills research, including peer-mediated social skills in childcare, school, and camp settings. For a number of years, her focus has been on skill-building and quality of life for adults with developmental disabilities.

Acknowledgements

Kimberly Maich: Thank you to my ever-patient and grown-up family: John, my husband of almost 30 years; my son, Robert (who taught me a great deal about ASD); my daughter Grace and her husband Mark; my daughter Hannah and her partner Steven; and adorable Quincey, my first grandchild. They are the prime motivators for all of life's events, including this book. The contributions of Shelley McLean deserve special mention, as well as the work of our publisher, editor, research assistants, and the many parents, professionals, and clinicians who contributed their valuable ideas.

Sharon C. Penney: Thank you to my family: my husband David, my daughters Heather and Julia, and my son Mark. It has been a special privilege to watch my grandson, Owen, grow and thrive throughout this process. My biggest thanks are to my son, Mark. He has been the most effective teacher in things related to autism. As a young child, he helped me learn and grow as a parent; as an adult, he has articulated what it has been like to live with autism. Thank you, Mark, for your insider knowledge.

Kelly Alves: Thank you to my husband and best friend, Jason; my beautiful daughter, Ellsa; and my inquisitive son, Dean, for their patience and understanding during this project. I also wish to thank the many wonderful families, students, and professionals that I have had the privilege to work with, and learn alongside, throughout this process.

Carmen Hall: Thank you to all the incredible mentors, students, and persons that I have been involved with in my career who have provided me with consistent motivation and inspiration for my research and passion in the field of ASD. Thanks are especially needed for my family (who has continued to stand by me unconditionally), including my husband Tony, and my son and daughter, Julian and Mikayla.

SECTION I

An Introduction to Autism Spectrum Disorder

Section I highlights the historical context leading to the naming and diagnosis of autism spectrum disorder (ASD) and how evidence-based interventions (EBIs) have come to be a primary, essential component in the ASD field. Chapter 1 focuses first on the historical context of how autism and Asperger's disorder characteristics were first discovered and how the classification and diagnosis of ASD changed through revisions to the *Diagnostic and Statistical Manual of Mental Disorders* (DSM) to the current version of the DSM-5. Chapter 2 highlights pseudoscience and "cures" that were presented to parents of children with ASD, which has led to a number of committees and reports that summarize research and categorize strategies into established EBIs, emerging interventions, and unestablished interventions. The procedures for establishing if an intervention is evidence-based, as well as an overview of the various interventions, are reviewed for the reader. Lastly, highlights across jurisdictions and their use of EBIs are presented to provide the reader with an overview of how these interventions are used across Canada.

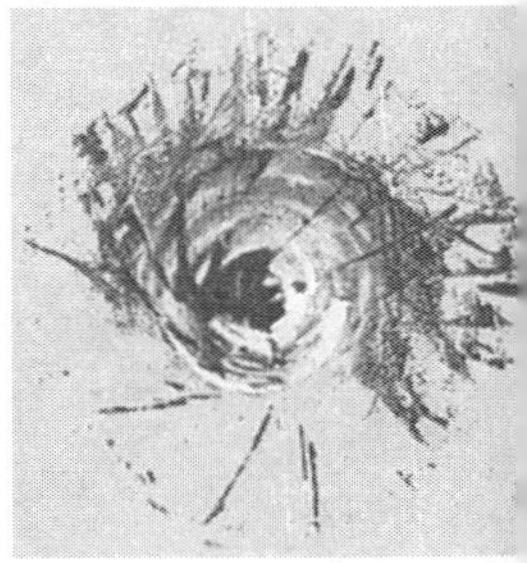

CHAPTER 1

Brief History of Autism Spectrum Disorder

LEARNING OBJECTIVES

- Recall highlights of ASD research and understanding from its first recognition, including the work of some influential pioneers in the field (e.g., Hans Asperger and Leo Kanner).
- Discuss the elasticity of terminology in the field of ASD over time.
- Discuss perspectives on ASD found in the media, including what everyday mass media teaches about ASD.
- State the definition and importance of self-advocacy.
- Identify recent service provision initiatives for those with ASD in the context of school and community, including resources, publications, research, and more.

This chapter provides a brief historical examination of autism spectrum disorder (ASD). First, some of the pioneering contributors to the field are introduced, those responsible for astutely observing individuals in their practices and subsequently constructing the characteristics and diagnostic criteria of ASD itself. Then those responsible for developing effective interventions and those part of historical controversy as our knowledge of ASD developed are highlighted. This chapter introduces Leo Kanner, Hans Asperger, Bruno Bettelheim, Lorna Wing, and O. Ivar Lovaas. These individuals and their contributions do not represent a comprehensive examination of the field of ASD and its history but rather highlight some individuals with notable influence. The chapter includes some key moments in the recent history of service provision for individuals and students with ASD. It also includes information about services and educational provisions in school systems and beyond. It examines directives and initiatives, research, publications, and various resources.

Next, this chapter traces the journey from the first described characteristics of autistic disorder to the current diagnostic criteria contained in the fifth edition of the *Diagnostic and Statistical Manual of Mental Disorders* (DSM-5). The text focuses on recent and current definitions of ASD, as presented in the two most recent editions of the DSM, and recent changes in their diagnostic criteria.

Finally, highlights of jurisdictional clinical ASD services, supports, and issues (including diagnostic pathways), and intensive behavioural intervention services are presented. The chapter closes with a discussion of media-based perspectives on ASD, including what everyday mass media teaches its audience about ASD, emphasizing the importance of advocacy in today's field.

CONTRIBUTORS TO THE FIELD OF AUTISM SPECTRUM DISORDER

Leo Kanner and Hans Asperger

Although some controversy remains about the identity of the primary figure who first recognized autism (Chown, 2012), infantile autism, or early infantile autism as a distinct diagnostic category, highly influential early contributors in the field include Leo Kanner and Hans Asperger, both working in the 1940s. Wing and Potter (2002), for example, referred to Kanner and Asperger this way: "Of all the early workers in this field, Leo Kanner in the USA and Hans Asperger in Austria are the only ones whose names are now legitimately famous" (p. 152). Often referenced as the "two pioneers of autism" (Lyons & Fitzgerald, 2007, p. 2002), Asperger and Kanner each published almost simultaneous and even similar descriptions of small groups of children with consistent and unusual social and behavioural characteristics. They then differentiated such children from those with the previously well-known diagnosis of childhood schizophrenia (Blacher & Christensen, 2011; Neumärker, 2003). Kanner's early writing was entitled *Autistic Disturbances of Affective Contact* (1943), and Asperger's early publication was named *Autistic Psychopathology in Childhood* (1944; translated in 1991 as per Pearce, 2005). Given their almost-simultaneous use of the term *autism* in the early 1940s, it is clear that neither Kanner nor Asperger truly originated it independently but rather brought this term into the wider public sphere. Kanner accomplished this more quickly than Asperger due to a range of social, cultural, and geopolitical factors occurring at the time of publication. For example, Kanner published in English (Lyons & Fitzgerald, 2007; Neumärker, 2003). Perhaps this explains why the term *Kanner syndrome* was documented quite quickly, while *Asperger's disorder*, used synonymously, did not find its way into the DSM until decades later.

child-onset schizophrenia: a rare and severe form of schizophrenia, defined by psychosis, or thoughts and beliefs that differ from reality, that appears before age 13 (Rapoport, Chavez, Greenstein, Addington, & Gogtay, 2009).

echolalia: the repetition of verbal language in an echoic manner, looping words and phrases around in a recurring way (Arora, 2012). For example, an inclusive classroom teacher says, "pretty flower," and the student with ASD repeats, "pretty flower," perhaps multiple times.

Kanner described this group of children in careful detail, following a clinical, systematic approach (Thompson, 2013). He introduced them as those who "[differ] so markedly and uniquely from anything reported so far, that each case merits ... a detailed consideration of its fascinating peculiarities" (Kanner, 1968, p. 217). Some characteristics of his *Autistic Disturbances of Affective Contact* that may be still familiar today include somewhat positive references to the cognitive capabilities of the involved children and their "cold-hearted" yet "highly intelligent families" (Neumärker, 2003, p. 207; Kanner, 1968), as well as the use of terms such as *echolalia*, *solitude*, *sameness*, *obsession*, and *stereotypy*. Following the initial work of Kanner and Asperger, little literature was published that moved the field of ASD forward in a hopeful, positive manner until the 1960s (Thompson, 2013).

Figure 1.1: Psychiatrist Leo Kanner, Pioneer of Autism

Source: Johns Hopkins University, via Wikipedia Commons.

Decades later, Blacher and Christensen (2011) published a detailed overview of Kanner's originally characterized children, along with descriptions of the characteristics Kanner had noted while claiming to develop the term himself. One of these children was referenced as Donald T. (see Table 1.1 for Kanner's description of Donald T.'s behaviour), whose father wrote extensively to Kanner and assisted with these first descriptive terms (Donvan & Zucker, 2010). Around the same time, *The Atlantic* published an article about the life of Donald Gray Triplett (also known as Donald T.) as a 77-year-old adult, more than 6 decades after Kanner's original description. This

> **stereotypy**: most commonly recognized stereotypies are motor stereotypies, which are "rhythmic movements that have a predictable pattern and location, seem purposeful but serve no obvious function, tend to be prolonged, and can be suppressed" (Thilinie & Tamara, 2010, p. 255). For example, a young girl with ASD sits at her desk in the classroom reading a book on dog breeds while repeatedly rocking her body from front to back. Other examples are waving one's hands, flapping one's arms, and nodding one's head (Thilinie & Tamara, 2010).

publication calls Triplett *autism's first child* (Donvan & Zucker, 2010) and answers the question, "What happened to Donald?" After being briefly institutionalized as a child, he was raised on a farm, went to college, and became employed. Although he was teased as a child and regarded as eccentric as an adult, he developed and sustained connections with his family and community, as well as interests and hobbies in the context of "freedom, independence and good health" (Donvan & Zucker, 2010, p. 81). Table 1.2 lists Donald Triplett's characteristics as an adult with ASD.

Table 1.1: Kanner's Original Symptoms Describing Donald T. as a Child

Kanner's Symptoms	Other: Predictive
	Donald T. (ages 1–5)
Does not look at the person while speaking	"Obsessive detail" from father's typewritten history
Does not use communicative gestures	Eating always a problem for Donald; sweets not a temptation
Not interested in playing with other children; ignores other children	Walked at 13 months
Prefers objects to people	Excellent rote memory for song lyrics, alphabet, and numbers
Father reports that he appears to "draw into his shell and live within himself." He does not seem to notice the coming or going of other people nor react to their coming with pleasure.	Had temper tantrums in which he was destructive
Does not come when called	Had difficulty associating his punishment with his behaviour
Regards other people as an interference or plays with their hands/feet as an object	Showed learning—better contact with the environment, became more imaginative over time
Delay in use of questions and ability to answer questions	Later learned to read and play the piano
Conversation obsessive in nature—inexhaustible questioning	No initiation of activities other than the limited interests in which he was absorbed; mother had to direct him in all other activities

Kanner's Symptoms	Other: Predictive
	Donald T. (ages 1–5)
Using words and sentences such as "chrysanthemum"	
Inflexible use of language	
Pronoun reversal	
A "mania" for spinning round objects	
Arranging beads, blocks, etc. in a certain manner	
Verbal rituals requiring others to repeat certain phrases during particular activities (e.g., bedtime)	
Stereotyped finger movements, shaking his head and whispering or singing the same three-note tune	
Difficulty in social communication (learning to ask and respond to questions) present at age 2	

Source: Blacher & Christensen, 2011.

Table 1.2: Characteristics of Donald T. as an Adult with ASD

Repetitive behaviours	Legendary skills
Prefers being alone	Appears content
Unusual gait	Active community life
Reliance on rituals	Engages in conversation
Conversation limited to pragmatics	Develops new skills into adulthood (e.g., driving)
Thinks concretely	Has activities, interests, and hobbies (e.g., golf)
No romantic relationships	Attended college
Needs financial support	Employed

Source: Donvan & Zucker, 2010.

Read about It. Think about It. Write about It.

- How do Donald T.'s characteristics of autism remain consistent, yet become more age-appropriate from childhood to adulthood?
- Examine how the characteristics were written by Kanner for Donald T. Would you say these are written in a positive, strengths-based manner? Why or why not?

Hans Asperger, a pediatrician in Vienna, described a group of boys as having *autistic psychopathy*. These boys had high intellectual functioning but difficulties with learning, attention, and social behaviour and seemed to have impairments in emotions and instincts (Hippler & Klicpera, 2003). Asperger published his work about 4 children in 1943, the same year as Kanner described 11 others (Lyons & Fitzgerald, 2007). Asperger's work did not become well known, because it was written in German and was only translated into English by Uta Frith in 1991 (Lyons & Fitzgerald, 2007). Lorna Wing, mentioned later in this chapter, first coined the term *Asperger's syndrome* in 1981, when she used Asperger's description of the individuals with a slight extension (Hippler & Klicpera, 2003). Later, with the publication of the *Diagnostic and Statistical Manual of Mental Disorders IV* in 1994, the term *Asperger's disorder* first appeared officially. In the DSM-IV, the diagnosis was slightly different than first described, including two criteria in social impairments and one in repetitive and restricted patterns of behaviour (Hippler & Klicpera, 2003). In 2013, with the introduction of the DSM-5, Asperger's disorder no longer appeared as a separate diagnosis, but was grouped under the umbrella term *autism spectrum disorder*.

Bruno Bettelheim

Bruno Bettelheim, a doctoral graduate of psychology and philosophy and a later proponent of the then-dominant psychoanalytic approach (Fleck & Müller, 1997), affected the direction of the field of ASD from the 1950s onward. His prominence was even to the point of holding what was described as "celebrity status" (Adelson, 1997, p. 67), a significant departure from his early experiences as a concentration camp prisoner (Fleck & Müller, 1997). In 1959, he described children with autism as "unable to relate themselves in the ordinary way to people and situations" (Bettelheim, 1959, p. 455), comparing them to children raised in the wild, who had been subjected to total abandonment and extreme environmental deprivation. He saw children with autism as victims of emotionally isolating, disengaged, rejecting parents whose "efforts to find their lost children have been more than lax" (Bettelheim, 1959, p. 457). In the 1967 publication

The Empty Fortress: Infantile Autism and the Birth of the Self, Bettelheim compares and contrasts children with ASD to "victims of concentration camps" (p. 7). He believed that "autistic children withdraw from the world before their humanity ever really develops" (p. 7).

> **refrigerator mother**: A mother described as typically cold, aloof, intellectual, and professional, whose rejecting demeanour was posited to cause the social withdrawal seen in children with autism. Such views are commonly attributed to Bettelheim but are also present in Kanner's work (Whittaker, 1976).

Whittaker (1976) explained this pattern with the family etiology hypothesis—commonly used in the mid-twentieth century—assuming that parental "pain and strain" in families of "troubled children" (p. 91), especially in the mother, influence the development of such children and are, directly or unconsciously, a pathological cause. In the most common version of this theory, the disorder was believed to be caused by cold, unaffectionate mothers (Barbera, 2010, p. 56; see Chapter 9). One of the outcomes of such a view was the separation or severing of the so-called refrigerator mother relationship, a process Bettelheim called a *parentectomy.* A parentectomy demanded separation, including residential separation from the family home. In Bettelheim's treatments, this meant a relocation to his well-known orthogenic schools, where intensive treatment could be implemented without interruption (Whittaker, 1976).

Bettelheim's reputation disintegrated after his death, as his background, experiences, credentials, and methodology were found to be more myth than reality (Adelson, 1997). However, this influential man (Raines, 2002) sowed the seeds of a dubious yet undeniable influence, reflected in his biographies (e.g., *Rising to the Light: A Portrait of Bruno Bettelheim* [Raines, 2002]) and in the stories of those who had encountered him (e.g., *Not the Thing I Was: Thirteen Years at Bruno Bettelheim's Orthogenic School* [Eliot, 2002]).

Read about It. Think about It. Write about It.

- Do you see any reflections of Bettelheim's work in the perception of autism today and the treatment of parents of children with ASD? If so, explain.
- How do you think the concept of the refrigerator mother influenced the progression of autism interventions and autism perceptions? Do you think autism awareness and positive perceptions would have been more advanced today without the introduction of this concept? Why or why not?

Lorna Wing

Lorna Wing, a respected UK-based psychiatrist and parent of a daughter diagnosed with ASD at the age of three, is credited with significant advances through her pioneering work expanding on and popularizing more modern notions of ASD. In particular, she popularized the term *Asperger's syndrome* and widened the narrow definition of autism by describing it as a *spectrum* of diagnoses and a *triad* of characteristics that make up the disorder (Hebert, 2014; Leekam, 2014). The three main characteristics that she described as notable in the disorder—and across diagnoses—were deficits in social interactions, difficulties with communication, and impairments in imagination, which most often were accompanied by repetitive and restricted patterns of behaviour (Wing, 1993). Later, when the triad of characteristics was published in the DSM-IV, impairments in imagination was removed, and repetitive and restricted patterns of behaviour became the third characteristic of the triad. Wing also advocated for a continuum of diagnoses, indicating the similarities of the disorders Kanner and Asperger described.

Her most well-known, foundational writing is *Autistic Children: A Guide for Parents and Professionals* (Wing, 1972), which emphasized that parents should first remember the positives: "He is first and foremost a child, with the same need as every other child for a home and family, love, security, guidance and a chance to develop his skills and positive assets to the full" (p. 13). This view differed significantly from other authors at the time, such as Bettelheim, who negatively characterized the parents of children with autism in their work. One of Wing's best-known publications, written with Judith Gould, was a 1979 epidemiological survey of children, helping to resolve the complexities of classifying social, language, and behavioural issues in the field. Importantly, "all the children with social impairments had repetitive stereotyped behavior and almost all had absence or abnormalities of language and symbolic activities. Thus, the study showed a marked tendency for these problems to occur together" (Wing & Gould, 1979, p. 25). This tendency was also referred to as a "cluster of abnormalities" (p. 26) and led to a recommendation that the "full range of conditions" (p. 27) must be included in a future system of classification—something "more suitable than 'autism' or 'psychosis'" (p. 27). With the current usage of *spectrum* and *triad* as commonly understood descriptors in the field, Wing's leadership toward new terminology and understanding was solidified, marking a broadened understanding of autism as an "autistic continuum" (Wing, 1993, p. 70).

Ole Ivar Lovaas

Ole Ivar Lovaas is considered a transformative pioneer of both applied behaviour analysis (ABA) applications for language development and challenging behaviour and interventions for children with ASD (Smith & Eikeseth, 2011). Born in Norway in 1927 and educated in the United States, he worked in the field from the 1960s until his death in 2010 (Smith & Eikeseth, 2011, p. 378). One listed achievement of many included a change in our understanding of children with autism, such as a greater focus on reducing serious self-injurious behaviours.

> The rapid reduction of even the most horrifying behavior—children's punching themselves hard in the face thousands of times every hour, chewing off their fingertips, smashing their heads against the sharpest object available, or poking their eyes—helped prove that children with autism were sensitive to consequences, contrary to the conventional wisdom in the 1960s. (Smith & Eikeseth, p. 376)

Lovaas built the foundation for successful, early, and intensive behaviour intervention (IBI) focused on skill-building for young children with ASD, which he developed using principles of behaviour modification. His foundational work was titled the *UCLA Young Autism Project* (Lovaas, 1987; Smith & Eikeseth, 2011). In this publication, Lovaas reported on his unique project, which "sought to maximize behavioural treatment by treating autistic children during most of their waking hours for many years" (Lovaas, 1987, p. 3) in a "special, intense, and comprehensive learning environment" (p. 4). His design included an experimental group that received 40 hours of individualized therapy per week (intensive treatment) using ABA intervention and two control groups, the first of which received 10 or fewer hours of individualized intervention and the second of which received no treatment. Each group had between 19 and 21 children, all aged 46 or fewer months at the beginning of this 2-year-or-longer intervention plan. Multiple interventions, including aversive interventions, were used, and data were recorded in multiple ways. Some significant findings included that 47% of the intensive treatment experimental group were successful in a "normal first grade in a public school" (p. 6), and there was an average gain of 30 intelligence quotient points in the intensive treatment group. In other words, many students who received this intensive therapy "achieved normal intellectual and educational functioning" (p. 7), with widespread improvement in multiple domains (such as language). Lovaas concluded:

> Given a group of children who show the kinds of behavioral deficits and excesses evident in our pretreatment measures, such children will continue to manifest similar severe psychological handicaps later in life unless subjected to intensive behavioral treatment that can indeed significantly alter that outcome. (Lovaas, 1987, p. 9)

Since this publication, Lovaas and many others (e.g., Strauss, Mancini, & Fava, 2013) have modelled multiple programs upon components of Lovaas's intensive early-intervention treatments. The goal of such programs has been to change the developmental trajectory of children with ASD by intervening early with ABA principles in intensive behaviour intervention programs. Since this seminal study, such programs have been similarly evaluated in various Canadian locales, typically with young children with ASD. The foundation of Lovaas's work continues to be strongly evident in early intervention programs, though also the subject of debate (Smith & Eikeseth, 2011). For example, across Canada, most jurisdictions have an early intensive behaviour intervention (EIBI) program that has components of Lovaas's discrete trial training (DTT) work, an intensive ABA approach, where skills are broken down into contrived, small components and learning occurs in trials (for a fuller discussion, see Chapter 3). Although many programs have shifted to have a hybrid approach of teaching methodologies, these DTT programs are still very prevalent.

intensive behaviour intervention (IBI): a high intensity, low-ratio approach to programming, sometimes called early intensive behaviour interventions (EIBIs), initially developed by Lovaas. These programs are based on applied behavioural analysis (ABA) principles specifically designed for working with children with ASD (de Rivera, 2008).

Read about It. Think about It. Write about It.

- How have autism services in your region been influenced by this seminal study of the effects of intensive behaviour intervention (IBI) by Ivar Lovaas in 1987?

ELASTICITY OF TERMINOLOGY

Moving ahead more than 40 years from Leo Kanner's original 1943 term, *early infantile autism*, it becomes evident that the terminology around autism is elastic over time. Since the *Diagnostic and Statistical Manual IV-TR* (2000), language around ASD has continued to shift, reflecting changes in our academic understanding, our professional approaches, and our everyday language emerging from the published literature; this language remains differentiated by geographical region (Jacobsen, 2010). Perhaps this is unsurprising given the significant time lapse between revisions of the DSM, which guides our language around psychological disorders. In the meantime, there is a tug-of-war between formal language and everyday terminology. For example, the DSM-IV-TR used the term *Asperger's disorder* (Neumärker, 2003), but the terms *Asperger's syndrome*, *Asperger syndrome*, and simply *Asperger's* are also commonly used. When the term *autism*,

Figure 1.2: Diagnostic and Statistical Manuals

Source: Authors.

for example, is heard or used in everyday conversation, it is often uncertain whether the speaker is referencing a specific former diagnosis (i.e., autistic disorder), a previous umbrella term (i.e., pervasive developmental disorders), or the current all-encompassing diagnosis (i.e., ASD).

CURRENT DEFINITIONS

As previously explained, shifting knowledge, understandings, and attitudes toward ASD are reflected in the language used in the field, the published literature on the topic of ASD, and most notably in the manuals guiding the diagnosis of ASD—most recently the fourth and fifth editions of the DSM.

Autism was first found in the DSM-III as a distinct category called *infantile autism*; before this, the characteristics of the disorder were listed under *childhood schizophrenia* (Watkins, n.d.). Six characteristics were originally listed for a diagnosis of infantile autism. Revisions for the DSM-III-R in 1987 renamed the term *autistic disorder*, with notable increases in the number and quality of observable and measurable characteristics to be diagnosed (Watkins, n.d.). Thompson (2013) highlights the literature of the autism diagnosis up to the mid-2000s (see Figure 1.3).

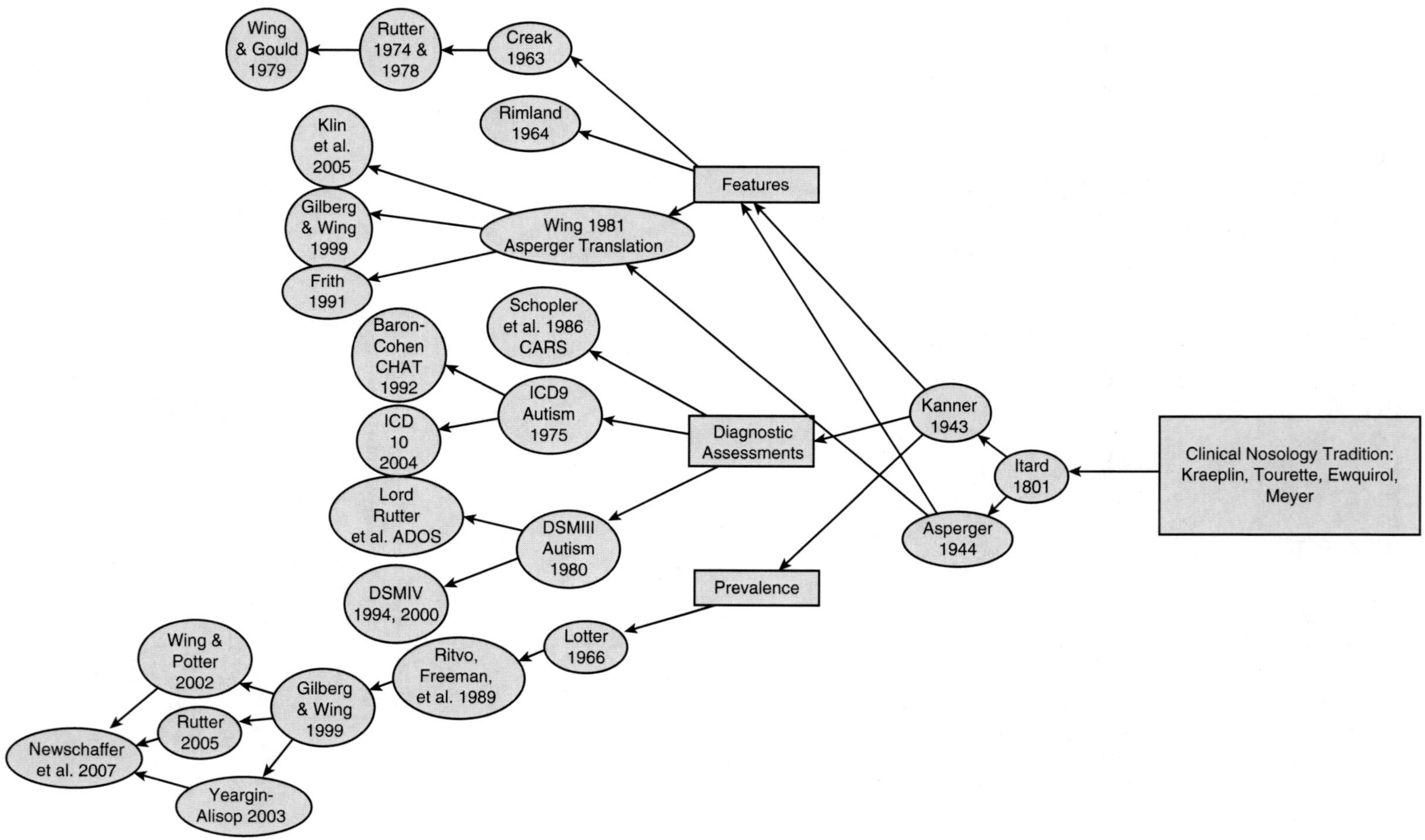

Figure 1.3: Theoretical Origins and Empirical Influences on Autism Diagnostic Nosology (Classification) and Prevalence

Source: Thompson, 2013, p. 87.

Studying Autism as a Non-autistic Scholar: Reviewing Autism in Canadian Literature between 1950 and 2018

Margaret Janse van Rensburg, MSW Candidate, Carleton University

Autism is among many identities that need to be promoted on a social justice agenda. Using Critical Discourse Analysis and Critical Autism Studies, I explore how social workers can engage in social justice. Autistic voices traditionally have been oppressed, and this is portrayed in popular and academic literature over time. Canadian academic and popular discourse surrounding autism between 1950 and 2018 has been framed by an agenda of "fixing" autistic children. I seek to challenge dominant-subordinate power relationships, to confront ableist perceptions of autism, and to increase inclusivity, while increasing awareness of the barriers for people with autism in Canadian society. Further, I explore how a non-autistic scholar can better research autism in an anti-oppressive way.

By breaking down Canadian literature between 1950 and 2018 into decades, discourse surrounding autism is placed in historical context and reviewed to highlight social oppression. Between 1950 and 1970, autism was dominated by medical discourse. Between 1970 and 2000, the focus was educational, with increased reliance on behaviour analysis. Literature between 2000 and 2018 continues to reveal these medical and educational foci but has also begun to shift into a broader understanding of autism that includes neurodiversity, intersectionality, inclusivity, and alternative understandings of autism. The results display a shift in Canadian academic and popular perceptions and publications about autism. An inclusive conceptualization of autism is necessary for fair treatment of autistic people in society. As a non-autistic scholar, I question how an autistic person would analyze the data and evaluate the presented analysis.

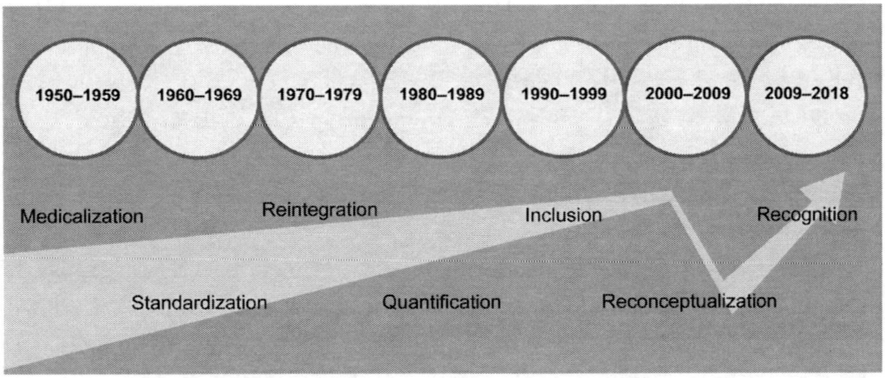

Figure 1.4: "Autism" in Canadian Literature

Source: Margaret Janse van Rensburg.

When doing research about autism, it is important to incorporate the voices of autistic people. Researching autism without doing so runs the risk of speaking for people with autism. Critical Autism Studies provides an opportunity for autistic people to create and to be included in research. My future research seeks a more inclusive methodology in direct interviews with autistic people, including autistic scholars and media sources, and inviting autistic people to provide feedback throughout the process.

DSM-IV-TR

The DSM-IV was published in 1994, and later the DSM-IV-TR in 2000, which provided additional diagnosis and the triad of characteristics earlier described by Wing (1993). The DSM-IV-TR included autism under the umbrella term *pervasive developmental disorders*, which encompassed five different but related disorders: autistic disorder; Asperger's disorder; pervasive developmental disorder–not otherwise specified; Rett's disorder; and childhood disintegrative disorder. Hartley and Sikora (2010) succinctly summarized two of these former subtypes, autistic disorder and pervasive developmental disorder–not otherwise specified:

> **diagnostic and statistical manual**: a manual typically used in the mental health and disability sector that provides information on the criteria, symptoms, and descriptions for diagnosis across many mental health disorders (American Psychiatric Association, 2013b). It is commonly referred to as the DSM.

> A *DSM-IV-TR* diagnosis of Autistic Disorder requires impairments in three domains, including Social Relatedness (i.e., deficits in social interest or interactions), Communication (i.e., deficits in language development or atypical speech), and Restricted/Repetitive/Stereotyped Patterns (i.e., odd or stereotyped interests or behaviors). A diagnosis of Pervasive Developmental Disorder–Not Otherwise Specified is given if some but not all criteria are met for Autistic Disorder, the onset of symptoms occurs after 3 years of age, or there is an atypical presentation of symptoms. (American Psychiatric Association, 2013c, pp. 85–86)

Less commonly recognized were Rett's disorder—characterized by cognitive delays, atypical motor movements, social disinterest, and its presence primarily in females—and childhood disintegrative disorder, which is typically marked by a regression later in childhood (Odle, Barstow, & Cataldo, 2011). Asperger's disorder, often called Asperger's syndrome, is commonly recognized, although this diagnosis is no longer in the DSM-5. A diagnosis of Asperger's disorder in the DSM-IV-TR required that the individual have two deficits in social interaction and one impairment in repetitive and restricted patterns of behaviour (the same as for a diagnosis of autistic disorder) with no characteristics of communication impairments or no delay of language onset (APA, 2000). Asperger's disorder is perhaps best distinguished from the other subtypes by what it *lacks*, such as a lack of delays in language and cognitive development (Woods, Mahdavi, & Ryan, 2013). These individuals are often described as being highly talented and gifted and achieving high-level cognitive tasks but are not able to relate socially and prefer repetitive and routine structure and behaviour. It is important to note, however, that each individual with ASD is unique—even within a diagnostic category.

Although the DSM-5 was published in 2013, many are still familiar and comfortable with the terminology in the earlier DSM-IV-TR (APA, 2000). Even though what Tsai

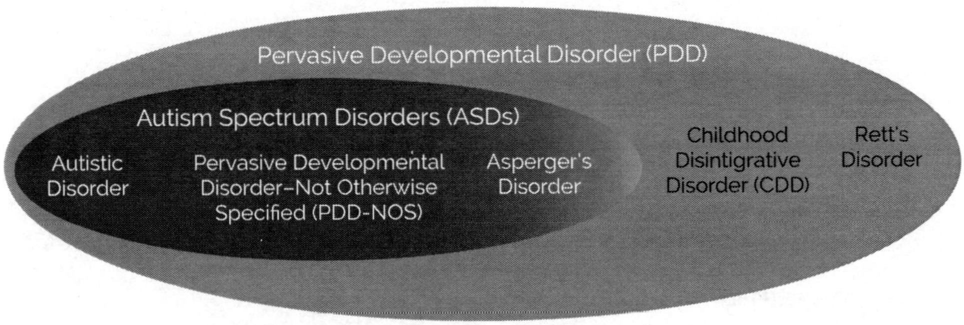

Figure 1.5: Pervasive Developmental Disorders
Source: Thames Valley Children's Centre (TVCC), 2008a, p. 2.

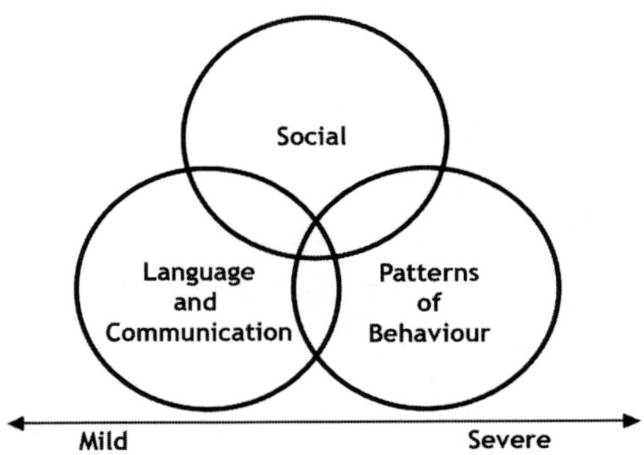

Autism is characterized by three areas of impairment:

1. Challenges with social interactions
2. Impairments in verbal and nonverbal communication
3. Repetitive and restricted patterns of behaviour

Figure 1.6: Previous Areas of Impairment
Source: Thames Valley Children's Centre (TVCC), 2008a, p. 3.

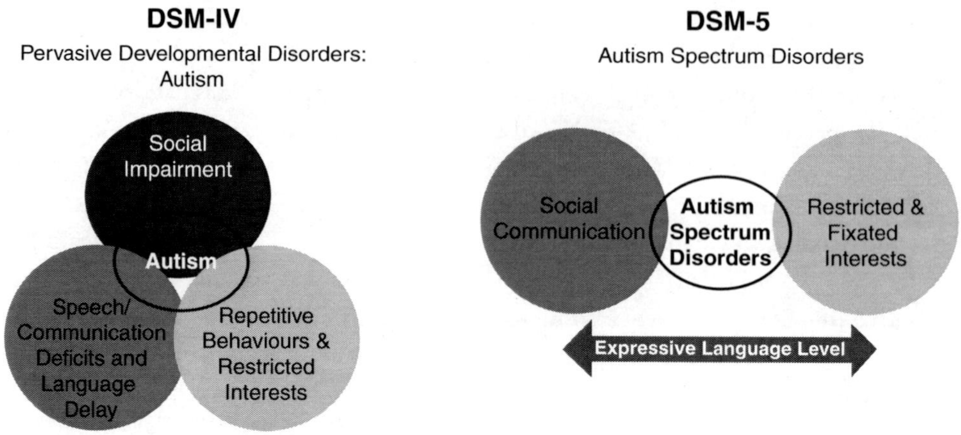

Figure 1.7: Characteristics of ASD from DSM-IV to DSM-5
Source: Lord & Jones, 2012, p. 31.

and Ghaziuddin (2013) describe as a "splitters" approach was intended to "support the taxonomic validity of each subtype" (p. 324), clinically differentiating between subtypes of pervasive developmental disorders continued to be challenging with this heterogeneous disorder (Falkmer, Anderson, Falkmer, & Horlin, 2013).

DSM-5 Definition

In a significant shift to diagnostic categorization in the field of ASD, the DSM-5 entered the picture in May 2013 as a newly updated diagnostic tool, after 6,000 hours of consideration through the American Psychiatric Association's Work Group on Neurodevelopmental Disorders, as well as field testing (Grzadzinski, Huerta, & Lord, 2013; Tsai & Ghaziuddin, 2013). The changes included replacing terminology (e.g., PDD), subsuming some subtypes (e.g., PDD-NOS), removing other subtypes (e.g., Rett's), and absorbing the entire category into a singular, yet adaptable term: ASD (Tsai & Ghaziuddin, 2013).

The DSM-5 criteria are presented in the box "Autism Spectrum Disorder Diagnostic Criteria." A new, related addition in the DSM-5—though not labelled as an ASD—is social (pragmatic) communication disorder, which, as its name implies, relates to "persistent difficulties in the social use of verbal and nonverbal communication" (para. 2; e.g., social relationships, listener-based

hidden curriculum: the set of implicit rules about what to do and what not to do in every context, communication, and situation (e.g., what to wear) that most children will successfully pick up through everyday interactions, without explicit instruction (Myles & Simpson, 2001).

flexibility, rule-following, and non-explicit information, or the "hidden curriculum"). Three other main diagnostic criteria are functional limitations in a range of areas, such as academic achievement; its onset at an earlier stage of development; and the exclusion of other diagnostic possibilities (e.g., ASD).

The former five pervasive developmental disorders described in the DSM-IV-TR (APA, 2000) have been collapsed and subsumed within the DSM-5 into a single diagnostic category called *autism spectrum disorder*. This change reflects the common usage adopted in the field, in everyday conversation, and in recent literature (e.g., Hall, 2013), the adaptation of the "common practice of diagnosing to the changes in society with respect to cultural and sociologic factors," even though the "official" terminology of pervasive developmental disorders had remained static for 14 years after its inception (Lauritsen, 2013, p. S37). Perhaps, though, some of these now-common usages that reflect, for example, the community, culture, and services of now-familiar Asperger's may continue, "just like the term 'high-functioning autism' (HFA) being commonly used despite the fact that it was never in the DSM" (Fung & Hardan, 2014, p. 95).

The 2013 ASD diagnosis in the DSM-5 is also outlined by multiple diagnostic criteria, specifications, and severity levels (Autism Speaks, 2015). These severity levels are graded on a scale of one to three, with level one requiring support, level two requiring substantial support, and level three requiring very substantial support. Examples of how characteristics are displayed at each level for the social communication and restricted, repetitive behaviour domains are presented in Table 1.3.

Five diagnostic criteria are currently required for a diagnosis of ASD:

1. "persistent deficits in social communication and social interaction across multiple contexts," such as social-emotional reciprocity, nonverbal communication, and interpersonal relationships;
2. two indications of "restricted, repetitive patterns of behavior, interests, or activities," including motor movements, inflexibility, and sensory-based issues;
3. an onset early during the developmental period;
4. clinical impairment (e.g., occupational) resulting from the deficits; and
5. exclusionary considerations (Autism Speaks, 2015, para. 3).

Lastly, the DSM emphasizes that any cognitive, language, medical, genetic, or environmental factors must be indicated (Autism Speaks, 2015). It is clear that subsumed in these changes is a move to a dual-deficit model of social communication and repetitive/restricted behaviour deficits, rather than the familiar triad of areas of deficit (Grzadzinski et al., 2013; Wing & Gould, 1979). Another noticeable change is the lack of

social-emotional reciprocity: a didactic, reciprocal social interaction between two persons in which both persons are equally reinforced by one another (Strain & Shores, 1977).

reference to a delay in language development (Fung & Hardan, 2014). Grzadzinski and colleagues (2013) reference this new framework as a "dimensional approach" (p. 2), and describe it as having positive possibilities for research typologies. Interestingly, they also note the philosophical shift indicated by the change from Roman numerals (e.g., IV) to digits (e.g., 5), describing the DSM now as a "living document." Incremental updates can be identified with decimals—DSM-5.1, DSM-5.2—instead of waiting for the sixth edition of the DSM to be released.

Autism Spectrum Disorder Diagnostic Criteria

Diagnostic Criteria 299.00 (F84.0)

A. Persistent deficits in social communication and social interaction across multiple contexts, as manifested by the following, currently or by history (examples are illustrative, not exhaustive):

1. Deficits in social-emotional reciprocity, ranging, for example, from abnormal social approach and failure of normal back-and-forth conversation; to reduced sharing of interests, emotions, or affect; to failure to initiate or respond to social interactions.
2. Deficits in nonverbal communicative behaviors used for social interaction, ranging, for example, from poorly integrated verbal and nonverbal communication; to abnormalities in eye contact and body language or deficits in understanding and use of gestures; to a total lack of facial expressions and nonverbal communication.
3. Deficits in developing, maintaining, and understanding relationships, ranging, for example, from difficulties adjusting behavior to suit various social contexts; to difficulties in sharing imaginative play or in making friends; to absence of interest in peers.

Specify current severity:

Severity is based on social communication impairments and restricted, repetitive patterns of behavior. [See Table 1.3.]

B. Restricted, repetitive patterns of behavior, interests, or activities, as manifested by at least two of the following, currently or by history (examples are illustrative, not exhaustive):

1. Stereotyped or repetitive motor movements, use of objects, or speech (e.g., simple motor stereotypies, lining up toys or flipping objects, echolalia, idiosyncratic phrases).

2. Insistence on sameness, inflexible adherence to routines, or ritualized patterns of verbal or nonverbal behavior (e.g., extreme distress at small changes, difficulties with transitions, rigid thinking patterns, greeting rituals, need to take same route or eat same food every day).
3. Highly restricted, fixated interests that are abnormal in intensity or focus (e.g., strong attachment to or preoccupation with unusual objects, excessively circumscribed or perseverative interests).
4. Hyper- or hyporeactivity to sensory input or unusual interest in sensory aspects of the environment (e.g., apparent indifference to pain/temperature, adverse response to specific sounds or textures, excessive smelling or touching of objects, visual fascination with lights or movement).

Specify current severity:

Severity is based on social communication impairments and restricted, repetitive patterns of behavior.

C. Symptoms must be present in the early developmental period (but may not become fully manifest until social demands exceed limited capacities, or may be masked by learned strategies in later life).

D. Symptoms cause clinically significant impairment in social, occupational, or other important areas of current functioning.

E. These disturbances are not better explained by intellectual disability (intellectual developmental disorder) or global developmental delay. Intellectual disability and autism spectrum disorder frequently co-occur; to make comorbid diagnoses of autism spectrum disorder and intellectual disability, social communication should be below that expected for general developmental level.

Note: Individuals with a well-established DSM-IV diagnosis of autistic disorder, Asperger's disorder, or pervasive developmental disorder not otherwise specified should be given the diagnosis of autism spectrum disorder. Individuals who have marked deficits in social communication, but whose symptoms do not otherwise meet criteria for autism spectrum disorder, should be evaluated for social (pragmatic) communication disorder.

Specify if:

With or without accompanying intellectual impairment
With or without accompanying language impairment
Associated with a known medical or genetic condition or environmental factor
Associated with another neurodevelopmental, mental, or behavioral disorder
With catatonia

Source: American Psychiatric Association. (2013b). *Diagnostic and Statistical Manual of Mental Disorder* (5th ed., pp. 50–51). Arlington, VA: Author.

Table 1.3: Severity Levels for ASD in the DSM-5

Severity Level	Social Communication	Restricted, Repetitive Behaviours
Level 3 "Requiring very substantial support"	Severe deficits in verbal and nonverbal social communication skills cause severe impairments in functioning, very limited initiation of social interactions, and minimal response to social overtures from others. For example, a person with few words of intelligible speech who rarely initiates interaction and, when he or she does, makes unusual approaches to meet needs only and responds to only very direct social approaches.	Inflexibility of behaviour, extreme difficulty coping with change, or other restricted/repetitive behaviours markedly interfere with functioning in all spheres. Great distress/difficulty changing focus or action.
Level 2 "Requiring substantial support"	Marked deficits in verbal and nonverbal social communication skills; social impairments apparent even with supports in place; limited initiation of social interactions; and reduced or abnormal responses to social overtures from others. For example, a person who speaks simple sentences, whose interaction is limited to narrow special interests, and who has markedly odd nonverbal communication.	Inflexibility of behaviour, difficulty coping with change, or other restricted/repetitive behaviours appear frequently enough to be obvious to the clinical observer and interfere with functioning in a variety of contexts. Distress and/or difficulty changing focus or action.

Level 1 "Requiring support"	Without supports in place, deficits in social communication cause noticeable impairments. Difficulty initializing social interactions, and clear examples of atypical or unsuccessful responses to social overtures of others. May appear to have decreased interest in social interactions. For example, a person who is able to speak in full sentences and engages in communication but whose to-and-fro conversation with others fails, and whose attempts to make friends are odd and typically unsuccessful.	Inflexibility of behaviour causes significant interference with functioning in one or more contexts. Difficulty switching between activities. Problems of organization and planning hamper independence.

Source: American Psychiatric Association, 2013b, p. 52.

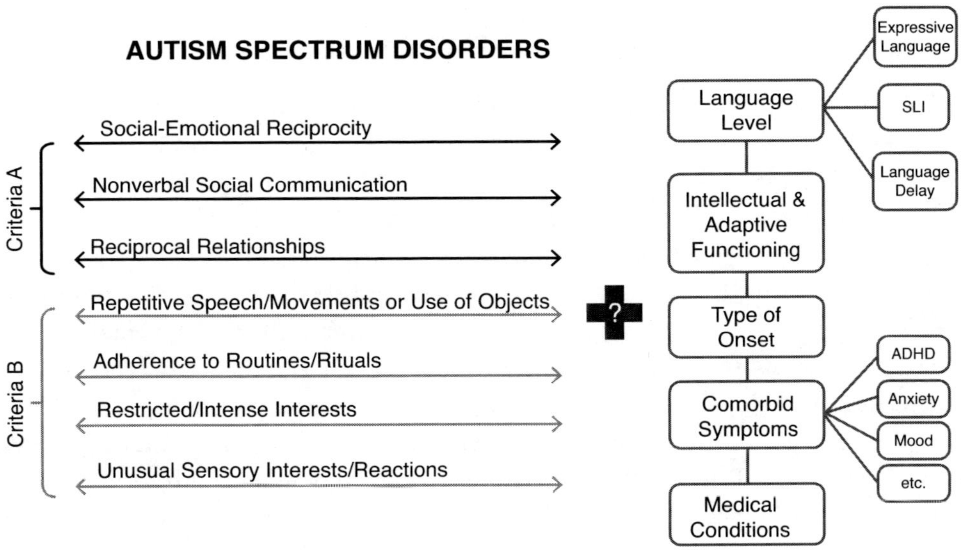

Figure 1.8: Characterization of ASD

Note: SLI: Specific Language Impairment

Source: Grzadzinski, R., Huerta, M., & Lord, C. (2013). DSM-5 and autism spectrum disorders (ASDs): An opportunity for identifying ASD subtypes. *Molecular Autism, 4*(1), 1–6.

According to Lauritsen (2013), these changes had been "widely anticipated" (p. S37), in part due to the frustrating lack of clarity that plagues classification systems in psychiatry, as well as the diagnostic processes families have endured (Fung & Hardan, 2014; Grzadzinski et al., 2013; Lord et al., 2012; Szatmari et al., 2002; Tsai & Ghaziuddin, 2013). However, it remains to be seen what the final outcomes of this dramatic—yet fully rationalized—change might be. For example, some argue that it would have been more beneficial to review and reconsider the criteria of the subtypes of PDDs, rather than completely abandoning them (Ghaziuddin, 2010) and caution that the current direction will limit potentially valuable research in this area (Tsai & Ghaziuddin, 2013). There are also fears that "eliminating the subtypes of PDDs and creating a single ASD will have an impact on services and may actually result in some patients being denied services" (Tsai & Ghaziuddin, 2013, p. 327). Such investigations are already underway, although the new diagnostic criteria for ASD does include a comment that those with some previous diagnoses (e.g., Asperger's disorder, PDD-NOS, autistic disorder) should be rediagnosed with ASD, with the exception of those who do not meet the criteria (Autism Speaks, 2015). In these cases, an examination of either the heightened restrictiveness (Fung & Hardan, 2014) or the inclusivity of "the new" ASD is needed. Taheri, Perry, and Factor (2014), for example, completed an Ontario-based file review and found that 45% of the 22 previously diagnosed participants would not meet DSM-5 criteria, with a bias toward excluding those with PDD-NOS diagnoses and/or higher cognitive scores.

DIAGNOSTIC PATHWAYS IN THE DSM-5

Typical diagnostic pathways vary by diagnostician, by region, and over time; however, both typical practice and best practice do exist. Across Canada, a range of professionals in varied roles can diagnose: for example, psychologists, psychiatrists, and physicians. Brian, Zwaigenbaum, and Ip (2019) outlined an eight-step process for diagnosing autism spectrum disorder in children. These steps included a review of the child's records, interviews with parents and/or caregivers, assessment of the core features of ASD, a physical examination, consideration of differential diagnoses including those diagnoses that mimic ASD, establishing the diagnosis (based on the interpretation of the collected data), communicating the diagnosis, as well as providing a comprehensive assessment report to inform programming for the individual and their families. Zwaigenbaum and Penner (2018) provided several suggestions regarding the assessment of individuals with potential ASD. They suggested that assessments should be ongoing, begin when symptoms appear, and continue throughout life to inform treatment and programming. Assessment and evaluation, therefore, need to inform both the diagnosis of ASD and what follows once the diagnosis is provided. Assessments should also consider the wishes of the individual with ASD and their families.

Brian and colleagues (2019) provided a list of areas of functioning that should be included in a comprehensive assessment of the individual. They included:

- Cognitive and academic
- Speech, language, and communication
- Sensory and motor functioning, and sensory sensitivities
- Adaptive functioning (e.g., self-help skills)
- Behavioural and emotional functioning (e.g., anxiety, self-esteem issues)
- Physical health and nutrition (p. 449)

Comprehensive assessments of children showing symptoms of autism is not new. Dua (2003), on behalf of the British Columbia Ministry of Health Planning, within *Standards and Guidelines for the Assessment and Diagnosis of Young Children with Autism Spectrum Disorder in British Columbia* indicated that an assessment should include multiple components, as follows:

> Assessment of a child with probable ASD must evaluate multiple domains of functioning. This must include:
>
> A) Psychological assessment of cognitive level and adaptive functioning using standardized norm-referenced instruments (See Section 7.3.2).
> B) A comprehensive speech-language-communication evaluation using standardized norm-referenced instruments (See Section 7.3.3).
> C) A comprehensive medical evaluation by a pediatrician including a detailed physical exam and appropriate laboratory investigations (See Section 7.3.4).
> D) The following additional assessments are required whenever the indicators, listed below are identified at any stage of the diagnostic process:
>   i) occupational therapy assessment (See Section 7.3.5)
>   - evidence of aberrant sensory based behaviours;
>   - evidence of motor skill deficits; and,
>   - need for adaptive functioning assessment related to child's activities of everyday living;
>   ii) psychiatric assessment for comorbid mental health issues (See Section 7.3.7)
>   - prominent self-injurious or aggressive behaviours;
>   - significant mood or anxiety symptoms;
>   - indications of attentional and/or hyperactive symptoms; and,
>   - evidence of tics and/or obsessive-compulsive symptoms;

iii) additional specialty assessments, as indicated, should be arranged for children who manifest abnormal findings at any stage of assessment including:
- neurology;
- nutrition;
- medical genetics; and,
- endocrinology. (Dua, 2003, pp. 15–16)

Brian and colleagues (2019) suggested that there does not need to be a one-size-fits-all approach to the assessment and diagnosis of the core features of ASD (p. 444). These authors suggested three approaches to the diagnostic process for children suspected of having ASD as they relate to the personnel/resources required for diagnosis. The first approach is an experienced sole clinician; the second, a shared-care model comprised of a clinician and a second health-care provider; and the third, a team-based approach where multidisciplinary teams are used to determine the diagnosis.

Brian and colleagues (2019) further suggested there are instances where sole and shared-care assessments of the core features of ASD are both efficient and practical. In some instances, the presentation of symptoms and the child's history makes for a clear diagnosis of ASD. In these cases, the diagnosis can easily be made by a sole clinician or in a shared-care model of two clinicians working together. Such approaches can help to eliminate the long waitlists associated with team-based approaches and allow children earlier access to treatment and/or programming interventions and potentially improved developmental outcomes (Brian et al., 2019; Penner, Anagnostou, & Ungar, 2018; Zwaigenbaum & Penner, 2018). In a Canada-wide survey examining the diagnostic practices of Canadian pediatricians, Penner and colleagues (2018) found that where pediatricians spent significant time completing multidisciplinary team-based assessments, there was a significant increase in the wait times for the diagnosis for children suspected of having ASD. While there have been many advances in the understanding and awareness of ASD, there are still inefficiencies in the diagnosis of ASD where the mean age of diagnosis is still between ages four and five (Zwaigenbaum & Penner, 2018).

Brian and colleagues (2018) further indicated that, in some instances, multidisciplinary teams are the most appropriate approach to the diagnosis. These authors suggested when the symptoms of ASD are subtle; where the child has other genetic, health, or developmental issues; or where the child has a complicated psychosocial history (e.g., attachment, abuse, neglect), it may be prudent to provide a multidisciplinary team approach to the assessment of ASD (Anagnostou et al., 2014; Brian et al., 2019; Penner et al., 2018; Zwaigenbaum & Penner, 2018).

Clinicians responsible for evaluating children for a diagnosis of ASD should use evidence-based measures in their evaluations (Randell et al., 2018). The Marian Foundation (2008) suggested that the use of the Autism Diagnostic Observation Schedule (ADOS) and the Autism Diagnostic Interview–Revised (ADI-R), along with clinical judgment, is considered the *gold standard* for the assessment of the core features of children suspected of having ASD (p. 48). A recent Cochrane Report (Randell et al., 2018) suggested that the ADOS provided the best results for correctly identifying children with ASD and tended to avoid falsely identifying children without ASD.

Although such diagnoses can and do happen in any geographic area—either rural or urban—some diagnostic and research centres are publicly funded and provincially, nationally, and internationally recognized in Canada. Yet other diagnoses happen by equally skilled clinicians working individually and privately. Dr. Adam McCrimmon from the University of Calgary (Werklund School of Education) in Alberta provides an example of such a diagnostic pathway.

Read about It. Think about It. Write about It.

- How have the changes in the diagnostic criteria for ASD influenced the evaluation and treatment of people with ASD?
- How would changes in the DSM-5 influence policy?

Assessment Practices for Autism Spectrum Disorder—Perspectives and Processes from Alberta

Adam W. McCrimmon, Andrea Rodgers, and Erin Kapler, Werklund School of Education, University of Calgary

Although clinical assessment and diagnostic practices for ASD remain complex, research has investigated the typical process through which parents and the child work with professionals (typically from a variety of disciplines) to better understand the nature of possible atypical development demonstrated by the child to obtain a diagnosis for the child (Mansell & Morris, 2004). Assessment and diagnosis of ASD most often, though not always, occurs before elementary school (Centers for Disease Control and Prevention, 2007; Shea & Mesibov, 2009). Indeed, clinicians often strive to diagnose children at or before the age of two as formal assessment and earlier diagnosis result in enhanced prognosis (Fernell, Eriksson, & Gillberg, 2012), enabling children to access interventions and supportive services at an earlier stage in development thus improving developmental outcomes (Remington et al., 2007).

The diagnostic process typically begins when a parent or another individual (i.e., a relative, family friend, teacher) notices developmental or behavioural atypicalities in the child. Such atypicalities may include delayed or lack of imitation, sharing of attention and focus with social partners, orienting to socially important stimuli, and/or language development (e.g., delayed acquisition of single words and/or phrase speech, delayed or atypical expansion of abilities, or loss of previously developed skills). These concerns subsequently lead parents to seek out professional opinion on the nature of the behavioural differences, including a possible diagnosis. Although there are many domains to be assessed (i.e., behavioural atypicalities, cognitive development, language development, sensory needs, gross and fine motor development) and many approaches to assess each domain, best practice standards dictate a comprehensive and developmental assessment that ascertains an accurate picture of the child's behaviours in relation to both typical developmental standards and in comparison to the child's previous development. In addition, the use of a multidisciplinary team (e.g., pediatricians, psychologists, speech-language pathologists, occupational therapists, etc.) is recommended so that professionals with specific training and experience can evaluate the child's skills and abilities across a variety of domains. The process of diagnosis often involves the use of formal tools designed to screen for and/or identify ASD-specific behaviours, such as the Autism Diagnostic Observation Schedule, Second Edition (ADOS-2; Lord et al., 2012); the Autism Diagnostic Interview–Revised (ADI-R; Lord, Rutter, & Le Couteur, 1994); the *Modified Checklist for Autism in Toddlers* (M-CHAT; Robins, Fein, Barton, & Green, 2001); Rapid Interactive Screening Test for Autism in Toddlers (RITA-T; Choueiri & Wagner, 2015); Developmental, Dimensional and Diagnostic Interview (3di; Skuse et al., 2004); Childhood Autism Rating Scale, Second Edition (CARS-2; Schopler, Van Bourgondien Wellman, & Love, 2010); and/or the Diagnostic Interview for Social and Communication Disorders (DISCO; Wing, Leekam, Libby, Gould, & Larcombe, 2002). Parents typically receive the results of the assessment upon its conclusion, and then seek support and services for their child.

There are two general pathways for parents who are seeking a diagnostic assessment for their child: through the health system or privately. Each approach has its pros and cons, and parents are encouraged to consider the cost of assessment (typically free through the health system), the comprehensive nature of the assessment (often more rigorous and involves more professionals in the health system), and the wait times to obtain an assessment (often quicker to get an assessment via a private clinic). Parents seeking to access the health system often have a referral from primary care physicians in collaboration with other professionals in the community (e.g., early childhood educators, school personnel, speech-language pathologists [SLPs], occupational therapists [OTs], audiologists, mental health providers, etc.) who may be the first ones to raise concerns about the child's development or behaviour. Additionally, different health-based ASD diagnostic clinics may have different assessment streams depending upon the child's identified needs and the composition of available professional teams. Decisions regarding the appropriate diagnostic route are often made at the intake level, based on the clinical issues identified at the time of referral. Team-based assessments are often delivered via a multidisciplinary team of professionals, including a licensed psychologist, SLP, OT, developmental pediatrician, and/or social worker.

Parents can access private clinics often via self-referral. Private clinics often utilize psychologists with specialized expertise in the assessment and diagnosis of ASD. Private assessments often utilize similar tools and diagnostic processes as health system-based processes; however, teams are less common.

Diagnostic Observation

Name: ______________________ **Date:** ______________________

Location: ______________________

Use these questions as a guide for observing the child/adolescent and your description of the child/adolescent. The description should be in narrative form rather than "yes" and "no" responses. Wherever possible, use examples.

Section	Observation Notes
(A) Free Play *Does the child ...* Spontaneously seek engagement with others (children or adults)? How does he/she do this? Does it involve joint reference to objects, such as giving and showing objects, or is it limited to seeking affection or help? Play by themselves or with others (children or adults)? How does he/she play? • engage in pretend situations? • use imagination, either alone or with others? Remain with the activity for an age-appropriate or developmentally appropriate amount of time, or jump from activity to activity more quickly than expected? Become fixated on any one activity (engage in one activity when change would be expected)? Change activities willingly when asked? Engage in any repetitive motor movements?	

Figure 1.9: Diagnostic Observation Form

Source: Cindy Herbert.

(B) Response to Name *Call the child's name when he/she is not looking at you. Each time the child does not respond, call out his/her name slightly louder. Note if and how he/she responds. If there is no response, ask an adult who is familiar with the child to do the same. Repeat several times throughout the observation.* Does the child respond to you? Does the child respond to a familiar adult? Did you have to call his/her name several times before receiving a response? How did he/she respond (turn his/her head, make eye contact, etc.)?	
(C1) Communication General: How does the child communicate with adults? How does the child communicate with other children? Does the child use facial expression to communicate, or does facial expression remain the same regardless of the situation?	
(C2) Communication Speech: Does the child speak or use speech sounds to communicate? How much of the child's speech is directed toward others, as opposed to saying words to him/herself but not for the purpose of communicating with someone else?	

Figure 1.9: *Continued*

How long are his/her utterances (words or phrases)? In what situations does the child speak with others? Is it to get help, or for social reasons? Does his/her voice sound flat or monotonic? Is there anything unusual about his/her intonation?	
***If the child is nonverbal, bypass section C3.**	
<u>(C3) Communication</u> <u>Unusual or Idiosyncratic Speech:</u> *Does the child...* Use "you" or "he/she" or his/her own name instead of "I"? Have immediate echolalia? Use rehearsed/learned speech, even if it is used in the appropriate situation? Use more repetitive speech than what would be expected for his/her developmental level?	
<u>Pointing</u> *During your observation, make sure there is opportunity for the child to point. Ask where something is and see if he/she responds by pointing.* *Does the child point to objects or people ...* Out of reach, or only within arm's length? With his/her index finger, or with open hand? To request something of interest or to tell someone else about something?	

Figure 1.9: *Continued*

<table>
<tr><td><u>Other Gestures</u>

Gestures must have a communicative purpose and must not involve the use of other people's body parts.

Does the child use any other gestures to communicate?

If he/she does, are these gestures used to describe something, such as the size of an object?

Does the child use these gestures (besides pointing) to display his/her emotions?

Would the child wave goodbye in response to someone waving goodbye, or does he/she need to be prompted?</td><td></td></tr>
<tr><td><u>Use of Another Person's Body to Communicate</u>

Does the child take someone else's hand and lead him/her to another place?

Does the child ...

Use his/her hand to place someone else's hand (or other part of his/her body) on an object?

Move someone else's hand while the other person is holding an object to get him/her to do something with the object?

Move someone else's hand to get him/her to point to something?</td><td></td></tr>
</table>

Figure 1.9: *Continued*

Eye Contact *Observe the child for appropriate, socially modulated, and flexible eye contact. If the child seems shy or anxious initially but his/her eye contact changes significantly as he/she warms up or becomes more comfortable, use this more comfortable eye contact as the basis for description. If his/her eye contact is abnormal, note this regardless of whether it seems to be due to shyness or inattention. If it seems to be reduced due to either of these factors, make note of that as well.* Is there anything unusual about the child's eye contact? For example, is it much less than what would be expected, or looks more like "staring"? In what situations does the child use eye contact? *Do they use eye contact when ...* Someone is speaking to him/her? He/she is speaking to someone? He/she is giving something to someone or requesting help from another person?	

Figure 1.9: *Continued*

Read about It. Think about It. Write about It.

- Who are the professionals that can make a diagnosis of ASD in your region?
- What role do other professionals play in supporting the person and their family in making the diagnosis and supporting the family after the diagnosis?

The subsequent pathway between diagnosis and service provision, however, may be neither straightforward nor simple. In an Alberta-based study, Hodgetts, Zwaigenbaum, and Nicholas (2015) note significant heterogeneity in clinical phenotype and many potential comorbidities present in those diagnosed with ASD. Mansour and colleagues (2017) evaluated 99 children aged 6 to 13, diagnosed with a previous subtype of what is now termed ASD (autistic disorder, Asperger's disorder, or PDD-NOS) for comorbid disorders using a variety of standardized instruments and behavioural checklists. Their results indicated that attention deficit hyperactivity disorder (ADHD) is the most common comorbid disorder, with 86% of their sample meeting the criteria for the disorder. The next most common disorder was specific phobias (33%) followed by oppositional defiant disorder (21%) and obsessive-compulsive disorder (at 15%). The results of the study also indicated that 56% of the participants meet the diagnostic criteria for two comorbid disorders. Despite the obvious increase in need by families with children who have been diagnosed with ASD in comparison to families with children with other special healthcare needs, the former find it more challenging to gain access to healthcare and family support services. The researchers attributed this to a strain on services stemming from the prevalence of ASD.

It appears that there are few commonalities among the experiences of parents, families—even adults with ASD—as they traverse the diagnostic process related to assessing and diagnosing this neurodevelopmental disorder. The following anecdotes highlight the journeys of Olivia, and Anika and her son Nolan.

clinical phenotype: the characteristics or traits that are displayed in a clinical population such as ASD. The phenotype is described as heterogenous in examining the wide range of traits displayed in ASD (Oriane & Philippe, 2016).

Olivia's Journey

Suzy Marotta, Toronto, Ontario

At 16 months old, Olivia wasn't really showing any signs of verbal communication with us. She was making sounds but didn't identify familiar objects such as her bottle or family members. She also wasn't really showing too much interest in playing with toys; she would explore them but she did love dancing to music and was fascinated by Elmo on TV. I didn't worry too much about it and observed her for the next couple of months and would bring up my concerns at her next checkup.

At her 18-month-old checkup, the pediatrician asked me to fill out a questionnaire about her development, and I remember checking off "NO" to "does she speak more than 20 words" and "NO" to "follow one step direction" and "SOMETIMES" to "does she have eye contact during interaction." My heart was racing because that was the first time I felt something wasn't right. I know that some kids develop at their own pace, some slower or quicker than others but when we were in the examination room and before I even brought up my concerns, the pediatrician was interacting with Olivia and said the words that I didn't expect to hear: "I don't think it's autism ... but ... it's definitely a speech and language delay. Put her on the TPSLP waitlist and she'll get picked up in about 6 months."

Figure 1.10: Olivia Marotta

Source: Suzy Marotta.

The next six months I was overthinking everything Olivia was and wasn't doing. At Olivia's 2-year-old checkup, her pediatrician said it again: "I don't think it's autism ... she's looking at me as I'm interacting with her. She's responding." I told him I wanted a referral for her to be assessed for autism; he recommended to just do the speech therapy and wait another year, but I was persistent and told him I wanted it done because if it is autism, I didn't want to wait because she would be going to school in a couple of years. He warned me how long the waitlist is, and honestly, I didn't care, I just wanted the referral to have my mind at ease.

Olivia was put on the waitlist for Holland Bloorview Hospital, and I called them every week for seven months until I finally got a date for an assessment, and it all happened so quickly. Within three weeks she was assessed and diagnosed with "autism." "So, what do we do next?" we asked. "How do we help her?" The developmental pediatrician was very helpful, providing many resources and pointing us in the right direction for ABA therapy, which meant another waitlist, so we started private one-on-one ABA therapy and couldn't believe how quickly Olivia learned new skills and how she was interacting with us.

Olivia's expressive language bloomed. Her first word was "cookie" and then it expanded to "want cookie" and then to "I want cookie." She was learning quickly by using visual pictures to communicate but soon we noticed that she was so compelled by YouTube videos of kids performing ballet and playing, and she was imitating their behaviours. We decided to start making short home videos on her iPad to help Olivia to accomplish specific tasks, such as introducing yourself to a new friend, or asking for more food at dinner time. This technique was really supporting her in many ways.

After two years of one-on-one therapy, we decided that Olivia would benefit from a group-based therapy program and enrolled her in a one-to-five ratio social skills group where she had the opportunity to learn and cooperate in simple games with other kids such as musical chairs or snake and ladders. She learned how to take turns in a baking activity, and she was able to be involved in simple conversations with other children by sharing information and asking questions. Olivia became a social butterfly. She would enjoy meeting new children at the playground or at school and was at ease "making friends."

Since the age of five, Olivia has showed a great interest in dance, gymnastics, and drawing. Watching all those YouTube videos, she taught herself the basic ballet steps, she began to do cartwheels and handstands; she also was able to draw characters with details. We enrolled her in a dance school and she's been participating for three years now dancing ballet, acro, and jazz. She also has been attending an art class once a week and learning the techniques of drawing and painting by creating many kinds of creative art pieces.

Olivia may sound like a child who had it all together, but there are some struggles she still needs to overcome, such as keeping on task and completing it on time or following with what needs to be done instead of making her own choice on what to do; for example, at school, the teacher says it's time to review a math lesson but Olivia prefers to go to the quiet table and mould clay instead. Olivia loves attending school; she has always been eager to go but has a difficult time completing her school work. She's very capable of knowing all she learned but requires many "mini breaks" and positive reinforcements to complete her school work.

The main struggle Olivia has is self-regulation. She isn't able to calm herself down when she gets upset or angry. She starts off by yelling and then she throws herself on the floor and screams and cries as she flings her arms and legs. She described it one day as "I have fireworks in my brain and I don't know how to make them stop." The breathing technique was introduced to Olivia and until today it triggers her behaviour, but since she shared about the fireworks in her brain, we have been telling her to "Calm your brain down—relax your brain," and it's been helping. She also prefers to be held when she's calming down.

Olivia must have a scheduled routine to follow on a daily basis. We use a monthly calendar and write down all the events for the month. If something changes in her routine, she requires advanced notice, if possible, about the change. If the event is cancelled, we cross it out with an X. We tell her that if something changes in the day unexpectedly that it's OK and to deal with the change and then everything will go back to regular.

Since Olivia's diagnosis, we have been so proud of all her accomplishments, such as getting over the fear of being in overcrowded places or a loud environment. Now Olivia enjoys going shopping at the mall, eating at a restaurant, dancing at a school dance, and performing in front of other people at dance recitals and school assemblies.

There are so many things that we wish for Olivia's future:

- Have positive involvement in her schooling years
- Have some close and trusting friends she can rely on
- May she find a meaningful career that she is passionate about
- Continue to be independent with her daily skills and routines
- Hopefully she will find someone who will love her and take care of her as an equal partner in life and maybe have children of her own
- A lifetime of health and wellness
- Being kind and compassionate to others
- Most importantly always to be happy in life. Every morning Olivia wakes up with a smile on her face and is always in a good mood, and we hope she continues this every day of her life.

Anika and Nolan

Anika Blum O'Connor

When Anika Blum O'Connor, a mother in southern Ontario, and her husband, Patrick, went to one of their son Nolan's regular check-ups soon after he turned 18 months old, the physician didn't hold back. Almost immediately, he asked if there was "something wrong" with their young son or if she and her husband had noticed "anything odd." The doctor continued: he called Nolan's name but received no response; he asked if Nolan was talking. This was the first of many of Anika's "Aha!" moments in the next four months. Though Anika and Patrick had indeed noticed some issues, they were able to ignore most of them and convince themselves that he was fine and "just slow," encouraged by well-meaning friends with comforting platitudes such as "Don't compare your children." When

Figure 1.11: Anika's Son, Nolan, Diagnosed with ASD before Age Two
Source: Anika Blum O'Connor.

prompted to think in-depth about his development, they recalled that he had been talking—some—at his 12-month appointment but had stopped. He was not blowing kisses. He was, however, affectionate and cuddly and didn't mind eye contact. They wrote themselves a "laundry list" of reasons that he was fine, such as the development of some word approximations in the coming weeks. But it turns out that he was, indeed, quite different in development than his gifted older sister, who was close in age. These differences were underscored by this visit to the doctor, who recorded a query of "PDD?" in his notes, they later discovered.

What happened next? Anika was told to take Nolan to get his hearing tested—and it was normal. He was put on a waiting list for services with speech-language pathology. He also went on a waitlist for further assessment at the local children's centre—and Anika found out how difficult it was to obtain access to the fragmented local services. When the speech-language pathologist met with Nolan, Anika was told the assessment would take 20 minutes—but it was over an hour and a half. Though the pathologist could not diagnose, she did express her concerns and was the first to use the word *autism*. Anika left the children's centre and vomited outside, shaken by both physical and emotional reactions to "that word." To her, it meant "worst-case scenario behaviours" and self-injurious children.

The next step was yet another referral, for that ominous "*a*-word" diagnosis, which came readily—even surprisingly—within four months. The process had its odd moments, such as the pediatrician elbowing Nolan to see his reaction. They were asked to complete standardized assessments as well. Then came their second "Aha!" moment. No further denial was possible. Anika and her husband realized this as-yet-unconfirmed diagnosis was probably correct and likely quite severe. It only took two appointments to confirm autism. "The best part," Anika reflected, "was the pediatrician allowing *us* to go through the assessment and come to conclusions. We had already processed this conclusion by the time he confirmed it." The worst part was the questions about IQ. Anika recalls, "I did not like these; I would not answer them. Who would know this? How do you tell? This memory still hurts."

Unlike the experiences of other families, the diagnostic process was fast, and no fighting was necessary. "It fell on our laps," said Anika. "We were fortunate that our family doctor was astute, even with almost no experience in the field." However, getting services was another story: "He was on the IBI waitlist for 17 months." She continued with her poignant memories of these now long-past days: "A diagnosis is like a precipice—a very scary thing. I looked for everything online. I made a list for the doctor, who went through everything with me. And it came down to IBI (we couldn't afford private), and the gluten-free, casein-free diet.

"My biggest piece of advice is that we did everything so quickly. Crying and cookies were both key. I was a stay-at-home mom, and I made it my mission to be sure that Nolan was not forgotten. I would call the centre daily and pop in with cookies for the staff. I went to every parent-training course to avoid that awful feeling of impotence where you feel you can't help your child."

Her advice for other parents? "Any financial sacrifices you make are paid back ten-fold. It helps the siblings of your child: everything is planned around that one child, it's the whole family, everyone benefits, and it changes the quality of life for everyone. As daunting and as overwhelming as it is, really look at it as your full-time job." Though Anika says she once mourned for the child she thought she would have, she never blamed herself for one second, and she continued to love, honour, value, and treasure her now 10-year-old son, who came to be a poster child and video model for other families and many students in the ASD field. As her copy of *More Than Words* (Sussman, 1999) became a dog-eared bible for helping her son, all these years later, her "head is still sore from the advocate hat," Anika laughingly explained. However, she won't have time to rest that hat or that head. She is continuing her education with a post-graduate diploma and plans to continue to take an active role in the field as a full-time, front-line worker, supporting children with ASD, as her son was—and still is—supported by the professionals around him.

These diverse sets of needs and experiences in navigating the diagnostic pathways of ASD are just the beginning of experiences in the lifespan throughout Canada. It is inevitable that families like Nolan's—families in all of their diversity—will continue the search for services and supports, highlighting the need for advocacy, including self-advocacy.

Self-Advocacy

Likely the most well-known advocate in the field of ASD is animal behavioural scientist, and adult with ASD, Dr. Temple Grandin. Dr. Grandin is multitalented; she is a strong visual learner and a highly prolific author in her field of animal science, as well as in the field of ASD. Not only was she named to the Colorado Women's Hall of Fame (Colorado State University, 2012) and one of *Time*'s (2010) top 100 inspirational people but she was also the subject of an award-winning biographical movie, *Temple Grandin* (2010), in which she was played by Claire Danes (Bellows et al., 2010). Recently she was featured in children's picture books: *The Girl Who Thought in Pictures: The Story of Dr. Temple Grandin* (Mosca, 2017) and *How to Build a Hug: Temple Grandin and Her Amazing Squeeze Machine* (Guglielmo & Tourville, 2018). Canada has its own advocate: Carly Fleischmann. Fleischmann, who was born and raised in Toronto, Ontario, is a young adult and a well-known figure with a strong following locally, nationally, and internationally. In her own words, Carly exemplifies self-advocacy in her online introduction:

> My name is Carly Fleischmann and as long as I can remember I've been diagnosed with autism. I am not able to talk out of my mouth, however I have found another

> way to communicate by spelling on my computer. (and yes that is me typing on the computer by myself) I used to think I was the only kid with autism who communicates by spelling but last year I met a group of kids that communicate the same way. In fact some are even faster at typing then I am. Last year a story about my life was shown on ABC news, CNN and CTV here in Canada. After my story was played I kept on getting lots of emails from moms, dads, kids and people from different countries asking me all sorts of questions about autism. I think people get a lot of their information from so-called experts but I think what happens is that experts can't give an explanation to certain questions. How can you explain something you have not lived or if you don't know what it's like to have it? If a horse is sick, you don't ask a fish what's wrong with the horse. You go right to the horse's mouth. (CarlysVoice, 2013, para. 1)

Carly and her family members are certainly that horse's mouth. Hailed as a leader of self-advocacy in the field of ASD and beyond, Carly demonstrates, invites, and inspires independence through advocacy, struggle, and community. She represents a growing group of adults, adolescents, and even children who are turning to online social media in a movement to not only learn about others and share their stories as persons with ASD but also to teach and preach about ASD directly from lived experiences, with enthusiasm and deep self-understanding.

> **self-advocacy**: in the field of ASD, self-advocacy can be referred to as a group process of struggling for needs and rights: "the emergence of autistic self-advocacy movements in several Western countries in the late 1990s ... challenged the dominating views of autism and argued for their right to speak for themselves" (Bertilsdotter Rosqvist, 2014, p. 353).

Carly Fleischmann shares her struggles with sensory processing—among other issues and skills such as self-advocacy. Carly utilizes social media sites such as Twitter and Facebook and blogs about her journeys in ASD, from a diagnosis of severe intellectual disability to a recognition of giftedness. Some of the essential topics Carly has delved into include her struggles in advocating for use of her communication device on airplane flights, promoting the successful use of assistive technology, and demonstrating what sensory overload is like to those who have not experienced it firsthand in the interactive Carly's Café. Additionally, she and Arthur Fleischmann (her father) have penned a semi-autobiographical account of

> **intellectual disability**: formally titled mental retardation, this is a DSM diagnosis of an impairment in general cognitive abilities that affect a person's functioning ability in three main areas: conceptual, practical, and social domains (American Psychiatric Association, 2013b).

Carly's life and family—which includes a twin sister, Taryn—from childhood to adolescence in *Carly's Voice: Breaking through Autism* (Fleischmann & Fleischmann, 2012). Its introductory chapter includes a reminiscence of when seven-year-old Carly went, unaccompanied and naked, from her home to the park, and her father's well-practised response for well-meaning onlookers:

> One lapse in scrutiny and here we were—Carly, in the park, naked, at dusk, alone. I felt happy to have found her, but I also felt the crush of frustration and desperation, knowing that this would not be a onetime near-catastrophe. It was just a moment in our lives. And we would have many more. ... "Carly has autism." Three words must suffice to explain a tome of weird behaviours and limitations. It's shorthand for Carly-is-different-she-acts-in-odd-ways-she-loves-taking-off-her-clothes-especially-if-what-she-is-wearing-has-a-spot-of-water-on-it-she-likes-repetitive-motion-like-that-of-the-swing-she-doesn't-speak. We didn't know what Carly knew and what she was incapable of knowing. She made odd movements and sounds and covered her ears when it was noisy. She cried often. And she never, ever stopped moving. Never. (pp. 4–5)

NATIONAL PERSPECTIVES

Since, for the most part, clinical and education services are jurisdictionally controlled, eliciting information about ASD from a cross-Canada perspective is challenging. One issue that has certainly affected multiple jurisdictions is conflict, acrimony, and litigation around ASD (Shepherd & Waddell, 2015). Such litigation (including high-profile cases) has focused on services and their funding from both health-care and school perspectives, leaning on issues such as human rights, human rights legislation, and discrimination. From the outcomes of such cases, Shepherd and Waddell further conclude, "The implication for Canadians is that these services will continue to vary considerably across the country, particularly in an era of waning federal funding and oversight" (2015, p. 3552). Estimates of the prevalence of ASD are generally reported in national numbers; however, it is important to understand that national numbers may not be representative of the local numbers and needs. For example, Alberta may have a higher rate of persons with ASD since families move to obtain higher levels of funding than what is offered in other provinces (Dudley & Zwicker, 2016, p. 1). National-level ASD prevalence rates are difficult and expensive to acquire; furthermore, surveillance methods are limited, and international rates may not reflect Canadian rates. One method used to obtain prevalence data is from school census reporting; however, these censuses may not include all diagnosed individuals. In Calgary, 1 in 94 school-aged children has been diagnosed with ASD, which is different from the 1 in 68 reported by the Centers for Disease Control (CDC, 2018, p. 2). According to this document, 1 in 86 children had been diagnosed with ASD in one school board zone. The authors of this document suggest that policymakers make use of school census material to monitor local prevalence levels of ASD, use school censuses as a tool to "track future needs beyond Grade 12," and to collect information on the mental health needs of those with ASD (p. 3).

In recent years, helpful compilations have appeared in the open access body of literature examining ASD from a national perspective—as well as funding. One example is the Autism Spectrum Disorder Strategic Fund, which offers $9.1 million for "innovative community-based projects" in order to provide "tangible opportunities for Canadians living with autism, their families and caregivers to gain knowledge, resources, and skills" (Public Health Agency of Canada, 2018a). One compilation of projects relates to funding and the second relates to prevalence rates. In 2017, Autism Canada released *Provincial and Territorial Funding Programs for Autism Therapy*.

Built on jurisdictional policies, practices, and legislation, this province-by-province overview includes all 13 geopolitical jurisdictions in Canada, with Yukon and Nunavut combined. It is important to note that, according to Autism Canada, Nunavut and Yukon do not offer funded programs specific to ASD. This online report presents program-by-program information for one to four related programs in each province or territory. Each program is then broken down by related ministry, eligibility criteria, whether ABA and IBI are offered, a description of the program, and its related funding—if any. Shepherd and Waddell summarize the state of early intervention services, noting that they "now vary along three dimensions: (1) the relative mix of public and private funding; (2) the degree of integration across services; and (3) the extent of population coverage" (2015, p. 3550). It is important to note that the diagnosis of—and support for—ASD must be understood and interpreted in a much broader framework: that of disability policy, accessibility legislation, and human rights legislation, in Canada and internationally. McColl, Jaiswal, Jones, Robert, and Murphy (2017), through the Canadian Disability Policy Alliance, provided a comprehensive overview of Canadian disability policy in the unique *Review of Disability Policy in Canada*:

> a national collaboration of disability researchers, community disability organizations, and federal and provincial policy-makers, aimed at creating and mobilizing knowledge to enhance disability policy in Canada, and to promote equity and opportunity for disabled Canadians. (p. 4)

Due to its broad nature and focus, the only mention of ASD in this recent and comprehensive review is within Newfoundland and Labrador's *Health and Community Services Act* (1995), which provides the parameters around intensive ABA services for young children with ASD. An additional new resource is *Autism Spectrum Disorder among Children and Youth in Canada 2018: A Report of the National Autism Spectrum Disorder Surveillance Team*. This report on diagnoses of ASD from ages 5 to 17 is the first compilation of all the Canadian jurisdictions, using data collected from 2011 to 2015.

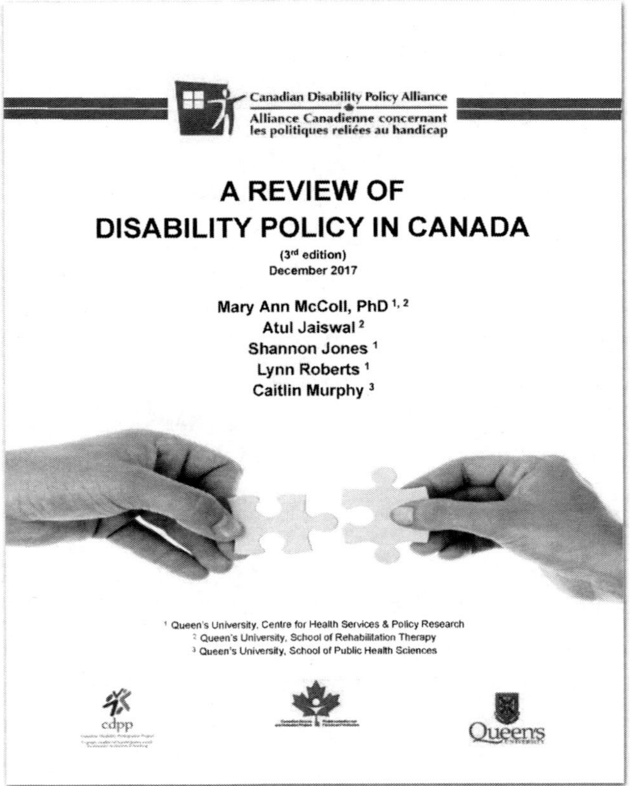

Canadian Disability Policy Alliance
Alliance Canadienne concernant les politiques reliées au handicap

A REVIEW OF
DISABILITY POLICY IN CANADA
(3rd edition)
December 2017

Mary Ann McColl, PhD [1,2]
Atul Jaiswal [2]
Shannon Jones [1]
Lynn Roberts [1]
Caitlin Murphy [3]

[1] Queen's University, Centre for Health Services & Policy Research
[2] Queen's University, School of Rehabilitation Therapy
[3] Queen's University, School of Public Health Sciences

Figure 1.12: *A Review of Disability Policy in Canada*
Source: McColl, Jaiswal, Jones, Roberts, & Murphy, 2017.

Though it is published from a public health perspective, this cross-Canada compilation is an invaluable 33-page reference document for students, clinicians, educators, and parents and is published in an online open-access format. A look at its table of contents shows that care has been taken to provide background information not only on ASD but also the multiple methods and multiple sectors (e.g., health, social services, and education) used to compile current prevalence and incidence rates shared in this resource.

The National Autism Spectrum Disorder Surveillance System

Bryson, Clark, and Smith's 1998 epidemiological investigation marked the first effort among researchers in Canada to conduct a large-scale study of autism in children between the ages of 6 and 14 years in a defined geographic region. The researchers screened 20,800 children living in both urban and rural areas of Nova Scotia by distributing questionnaires to their school teachers and counsellors. Questions focused on social and language skills, repetitive behaviours, and academic achievement. For children identified as having difficulties in these areas, follow-up assessments were completed and interviews were conducted with parents and caregivers. The results of the study provided an initial prevalence of 10.1 per 10,000 with a ratio of 2.5:1 male to female. *The National Epidemiologic Database for the Study of Autism in Canada* (Ouellette-Kuntz et al., 2014) collated results from three Canadian jurisdictions: southeastern Ontario, Prince Edward Island, and Newfoundland and Labrador. They discovered an increasing prevalence rate in all three areas but no decreased diagnostic ages; rather, one region had an increase. Both changes were significant, and many factors were identified as potentially impacting these estimates within a challenging field of study (Ouellette-Kuntz et al., 2014).

Around a decade after Bryson and colleagues' work, the Government of Canada identified a need to obtain accurate information about the number of Canadian children living with autism spectrum disorder (ASD). Up to that time, prevalence rates for ASD had typically been reported by the United States CDC, with rates ranging from 1 in 150 in 2000, to 1 in 110 in 2006, and 1 in 68 in 2012 (CDC, 2017); however, no comprehensive Canadian data had been collected. With the establishment of the Canadian federal government's Action Plan to Protect Human Health from Environmental Contaminants (Government of Canada, 2014) in 2008 came a call to create a system to collect data on the number of children living with ASD in Canada. The result was the development of the National Autism Spectrum Disorder Surveillance System (NASS).

The NASS was tasked with four key objectives: estimating the number of children who had been diagnosed with ASD across Canada and how many new cases were emerging; describing the population of children diagnosed with ASD in Canada, identifying patterns, and comparing those patterns with other countries; increasing awareness and understanding of ASD among the Canadian public; and using the information gathered to inform ongoing research and policy. The initial findings and first report of the NASS were released in March 2018—another decade later again.

> **epidemiology**: A field of research that examines the incidence of a particular disorder.

Key findings from the report include:

- Approximately 1 in 66 children between the ages of 5 and 17 in Canada has been diagnosed with ASD
- Males (1 in 42) are approximately 4 times more likely to be diagnosed with ASD than females (1 in 165)
- More than half (56%) of children diagnosed with ASD had received the diagnosis by the age of 6, and three-quarters had received the diagnosis by the age of 8

- Of the 7 Canadian provinces and territories that participated in the initial NASS research, Newfoundland and Labrador reported the highest prevalence of ASD, at 17.5 per 1,000, and Yukon reported the lowest prevalence at 8.0 per 1,000

Details of the findings of the NASS can be found in the full report from the Public Health Agency of Canada (2018c; see Figure 1.13).

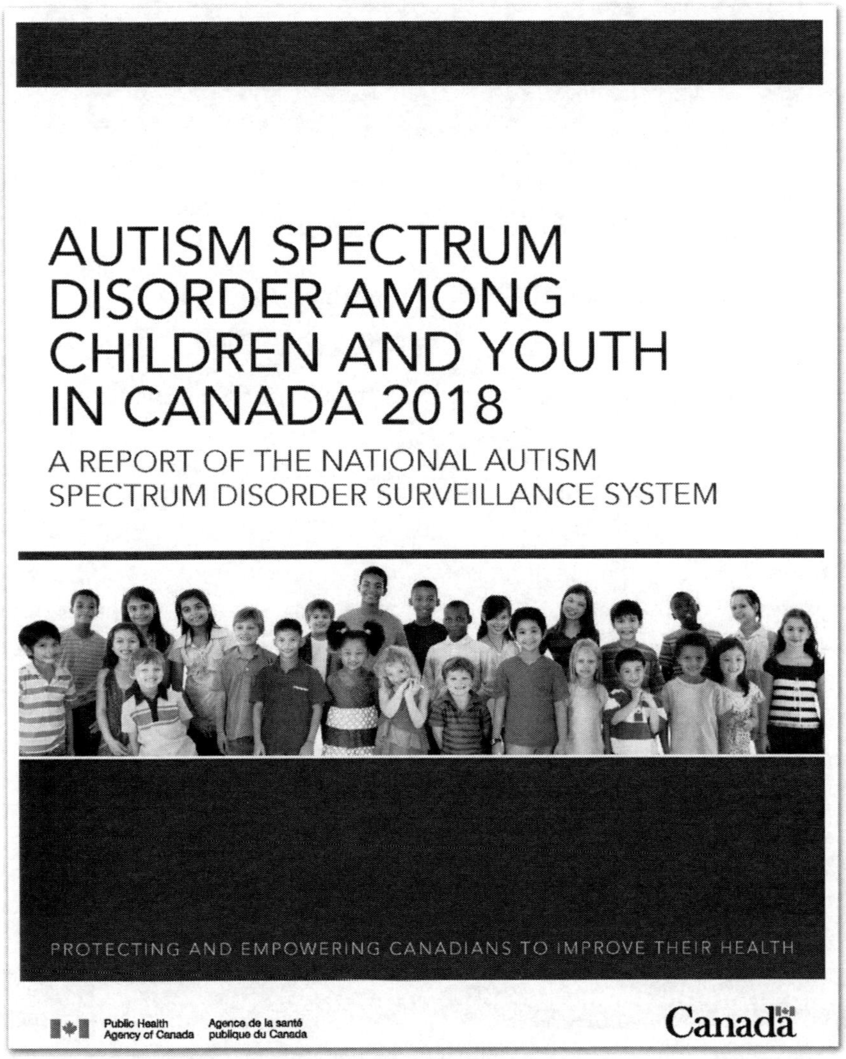

Figure 1.13: *Autism Spectrum Disorder among Children and Youth in Canada 2018: A Report of the National Autism Spectrum Disorder Surveillance System*
Source: Public Health Agency of Canada, 2018c.

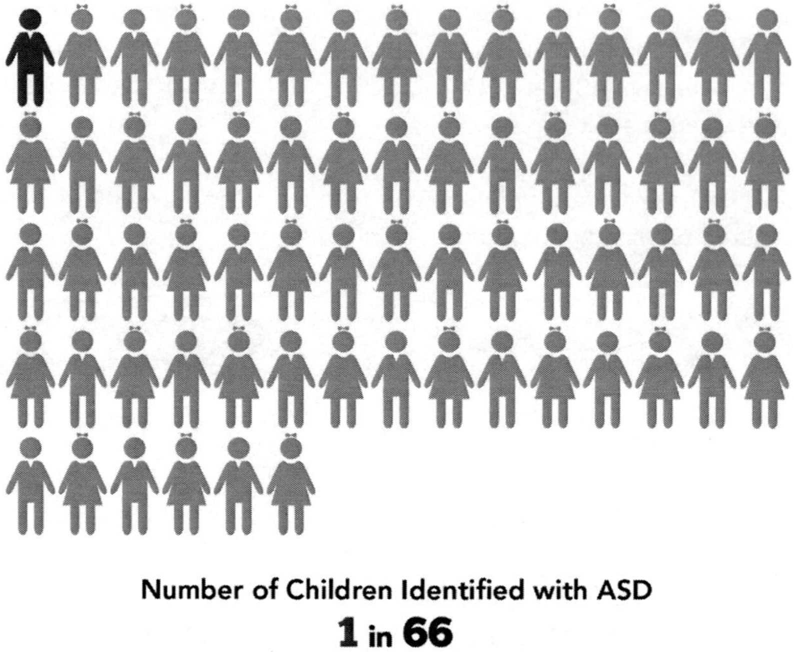

Figure 1.14: Prevalence of ASD among 5- to 17-Year-Old Children and Youth in Canada, 2015

Source: Public Health Agency of Canada, 2018c, p. 8, Figure 3.

This initiative and the resulting data provide an important first step toward obtaining information that may be used to inform future research and public policy for the benefit of Canadian children living with ASD and their families and caregivers. See Figure 1.14 for an overview of prevalence rates. It is important to note that this report does not include specific information related to Indigenous children in Canada, a population that Lindblom (2014) found to be underdiagnosed in British Columbia.

Source: Public Health Agency of Canada, 2018c.

Read about It. Think about It. Write about It.

- What are some reasons for the increases in diagnosis of ASD? Support your responses.
- How do you think regional epidemiology studies impact regional government and service providers?

- **Prevalence:** The total number of cases diagnosed compared to the total number of individuals in a population for a specific time period (e.g., a specific year—2015 or a specific date within a year), supporting comparisons by age, sex, region, time and/or other factors.
- **Incidence:** The number of newly diagnosed cases in a specific time period (e.g., a specific year—2015) in a defined population. This may inform a more targeted understanding of any changes (increases/decreases) by age, sex, region, time and/or other factors. For NASS, the incidence year is attributed to the year in which cases are first diagnosed.

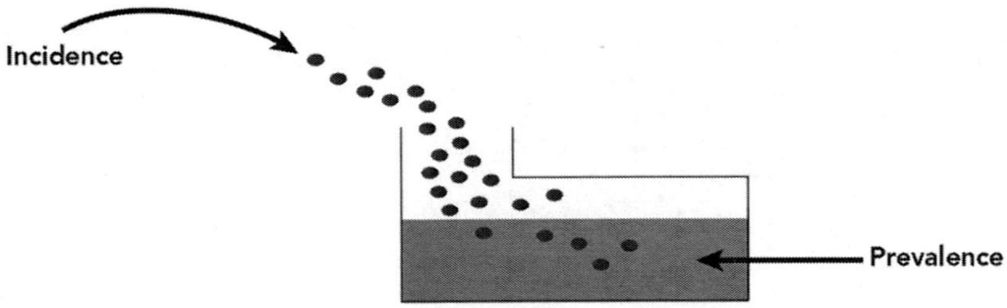

Figure 1.15: Prevalence versus Incidence Explained
Source: Public Health Agency of Canada, 2018c, p. 6, Figure 1.

> **disability tax credit (DTC)**: "a non-refundable tax credit that helps persons with disabilities or their supporting persons reduce the amount of income tax they may have to pay. An individual may claim the disability amount once they are eligible for the DTC. This amount includes a supplement for persons under 18 years of age at the end of the year" (Canada Revenue Agency, 2019a, para. 1).

Autism Spectrum Disorder among Children and Youth in Canada 2018 provides a cross-Canada prevalence rate of this age group as 1 in 66 or 15.2 children and youth per 1,000 children and youth in Canada. The report also provides more detailed breakdowns, including prevalence rates by gender and age at diagnosis (see box "The National Autism Spectrum Disorder Surveillance System").

It is also important to realize that many community members base information about ASD on someone they know—a friend's child or a relative, for example—but also tend to consume mass media representations of ASD as learning tools rather than professional literature or scholarly research articles. A brief look at these representations provide some insight into everyday influence on community knowledge of ASD.

MESSAGES FROM POPULAR MEDIA

Even with the regular dissemination of evidence-based interventions, many people receive, process, and accept information about disabilities, including ASD, from popular media: television, movies, and fictional books. Currently, characters with ASD or

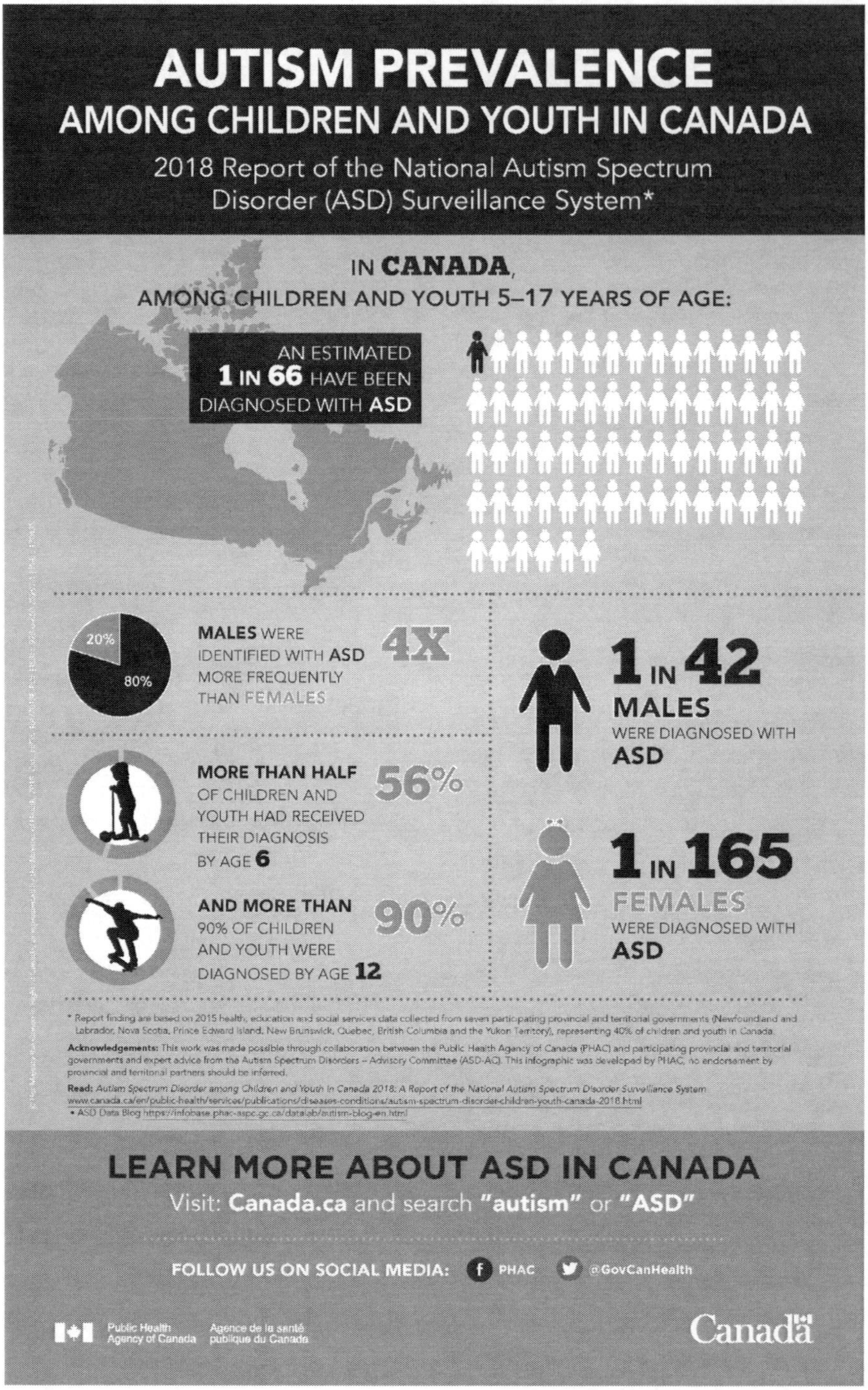

Figure 1.16: *Autism Prevalence among Children and Youth in Canada: 2018 Report of the National Autism Spectrum Disorder (ASD) Surveillance System*

Source: Public Health Agency of Canada, 2018c.

features of ASD appear to be a popular trend in entertainment-based mass media. It is difficult not to notice what appear to be traits designed to attain and maintain interest in characters portrayed as quirky, eccentric, or offbeat. Modern pop culture is exposing our society to a whole new typology of ASD, creating a new characteristic stereotype. For example, the 2014 release of *The Imitation Game* (Tyldum, 2014) no doubt leaves some audience members—especially those with a background in ASD—wondering if the brilliant, troubled, and socially awkward mathematician depicted in the film, Alan Turing, should or could be retroactively diagnosed with ASD. It only takes a few moments online to see that many others have indeed wondered, investigated, and published articles in the popular media on this very topic. On the television show *The Big Bang Theory* (Lorre & Prady, 2007), the popular character Sheldon Cooper is similarly portrayed as a socially awkward man but a brilliant physicist. Indeed, Sheldon's character may have finally outpaced Raymond Babbit, better known as *Rain Man* (Guber et al., 1988), as the average person's go-to reference for ASD. Only one of the two, however, is directly referenced as a person with ASD (Babbit, as an "autistic savant" [Guber et al., 1988]), despite the readily available assumptions that audiences may make or that producers may intentionally or unintentionally imply. Netflix's *Atypical* (Rashid, 2017) has now jumped into the mix, featuring an adolescent character diagnosed and identified with ASD moving into adulthood in the context of a tumultuous family environment. As forward-thinking as it may first appear that media creators are educating mass audiences about ASD, this depiction of neurodiversity shows only stereotypes of extremely high-functioning adult males with features of ASD-like behaviour (e.g., social difficulties) that do not impinge on everyday functioning, such as professional success. Belcher and Maich (2014, p. 98) described such public perception in detail.

> **neurodiversity**: "a concept akin to biodiversity or cultural diversity that recognizes neurological disorders as a natural human variation [advocating] to promote social support systems and spotlight the value of neurological differences, in the same vein as variations in learning styles or social tendencies like introversion and extroversion" (Public Broadcasting System, 2013).

Journalist Maggie Furlong (2013) recently noticed the rising prevalence of characters with Asperger's disorder—a former subtype of ASD—on television shows and wondered whether this is a "new, popular character quirk, or … a sign of society's efforts to embrace and personify a disorder that has become more and more prevalent" (para. 1). Draaisma (2009) describes many media-based portrayals of ASD as misrepresentative, even potentially harmful; however, the public appears to prefer these stereotypical, fictional examples. Similarly, Kanner and Asperger communicated an "essence of autism" (Lyons & Fitzgerald, 2007, p. 1475). Through case examples to further clinical understanding, they explained the "'Zusammenklang' or Gestalt of the child—his voice, face, body, language, intonation, gestures, gaze, expression and diction" (p. 1475). Perhaps popular media is doing the same for the everyday viewer in a stereotypical manner. Draaisma (2009) reflects,

> There is a strange discrepancy between the research that their directors, script writers and actors put in when they make a film featuring autistic persons and the actual characters they come up with ... they all want an absolutely sincere and truthful rendition of autism; what they come up with is an autistic character with freak-like savant skills, unlike anything resembling a normal autistic person. (p. 1478)

> **Asperger's disorder**: a diagnosis in the DSM-IV-TR (American Psychiatric Association, 2000) that included impairments in social interaction and repetitive and restricted patterns of behaviour but did not have early language delays or cognitive delays. It has since been removed in the DSM-5 (2013).

While the mass media helping to educate the public on ASD can be viewed positively, perhaps it is time to go beyond a mere mass media perspective, avoiding unrealistic depictions such as "highly skilled 'superheroes'" (Belcher & Maich, 2014, p. 103), superior savants who are "worthy of awe" (p. 104), those with "comically portrayed difficulties" (p. 104), or, on the other end of the perception spectrum, excessive "fuzziness or normalization" (p. 105) of ASD-driven difficulties as something "everyone has" to a certain extent. The next step is a move to an individualized, authentic—even insider—reality based on the lived experiences of people diagnosed with ASD. Moving from a concept of ASD based on a medical model of deficits within a disorder to a neurological *difference*—even a *culture* of neurodiversity—has certainly been initiated, encouraged, and underscored by "autistic people" (Owren, 2013, p. 32), who utilize this terminology simply as a descriptor. In other words, "many autistic self-advocates reject that their autism in itself is a disorder. They claim that, apart from differences such as race, gender and sexual orientation, people are also born with different minds" (p. 32). The movement focuses not on "fixing" ASD but on accessing equal rights and freedoms afforded to all human beings with diverse characteristics, and the positive attitudes and treatment that should accompany these.

Read about It. Think about It. Write about It.

- What has a movie, television, or book character taught you about ASD? Do you think these portrayals were accurate or inaccurate? Why?

SPOTLIGHTS ACROSS CANADA

Policy: Alberta

Policy development around ASD is another important component of services and supports in the field, underscoring clinical practice in varied jurisdictions, such as Alberta. It is also important because the prevalence of ASD appears to be rising, which translates to an increase in needs: "The reason for the dramatic rise is uncertain and may be a result of a combination of a true rise in incidence, changing diagnostic criteria and increased awareness. It has been speculated that Alberta may have higher numbers of persons with ASD due to family in-migration to utilize higher levels of funding for ASD supports compared to other provinces" (University of Calgary School of Public Policy, 2016, p. 1). The estimated cost of ASD at the national level can be high and may not accurately reflect local need. Issues with data collection are rooted in the limitations of different surveillance methods, such as the need for appropriate infrastructure, labour, sample sizes, and consistent diagnostic criteria (p. 2). With rising ASD prevalence, there is added urgency to government policy discussions. "These types of estimates are critical for managing the needs of the ASD population across the lifespan, informing policy and planning for the costs required to support students, and streamlining resources" (p. 3). The University of Calgary School of Public Policy (2016) made three recommendations for estimation of ASD for the creation of effective policies. These recommendations are that the provincial government could consider using school records to monitor local numbers, use school records to track future needs beyond Grade 12, and collect information on the mental health needs of those with ASD. Some of these issues have been addressed with the National Autism Spectrum Disorder Surveillance System (Public Health Agency of Canada, 2018c).

Policy: Ontario

The Ontario Ministry of Education issued an information bulletin in 2007: *Policy/Program Memorandum No. 140 (PPM 140), Incorporating Methods of Applied Behaviour Analysis (ABA) into Programs for Students with Autism Spectrum Disorder (ASD).* Its communicated purpose was to provide "a policy framework to support incorporation of ABA methods into school boards' practices" and to give "direction to school boards to support their use of applied behaviour analysis (ABA) as an effective instructional approach in the education of many students with Autism Spectrum Disorder (ASD)" (Ontario Ministry of Education, 2007b, para. 1). *PPM 140* focused on the following:

- Describing ABA practices in the school setting, and
- Explaining the foundational principles of ABA-based programming (e.g., individualization, data collection, positive reinforcement, generalization).

Two specific directives are provided within its text:

- "School boards must offer students with ASD special education programs and services, including, where appropriate, special education programs using ABA methods" (para. 13)
- "School board staff must plan for the transition between various activities and settings involving students with ASD" (para. 20)

In *Autism Matters*, Laurie Pearce (2008) clarifies what this memorandum means at a practical level, stating, "The PPM makes it possible for you to insist that ABA strategies be included in your child's IEP [individual education plan]: it does not make it possible for you to insist that a board-certified behavior analyst or other behavioural expert be involved in developing (or delivering) your child's education" (p. 6).

Each school board employs staff with ABA expertise, which may or may not include an external behaviour consultant or board-certified behavior analyst (BCBA) who will assist the team working with the individual to incorporate ABA programming into their IEP. Pearce (2008) also clarifies that this initiative does not apply to IBI and its clinical presence or therapists in the school environment. Weiss, White, and Spoelstra (2008) followed up the implementation of *PPM 140* with an online parent survey supported by Autism Ontario that resulted in 640 responses. Among other conclusions, quantitative results showed that only 6% of participants rated the use of ABA principles in school environments as happening "all of the time." Forty-five percent rated its implementation as "never," 34% as "some of the time," and 15% as "most of the time." Qualitatively, "the most frequently occurring theme to emerge from parent comments involved concerns that ABA was not being implemented effectively with their children, as it is described by PPM-140" (p. 13).

The obvious direction and intention here is the movement toward strategies involving evidence-based ABA interventions, as well as the subtler move to embed transition plans in IEPs for all students with ASD, previously accessible only for students 14 years of age and older (excluding those with a giftedness identification alone; Ontario Ministry of Education, 2004). This directive became less unique when the ministry required transition plans in IEPs as a universal component for all students who are supported by an IEP, through *Policy/Program Memorandum 156 (PPM 156)* in 2013 (Ontario Ministry of Education, 2013).

Research: Quebec

Researchers Perez Repetto, Jasmin, Fombonne, Gisel, and Couture (2017) measured the sensory features of children with ASD at two time points (three/four years old; and five/six years old). Sixty-eight children diagnosed with ASD from the Autism Clinic of the Montreal Children's Hospital participated during the first time point, and 29 participated in the follow-up time point. Results from multiple standardized measures showed scores of children remained stable during the two time points. They did not demonstrate improvement in children with ASD as they age, unlike typically developing children. The results support the hypothesis that sensory features of children with ASD would remain stable over time.

Research: Newfoundland and Labrador

Pelly, Vardy, Fernandez, Newhook, and Chafe (2015) studied the cases of ASD in the Avalon Peninsula of Newfoundland and Labrador and noticed a significant increase in cases: from 10.1 to 16.7 per 10,000 reported from 2006 to 2010. The study found that only 72.4% of the diagnosed cases were referred to the provincial health services. On the basis of these findings, Pelly and colleagues recommended the need to establish improved methods of tracking ASD, the need for a provincial ASD registry, and further research in ASD in this population.

Read about It. Think about It. Write about It.

- What do you think the benefits and downfalls would be to develop a national autism strategy as compared to the regionalized approach currently implemented?

A LOOK BACK

Chapter 1, "Brief History of Autism Spectrum Disorder," focused on:

- The history of autism, early accounts of autism characteristics, the formation of the diagnosis, and changes in the DSM criteria to the current DSM-5 and the amalgamation of disorders to the autism spectrum disorder diagnosis
- Epidemiology of autism spectrum disorder, changes in epidemiology over time, and the focus in the Canadian context
- How ASD is portrayed in the mass media and potential benefits and drawbacks of this exposure, and self-advocacy
- Regional initiatives in ASD service provision

ADDITIONAL RESOURCES

"Autism's First Child"

http://www.theatlantic.com/magazine/archive/2010/10/autisms-first-child/308227

This comprehensive article profiles Donald T., the first child diagnosed with autism by Dr. Leo Kanner. Authors provide an in-depth overview of Donald's early life, as well as a summary of common social challenges individuals with ASD experience.

DSM-5 (American Psychiatric Association)

http://www.dsm5.org/Pages/Default.aspx

This informative website provides a detailed list of updates to DSM–5 criteria. Parents and/or professionals can review sample assessments and fact sheets, as well as view informational webinars related to the DSM–5.

Leo Kanner Collection (Johns Hopkins Medical Institution)

http://www.medicalarchives.jhmi.edu/papers/kanner.html

The Medical Archives of the Johns Hopkins Medical Institution house several articles authored by Dr. Leo Kanner as well as audio-recorded interviews. In these interviews, Dr. Kanner recounts his time in medical school as well as his initial impressions of Johns Hopkins Hospital, where he served in various clinical and academic roles from 1928 to 1981.

ASD in the DSM-5 (Autism Speaks)

www.autismspeaks.org/what-autism/diagnosis/dsm-5-diagnostic-criteria

This website provides a comprehensive list of the DSM-5 criteria for a diagnosis of ASD. Social communication issues and restricted, repetitive behaviours associated with a diagnosis of ASD are categorized as level 1, 2, or 3, depending on the level of support required. A summary of Social (Pragmatic) Communication Disorder is also included. This new addition to the DSM-5 presents with similar behaviours to ASD.

ASD Studies (Simon Fraser University)

http://autismlab.psyc.sfu.ca/studies

This website, housed by Simon Fraser University, lists current ASD-related studies. Parents and/or individuals with ASD can browse and sign up to participate in research on a variety of topics related to ASD. Additionally, this website includes useful links to funding resources, as well as governmental and academic institutions.

Carly's Café

www.carlyscafe.com

This short video clip by Carly Fleischmann provides her first-person account of her experience living with ASD. This video demonstrates Carly's sensory challenges and the frustration individuals may experience without an effective communication system.

Temple Grandin (Colorado State University)

www.colostate.edu/templegrandin

Dr. Temple Grandin is an author, presenter, animal advocate, and individual with ASD. This website provides an informative account of her impactful career in animal behaviour. Dr. Grandin has a unique ability to connect with animals, leading to ground-breaking innovations in methods used to handle animals.

Autism Spectrum Disorder among Children and Youth in Canada 2018: A Report of the National Autism Spectrum Disorder Surveillance System

https://www.canada.ca/en/public-health/services/publications/diseases-conditions/autism-spectrum-disorder-children-youth-canada-2018.html

This website links to a lengthy document authored by the National Autism Spectrum Disorder Surveillance System. Published in March 2018, this document included recent statistics on national, provincial, and territorial prevalence rates of ASD.

Government of Canada: ASD

https://www.canada.ca/en/public-health/services/diseases/autism-spectrum-disorder-asd.html

This Government of Canada website provides information on diagnostic features of ASD, as well as therapies and supports available to individuals with ASD and their families.

Autism Speaks Canada

https://www.autismspeaks.ca

Autism Speaks Canada is a national, charitable organization committed to helping individuals and families impacted by ASD. Autism Speaks Canada organizes a variety of fundraising events across Canada. Their mission is to improve services and resources and further acceptance and inclusion.

CHAPTER 2

Foundations of Autism Spectrum Disorder

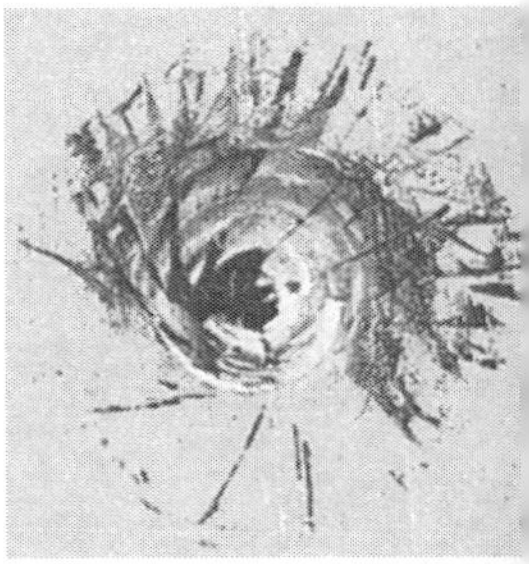

LEARNING OBJECTIVES

- Understand science, pseudoscience, and the most common types of research with respect to ASD.
- Be familiar with systematic reviews of research for ASD, evidence-based practices, and related Canadian contributions.
- Review *National Standards Project—Phase 2*'s results and methodology.
- Identify established evidence-based and emerging practices, as listed by NAC.

This chapter provides an overview of the science and research behind autism spectrum disorder (ASD). As a field that has had many unfortunate and unproven interventions made public, often at the expense of parents and children with ASD, the importance of evidence-based practice and interventions has become a focus. Recent reviews of literature pertaining to effective interventions for children and adults with ASD now exist. These will be covered, along with criteria for evidence-based interventions (EBIs). The type of research used and how these reviews were completed will be explored. A broad overview of the strategies found to be effective from the Phase 2 review by the National Autism Center (NAC; 2015) will be provided (see Chapters 3 and 4 for further details). Lastly, strategies that are found to be emerging and to be implemented with caution and awareness and those strategies that are unsupported in the literature will be noted.

A January 2020 Google search of the term *Autism Spectrum Disorder* returned 107,000,000 results in 0.55 seconds. This abundance of easily accessible information, ranging in quality and accuracy, highlights the need for stakeholders involved in intervention selections for individuals with ASD to develop a skill set in critiquing sources of information. Skills in this area are essential, as educators and clinicians are faced with a lengthy list of intervention options, each with varying quantity and quality of outcome-related evidence. In broad terms, ASD-related interventions can be grouped into two general categories: interventions based on science and interventions based on pseudoscience.

SCIENCE

To qualify as *science*, several important components need to be present. In the field of applied behaviour analysis (ABA), scientific interventions include an *operational definition* of the behaviour(s) targeted for change. An operational definition is different than a dictionary definition.

operational definition: a definition that breaks a broad concept, such as aggression, into *observable* and *measurable* actions, such as how often hitting or biting happens (Mayer, Sulzer-Azaroff, & Wallace, 2018).

It is necessary for behaviour to be defined in observable terms as behavioural science also includes direct, accurate, and repeated measurement of what are termed observable dimensions of behaviour (i.e., frequency, duration, latency; Horner et al., 2005).

Single-Subject Research

Behavioural science also includes controlled experiments. An experiment is a test that includes at least one independent variable and one dependent variable. An experiment includes a test condition that includes the independent variable and a control condition, where the independent variable is not present.

independent variable: "the variable the experimenter systematically manipulates," which may show its effect on the dependent variable (Malott & Shane, 2014, p. 73).

dependent variable: the variable measured throughout a controlled research experiment, which is affected by the manipulation of the independent variable.

Many of the experiments assessing interventions for individuals with ASD are designed using what is known as a single-subject research framework. This type of research design is effective for demonstrating individual behaviour change (Horner et al., 2005; ONTABA, 2017; Tankersley, Harjusola-Webb, & Landrum, 2008). Single-subject research, sometimes referred to as single-case design, does not mean there is only a single subject or participant. Rather, this term means that all participants receive all intervention conditions, allowing researchers to analyze and compare behaviour change across time and treatment conditions where the research participants are their own controls.

single-subject research: a type of research design whereby individual participants' data are compared to themselves, and they serve as their own controls.

The first step in a well-designed single-subject experiment is to collect baseline data. Baseline data are quantitative assessments of behaviour prior to treatment status. The behaviour targeted for change is typically referred to as the *target behaviour* (Alberto & Troutman, 2017). When baseline data are *stable* (i.e., a range of data points at or near the same level), researchers apply the interventions to the target behaviour. In research terms, the intervention is called the independent variable. When researchers apply the independent variable(s) to the target behaviour, this is called the *treatment phase*. Researchers continue to collect data on the target behaviour during the treatment phase to determine if the independent variable is having any effect. The purpose of a controlled experiment is to demonstrate that any change in the target behaviour (dependent variable) occurred as a result of the treatment or intervention (independent variable).

If a researcher can demonstrate that the treatment—and treatment alone—led to target behaviour change, then a *functional relationship* can be established. Researchers can claim a functional relationship is present if there is a significant change in the target behaviour that coincides with the introduction of the independent variable—repeatedly. If behaviour change only occurred during the treatment phase, the researcher has demonstrated that the change in behaviour occurred as a function of the treatment. A functional relationship between an independent and dependent variable demonstrates the highest level of behavioural science: experimental control (Mayer et al., 2018).

Authors of well-designed single-subject experiments publish their work in peer-reviewed journals. Single-subject research provides a detailed account of individual behaviour change and is the primary research design methodology to assess behavioural interventions for individuals with ASD (Horner et. al, 2005).

experimental control: The highest level of behavioural science, which demonstrates a functional relationship between the dependent and independent variables. It is deemed to be established in a controlled research study when three demonstrations of experimental effect occur at three different points in time (Horner et al., 2005, p. 168).

peer review: a process for journal publications and other academic work whereby researchers submit their work to field experts through a publisher. These experts scrutinize studies to determine if they make important contributions to the behavioural literature. Experts assess the quality of research and its results (NAC, 2015).

Group Design

A second type of research design used to evaluate ASD-related interventions is group design. Researchers using group design recruit large numbers of participants. Potential participants are divided into two separate research groups: an experimental group and a control group (Alberto & Troutman, 2017). Researchers tend to gather demographic information about participants such as age, gender, and diagnosis. Participants are placed in either the experimental or the control group with a result of balanced, matched groups. In group design research, the independent variable is applied to participants in the experimental group. The participants in the control group do not receive the intervention. The premise of this research design is that any improvements in the treatment group are attributed to the intervention, as this should be the only notable difference (Alberto & Troutman, 2017; Tankersley et al., 2008).

Comparing Single-Subject and Group Design Research

There are a few important differences between single-subject research and group design. Single-subject research records the *direct* measurement of observable behaviour (Horner et al., 2005; Mayer et al., 2018). Direct data collection means that the observer watches participants either in person or through video, while the researcher records data on the target behaviour. Group design research includes primarily *indirect* data collection tools to measure change. Participants (or others familiar with participants) complete assessments, surveys, or questionnaires, providing indirect information about perceived treatment effects.

Another important difference between group design and single-subject research relates to when data are collected. In group design research, data are collected during a few fixed points in time (i.e., Time 1, Time 2), usually at the beginning and end of an intervention. This differs from the frequent, consistent data collection during single-subject research. As noted, the ongoing, repeated measurement of a dependent variable across different conditions is a defining feature of single-subject research (Horner et al., 2005).

Single-subject research and group design also differ in how results are interpreted. Single-subject research collects raw data on a target behaviour and then this information is transferred to a line graph for interpretation. Line graphs can be constructed on graph paper or from data entered into a program like Microsoft Office *Excel* software (2019). Researchers, clinicians, or educators visually analyze graphed data to assesses the effectiveness of a treatment. Researchers evaluate whether behaviour data changed in level, trend, or variability from the baseline phase to the treatment phase. See Figures 2.1–2.3 for examples of data changing in level, trend, and variability.

Group Design Research Compared to Single-Subject Research

How could researchers use either group design or single-subject design to implement an investigation? The research question is: Does educational video game practice affect spatial skills? In this example, the independent variable is educational video game practice, and the dependent variable is spatial skills.

Researcher 1 uses group design for his study. He recruits 300 participants and randomly assigns each participant to either the treatment group or the control group.

At Time 1, the researcher provides all participants with an indirect assessment to complete, such as a questionnaire related to spatial skills. The participants in the treatment group receive the intervention (educational video game practice) while the participants in the control group do not. At Time 2 (e.g., six months later), the researcher re-administers the indirect assessment and statistically analyzes the results. Any differences in the scores between the treatment group and the control group may be attributed to the independent variable.

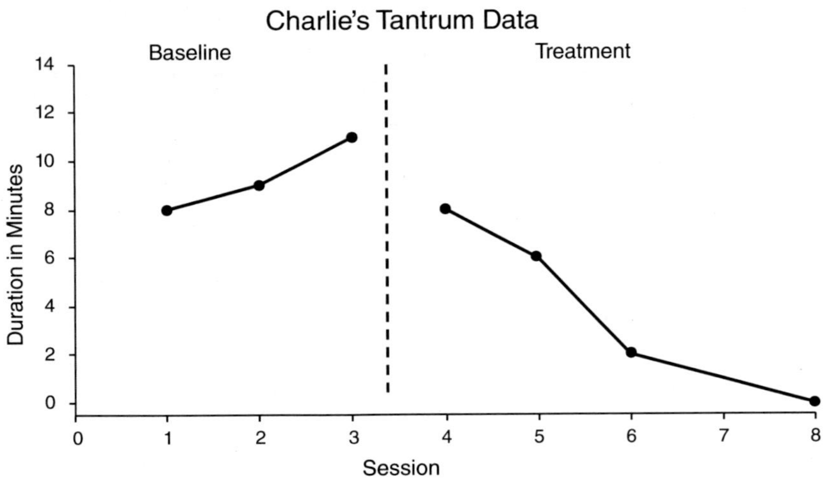

Figure 2.1: Data Changing in Trend

Source: Authors.

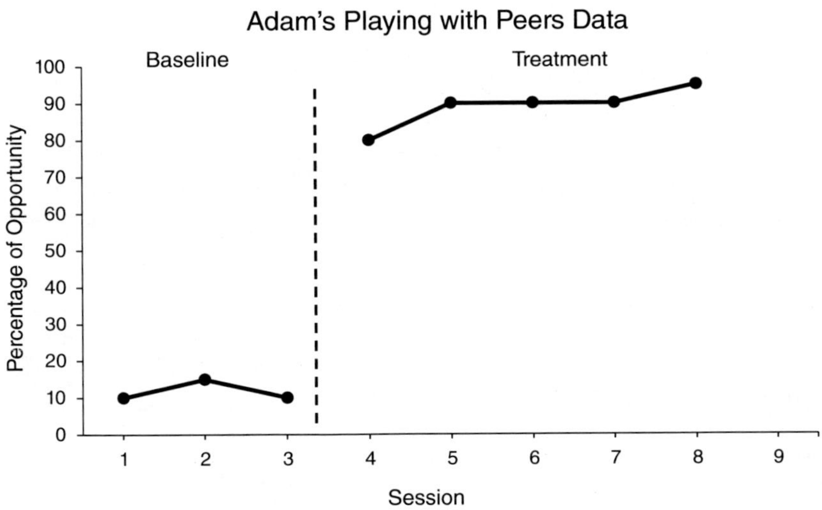

Figure 2.2: Data Changing in Level

Source: Authors.

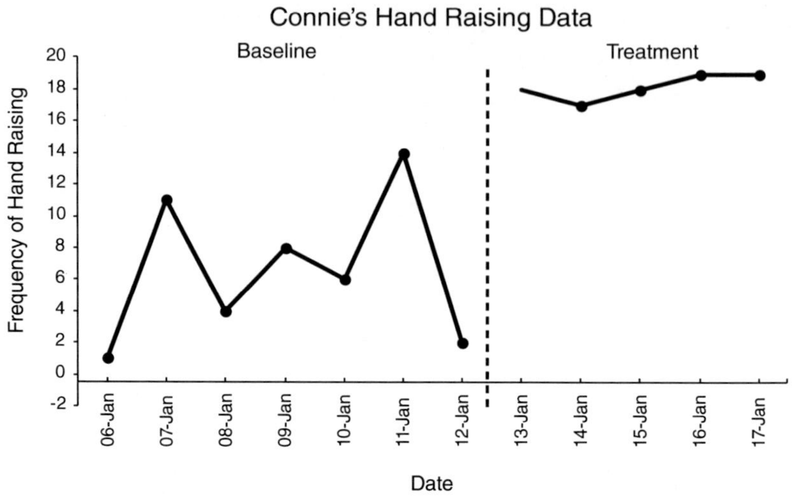

Figure 2.3: Data Changing in Variability
Source: Authors.

Researcher 2 uses single-subject design for her study. She operationally defines spatial skills into a directly observable behaviour (e.g., duration of time to complete a maze). She recruits three individuals to participate. She begins by collecting baseline data, measuring the duration of time it currently takes each participant to complete a maze. After three or more days of baseline measurements, the researcher provides each participant with the independent variable (educational video game practice). Each day, the researcher collects duration data on each participant. The researcher transfers her raw data to a graph. She carefully examines each participant's visual data to determine whether the independent variable had an effect on the dependent variable.

Group design research evaluates treatment effects using statistical analysis. Statistics are gathered from indirect data collection measures and analyzed using appropriate statistical calculations. Based on the results of these computations, the intervention is labelled as effective or as ineffective. Group design research typically presents statistical findings in tabular format.

PSEUDOSCIENCE

Even though the word *science* is found within the term *pseudoscience*, practitioners should be wary of pseudoscience and not equate this word with true science. The prefix *pseudo-* originates from the Greek term *pseudes,* alluding to something that appears at face-value to be one thing but is found to be another upon closer inspection. Unfortunately, for concerned parents, professionals, and educators, there are times and reasons that allow pseudoscientific interventions to prevail in the field of ASD. Factors such as the unique presentation of symptoms, the absence of consistent diagnostic processes, and no universal treatment approach provide opportunities for pseudoscience to continue to make unfounded claims (Smith & MacDonald, 2017). As mentioned previously, science relies on empirical, objective, and quantifiable evidence. This is not true of pseudoscience. Pseudoscience relies on very subjective forms of support such as testimonials and other first-person accounts (Green, 2010). Testimonials are subjective, unsubstantiated, first-person descriptions of the impact that a treatment may have had on one person or family (Green & Perry, 1999). Parents, clinicians, and educators should look out for *red flags* to help identify pseudoscience.

pseudoscience: a theory, approach, or intervention that claims scientific rigour and authority when there is no science and/or research that has been applied to the claim.

Pseudoscientific Therapies: Some Warning Signs

- High "success" rates are claimed.
- Rapid effects are promised.
- The therapy is said to be effective for many symptoms or disorders.
- The "theory" behind the therapy contradicts objective knowledge (and sometimes common sense).
- The therapy is said to be easy to administer, requiring little training or expertise.
- Other, proven treatments are said to be unnecessary, inferior, or harmful.
- Promoters of the therapy are working outside their area of expertise.
- Promoters benefit financially or otherwise from adoption of the therapy.
- Testimonials, anecdotes, or personal accounts are offered in support of claims about the therapy's effectiveness, but little or no objective evidence is provided.
- Catchy, emotionally appealing slogans are used in marketing the therapy.
- Belief and faith are said to be necessary for the therapy to "work."
- Skepticism and critical evaluation are said to make the therapy's effect evaporate.
- Promoters resist objective evaluation and scrutiny of the therapy by others.
- Negative findings from scientific studies are ignored or dismissed.
- Critics and scientific investigators are often met with hostility, and are accused of persecuting the promoters, being "closed-minded," or having some ulterior motive for "debunking" the therapy.

Source: Green & Perry, 1999; adapted from the American Arthritis Foundation.

Those who endorse pseudoscientific treatments often make grandiose, misleading claims which describe results that are typically impossible. Individuals may claim they are "cured" or that the intervention had a significant impact on many areas of functioning. Pseudoscientific claims of effectiveness are *not* included in peer-reviewed journals. Individuals publicize results in newsletters, videos, and on social media. Individuals promoting such interventions often have financial stakes in their success (Green & Perry, 1999). Practitioners need to be pseudoscience detectives and pay close attention to researcher claims. Pseudoscientists will go to great lengths to make their claims appear scientific by including deceptive graphs and figures.

Pseudoscientific Claim

The implications of selecting a pseudoscientific intervention to treat an ASD-related characteristic range from having little to no impact at all to significant, potentially harmful outcomes (Green & Perry, 1999). Interventions based on pseudoscience should be avoided.

Be a Pseudoscience Detective

Mr. Black, a homeopathic practitioner, recently posted a video to Facebook. In this short clip, Mr. Black described a recent consultation he had with a father. During this visit, the father reported that his young son flapped his hands and walked on the tips of his toes. Mr. Black prescribed the father two homeopathic medicines to give to his son. Mr. Black shared that in just three weeks of taking these medicines, there was a miraculous improvement. The father returns to visit Mr. Black and reports that almost 100% of the hand flapping is gone. Not only that, but the young boy is now reading! Mr. Black ends the video by inviting other families to contact his office to sign up for a reasonably priced consultation.

Look at the warning signs for pseudoscientific therapies listed by Green and Perry (1999). How many red flags can you detect in this example?

Read about It. Think about It. Write about It.

- Looking at the characteristics of pseudoscience versus science, have you ever mistakenly been taken advantage of by pseudoscience? What about in the field of ASD?

- Look at a single-subject study and group design research paper. Which one is easier for you to understand? What do you think the benefits and drawbacks are for each approach?
- Given that understanding research is a difficult and cumbersome task, how can we better communicate with and equip families of children with ASD to navigate toward high-quality research?

EVIDENCE-BASED PRACTICE AND ASD

Timeliness is important in ASD interventions. Practitioners want to prevent any of the possible negative implications associated with choosing a non-evidence-based, possibly ineffective, intervention. Yet selecting a suitable treatment to address specific target behaviours can be an overwhelming task for clinicians, educators, and parents. Hundreds of new articles are published in several journals every month, making it unrealistic for many stakeholders to stay up to date on all of the diverse literature. *So, what do we do?* In the last few years, credible groups have been developing comprehensive research reviews. These documents evaluate and classify ASD-related interventions based on the quality and quantity of evidence to support them (Gibbs & Gambrill, 2002). This information is compiled so that parents, clinicians, and educators have easy-to-access, vetted information on the outcomes associated with the wide range of intervention options (NAC, 2015). Another reason that researchers publish this information is to build capacity in stakeholders to assess intervention-specific research (Bulmer et al., 2012/2016). Developing such skills in evaluating research findings is a necessary prerequisite to

research quality: assessing the quality of research studies refers to how well studies are designed. Reviewers evaluate numbers of participants and types of data collection methodologies. High-quality studies will include detailed methodology sections that explain how studies were implemented (NAC, 2009, 2015).

quantity of evidence: reviewers assess the number of studies published about a particular intervention. They also quantify the number of different authors that have evaluated an intervention. The more often a successful study is carried out, the more potential evidence there is to support its effectiveness (NAC, 2009, 2015).

reliability: reviewers assess the results of each intervention to evaluate consistency. Reliable interventions will show consistent findings over time (NAC, 2009, 2015).

selecting appropriate interventions. Lastly, authors of comprehensive reviews describe limitations attached to current treatment literature. This is useful information to inform the direction of future studies (NAC, 2009, 2015; Wong et al., 2014).

Parents, professionals, and educators should consider a comprehensive, systematic research review as a credible and reputable source of information. Authors of these documents use rigorous methods when searching for, screening, and evaluating research studies. One way that researchers determine whether an intervention has the potential to be evidence-based is by examining the *strength of evidence* supporting that intervention (NAC, 2015). Reviewers determine strength of evidence by scoring the quality of the study, quantity of evidence, and consistency or reliability of evidence over time (NAC, 2015).

Prior to choosing interventions to change challenging behaviour, improve skills in socially significant areas, or teach new skills, practitioners should take time to review systematic studies. Below is a list of noteworthy comprehensive research reviews available to guide treatment selection for children, youth, and adults with ASD:

- The National Autism Center. (2009, 2015). *The national standards project report (phase 1 and 2).*
- Wong, C., Odom, S. L., Hume, K. Cox, A. W., Fettig, A., Kucharczyk, S., … & Schultz, T. R. (2014). *Evidence-based practices for children, youth, and young adults with autism spectrum disorder.*
- Ontario Association for Behaviour Analysis (ONTABA). (2017). *Evidence-based practices for individuals with autism spectrum disorder: Recommendations for caregivers, practitioners, and policy makers.*

For the information included in a comprehensive research review to be meaningful, readers need to be familiar with terminology and phrases used to describe outcomes and evidence associated with specific interventions. A variety of descriptive terms are used to classify interventions (see Table 2.1). These terms can be understood along a continuum, ranging from well-established to unsupported. Interventions labelled as promising or emerging fall somewhere between.

Read about It. Think about It. Write about It.

- Before reading this chapter, how did you think evidence-based interventions (EBIs) were determined? Is this different than your original perception?
- Search to see if you can find EBI documents for other disabilities. Are they as readily available as in the field of ASD?
- What are some downfalls to EBIs? Do a quick search to see what opponents of EBIs have to say.

Table 2.1: Summary of Terms for ASD Interventions

Evidence Based	**Emerging**	**Not Evidence Based**	
Good Evidence Showing Effectiveness	Some (Weaker) Positive Evidence	Insufficient Evidence to Inform Decision-Making	Good Evidence Showing Ineffectiveness/ Harmfulness
(Well) Established	Emerging	Unestablished	Ineffective
Empirically Validated	Evidence Informed		Not Recommended
Empirically Supported Treatment	Probably Efficacious		
	Practices with Some Support		Non-evidence Based
Definitely Use	**Use Only with Caution**	**Do Not Use**	**Definitely Do Not Use**

Source: Ontario Association for Behaviour Analysis (ONTABA), 2017, p. 14, Table 1.

COMPONENTS OF EVIDENCE-BASED PRACTICE

Another important term that practitioners, professionals, and caregivers should have a working understanding of is *evidence-based practice* (EBP). EBP is a broad decision-making framework made up of three individual but equally important skills: professional judgment; an awareness of the unique features of each client and family; and a thorough understanding of well-supported interventions (Bulmer et al., 2012/2016). Those who are acting in accordance with EBP demonstrate all of these valuable skills. The concept of EBP has been adopted in a variety of educational, medical, and social service sectors to assist with decisions related to treatment selection (Slocum et al., 2014). EBP is emphasized in many other health and social service sectors such as psychology, nursing, and social work. Professionals, clinicians, and educators supporting individuals and families around ASD should strive to develop a skill set that includes expertise in all components of EBP.

Professional Judgment

Professional judgment, sometimes referred to as professional expertise, relates to the skill set professionals acquire through education, training, and experience. This professional judgment or expertise results in effective practice (APA, 2013b). The clinical and interpersonal skills professionals acquire are also an important component of expertise. Professional judgment often correlates with the length of time a professional has been practising (i.e., longer careers result in more developed skills). Professionals also develop such judgment by engaging in a range of work-related activities. Practitioners and educators should continue to read and interpret literature and communicate with a wide variety of audiences (e.g., parents, professionals, students). Professionals demonstrate strong judgment by having an awareness of situations that warrant the involvement of another professional discipline (Bulmer et al., 2012/2016; Slocum et al., 2014). Individuals within the field of ASD improve expertise through ongoing professional development, reading research, attending and presenting at conferences, and remaining connected to professional colleagues—within and beyond their own disciplines.

Client and Family Values

In studies involving individuals with ASD, the terms *client*, *student*, or *participant* are often used to describe the individual whose behaviour has been targeted for change. The term *client* can also extend to include others who may indirectly benefit from the behaviour change, such as parents, caregivers, and siblings (Slocum et al., 2014). Professionals practising in an evidence-based manner should collaboratively consider the values, opinions, and preferences of their clients when selecting interventions.

Evidence-based Interventions (EBIs)

It is essential for professionals involved in intervention selection for individuals with ASD to have a thorough knowledge of well-established interventions. EBIs are a necessary component of evidence-based practice but are not the sole component (Bulmer et al., 2012/2016).

> **evidence-based interventions (EBIs):** "specific interventions that have led to successful outcomes for specific target behaviour in learners that share particular characteristics, in well-designed scientific studies" (Bulmer et al., 2012/2016, p. 3).

Read about It. Think about It. Write about It.

- What is the difference between EBP and EBIs?
- Given that professional judgment is so important in implementing any of the evidence-supported strategies, how valid is the categorical approach to classifying an intervention as evidence-based?

A TIMELINE OF SYSTEMATIC RESEARCH REVIEWS

Researchers have compiled several large-scale, comprehensive literature reviews to assist with selecting EBIs. There are a number of high-quality, detailed reports to assist with this task, which are described below.

National Standards Project—Phase 1

In 2009, a panel of expert clinicians and educators from a variety of ASD-related professions convened to update documented clinical practices guiding treatment and educational supports for young children with ASD. Practitioners revised existing guidelines to reflect the recent increase in research evaluating educational and behavioural interventions (NAC, 2009). As the number of studies evaluating treatments for young children with ASD expand, practice guidelines were and are updated to account for this growing body of research. At the time, this comprehensive project was the largest ASD-related research review (NAC, 2009). This expert panel of authors produced a 174-page document titled *National Standards Project—Assessing the Need for Evidence-based Practice Guidelines for Autism Spectrum Disorders*. The National Standards Project reviewed research studies published between 1957 and 2007 involving participants under 22 years of age diagnosed with autistic disorder, Asperger's disorder, or PDD-NOS (NAC, 2009).

An important first step in planning a large-scale literature summary is to develop criteria to determine which articles will be included. Articles can be excluded for several reasons, such as sample size, data collection, or methodology (NAC, 2009, 2015; Wong et al., 2014). To avoid any perceptions of bias, it is good practice for such exclusion or inclusion rationales to be shared. Consumers of research who read large-scale, comprehensive reviews of literature should pay close attention to inclusion criteria, as they are often a defining reason for differing results between publications (Bulmer et al., 2012/2016). Authors of the National Standards Project included a detailed overview of the decision-making model used to include or omit research articles (NAC, 2009).

To meet inclusion criteria for this project:

- The main focus of the research article had to evaluate a behavioural or educational intervention.
- The research article needed to include statistical analyses or graphic display of data.
- The article had to be published in an English-language, print, peer-reviewed journal (NAC, 2009).

In total, 775 research articles met these criteria and were reviewed (NAC, 2009).

The results of *National Standards Project—Phase 1* provided meaningful information for parents, educators, and clinicians on outcomes associated with various interventions for young individuals with ASD. After vetting, reading, and evaluating each research study, authors labelled 11 interventions as *established*. This group of interventions led to meaningful behaviour change in participants and could be considered effective for individuals with ASD under 22 years of age (NAC, 2009). Twenty-two treatments were labelled as *emerging*, meaning there was some support that these treatments contributed to behaviour change, but more research was warranted. A third category, titled *unestablished*, included five treatments described as ineffective and potentially harmful (NAC, 2009).

Evidence-based Practices for Children, Youth, and Young Adults with Autism Spectrum Disorder

Subsequent to the *National Standards Project—Phase 1*, several authors released *Evidence-based Practices for Children, Youth, and Young Adults with Autism Spectrum Disorder* (Wong et al., 2014). This comprehensive review of literature developed through the National Professional Development Center on Autism Spectrum Disorder (NPDC) categorized interventions as either comprehensive treatment models (CTM) or focused intervention practices (Wong et al., 2014).

> **comprehensive treatment model**: an intervention that focuses on the core deficits of ASD where multiple strategies and practices are combined together around a core theory (Wong et al., 2014).

> **focused intervention packages**: interventions that are typically operationally defined, customized to learners, and delivered in a shorter time frame than a comprehensive treatment model (Wong et al., 2014).

Evidence-based Practices for Children, Youth, and Young Adults with Autism Spectrum Disorder reviewed updated, evidence-specific, focused interventions with the intent of assisting educators in the selection of interventions for developing individual education plans (IEPs) for students with ASD (Wong et al., 2014). Using slightly different inclusion criteria than the *National Standards Project—Phase 1*, Wong and colleagues' (2014) review included 456 research articles. After a detailed analysis of each article, Wong and colleagues categorized 27 interventions for ASD as EBP. These interventions demonstrated significant, positive outcomes across several well-designed studies. The authors grouped several other interventions together in a category called *Other Practices with Some Support*. Many of the practices included in this category were combinations of EBP that did not have enough empirical support evaluating them in a grouped format (Wong et al., 2014).

Canadian Contributions to Evidence-based Practice

A Canadian publication authored by Dr. Adrienne Perry and Dr. Rosemary Condillac titled *Evidence-based Practices for Children and Adolescents with Autism Spectrum Disorders*

Table 2.2: Overview of Comprehensive Research Review

Intervention	NAC (2015)	NPDC on ASD (2014)	Maine (2009)
Behavioural Interventions; Comprehensive/ Intensive Behavioural Treatment for Young Children	The NPDC on ASD and the Maine Departments of Health & Human Services/Education did not report on specific "comprehensive programs for young children" or "behavioural packages"; however, many of the components in the intervention packages identified as effective by the National Autism Center overlap with individual interventions identified as effective by NPDC on ASD and the Maine Departments of Health & Human Services/Education.		
Antecedent-based Interventions	X	X	X
Cognitive Behaviour Intervention	X	X	promising evidence[1]
Differential Reinforcement	X	X	X
Discrete Trial Training	X	X	X
Exercise	emerging[2]	X	X
Extinction	X	X	X
Functional Behaviour Assessment	X	X	X
Functional Communication Training	emerging[2]	X	X
Modelling	X	X	X
Parent-Implemented Intervention	X	X	X
Peer-Mediated Instruction and Intervention	X	X	X
Picture Exchange Communication System (PECS)	emerging[2]	X	X

(*continued*)

Table 2.2: *Continued*

Intervention	NAC (2015)	NPDC on ASD (2014)	Maine (2009)
Pivotal Response Training (PRT)	X	X	X
Prompting	X	X	X
Naturalistic Intervention/ Incidental Teaching	X	X	X
Reinforcement	X	X	X
Response Interruption/ Redirection	X	X	X
Scripting	X	X	not reviewed
Self-Management	X	X	X
Social Narratives/ Story-based Interventions	X	X	insufficient evidence
Social Skills Training	X	X	insufficient evidence
Task Analysis	X	X	X
Technology Aided Instruction and Intervention	emerging[2]	X	promising evidence[1]
Time Delay	X	X	X
Video Modelling	X	X	X
Visual Supports/ Schedules	X	X	X

1. The Maine Departments of Health & Human Services/Education identified an intervention as having "promising evidence" when it had shown positive effects in two or more well-controlled research studies, but the reviewers judged that additional research by independent teams was necessary to further support the effectiveness of the intervention.
2. The National Autism Center review identified interventions as "emerging" when at least one well-controlled study indicated that the intervention may show beneficial results, but "additional high-quality studies are needed that consistently show these interventions to be effective for individuals with ASD."
Source: Bulmer et al., 2012/2016.

(2003) was the first large-scale review of ASD interventions geared toward Canadian professionals. Using DSM-IV criteria, this document referred to a subset of pervasive developmental disorders (PDDs) sharing common features of impairments in social skills, verbal and nonverbal communication, and restricted and repetitive behaviours (APA, 2000; Perry & Condillac, 2003). At the time of publication, this document was intended to assist mental health professionals with treatment selection, with the additional goal of extending to families and professionals in other relevant sectors (Perry & Condillac, 2003).

Even though diagnostic terminology and prevalence rates have changed, the role of literature summaries in the field of ASD remains consistent. In 2016, a group of authors in Atlantic Canada updated an information paper titled *Evidence-based Practice for Learners with Autism Spectrum Disorder* (Bulmer et al., 2012/2016). Like earlier publications, this paper is intended to assist practitioners with selecting EBIs, as well as to further the discussion of possible risks and potential benefits associated with treating ASD. See Table 2.2 for a comparison of results across comprehensive literature reviews.

Findings and Conclusions: National Standards Project—Phase 2

On April 2, 2015 (World Autism Day), the National Autism Center released an updated review of interventions for individuals with ASD. This report, titled *National Standards Project—Phase 2* reviewed research articles from 2007–2012 (NAC, 2015). Unique to this publication, articles involving interventions for adults over 22 years of age were systematically reviewed for the first time. Based on similar inclusion criteria to the earlier Phase 1, 27 articles assessing interventions for adults met criteria for this project (NAC, 2015). Authors of this comprehensive review grouped treatment outcomes as established, emerging, or unestablished (NAC, 2015).

> **established interventions**: a category of interventions grouped and defined by the NAC. Interventions with this classification have scientific evidence indicating favourable outcomes for individuals on the autism spectrum (NAC, 2015).

> **emerging interventions**: a category of interventions grouped and defined by the NAC based on scientific evidence, where "one or more studies suggest that an intervention produces favorable outcomes for individuals with ASD. Additional high-quality studies must consistently show this outcome before firm conclusions about intervention effectiveness can be made" (NAC, 2015, p. 34).

Findings and Conclusions from Phase 2

The National Autism Center's *Findings and Conclusions: National Standards Project—Phase 2* (2015) classified interventions as either established, emerging, or unestablished. Additionally, established interventions were further subclassified based on variables such as target skill area and age group. Age groups were children, adolescents, and young adults (i.e., 0–22 years of age), and adult (22 years of age and older). Target skills were also classified as either skill increase or behaviour reduction (NAC, 2015). Such categorization may increase confidence with outcomes associated with a specific intervention. Practitioners, parents, or educators could use this subclassification system to quickly identify interventions with favourable outcomes based on the age of the student/child, the specific target area to increase, or the challenging behaviour to be reduced (see Tables 2.3 and 2.4). This subclassification system also identifies current gaps in available literature. It is anticipated that practitioners and educators will be motivated to carry out well-designed research studies to address some of the current limitations.

> **unestablished interventions**: a category of interventions grouped and defined by the NAC as having little or no scientific evidence to base conclusions about intervention effectiveness for individuals with ASD. Future research could show such interventions to be effective, ineffective, or harmful (NAC, 2015).

Table 2.3: Skill Areas Targeted for Increase

Target Area	Description
Academic	• Prerequisite skills necessary for success in school tasks • Includes behaviours such as sequencing, letter/number/colour recognition, as well as mathematics, literacy
Communication	• Verbal and/or nonverbal acknowledgement toward a social partner • Includes behaviours such as requesting, conversation, vocabulary, and articulation
Higher Cognitive Functions	• Problem-solving skills that do not require a social partner • Includes such areas as IQ, memory, organizational skills, and executive functions
Interpersonal	• Social interaction between at least two people • Includes such areas as joint attention, pretend play, participating in a group
Learning Readiness	• Foundational skills needed to learn more complex tasks • Includes behaviours such as following instructions, waiting, and attending to environment

Target Area	Description
Motor Skills	• Coordination of fine or gross motor muscles • Includes behaviours such as cutting, typing, walking, throwing/catching a ball
Personal Responsibility	• Everyday, routine activities or events • Includes behaviours such as feeding, sleeping, toileting, time/money management
Placement	• Studies that mentioned restricted school, home, or community placement • Examples include general education setting
Play	• Non-academic, leisure tasks that do not necessarily involve a social partner • Includes behaviours such as appropriate independent toy use
Self-Regulation	• Ability to manage own behaviour to achieve a goal • Includes behaviours such as persistence, remaining on-task, and coping with change

Source: NAC, 2015.

Table 2.4: Behaviour Areas Targeted for Reduction

Behaviour	Description
General Symptoms	• Symptoms directly associated with a diagnosis of ASD
Problem Behaviours	• Behaviours that may harm the individual and/or others • Behaviours that may be a barrier to participating in community/school routines • Includes behaviours such as self-injury, aggression, property destruction
Restricted, Repetitive, Non-functional Patterns of Behaviour, Interests, or Activity (RRN)	• Frequent, maladaptive motor, vocal, or cognitive behaviour • Includes behaviours such as stereotypy, restricted interests
Sensory or Emotional Regulation (SER)	• Managing arousal level to be an active member of community • Includes behaviours such as sleep disturbance, anxiety, depression

Source: NAC, 2015.

Read about It. Think about It. Write about It.

- Review the evidence-based documents for ASD described in this chapter. What similarities and differences did you notice between them? What was most appealing to you?
- Examine the different methodologies that were used in the various evidence-based review documents. Do you think their methodologies influenced their results? Why or why not?
- Do you feel that the evidence-based practice documents for ASD are accessible to all, including parents and individuals with ASD?

ESTABLISHED INTERVENTIONS

The remainder of this chapter will provide a brief description of the established interventions listed in *Findings and Conclusions: National Standards Project—Phase 2*.

Behavioural Interventions

The *National Standards Project—Phase 2* uses the term *behavioural interventions* to describe a broad class of practices largely based in applied behaviour analysis (ABA).

ABA changes behaviour (increasing skills or reducing problematic behaviours) in a very systematic manner. This teaching method breaks learning opportunities down into smaller interactions to promote effective analysis. ABA uses a three-term contingency to describe learning (see Figure 2.4). ABA analyzes the events that occur before and after a specific behaviour. The events that occur immediately before target behaviours are called antecedents, and the events that follow a target behaviour are called consequences (Alberto & Troutman 2017; Mayer et al., 2018).

> **applied behaviour analysis (ABA)**: a broad field of intervention using scientific principles of learning and behaviour to effect change by increasing desirable skills and decreasing undesirable behaviours. ABA has been proven effective with people of all ages. It is based on analysis of individual behaviours, the use of specific reinforcers, ongoing data collection, frequent assessment of progress, and program adjustments as required (Kearney, 2008).

ABA continues to be one of the most established treatments for individuals with ASD and is the basis for many provincially funded clinical intervention programs, as well as policies in Canadian schools. After reviewing 155 articles related to behavioural interventions, the authors of the *Findings and Conclusions: National Standards Project—Phase 2* determined this class of practices to be effective for increasing a variety of skills and reducing a range of problematic behaviours in individuals with ASD aged 3 to 22

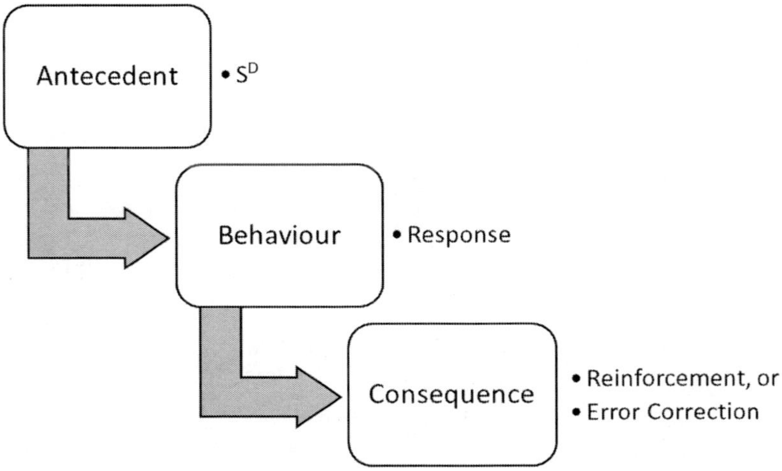

Figure 2.4: Three-term Contingency

Source: Authors.

Example

Examples of Behavioral Interventions consisting of one identified component:

- Joint Attention Intervention
- Chaining
- Differential Observing Response (DOR)
- Forward Chaining
- Function-based Intervention
- Imitation Training
- Reinforcement Schedule (schedule specified)
- Response Interruption and Redirection (RIRD)
- Repeated Practice
- Standard Echoic Training

Examples of Behavioral Interventions consisting of two identified components:

- Extinction + Reinforcement
- Function-based intervention + prompts
- Sign Extinction + Differential Reinforcement of Alternative Behavior (DRA)
- Stimulus Fading + Positive Reinforcement

Examples of Behavioral Interventions consisting of three identified components:

- Choice + Task Interspersal + Positive Reinforcement
- Discrete-trial Training + Natural Consequences + Error Correction
- Most to Least Prompting + Natural Consequences + Activity Interspersal
- Preteaching + Prompting + Positive Reinforcement

Examples of Behavioral Interventions consisting of four or more identified components:

- Combined Task Direction + Contingent Reinforcement + Physical Prompts + Stimulus Fading
- Modeling + Prompting + Reinforcement + Redirection + Abolishing Operation Component
- Prompt Delay + Auditory Scripts + Manual Prompts + Behavioral Rehearsal + Tokens
- Reinforcement Pairing + Habit Reversal + GaitSpot Squeakers + Differential Reinforcement of Incompatible Behavior (DRI)
- Video Modeling + DRA + Escape Extinction + Stimulus Fading + Photo Prompting
- Video Modeling + Highlighting + Prompting/Fading + Reinforcement
- Video Modeling + Photo Prompts + Contact Desensitization + Shaping + Differential Reinforcement of Other Behavior (DRO) + Escape Extinction
- Written Task Analysis + Social Scripts + Prompting + Self-monitoring + Fading

Figure 2.5: Examples of Behavioural Interventions

Source: NAC, 2015, p. 44.

and over (NAC, 2015). Some of the reviewed studies assessed the effectiveness of a single-behaviour intervention (e.g., chaining); however, most included a combination or package of interventions addressing antecedent and consequent events.

Cognitive Behavioural Interventions Package

Recently, there has been an increase in the number of well-designed studies evaluating cognitive behavioural interventions (CBI) for individuals with ASD (NAC, 2015). Earlier large-scale research reviews listed cognitive behavioural intervention packages (CBIPs) as emerging interventions (NAC, 2009; Wong et al., 2014). The *National Standards Project—Phase 2* reviewed 10 articles evaluating CBIPs and classified it as established for youth 6 to 14 years old (NAC, 2015). CBIPs are demonstrated as effective for sensory regulation, increasing cognitive and interpersonal skills, and reducing problem behaviour (NAC, 2015). Typically, these practices follow a manualized curriculum that includes education, strategies for stress and anxiety, homework, and parent involvement (NAC, 2015).

Comprehensive Behavioural Treatment for Young Children

Comprehensive behavioural treatment for young children (CBTYC) is a broad, systematic program that addresses skills across a range of developmental areas (e.g., communication, social skills, self-help skills; NAC, 2015). Skills addressed in these comprehensive programs are taught using principles of ABA. The *National Standards Project—Phase 2* reviewed 20 articles and labelled these programs effective for children up to nine years old (NAC, 2015). CBTYC was demonstrated to be effective for increasing skills such as play, communication, and motor skills, as well as reducing general ASD symptoms and specific problematic behaviour (NAC, 2015).

Across Canada, many government-funded autism intervention programs resemble comprehensive behaviour treatment. Canadian versions of these programs are called intensive behaviour intervention (IBI) or early intensive behaviour intervention (EIBI; de Rivera, 2008). IBI is typically delivered several hours per day (approximately 20–30 hours per week) for 2 to 3 years, with the primary goal of improving the developmental trajectory for children with ASD to more closely match their same-age peers. The framework of this intervention is based on research carried out by Lovaas and his students at the University of California at Los Angeles. It was Lovaas's hypothesis that "construction of a special, intense, and comprehensive learning environment for very young autistic children would allow some of them to catch up with their peers by first grade" (Lovaas, 1987, p. 4).

IBI includes a variety of ABA-based teaching methods, such as discrete trial training (DTT), and naturalistic methods, such as incidental teaching. It necessitates the collection and analysis of data to guide decisions about progress. IBI can be delivered across several learning environments such as home, community, and specialized learning centres. This teaching method can be implemented individually or with small groups of children.

Read about It. Think about It. Write about It.

- Many of the ASD EBIs are presented in packages for ease and to make larger categories of interventions. What are the benefits and downfalls of this approach to categorization?

Language Training (Production)

Language training (production) involves selecting developmentally appropriate vocal targets and using strategies such as modelling, prompting, and reinforcement to elicit spoken communication (NAC, 2015). Previously classified as emerging, the *National Standards Project—Phase 2* reviewed two articles including language training (production) and labelled it effective for increasing communication skills and as considered established for children three to nine years old (NAC, 2015).

Modelling

Showing someone how to perform a skill is one of the easiest and most effective ways to teach. Modelling is "teaching by correctly demonstrating the target behaviour to be learned" (NAC, 2015, p. 51). Modelled responses can be delivered *in vivo*, which means the target behaviour is presented live in front of the individual with ASD, or via video, where a recorded demonstration of the target behaviour is presented on a monitor (see Figure 2.6). When teaching using either live or video modelling, it is important that

- The target behaviour is clearly performed; and,
- The learner is paying attention to the model.

National Standards Project—Phase 2 reviewed 28 articles that included modelling as the primary intervention. This intervention is classified as established for increasing communication, interpersonal, and play skills; academics; and personal responsibility, as well as reducing problem behaviour in children and youth 3 to 18 years old (NAC, 2015).

VIDEO MODELLING

Video Modelling: when an individual is pre-recorded while performing a target behaviour. This video can later be watched by individuals with ASD. Any individual can be pre-recorded, even individuals with ASD (National Autism Center, 2015).

Video Modelling:

(1) (2) (3) (4)

(1) A model is pre-recorded demonstrating the behaviour.
(2) An individual with ASD can watch this video on a TV or computer screen.
(3) The individual with ASD needs to be encouraged to pay attention to the video.
(4) Important steps need to be identified (National Autism Center, 2015).

Figure 2.6: Video Modelling

Source: Authors.

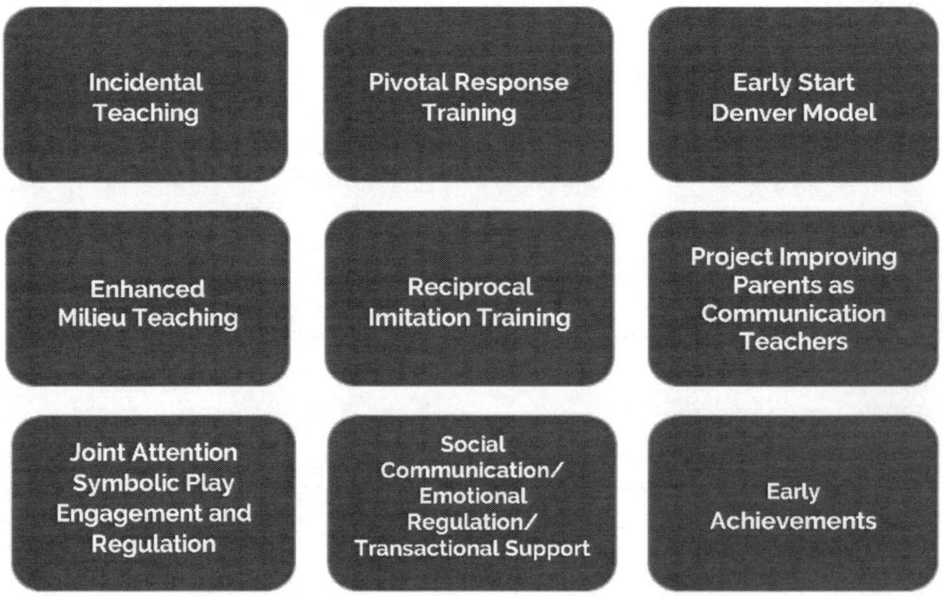

Figure 2.7: Examples of Naturalistic Teaching Strategies

Source: Authors.

Naturalistic Teaching Strategies

Naturalistic teaching strategies (NTS) use current interests and motivations, as well as familiar items and common home, school, and community routines to teach communication, adaptive living, and play skills (NAC, 2015). Another important component of naturalistic teaching is delivering reinforcement that is naturally connected to the target behaviour. This means there is a link between the response the learner performs and the reinforcer that follows (NAC, 2015).

Naturalistic Teaching Example

Alex, a young child with ASD, is showing interest in playing with bubbles. He is staring at the jar of bubbles on the shelf, reaching toward the jar, and vocalizing. His mother recognizes these behaviours as indicators that Alex is likely motivated now by bubbles and uses this opportunity to target communication. Alex's mother bends down close to Alex and models the sound /b/. Alex imitates this sound (the target behaviour). His mother provides the naturally connected reinforcer and blows bubbles for Alex to pop!

Figure 2.8: Blowing Bubbles

Source: marvelmozhko, Pixabay.

National Standards Project—Phase 2 reviewed three articles that included naturalistic teaching strategies. This intervention is effective for children up to nine years old and for increasing learning readiness and communication (NAC, 2015). Interventions such as milieu teaching, incidental teaching, and embedded learning include similar teaching presentations and are often grouped under NTS (NAC, 2009, 2015).

Parent-Training Package

Parent training as an intervention was evaluated in earlier large-scale research reviews, which evaluated parent-training literature focused on studies that trained parents to act as therapists (NAC, 2015). *National Standards Project—Phase 2* included studies related to general parent education and the important, therapeutic support role parents of individuals with ASD play (NAC, 2015). Parent education can be delivered in a variety of formats and address a range of skill areas. The *National Standards Project—Phase 2* reviewed 11 articles and identified parent-training packages to be effective for increasing interpersonal and play skills, as well as reducing general ASD symptoms, problem behaviours, and restricted interests (NAC, 2015).

Peer-Training Package

Peer-training packages train similar-aged peers to initiate and respond to social interaction attempts from children and youth with ASD (NAC, 2015). These interventions are carried out in the school and community settings with the goal of reducing the need for adults to prompt social skills (NAC, 2015). It is advantageous if the selected peer and the individual with ASD have a common interest to promote meaningful social interactions. Peer training focuses on social skills such as sharing, turn-taking, and appropriate play skills. The *National Standards Project—Phase 2* reviewed three articles and classified peer training as an established intervention effective for increasing learning readiness, communication, and interpersonal skills with children and youth aged 3 to 14 (NAC, 2015).

Pivotal Response Treatment

Pivotal response treatment, or pivotal response training (PRT), is a comprehensive teaching approach primarily used with young children with ASD. This intervention highlights key developmental areas such as motivation, initiation, self-management, and generalization, with teaching opportunities presented through naturally occurring routines (NAC, 2015). After reviewing six research studies on PRT, the NAC classified this intervention as effective for increasing learning readiness, communication, and play skills with children aged three to nine (NAC, 2015).

Schedules

Schedules provide individuals with ASD information about the order of activities to be completed within a specified time period (NAC, 2015). They are flexible interventions and can be used to present small amounts of simple information, such as two activities and a break, or to list a sequence of steps required to complete a work task. Schedules can be used during leisure activities, social interactions, academic lessons, or self-care routines (NAC, 2015). Schedules can present information using objects, real photos, abstract images, words, or a combination of these options. Prior to selecting a schedule as an intervention method, it is necessary that the learner demonstrates picture-identification skills, an essential prerequisite. *National Standards Project—Phase 2* reviewed two articles evaluating schedules and determined schedules to be an established intervention to address self-regulation in children aged three to nine (NAC, 2015).

Scripting

Scripting is an intervention that includes a written and/or verbal script about expected behaviour during a specific situation or event (NAC, 2015). Scripts are repeatedly reviewed and practised before the individual is expected to use the target skills in the specific situation. Scripting has shown its effectiveness for children aged 3 to 14 to increase play, communication, and interpersonal skills (NAC, 2015). Previously labelled as emerging (NAC, 2009), *National Standards Project—Phase 2* categorizes scripting as established (NAC, 2015). Prior to choosing scripting as a potential intervention, practitioners should assess for verbal imitation and reading abilities. Scripts are often taught using additional ABA-based strategies, such as prompting and reinforcement (NAC, 2015).

Self-management

Managing behaviour in the absence of adult supervision is a necessary and valued skill in society and very important to teach to children, youth, and adults with ASD (NAC 2009, 2015; Wong et al., 2014). It is a complex skill that involves assessing and monitoring behaviour, as well as the ability to work for longer periods of time without external reinforcement. Prior to teaching self-management, practitioners need to:

- Assess that the individual *can* complete the specific task required
- Determine reinforcers (conduct a preference assessment)
- Establish a clear criterion for target behaviour (NAC, 2015)

As part of *National Standards Project—Phase 2*, 10 articles specific to self-management were reviewed. This intervention is effective for youth aged 15–21 to increase academic, self-regulation, and communication skills, as well as reduce restrictive interests and repetitive behaviours (NAC, 2015).

Social Skills Package

Challenges in social skills are a core characteristic of ASD (APA, 2013). Impairments in this area can include lack of eye contact; difficulty beginning, maintaining, or ending a conversation; and inaccurate or inconsistent use of nonverbal body language (e.g., facial expressions, gestures; APA, 2013b; NAC, 2015; Taheri & Perry, 2012). Social skills interventions use prompting, modelling, and reinforcement to teach a variety of social behaviours (NAC, 2015). These interventions can be delivered individually or in groups in home, school, or community settings. *National Standards Project—Phase 2* reviewed 21 articles and determined this group of interventions to be effective for learners 13–18 years old, and they are effective to increase communication, interpersonal, and play skills, as well as reduce general ASD symptoms and restricted and repetitive behaviours (NAC, 2015).

Story-based Intervention

Story-based interventions describe appropriate social behaviour that should be demonstrated in a specific situation (NAC, 2015). They often describe the social scenario from the perspective of others involved (e.g., my friends don't like it when I take something from their desk without asking). Looking at an interaction from another person's perspective is often an area of difficulty for individuals with ASD. Using story formats, these interventions include information such as:

- a description of a target behaviour;
- the situation the target behaviour should occur in;
- a brief rationale explaining the importance of demonstrating the target behaviour;
- an overview of consequences that will follow the target behaviour; and
- a description of other potential consequences for unwanted, inappropriate behaviours. (Gray, 2019)

Story-based interventions can also include pictures and comprehension (NAC, 2015). *National Standards Project—Phase 2* reviewed 15 articles related to story-based interventions and determined them to be effective for increasing communication, learning readiness, and self-regulation, as well as reducing problematic behaviour (NAC, 2015).

ESTABLISHED INTERVENTIONS FOR INDIVIDUALS WITH ASD OVER 22 YEARS OLD

For the first time, interventions for adults (over 22 years old) were included as part of the *National Standards Project—Phase 2*. This addition reflects the growing body of research that includes adults as participants. Authors of this comprehensive publication reviewed 17 articles and determined behavioural interventions as the only effective intervention that meets established criteria. Behavioural interventions are based on ABA and include antecedent strategies to increase behaviour, as well as consequence-based interventions (see Figure 2.9). This set of practices increased communication, personal responsibility, and self-regulation, as well as reducing problematic behaviour (NAC, 2015).

Read about It. Think about It. Write about It.

- There is a substantially shorter list of effective EBIs for adults 22 years and older. Why do you think there are fewer EBIs for this age group?
- Look up critical issues for adults with ASD on the Internet—or discuss. Does the lack of EBIs contribute to some of these issues?

Established Intervention & Detailed Description	The Behavioral Intervention category is comprised of interventions typically described as antecedent interventions and consequent interventions. Antecedent interventions involve the modification of situational events that typically precede the occurrence of a target behavior. These alterations are made to increase the likelihood of success or reduce the likelihood of problems occurring. Consequent interventions involve making changes to the environment following the occurrence of a targeted behavior. Many of the consequent interventions are designed to reduce problem behavior and teach functional alternative behaviors or skills through the application of basic principles of behavior change.
Basic Facts	Number of articles reviewed: NSP2 = **17** Effective ages: Adults 22+ years Skills increased: • communication • personal responsibility • self-regulation Behaviors decreased: • problem behaviors

Figure 2.9: Behavioural Interventions for Adults

Source: NAC, 2015, pp. 74–75.

Example

Examples of Behavioral Interventions consisting of one identified component:

- Prompting
- Extinction (sensory and escape)
- Differential Reinforcement of Incompatible Behavior (DRI)
- Choice
- Functional Communication Training

Examples of Behavioral Interventions consisting of two identified components:

- Prompting + Error Correction
- Prompting + Blocking
- Escape Extinction + Sensory Extinction
- Differential Reinforcement of Alternative Behavior (DRA) + Extinction
- DRI + Response Interruption

Example *{cont.}*

Examples of Behavioral Interventions consisting of three or more identified components:

- Prompting + Blocking + DRA
- DRI + Reprimand + Overcorrection
- Rapport Building + Choice Making + Embedding + Functional Communication Training

Recommended Readings

Danya International, Inc., Organization for Autism Research & Southwest Autism Research & Resource Center. (2006). *Life journey through autism: A guide for transition to adulthood.* Arlington, VA: Organization for Autism Research, Inc. Retrieved from http://www.researchautism.org/resources/reading/index.asp#Transition

Luiselli, J. K. (Ed.) (2011). *Teaching and behavior support for children and adults with autism spectrum disorder: A practitioner's guide.* New York, NY: Oxford University Press.

Wehman, P. (2011). *Essentials of transition planning.* Baltimore, MD: Paul H. Brookes Publishing Co.

Wehman, P., Smith, M. D. & Schall, C. (2009). *Autism and the transition to adulthood.* Baltimore, MD: Paul H. Brookes Publishing Co.

Figure 2.9: *Continued*

EMERGING INTERVENTIONS

There is a wide range of intervention options available to address issues in ASD. Each option has varying evidence to support its effectiveness. Authors of the *National Standards Project—Phase 2* used the term *emerging* to describe a lengthy list of ASD-related interventions that had some empirical evidence to support their use (NAC, 2015). An emerging intervention could be a practice that has a few published studies, possibly including a small number of participants. The results show that an emerging practice may contribute to favourable outcomes; however, more research is needed. For an emerging practice to become classified as an established practice, researchers would need to show favourable treatment effects across wider-scale studies. *National Standards Project—Phase 2* classified 18 interventions as emerging for individuals under the age of 22. In addition to the interventions listed below, vocational skills package was labelled emerging for individuals with ASD 22 years or older (NAC, 2015).

Emerging interventions for individuals under age 22 include:

- augmentative and alternative communication devices
- developmental relationship-based treatment
- exercise
- exposure package
- functional communication training
- imitation-based intervention
- initiation training
- language training (production and understanding)
- massage therapy
- multi-component package
- music therapy
- picture exchange communication system
- reductive package
- sign instruction
- social communication intervention
- structured teaching
- technology-based intervention
- theory of mind training (NAC, 2015, p. 71)

Read about It. Think about It. Write about It.

- Emerging interventions are starting to have sufficient research support. Should they be implemented in the field? Why or why not?
- What precautions need to be taken with emerging practices?
- Were there strategies on the emerging interventions list that surprised you? Did you think they were established interventions? Why or why not?

UNESTABLISHED INTERVENTIONS

Individuals with ASD, parents, educators, and clinicians should be wary of unestablished interventions. They should be considered non–evidence-based. These practices have little to no empirical evidence from well-designed studies demonstrating effectiveness (see Table 2.5). Stakeholders involved in supporting individuals with ASD should avoid including unestablished practices in intervention plans due to potential ineffectiveness and harm (NAC, 2015). Unestablished interventions are often similar to pseudoscience, in that claims of effectiveness relate to low-quality methods of disseminating information, such as testimonials, opinions, and unverifiable accounts (NAC, 2015).

Table 2.5: Unestablished Interventions for Individuals with ASD

Age Group	Intervention
0–22 years old	• Animal-assisted Therapy • Auditory Integration Training • Concept Mapping • DIR/Floor Time • Gluten-free/Casein-free diet • Movement-based Intervention • SENSE Theatre Intervention • Sensory Intervention Package • Shock Therapy • Social Behavioural Learning Strategy • Social Cognition Intervention • Social Thinking Intervention
+ 22 years old	• Cognitive Behavioural Intervention Package • Modelling • Music Therapy • Sensory Integration Package

Source: NAC, 2015.

A LOOK BACK

Chapter 2, "Foundations of Autism Spectrum Disorder," focused on:

- The definition of *science* and *pseudoscience* and the research behind EBIs.
- A definition of *evidence-based interventions*, current reviews of the literature to determine EBIs, and research required to determine EBIs.

- A review of established interventions, emerging interventions, and non-supported interventions from *National Standards Project—Phase 2* (NAC, 2015).

ADDITIONAL RESOURCES

National Professional Development Center on Autism Spectrum Disorder—Evidence-based Practices

https://autismpdc.fpg.unc.edu/evidence-based-practices

The National Professional Development Center on Autism Spectrum Disorder develops free resources for a wide range of professionals supporting individuals with ASD. This website provides a list of commonly used therapeutic approaches and summarizes literature specific to each intervention. This website includes online learning modules, as well as case studies that could be used for academic purposes.

IRIS Center: 27 Evidence-based Practices for Students with ASD

https://iris.peabody.vanderbilt.edu/module/asd2/cresource/q2/p06/27-evidence-based-practices-for-students-with-asd/

This website presents an alphabetized list of EBIs for individuals with ASD. This resource provides a high-level description of 27 interventions that have substantial empirical support on their effectiveness.

Autism Science Foundation: Beware of Non–Evidence-based Treatments

https://autismsciencefoundation.org/what-is-autism/beware-of-non-evidence-based-treatments/

Parents and professionals are encouraged to assess the evidence supporting an intervention prior to implementation. This website, hosted by the Autism Science Foundation, outlines indicators that research is high quality. Additionally, this website lists non-evidence-based, potentially harmful interventions that should be avoided.

Texas Statewide Leadership for Autism Training: EBI Search

http://www.txautism.net/interventions

This website allows users to sort EBIs by domain and/or age group. A summary of established interventions is provided, as well as a detailed list of procedural steps to implement each intervention.

ONTABA—Evidence-based Practices for the Treatment of Challenging Behaviour

https://www.ontaba.org/pdf/ONTABA_OSETT-CB_Final_Report_Jan_2019.pdf

The Ontario Association for Behaviour Analysis is an affiliate chapter of the Association for Behavior Analysis International. This organization provides leadership and professional development opportunities on applied behaviour analysis. Members of this organization authored a report titled *Evidence-based Practices for the Treatment of Challenging Behaviour in Intellectual and Developmental Disabilities* (2019). This is a comprehensive research review summarizing evidence supporting a wide range of ASD-related interventions.

National Autism Center, *Findings and Conclusions: National Standards Project—Phase 2*

http://www.autismdiagnostics.com/assests/Resources/NSP2.pdf

From this website, parents and professionals can access *Findings and Conclusions: National Standards Project—Phase 2*. This report is a follow-up to an earlier publication. This document reviewed studies published between 2007 and 2012. Intervention outcomes were evaluated for children, youth, and adults with ASD.

Evidence-based Practices for Children, Youth, and Adults with Autism Spectrum Disorder

http://www.cidd.unc.edu/Registry/Research/Docs/31.pdf

This website links to a comprehensive research review authored by Wong and colleagues (2014). In this review, ASD interventions were classified as either focused (addressing a single goal) or comprehensive (addressing broad learning goals).

Asset Map of Resources for Autism Spectrum Disorders (ASD) Research in Canada

https://www.casda.ca/wp-content/uploads/2019/02/CASDA_Asset_map.pdf

The Canadian Autism Spectrum Disorder Alliance (CASDA) advocates for a national autism strategy. This resource lists funding allocations for ASD research across Canada. There are several funding sources supporting high-quality, ASD-related research across Canada.

SECTION II

Characteristics of and Interventions in Autism Spectrum Disorder

This section examines strategies shown to be effective in learning and overcoming challenges in the core areas of a diagnosis of autism spectrum disorder (ASD). The chapters are organized based on the fifth edition of the Diagnostic and Statistical Manual (DSM-5; American Psychiatric Association, 2013b). First, the two core areas where people with ASD struggle, both necessary to make a diagnosis of ASD, are covered. Chapter 3 examines evidence-based strategies that focus on social communication difficulties highlighted in the DSM-5. The structure of the chapter follows the interventions found to be classified as evidence-based interventions (EBIs) according to *Findings and Conclusions: National Standards Project—Phase 2* by the National Autism Center (2015). Chapter 4 covers common strategies used to work with challenging behaviours and repetitive and restricted patterns of behaviour as defined in the DSM-5. These are strategies that were found to be effective in Phases 1 and 2 of the National Standards Project. Lastly, the changing of the name of ASD and the diagnostic criteria brought with it an additional mention of sensory needs in relation to hyper- or hyposensory sensitivity or preoccupation with sensory needs in the environment under repetitive and restricted patterns of behaviour. Due to this new addition to the DSM-5, Chapter 5 focuses on sensory needs common in persons with ASD and common interventions focused on those needs.

CHAPTER 3

Social Communication–based Interventions

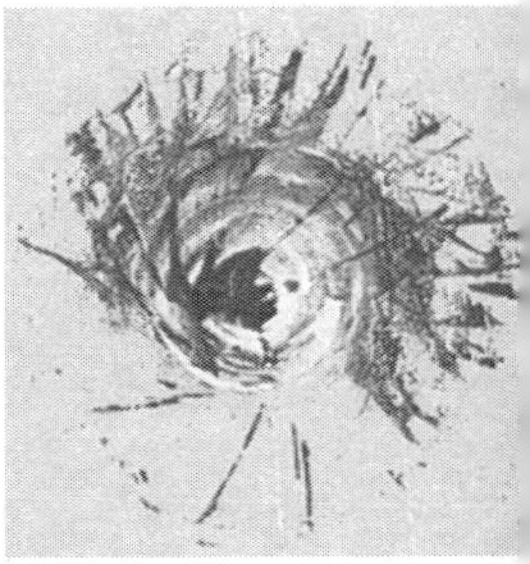

LEARNING OBJECTIVES

- Describe social communication as it relates to the DSM-5 diagnostic criteria for ASD and common social communication difficulties for individuals with ASD.
- Recognize evidence-based interventions that increase communication and interpersonal skills, including cognitive behaviour interventions, behavioural interventions, modelling, naturalistic teaching strategies, parent-training packages, peer-training packages, pivotal response treatment, self-management, social skills packages, and story-based interventions.
- Articulate a more in-depth understanding of different types of behavioural and social skills assessments and interventions for people with ASD.
- Highlight different social communication interventions used in different jurisdictions across Canada.

This chapter focuses on effective, evidence-based interventions (EBIs) that are based on assisting, improving, or enhancing communication and social skills for individuals with autism spectrum disorder (ASD). It examines the different interventions shown to be evidence-based in *National Standards Project—Phase 2* (NAC, 2015). Many of these interventions are packages of multiple approaches that focus on social and communication development. These interventions have included various approaches to early intensive behaviour intervention (EIBI), which include many different types of behavioural approaches. These multiple approaches are broken down and explained where needed. Examples of how these have been implemented with persons with ASD across Canada are included throughout, and examples are highlighted at the end in Spotlights across Canada.

SOCIAL COMMUNICATION

Social communication difficulties are common across individuals with ASD; however, there is significant variability in how they appear. Social communication challenges are broad and impactful. They can range from what may appear to be quite minor, like rarely looking toward others during communication or socialization, to what comes across as highly impactful, such as forming friendships (Ten Eycke & Müller, 2015). As described previously, the most recent edition of the Diagnostic and Statistical Manual (DSM-5) includes substantially different assessment criteria for ASD diagnoses than previous editions (American Psychiatric Association, 2013b). One of the noteworthy differences between diagnostic criteria listed in earlier versions and the current version relates to the social and communication domains. Under the DSM-5, the diagnosis of autistic disorder and other subtypes were replaced with a single term, *autism spectrum disorder*, and two characteristics—social interaction and communication—were combined into one diagnostic criterion labelled social communication (American Psychiatric Association, 2013b). Authors of the DSM-5 indicate there is often an overlap between the communication challenges that individuals with ASD face and their challenges with social interactions, lending support to joint assessment of these areas (American Psychiatric Association, 2013b).

Under the revised DSM-5 criteria, social communication delays are broadly classified as impairments in social-emotional reciprocity, nonverbal communication, and social relationships often demonstrated by a lack of imaginative and make-believe play (Anagnostou et al., 2015; Taheri & Perry, 2012). To receive a confirmed diagnosis, individuals must demonstrate symptoms in all three of these areas across several environments (American Psychiatric Association, 2013b). Delays in these areas are two of the earliest concerns most frequently reported by mothers of children who are later diagnosed with ASD (Herlihy, Knoch, Vibert, & Fein, 2013). Researchers are interested in developing and testing assessment methods to accurately and reliably diagnose ASD as young as possible, as it is highly plausible that diagnoses at earlier ages may hasten access to intervention and create more positive outcomes over time. A 2010 prospective study by Ozonoff and colleagues measured social and communicative behaviours in low- and high-risk children diagnosed with ASD later. No observable differences were noted between groups at 6 months of age; however, by 12 months, the infants diagnosed with ASD later showed limited eye gaze directed toward others, fewer shared smiles, and minimal social vocalizations. This pattern indicates that social communication delays are present very early in atypical development (Ozonoff et al., 2010). Since impairments in social communication skills are predominant in all individuals with ASD, interventions targeting skills in these areas are widely researched.

Social-Emotional Reciprocity

Social-emotional reciprocity refers to a set of behaviours describing the back-and-forth nature of a social situation. The ability to respond to an interaction initiated by another and to maintain that interaction are examples of social reciprocity (Anagnostou et al., 2015; Bennett et al., 2015). Typically developing infants show social reciprocal behaviour at a very young age by returning social smiles and back-and-forth babbling with parents (Autism Speaks Canada, 2019; Rogers & Dawson, 2010; Rogers, Dawson, & Vismara,

2012). As children grow, social reciprocal behaviours mature from quite basic to more sophisticated. Toddlers engage in parallel play, observing and imitating one another. By school-entry age (e.g., kindergarten), typically developing children demonstrate more sophisticated social-emotional reciprocity. In early adolescence, typically developing adolescents recognize that others have their own thoughts, feelings, and opinions (Autism Society of Baltimore-Chesapeake, 2019). Regardless of age, a willingness to interact and maintain social interactions is central to social-emotional reciprocity. There are several ways that individuals with ASD demonstrate issues with social reciprocity. They may have difficulty initiating and responding to social interactions, maintaining conversations, and may share their interests only infrequently with others (APA, 2013b). Social-emotional reciprocity also refers to an inability to match behaviour with the expected behaviour of a social context (e.g., giggling loudly at a solemn funeral service). Another notable challenge related to social-emotional reciprocity is accurately responding to the emotional state of others. An individual with delays in this area may not pick up on the cues people use to communicate sadness, joy, frustration, or annoyance. It is necessary to teach skills in this area as competence in social-emotional reciprocity is strongly linked to positive adult outcomes in employment, relationships, and independence (Bennett et al., 2015).

parallel play: one of six phases of play in preschoolers, as developed in research by Mildred Parten (1932), where children are playing independently, but beside one another, and may share similar objects or toys.

Nonverbal Communication

Typically developing individuals almost instinctively integrate nonverbal and verbal communication into social interactions. Nonverbal behaviours such as gestures, body posture, and facial expressions play an important part in communication. Common nonverbal behaviour characteristics associated with ASD are a lack of eye contact and failing to look toward the faces of others. Atypical eye contact can be observed early in children with ASD. One study of 12 infants labelled high-risk for ASD, who were later diagnosed, demonstrated atypical eye gaze patterns as young as 2 months of age (Rutherford, Walsh, & Lee, 2015). Orienting toward faces is an important social communication skill, as people express feelings, thoughts, and emotions through facial expressions (Tanaka & Sung, 2016). Nonverbal movements such as raising an eyebrow, sighing, or eye-rolling can be very communicative and can quickly change the meaning of social interactions. In one research study, eye-tracking patterns were assessed while looking at a static image of a face. Adults with ASD demonstrated disorganized eye tracking that concentrated *less* on core facial features of eyes, noses, and mouths and *more* on external features such as hair, chins, and clothing (Tanaka & Sung, 2016). Individuals with ASD who have atypical eye contact and difficulty orienting toward faces are likely to face challenges in everyday social situations, when interpreting nonverbal facial expressions is required (Tanaka & Sung, 2016). Researchers have commented that individuals with ASD fail to read "the language of the eyes" and miss subtle yet important cues shared through the eyes (Tanaka & Sung, 2016, p. 1545).

Teaching eye contact to young children with ASD may be a valuable, socially significant skill to introduce. In a recent Ontario study, researchers attempted to increase eye contact in individuals with ASD between 3 and 12 years old. Using discrete trial training, researchers assessed the effectiveness of various independent variables (snacks, social praise, and access to an iPad) on increasing eye contact. The intervention was effective for the majority of participants, who quickly demonstrated increased eye contact (Cook, Rapp, Mann, McHugh, Burji, & Nuta, 2017).

Social Relationships

Social relationships are meaningful, frequent interactions between people. Many skills needed to develop social relationships may be lacking in individuals with ASD. Young children with ASD have difficulty with imaginative play and making friends, often appearing disinterested in same-aged peers (APA, 2013b; Autism Speaks Canada, 2018c). At the time of diagnosis, assessing social relationships involves observing and inquiring about imaginative play. Challenges with imagination are most evident through limits around make-believe play and imaginative drawing. Imaginative play requires the recall and combination of past experiences and the generation of new ideas based on these recollections (Ten Eycke & Müller, 2015). Consider a young boy pretending to fix wood with tools. While engaging in this pretend play, the young boy recalls past experiences of observing adults or caregivers performing fixing duties such as using a hammer or a screwdriver. The young child's pretend play is based upon these recollections. Several well-designed research studies have demonstrated that individuals with ASD engage in less frequent, spontaneous pretend play than same-age, typically developing peers (Ten Eycke & Müller, 2015).

Researchers at the University of Victoria, British Columbia, recruited children with ASD and typically developing children to participate in a study investigating differences in imaginative drawings. After listening to brief scripts about a magical planet in a far-away land, participants were asked to either draw a strange-looking person or a funny-looking house (Ten Eycke & Müller, 2015). Differences were only observed in the images of the strange-looking person, with no noteworthy differences found between groups for drawings of the funny-looking house (Ten Eycke & Müller, 2015). Results of this coded drawing study indicate that impairments in imagination could be specific

> **communication**: nonverbal or verbal task cues to another person for the purpose of sharing emotions, information, or experiences (NAC, 2015).

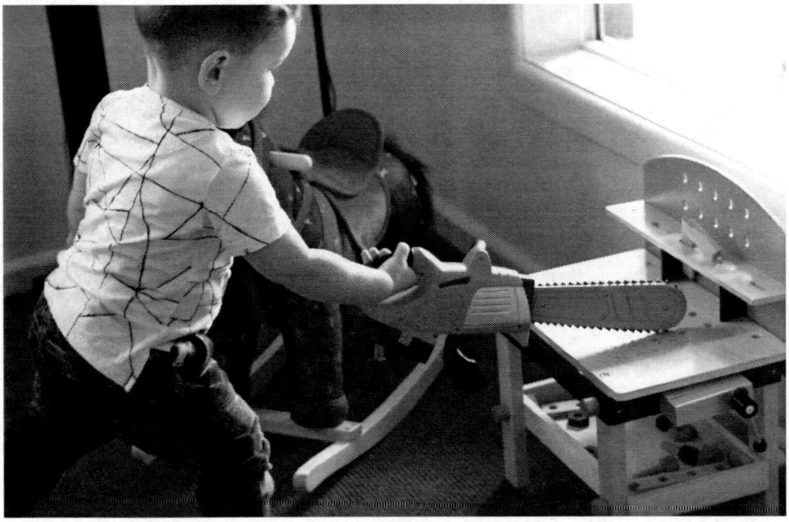

Figure 3.1: Young Boy Engaging in Imaginative Play
Source: trelismat/Pixabay.

to social stimuli. It is plausible that difficulty maintaining eye contact and orienting to facial features contribute to impairments in imagination. Individuals with ASD have quantitatively and qualitatively fewer experiences orienting toward faces and facial expressions, and this lack of experience could contribute to such minimal imaginative details related to people (Ten Eycke & Müller, 2015).

> **interpersonal skills**: skills requiring at least one other person. Common social skills investigated in the literature include joint attention, group participation, friendship skills, and play skills (NAC, 2015).

National Standards Project—Phase 2 lists a number of interventions with substantial evidence addressing the social communication skill deficits associated with a diagnosis of ASD. Interventions addressing social communication skills are included under two of the developmental areas targeted for increase: communication and interpersonal. As noted above, communication and interpersonal skills highly correlate; there is overlap with many of the EBIs included in *National Standards Project—Phase 2*.

Read about It. Think about It. Write about It.

- In the previous edition of the DSM, social and communication difficulties were two separate criteria. Is the new version with social and communication deficits combined logical? Why or why not? What are the benefits of separating or combining the two areas?

EVIDENCE-BASED INTERVENTIONS THAT INCREASE COMMUNICATION AND INTERPERSONAL SKILLS

Cognitive Behavioural Intervention Package

Cognitive behaviour therapy (CBT) is a behavioural analytic intervention used to modify an individual's thoughts or self-statements (Miltenberger, 2016). The National Autism Center (NAC) previously reviewed three studies assessing cognitive behavioural interventions and initially labelled this treatment as emerging (NAC, 2009). Recently, researchers have placed a focus on evaluating cognitive behavioural interventions, leading to an increase in publications. The most recent NAC document (*Phase 2*) reviewed 10 studies on cognitive behavioural interventions and now classifies this practice as established (NAC, 2015). Cognitive behavioural interventions are effective in increasing interpersonal skills and cognitive functions and decreasing problematic behaviours in children 6–14 years old (NAC, 2009, 2015).

Cognitive Behavioural Therapy

Diana Tajik-Parvinchi, PhD, York University, Toronto, Ontario

Cognitive behavioural therapy (CBT) is an evidence-based treatment approach based on the premise that maladaptive thought processes and behaviours lead to psychopathology, and altering these thoughts and behaviours may improve the psychological disorder. CBT was first pioneered by Ellis (1960s) and Beck (1970s; see review by Hofmann et al., 2012), whose notions of irrational beliefs (Ellis & Harper, 1961; Harper, 1975) and cognitive distortions (Beck, 1979) laid its groundwork. Beck observed that an excess of negative thoughts surfaced during therapeutic sessions, either about the self, the world, or the future, while treating clients with depression. He termed these negative thoughts *automatic thoughts* and helped his clients by evaluating and shifting these automatic thoughts to more realistic ones. CBT is based on three fundamental assumptions: that cognitive thoughts influence behaviour; that these thoughts can be examined and altered; and that as thoughts are modified, behaviour changes (Dobson & Dozois, 2001).

CBT is widely employed to treat a range of mental health conditions. It is considered an efficacious therapeutic intervention for anxiety disorders (Ollendick, King, & Chorpita, 2006), depression (Preschl, Maercker, & Wagner, 2011), and emotional regulation (Weiss et al., 2018). CBT is often delivered in manual-based treatment programs, either implemented in a group or individual formats (Pahnke, Lundgren, Hursti, & Hirvikoski, 2014; Russell et al., 2013; Weiss et al., 2018). CBT is consistent with the tripartite view of psychopathology (cognition, behaviour, emotion). CBT targets each of these areas by utilizing concepts such as cognitive restructuring strategies (Bandura, 1977) and problem-solving to facilitate the development of coping strategies. For example, anxiety-focused CBT aims to identify and modify thoughts about aversive stimuli and replace these maladaptive thoughts with more adaptive ones. This therapeutic approach provides graded exposure to the anxious stimuli, and, as the individual succeeds through these experiences, newly effective memories, positive perceptions, and adaptive emotion regulation skills replace the older, ineffective ones and become more readily available (Brewin, 2006).

Although many children and adolescents experience symptoms of anxiety, children with ASD are at greater risk for anxiety symptoms, maladaptive behaviour, and emotional difficulties (Brereton, Tonge, & Einfeld, 2006; Steinhausen & Metzke, 2004). For example, children with ASD 5–16 years of age commonly display tantrum behaviour, hyperactivity, conduct problems, and emotional difficulties (Konst & Matson, 2014; Totsika, Hastings, Emerson, Berridge, & Lancaster, 2011). In fact, these are often key reasons parents initially seek treatment (Robb, 2010).

CBT has been successfully utilized to treat the core symptoms of ASD such as social communication, as well as comorbid disorders of anxiety, aggression, and emotion dysregulation. The ASD-specific CBT programs have been modified to address the unique needs of this population. For example, clinicians often include modules that address social skills development and self-care skills. These modules also utilize restricted interests commonly observed in individuals with autism to maintain therapy interest and engagement (Danial & Wood, 2013; Wood et al., 2009), or they implement visual stimuli such as emotion thermometers to discuss different intensities of anxious and angry emotions (Weiss et al., 2018).

Anxiety-focused CBT approaches commonly include recognition or detection of emotion, anxiety ratings, introduction of adaptive coping strategies, emotion regulation strategies, and cognitive restructuring. ASD-specific CBT treatment sessions can last from 90 minutes to 30 hours a week (see review by Danial & Wood, 2013). Although CBT sessions can be individual or family-based, children with ASD appear to benefit from family-based CBT more than individual-based sessions (Danial & Wood, 2013).

While promising, individual treatment response varies. Some children display significant improvements following CBT, and others do not. In CBT studies focused on addressing anxiety in children with autism, about 40–50% of children continue to experience clinical levels of anxiety following treatment (Reaven, 2011). Research is currently being directed to investigate the circumstances under which treatment is effective, as well as identify those individuals who may be at risk of poor treatment response. This line of research can help maximize therapeutic benefits.

Comprehensive Behavioural Treatment for Young Children

Comprehensive behavioural treatment for young children (CBTYC), also referred to as early intensive behaviour intervention (EIBI), is a common intervention for ASD. This broad, intensive, applied behaviour analysis (ABA)-based program targets adaptive, language, and social skills, while reducing interfering behaviours (Caron, Bérubé, & Paquet, 2017; NAC, 2015; Wong et al., 2014). Following high-profile court rulings and vocal parent advocacy, some jurisdictions have increased provincial funding for EIBI programs (Volden et al., 2015). A service utilization study involving families across Canada assessed which services families of preschoolers received during the five-year period post-diagnosis (Volden et al., 2015). Twelve months post-diagnosis, the most common service accessed was behavioural. Across urban cities in five Canadian provinces (Nova Scotia, Quebec, Ontario, Alberta, and British Columbia), approximately 58% of preschoolers were reported to be receiving behavioural services, including EIBI (Volden et al., 2015).

Several factors are commonly reported as contributing to the effectiveness of EIBI programs. Defining features of EIBI include:

- Programming addresses core diagnostic characteristics of ASD
- Teaching is structured and predictable
- Low adult-to-child ratio
- Promotes family involvement
- Uses a functional approach to treating challenging behaviours
- Programming delivered and supervised by staff with training in ABA
- Intensive delivery (20 or more hours for at least 12 months; Reichow, Hume, Barton & Boyd, 2018)

Early Intensive Behaviour Intervention in Canada

Most provincial jurisdictions provide some form of EIBI for young children with ASD (Smith et al., 2019). These programs reportedly incorporate the core components deemed necessary for a quality program. Provincial EIBI programs are described as intensive programming (see above) across a variety of skill areas, delivered by well-trained and well-supervised clinicians. However, it does not appear that EIBI programs adequately document *how* these components are included in interventions. Researchers out of two Quebec universities carried out a systematic review of EIBI literature published between 2005 and

> **intensive behaviour intervention (IBI)**: an approach that uses ABA principles of learning in an intensive manner for a minimum of 25 hours per week. The goal of the intervention is to provide one-on-one or small group instruction that focuses on specific skills that help with future learning such as imitation, cooperation, and attention (Geneva Centre for Autism, 2006).

2015. The primary purpose of this review was to determine whether EIBI programs documented specific intervention practices (e.g., intensity of hours) and connected these practices to outcomes (Caron et al., 2017). The results of this review indicate that EIBI programs often fail to include descriptions outlining how the program incorporates these defining features of EIBI. Of the 28 articles included in this analysis, 21 described the intensity of hours through which intervention was provided, and only two articles described the training and skill sets of the interventionists (Caron et al., 2017). It is necessary for professionals who develop and deliver EIBI programs to document program practices to ensure delivery aligns with what is reported as effective in published literature.

While several common features are apparent across Canadian jurisdictions, there are variations in service delivery and program structure to accommodate for differences in provincial ministries, funding allocations, and the unique social service systems in each jurisdiction (Smith et al., 2019). Provinces provide access to EIBI through two primary options: (a) funds provided directly to families, referred to as direct funding in some jurisdictions, or (b) services provided through funded agencies, referred to as direct services. In some areas, parents can use direct funding to assist with the cost of hiring a team of therapists. Advocates of this model believe this option provides choice to access the services and supports that best fit with child needs (Ontario Ministry of Children, Community and Social Services, 2020). To help families hire qualified clinicians, some organizations host websites listing contact information of eligible professionals qualified to provide various clinical interventions. For example, in British Columbia, an organization called Autism Information Services manages the Registry of Autism Service Providers (RASP), and in Ontario, Autism Ontario manages the Ontario Autism Program provider list. These websites provide user-friendly resources for families with newly diagnosed children. Parents can access information on areas such as funding, invoicing, and helpful questions to ask when interviewing prospective candidates.

Hiring private providers to work as part of an EIBI treatment team, where relevant, is a significant decision, as there are a variety of professionals involved in delivering and supervising these programs. EIBI is typically an individualized intervention, meaning each client is assigned a personal, primary therapist. The primary therapist is responsible for day-to-day delivery of programming, as well as collecting and graphing data. Another important member of an EIBI program is

board-certified behavior analyst (BCBA): a master's-level clinician certified by the US-based Behavior Analyst Certification Board. To be certified, clinicians need to have coursework at the master's level specific to ABA, field work supervised by another BCBA, and take and pass an exam. BCBAs are required to follow the *Professional and Ethical Compliance Code* and to acquire continuing education credits to maintain certification (BACB, 2019).

a supervisor or a clinical supervisor. This individual oversees the overall quality of the program. This clinician may carry out initial assessments and set curriculum targets. It is common for staff employed in EIBI programs to obtain professional designation through the Behavior Analyst Certification Board (BACB). Professionals can be certified as a *board-certified behavior analyst* (BCBA) or at the assistant level as a *board-certified assistant behavior analyst* (BCaBA). This accreditation organization recently added a designation of *registered behavior technician* (RBT) for entry-level professionals. The BACB verifies education and ABA-related experience (BACB, 2019), providing several certification programs geared to the various roles and levels of education and experience.

Description of an ABA-based Treatment Facility

Tammy Frazer, Director/Clinical Supervisor of On Solid Ground, Barrie, Ontario

Figure 3.2: Tammy Frazer, Director/Clinical Supervisor, On Solid Ground
Source: Tammy Frazer.

Located in Barrie, Ontario, On Solid Ground, Inc. (OSG), was founded in January 2012 in an effort to meet the growing demand for qualified and professional ABA services in Simcoe and surrounding regions, for individuals with autism and other developmental disorders/delays. Servicing individuals between 2 and 25 years of age, OSG employs therapists with education and training in applied behaviour analysis and ASD: primary instructor therapists, BCaBAs, and BCBA clinicians with a wide range of experience. In our commitment to delivering quality, effective, evidence-based interventions, OSG provides individualized and group programming with the goal of maximizing each person's growth and development. Whether it is learning to communicate, listen, socialize, develop tolerance, perform workplace skills, or perform self-care skills such as using a toilet or dressing, OSG teaches the necessary skills aimed to improve overall quality of life.

Regulated and Unregulated Professionals

Many different professionals will likely be involved in programming for young children with ASD. It is common for families to seek input from a psychologist, an audiologist, a speech-language pathologist, and various other professionals. Families should be informed that some professionals involved in education and treatment for individuals with ASD are regulated, while other professions are not. Regulated professionals are required to follow guidelines and policies outlined by respective colleges, where applicable. This reliance provides parents, caregivers, and clients a level of consumer protection. Consumers know that a regulated professional has a certain minimum level of education and experience. The roles of instructor therapist, behaviour therapist, and clinical supervisor are not registered as health professions. Individuals with these titles may belong to registered colleges, in addition to their role in ABA. Currently, there is no regulatory college in Canada that monitors behaviour therapist roles.

Assessment

Comprehensive behavioural programming for young children with ASD is guided by a broad, skills-based assessment that focuses on early developmental milestones that assist with learning and skill deficits common in ASD. Three commonly used assessment

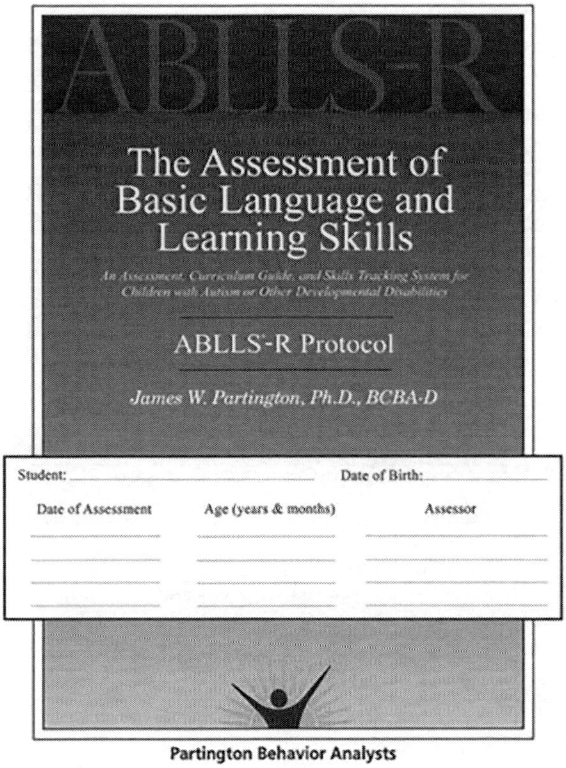

Figure 3.3: *The Assessment of Basic Language and Learning Skills—Revised*

Source: Partington, 2010.

tools are the *Assessment of Basic Language and Learning Skills—Revised* (ABLLS-R; Partington, 2010), the *Verbal Behaviour Milestones Assessment and Placement Program* (VB-MAPP; Sundberg, 2008), and the *Promoting Emergence of Advanced Knowledge Relational Training System* (PEAK; Dixon, 2014). The ABLLS-R includes 544 skills divided into 25 developmental domains that are alphabetically labelled. Assessment results are colour-coded to show learners' progress over time (see Figure 3.4 for an example of hypothetical assessment results for domains A–D).

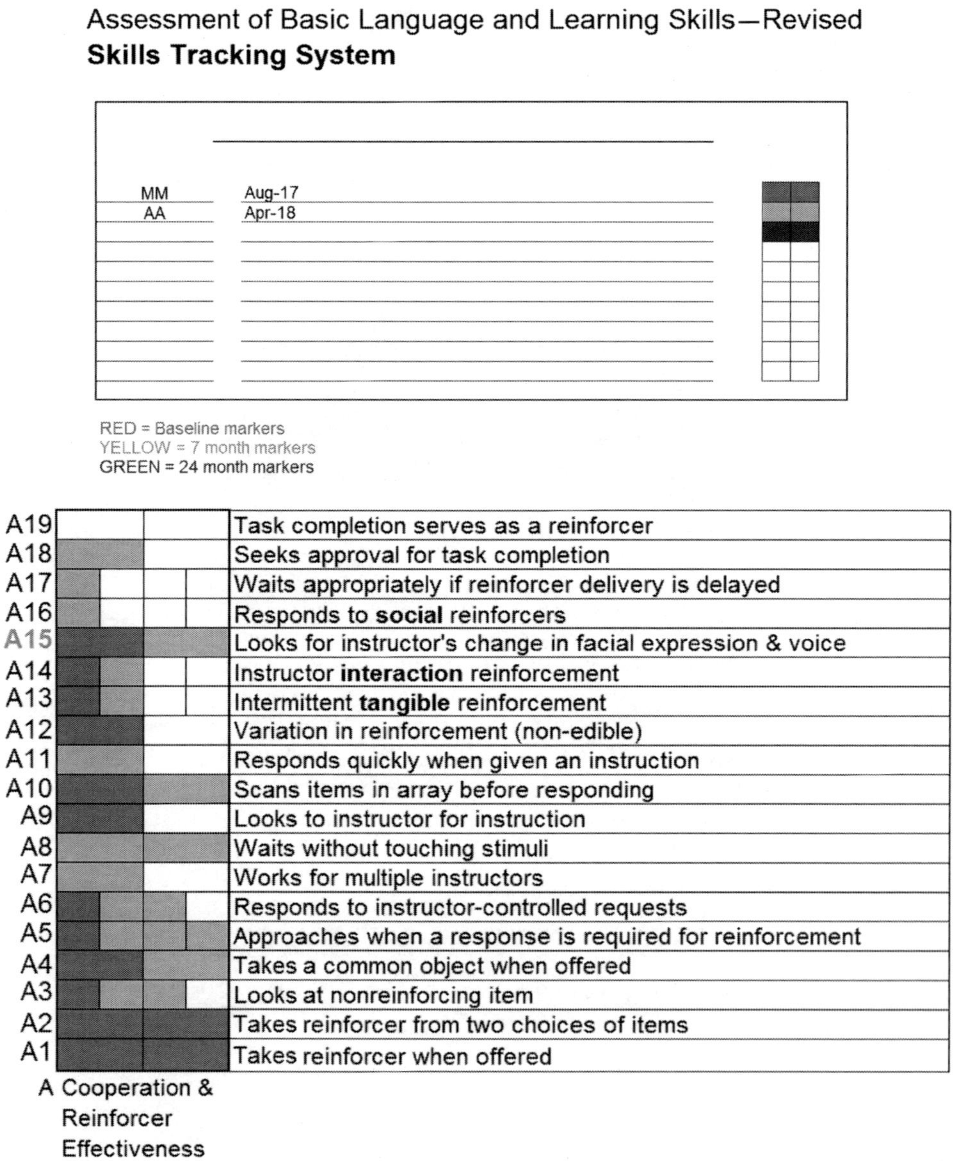

Figure 3.4: Hypothetical ABLLS-R Assessment Results

Source: Authors.

B27	Mazes
B26	Picture sequences
B25	Seriation - ordering by size, quantity, sequence, etc.
B24	Dependent matching sequence
B23	Replicate simple 3-dimensional objects
B22	Extend a sequence pattern
B21	Delayed finding a sample
B20	Delayed replication of a sequence
B19	Sort by class
B18	Sort by feature
B17	Sort by function
B16	Match associated pictures
B15	Jigsaw puzzles
B14	Puzzles with multiple pieces that must be juxtaposed
B13	Sequence pattern to match a visual model
B12	Block designs from picture
B11	Puzzles with a square-edged border frame
B10	Puzzles with multiple connecting pieces in inset-type frame
B9	Block designs on picture card
B8	Sort non-identical items
B7	Fluent matching 10 items in 30 sec.
B6	Match pictures to objects
B5	Match identical **pictures** to sample
B4	Match objects to pictures
B3	Match indentical **objects** to sample
B2	Form box
B1	Puzzle with a single-piece type inset

B Visual Performance

C57	Select pictures of social interactions
C56	Select non-examples
C55	Select "same" and "different"
C54	Select pictures representing emotions
C53	Select pics. representing a location/activity in a scene
C52	Receptive pronouns
C51	Receptive prepositions
C50	Follow a multiple component sequence instruction
C49	Select set of items with 2 specified characteristics
C48	Select set of items with a specifed characteristic
C47	Select single item with two specified characteristics
C46	Select all examples of an item
C45	Select common environmental sounds
C44	Locate objects from parts of objects in large, complex pic.
C43	Locate objects in larger, complex picture
C42	Select community helpers
C41	Select two items in **sequence** from larger set
C40	Select two items from larger set
C39	Select by class
C38	Select by feature
C37	Select by function
C36	Select associated pictures
C35	Select one of three pictures representing actions
C34	Demonstrates a specified pretend action
C33	Multiple actions with an object
C32	Demonstrates specific action with object from diff. obj.
C31	Specific motor responses in receptive tasks
C30	Follow instruction to go to a person and do an action
C29	Follow instruction to walk to person and get named item
C28	Follow instruction to give item to a person/place on obj.
C27	Follow instruction to go to a person
C26	Follows hand signals
C25	Selects items by following another's gaze
C24	Select adjectives
C23	Touches parts of items
C22	Touch own pieces of clothing
C21	Point to body parts on others or pictures
C20	Varied instructions to select using any response
C19	Fluent receptive discriminations (10 items in 30 sec.)
C18	Acquires new selection skills without instensive training
C17	Select one of six or more pictures on table

Figure 3.4: *Continued*

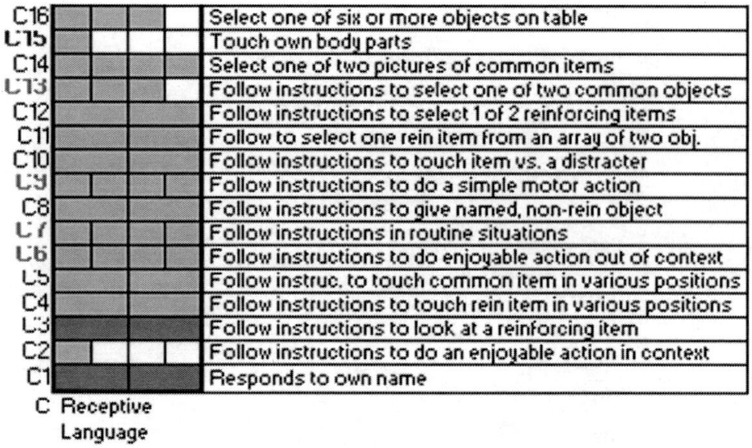

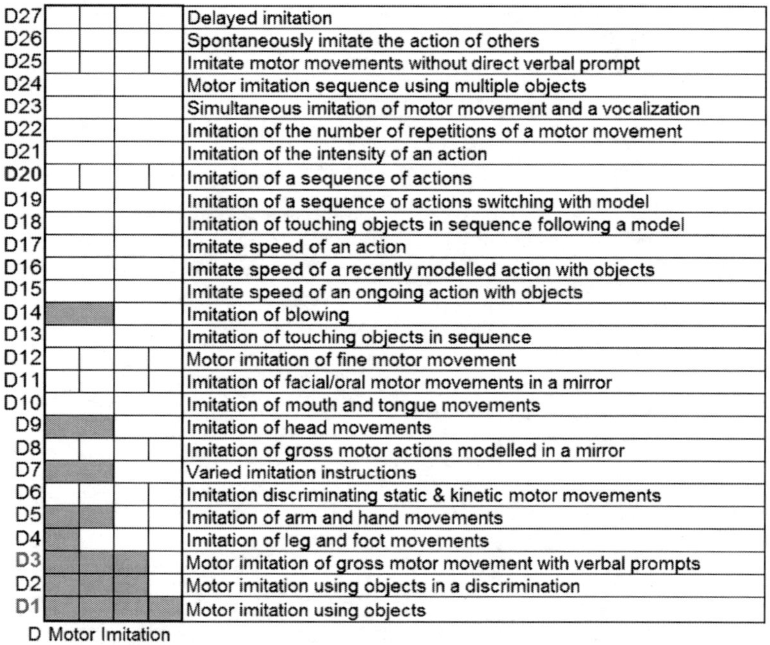

Figure 3.4: *Continued*

The VB-MAPP assessment tool prioritizes language development and strongly correlates to Skinner's analysis of verbal behaviour (Sundberg, 2008). This tool contains 170 skills grouped by chronological age: 0 to 18 months (level 1), 18 to 30 months (level 2), and 30 to 48 months (level 3). They emphasize Skinner's verbal operants—mands, echoics, tacts, intraverbals, and listener responding—as well as imitation, play and social skills, visual performance, group skills, and early academic skills (see Figure 3.5 for a sample of hypothetical assessment results). The VB-MAPP includes a supplementary barriers and transition assessment. These tools assist practitioners with identifying and

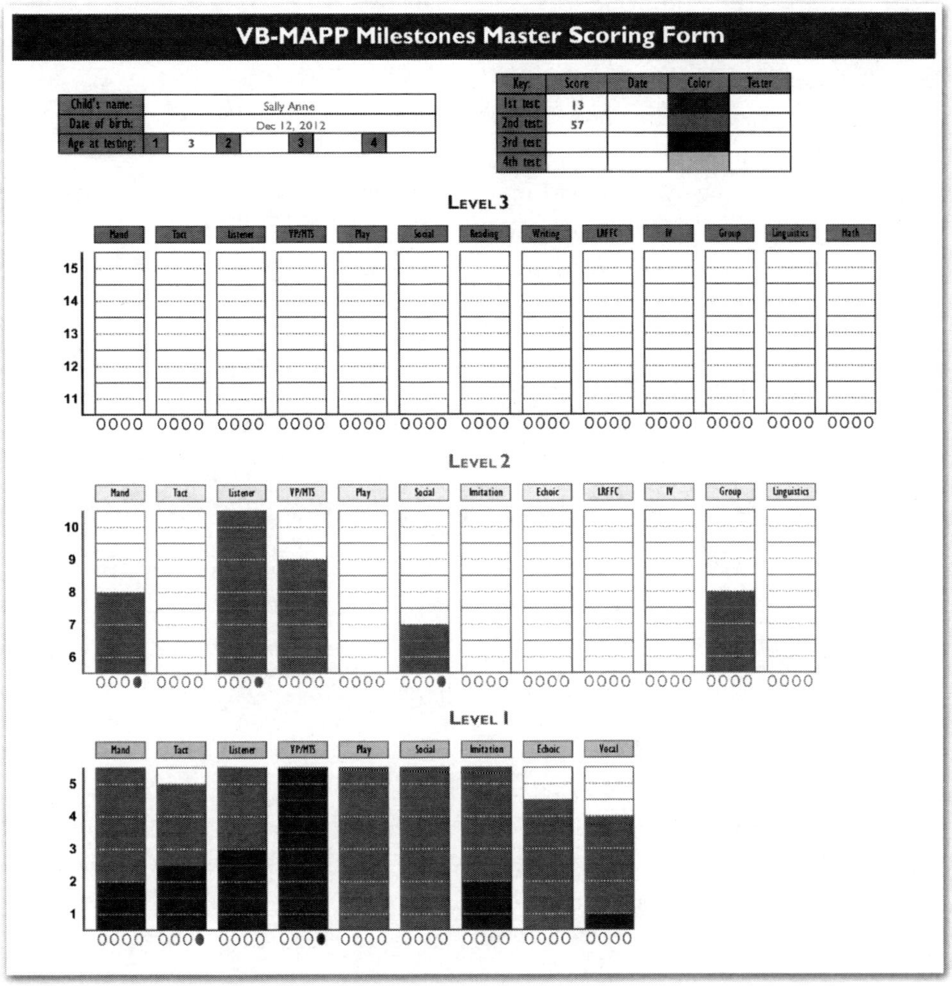

Figure 3.5: Hypothetical VB-MAPP Assessment Results

Source: Authors.

intervening on specific barriers to learning and measuring prosocial skills likely to contribute to a successful transition from EIBI programs to school.

PEAK is a 184-item assessment tool that includes basic learning skills such as eye contact and turn-taking, as well as complex cognitive, social, and inferencing skills not included in the ABLLS-R or VB-MAPP (Malkin, Dixon, Speelman, & Luke, 2017). These tools take broad, developmental domains such as self-help skills, academics, and language and break them into smaller, observable behaviours. During assessment, assessors present a variety of instructional tasks and observe responses. Performance levels are then compared to criterion-referenced scores and recorded on a skill-tracking data sheet. Based on assessment results, developmentally appropriate, skill-acquisition targets from a variety of domains are implemented. Selecting which teaching targets to include can be challenging, as there are many options and areas. Well-ordered, developmentally sequenced assessments allow practitioners to address skills in logical sequences, ensuring prerequisite skills are mastered prior to introducing more difficult skills (Malkin et al., 2017).

> **criterion-referenced scores**: a type of assessment where the scores on the assessment are based on the student's performance. This is in contrast to norm-based assessment, where the scores are reported in comparison to others.

TEACHING METHODS INCLUDED IN EIBI PROGRAMS

EIBI programs for young children are taught using several behavioural-based methods. Practitioners select different teaching methods depending on the age of the learner, the skill being taught, or the setting. Related instructional methods vary (Smith, 2001; Weiss, 2005).

Discrete Trial Training

Discrete trial training (DTT) is an intensive, ABA-based teaching method that is effective at teaching a wide range of skills (Weiss, 2005). It is a contrived method of teaching that breaks learning opportunities down into trials. Each trial includes five distinct components: cue, prompt, response, consequence, and intertrial interval (Smith, 2001).

Cue

A learning opportunity begins with a distinct signal that a specific response is expected. The technical ABA-term for cue is *discriminative stimulus*, often referred to as an S^D. A cue can be presented in many ways. In DTT, cues are often specific verbal teaching instructions such as *copy me*, *match*, or *sort*. However, cues are included in phrases in everyday routines, such as a parent calling out, "Time for dinner!" Each of these verbal instructions cue a specific response: copying the action of another, matching or sorting items, or walking to the dinner table. Cues can be nonvocal gestures, such as pointing, environmental sounds like a school bell ringing or a firetruck siren that cues drivers to move out of the way. In DTT, cues are delivered in a brief, clear manner to increase the likelihood that the learner will respond (Smith, 2001).

Prompt

The second component of DTT is the prompt. Prompts are gestures, touches, or visuals that assist learners to complete a task correctly (McClannahan & Krantz, 1999). In DTT, prompts are provided at the same time or immediately after the cue to prevent the learner from making an error. Prompts are usually presented in a hierarchy and systematically inserted, with the goal to *fade out* the prompt altogether. Preventing errors as part of teaching is called errorless teaching (Alberto & Troutman, 2017; Smith, 2001; Weiss, 2005). (See Chapter 4 for further information.)

Response

The third component is the learner's response. In DTT, each response has an operational definition, describing the precise actions of a correct response. If the learner's response is the same as the operational definition, it is considered a correct response. Any response other than the operational definition is considered incorrect (Alberto & Troutman, 2017; Smith, 2001; Weiss, 2005).

Consequence

After the learner responds, the instructor delivers a consequence. The type of consequence that is provided depends if the learner's response is correct or incorrect. The consequence for correct responses is reinforcement. Reinforcement can be a praise statement (*amazing work*), a high-five, or time-limited access to a toy, book, or other preferred items (Smith, 2001). Potential reinforcing items can be selected through a preference assessment (see Chapter 4). It is important to deliver the reinforcer immediately after the learner's correct response to help the learner understand the relationship between the correct response and the preferred event that followed. If the learner performed an incorrect response, the instructor implements an error correction procedure, ideally to prevent future errors (Smith, 2001). Error correction procedures can vary from an instructor delivering a brief *no* statement to more complex procedures that involve repeating the instruction and increasing the prompt provided (Alberto & Troutman, 2017; Smith, 2001; Weiss, 2005).

> **consequence**: an event that happens after a behaviour occurs that increases or decreases the likelihood of the behaviour occurring again in the future. In the case of DTT, consequences are either reinforcement or error correction (a mild form of punishment).

Intertrial Interval

The last component of the sequence is the intertrial interval. Following the consequence, the instructor pauses briefly (about one to five seconds) before presenting another cue and beginning the DTT sequence again (Smith, 2001).

Figure 3.6 shows the delivery sequence of the discrete trial. The sequence begins with the cue or instruction, immediately followed by a prompt, then the learner responds and, depending on the response, the instructor provides reinforcement or error correction.

It is important that instructors deliver DTT sequences accurately. Implementing interventions as planned is referred to as treatment integrity. Therapists practising out of the St. Amant Autism Program in Manitoba developed a 20-item Discrete Trial

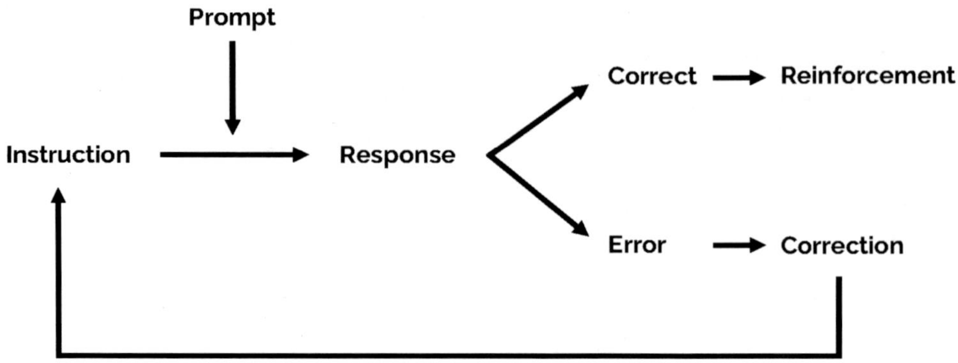

Figure 3.6: Discrete Trial Sequence
Source: Authors.

> **treatment integrity**: also called treatment fidelity, the extent to which a treatment or intervention is implemented as it is subscribed. Often in ABA, treatment procedure checklists are created, and implementer accuracy is measured by an observer.

Training Evaluation Form and assessed whether this tool measured accurate implementation of DTT (Ellement, Boris, Martin, & Fazzio, 2017). Following a self-instruction training package, senior staff overseeing DTT-based early intervention programs for young children with ASD increased supervisory skills assessing accurate DTT-delivery (Ellement et al., 2017). DTT is an effective instructional strategy for teaching new skills to learners with ASD. DTT has shown favourable outcomes for teaching imitation, receptive language, conversation skills, and alternative forms of communication such as picture exchange communication system (PECS) or sign language (Weiss, 2005). See Table 3.1 for a sample of a skill acquisition program that could be taught through discrete trial teaching.

Verbal Behaviour Approach

Verbal behaviour (VB) is an ABA-based teaching approach that prioritizes language acquisition. This teaching method focuses on increasing communication skills and creates communication opportunities for learners (Ingvarsson, 2017). VB is based on Skinner's interpretation of language and communication, explained in the book *Verbal Behavior* (1957). In this well-known text, Skinner explained that communication (referred to as *verbal behaviour*) is like motor behaviours such as crawling, running, and jumping. Skinner described all behaviour as influencing the environment (Ingvarsson, 2017). He claimed that it is more important to analyze the function of communication (*why* we communicate) than the form of communication (*how* we communicate).

Table 3.1: Discrete Trial Program Sample

<table>
<tr><td>Program Name</td><td colspan="2">Money Skills</td></tr>
<tr><td>Domain</td><td colspan="2">Core Academics</td></tr>
<tr><td>Rationale</td><td colspan="2">Identifying and counting money is a vital functional skill necessary for independence in the community.</td></tr>
<tr><td>Mastery Criteria</td><td colspan="2">3 consecutive Yes probes</td></tr>
<tr><td>Prompts</td><td>Least to Most Prompting
(Physical Skills)
• Model
• Gesture</td><td>Full Verbal + Time Delay
(Verbal Skills)</td></tr>
<tr><td>Teaching Procedure</td><td colspan="2">• Teach at table
• Use real coins
• Teach 3 acquisition targets at a time
• Conduct transfer trails across operants
• Receptive → Tact
• Tact → Intraverbal</td></tr>
<tr><td>Measurement Procedure & Graphing</td><td colspan="2">Probe data; graph cumulative number of targets acquired on a weekly basis</td></tr>
<tr><td>Revision Criteria</td><td colspan="2">1 week with no new targets acquired</td></tr>
<tr><td>Reinforcement Schedule</td><td colspan="2">FR 1 checkmark/point for acquisition
VR 3–5 for maintenance</td></tr>
<tr><td>Error Correction Procedure</td><td colspan="2">Extinction (no social consequence for error)
Represent S^D with prompt – differentially reinforce prompted correct (modulated social praise)</td></tr>
<tr><td>Target Suggestions</td><td colspan="2">• Receptive Identification of coins (penny–toonie)
• Receptive Identification of bills ($5.00–$50.00)
• Receptive Identification of coin value (penny–$100.00)
• Expressive Identification of coin value (penny–$100.00)
• Add value of coins
  ◦ Variety of coins = same value
  ◦ Mixture of coins and bills ("How much is this worth?")</td></tr>
<tr><td>Generalization</td><td colspan="2">• Across settings
• Across people</td></tr>
</table>

Source: Authors.

Skinner used the term *operant* to categorize the various ways a word, sign, or gesture functions on the environment (see Figure 3.7 for a visual explanation of a behavioural description of communication). Verbal operants frequently included in EIBI programs are defined later on in this chapter.

An EIBI program that uses a VB teaching approach teaches young children to communicate across several verbal operants. Communication can be taught using words, pictures, a voice output device, or a combination of communication methods. Parents, practitioners, and educators may hear the term *augmentative and alternative communication* (AAC) used to describe various forms of communication (see Figure 3.8).

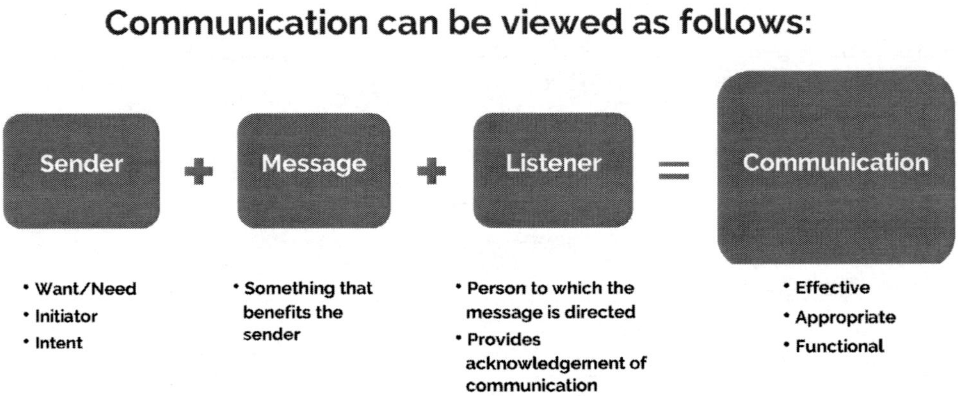

Figure 3.7: Behavioural Explanation of Communication
Source: Authors.

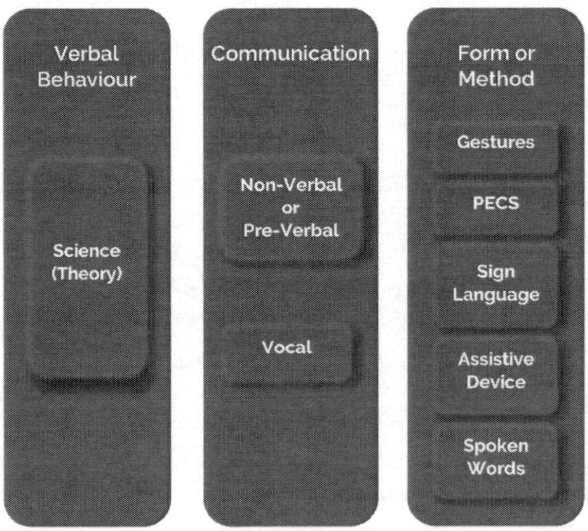

Figure 3.8: Forms of Communication
Source: Authors.

Augmentative and Alternative Communication

Tracie Lindblad, Clinical Director, Eastern Canada, Monarch House, Oakville, Ontario

After a diagnosis of ASD, often the first question to any professional by any parent is about their child's ability and future potential to use speech to communicate. This is a valid question as parents may have witnessed the regression in speech and vocal communication between 12 and 24 months of age and anxiously await its return. There are as yet many unanswered questions about the cause(s) of speech delay and/or complete absence of spoken language within this population. However, we do know that approximately 30 to 50% of individuals with ASD remain minimally verbal throughout their lives, with little to no functional speech (Johnson, 2004; Mirenda, 2003; National Institutes of Health & National Institute on Deafness and Other Communication Disorders, 2010). The primary goal of the field of augmentative and alternative communication (AAC) is supporting the communication and participation of persons with complex communication needs (McNaughton & Light, 2015). AAC is an umbrella term that encompasses the communication methods used to supplement (add to) or replace speech for those with impairments in the production or comprehension of spoken or written language. AAC is used by those with a wide range of speech and language impairments. Since communication is one of the central deficits of ASD, the need for AAC is a critical component for optimal outcomes for these individuals.

AAC encompasses many types of systems categorized into aided systems (e.g., book, picture, item, board, or device) or unaided systems (e.g., gestures, vocalizations, body language, facial expressions, and sign language) and further categorized into low-tech (e.g., picture-based communication boards), medium-tech (e.g., static speech generating devices), and high-tech (e.g., dedicated electronic devices) systems. The use of AAC for ASD is imperative for the development of language skills, increasing vocalizations or speech production, as well as decreasing problem behaviour, which is often attributed to a deficit in communication (though not all problem behaviour is the result of a communication deficit).

Parents and professionals alike face a difficult task in choosing an appropriate AAC system for minimally verbal individuals with ASD. A wide range of techniques and devices are routinely used by speech-language pathologists and behaviour analysts with varying degrees of success, varying degrees of evidence, and contradictory and anecdotal information from research and professionals, which adds to the complexity of this task.

What do we currently know about the use of AAC for ASD?

- Empirical evidence to support the use of speech-generating devices with learners with ASD is weak as a standalone treatment. There is evidence for the use of PECS (Bondy & Frost, 2001) as an AAC system for individuals with ASD.

- AAC use for increasing speech output is strengthened when used as part of a behaviour treatment package, but there is no guarantee that speech will increase nor that current vocalizations will be maintained.
- There is no standard assessment for determining appropriate AAC prerequisites nor for AAC system choice; however, a thorough assessment of the individual's prerequisite skills (e.g., joint attention, generalized imitation skills, ability to tolerate a delay to obtaining items, quality and quantity of vocalizations) is required prior to determining an appropriate AAC system. As Lorah, Parnell, Whitby, and Hantula (2015) stated, "the research is not about 'iPads® as SGDs' [speech-generating devices] but rather is about the combination of hardware, software, and training protocols. All three must work together to provide support for the individuals." Moreover, the use of AAC is about teaching language skills and effective communication so that the individual is accurate, effective in delivering their message, and efficient in communicating. The teaching of AAC is the most important piece of the equation and as such will require specific training, competency in AAC systems, and adequate intervention time on the part of the clinician. There is *no* one-size-fits all AAC system, and at this time, there is no empirical evidence to suggest one device is better than the other. It's all about assessment, fit, training, support, and teaching.

Table 3.2: Accessible Definitions for Skinner's Verbal Operants

Mand	Asking for reinforcers that you want. Saying "water" because you want it.
Tact	Naming or identifying objects, actions, events, etc. Saying "water" because you see water.
Echoic	Repeating what is heard. Saying "water" after someone else says "water."
Intraverbal	Answering questions or having conversations in which your words are controlled by other words. Saying "water" when someone else says, "What do you want to drink?"
Textual	Reading written words. Saying "water" because you see the written word water.
Transcription	Writing and spelling words spoken to you. Writing *water* because you hear "water" spoken.

Source: Cooper, Heron, & Heward, 2007, p. 529.

SKINNER'S VERBAL OPERANTS

Echoic

The echoic is a verbal operant where the learner repeats what is heard. It is helpful to think of the echoic as *echoing*. An example of an early echoic is when a young baby repeats a morpheme like *mama*. Echoics are important verbal operants to teach as more advanced verbal operants are taught using echoics as prompts.

Mand

The mand is a very important part of communication. As much as half of adult daily communication is made up of mands (Wallace, 2007). In everyday terms, mands are similar to requests. Individuals mand (or request) for a wide variety of reasons (see Table 3.3).

The defining feature of a mand is that it begins with an internal feeling, or state, of wanting or needing something. There are two internal states that prompt a learner to mand: *deprivation* and *satiation*. *Deprivation* is the state of being deprived of an item or event. An individual experiences deprivation and mands to satisfy the internal state. *Satiation* is associated with too much of an object or event (Miklos & Dipuglia, 2010).

"Pass the salt," "Where's my umbrella?", and "Turn down that loud music!" are all examples of mands. When manding for the salt and the umbrella, the speaker is in a state of deprivation for salt or an umbrella. A speaker mands for these items to satisfy, or get rid of, this internal feeling. When manding for someone to turn loud music down, the speaker is satiated by too much music.

In typically developing infants, mands are the first verbal operants to develop (Miklos & Dipuglia, 2010). This is because mands are an effective way to get wants and needs met. The first mands of babies typically occur in the form of crying, which infants use to communicate wants or needs.

Table 3.3: Various Types of Mands

Mand for Missing Item	"Have you seen my keys?"
Mand to Stop an Event	"Stop tickling me!"
Mand for Information	"Excuse me, which way to the closest washroom?"
Mand for Help	"Could you hold the door open for me?"
Mand for an Item	"Juice, please!"
Mand for an Activity	"Chase me!"

Source: Miklos & Dipuglia, 2010.

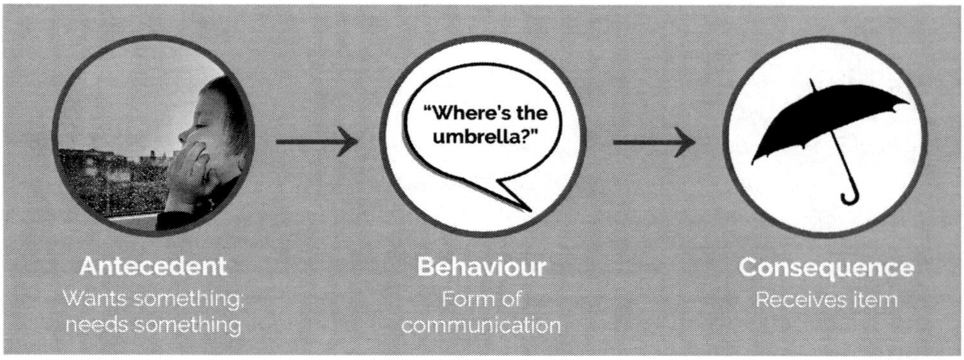

Figure 3.9: Mand for Missing Items—Umbrella
Source: Authors.

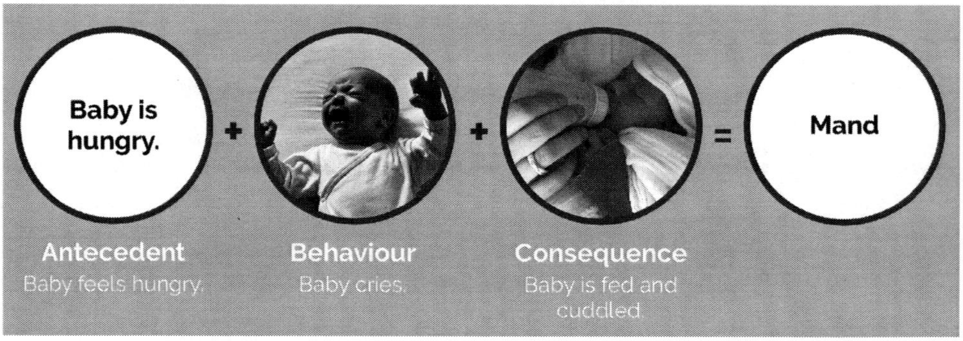

Figure 3.10: Baby's First Mand
Source: Authors.

Research supports that young children with ASD typically do not readily mand without specific teaching (Albert, Carbone, Murray, Hagerty, & Sweeney-Kerwin, 2012). In verbal behaviour–based EIBI programs, a significant focus is placed on increasing manding skills for young children with ASD. Therapists collect and graph data on frequency of independent and prompted mands.

Prompted Mand

A child is thirsty and reaches toward a juice box. The educator says, "Juice." The child repeats, "Juice." The educator gives the child the juice box. In this example, the educator prompted the child using an echoic prompt. The child repeated the echoic, and the educator reinforced this behaviour with juice. Across several learning opportunities, the educator would fade the echoic prompt, teaching the child to mand for juice when thirsty.

Tact

Tacts are also verbal operants commonly included in social interactions. Labelling events and items are a common way to initiate social communication exchanges. Tacts are verbal behaviours that occur after events trigger one of the senses. Tacts are communication that occur after hearing, smelling, feeling, seeing, or tasting something (Ingvarsson, 2017). When learning about the tact, it can be helpful to think about an event coming into con*tact* with a sensory system. Tacting is communicating about something nonverbal in the environment (Ingvarsson, 2017). Attending to objects and events and sharing those experiences with others is often an area of difficulty for individuals with ASD. EIBI includes programs that teach young children to label common items in books, as well as label actions, attributes, and emotions.

Figure 3.11: Tacting a Painting
Source: Authors.

Figure 3.12: Tacting a Firetruck
Source: Authors.

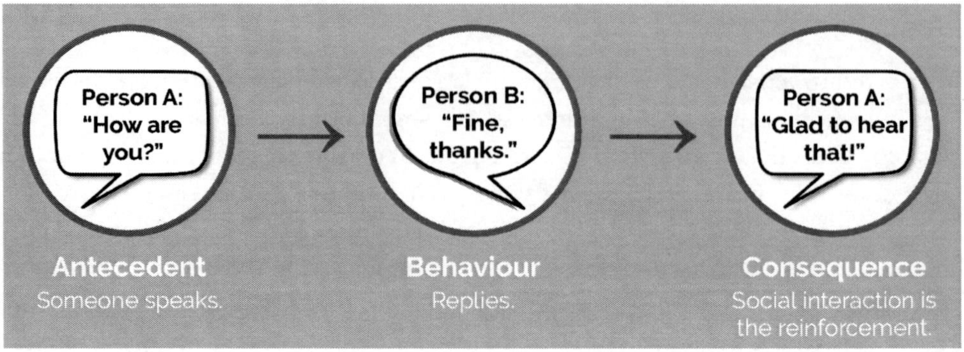

Figure 3.13: Intraverbal Example
Source: Authors.

Intraverbal

The intraverbal is a verbal operant exchanged between two communication partners; one speaker says something, and the other replies. The intraverbal is different than the echoic. With the echoic operant, the speaker repeats exactly the same phrase.

> *Person A:* "Hi, how are you?"
> *Person B:* "Great, thanks. How about you?"

Intraverbal skills are essential for social interactions. Social games, academic lessons, and conversations all include intraverbal exchanges. EIBI programs introduce intraverbals with simple fill-in-the-blank programs. These early intraverbals teach children to say different things in response to other people. This skill can develop into more advanced intraverbal exchanges. An intraverbal fill-in example is as follows:

> *Therapist:* "Twinkle, twinkle little ..."
> *Child:* "Star."
> *Therapist:* "How I wonder what you are."

INCIDENTAL TEACHING

Incidental teaching is an effective ABA-based intervention used to teach skills such as labelling, requesting, social initiation, and conversation; it is often included in comprehensive behaviour treatment programs for young children. The learning environment plays an important role in incidental teaching. Before using incidental teaching, therapists, educators, or parents alter settings to create an environment that will pique the child's interest and increase communication opportunities (often termed *communication temptations*). A common way to adapt the learning setting is to place preferred items in sight but out of reach. This is an effective way to create motivation as learners see and want these preferred items. Creating motivation is an important first step to using incidental teaching. Some other ways to set up incidental teaching opportunities are by placing items in clear containers on shelves, providing children with only part of the materials needed for tasks (e.g., a juice box without a straw), or pausing during a familiar routine (e.g., walking to the car door and pausing before opening it; Neely, Rispoli, Gerow, & Hong, 2016). Situations like these create opportunities for learners to initiate.

Children can show interest through initiation. An initiation can be verbal, such as requesting the item, or physical, by reaching for or pointing to the item. Therefore, the child is leading the learning (Ingersoll & Dvortcsak, 2010). Incidental teaching sets up opportunities to practise initiating, one of the noteworthy communication delays observed in individuals with ASD. Following initiation, the instructor models communication. Communication goals are individualized and can include vocal approximations, single words, or short phrases. If the child imitates the target behaviour, reinforcement is provided. Another unique feature of incidental teaching is the relationship between reinforcement and communication. The reinforcer (or reward) delivered by the therapist is connected to the communication response.

Incidental Teaching

- A therapist and child are sitting on the carpet playing with a car and car ramp. The therapist begins to drive the car up and down the road (*item is in sight but out of reach*).
- The therapist is labelling her actions and making car noises: "Beep beep! My car is driving so fast" (*this is a strategy to create motivation*).
- The young child reaches for the car (*initiation*).
- The therapist models communication: "Want car."
- The child imitates with "Want car."
- The therapist provides animated social praise and gives the car to the child (*the reward of receiving the car is connected to the behaviour of saying* want car).

Joint attention behaviours are often taught during incidental teaching opportunities.

Joint Attention in a Young Child

A young child is at the park with his dad when a cute, playful puppy runs up to the little boy. The little boy looks quickly at the puppy and then turns to his dad and smiles. In this brief interaction, the little boy is demonstrating joint attention. The boy is shifting his attention between the puppy (an interesting event) and his dad (a communication partner). Joint attention is *triadic attention* (Rogers et al., 2012, p. 220). It is communication between two people about an object or event (Rogers & Dawson, 2010).

Figure 3.14: Triadic Communication
Source: Authors.

Many social interactions begin when one person shares thoughts or feelings about an object or event.

Joint Attention in High School Students

You are sitting in chemistry class when the teacher writes a long, difficult question on the board. The teacher tells the class, "Open your notebooks and solve this problem." You look at the question, turn to your friend, and roll your eyes. She sighs and nods her head in return.

The high school scenario further demonstrates joint attention. An interaction occurred where one communicative partner shared personal thoughts and feelings about the chemistry question. The other communicator understood and responded.

There are a variety of ways young children demonstrate joint attention. Joint attention behaviours include looking at, showing, giving, and pointing to items (Rogers & Dawson, 2010; Rogers et al., 2012; Waddington, van der Meer, & Sigafoos, 2016). These behaviours begin to emerge in typically developing children between 6 and 12 months of age (Rogers & Dawson, 2010). However, many of the diagnostic features of ASD make joint attention difficult. As mentioned, individuals with ASD likely have difficulty shifting eye gaze between objects and people, often appearing over-interested in objects and less interested in faces (Cook et al., 2017; Tanaka & Sung, 2016). Joint attention skills are important to target as these behaviours are used to share thoughts and feelings. Joint attention behaviours of pointing, showing, and looking are typically paired with other nonverbal means of communication like smiles or frowns, showing feelings about an event (Rogers & Dawson, 2010). Individuals with ASD may not readily recognize when other people use joint attention behaviours to initiate interactions, leading to missed learning and missed social opportunities.

Godin, an occupational therapist practising out of Quebec City, Quebec, and Freeman and Rigby conducted a scoping study of playful engagement in social interactions of preschool-aged children with ASD (2017). This study outlines the importance of joint activity interventions which teach young children with ASD to initiate interactions through joint attention behaviours (pointing to and showing items), as well as to respond to other's joint attention behaviours (Godin et al., 2017; NAC, 2009, 2015). As joint attention behaviours emerge very early in typical development, most of the research in this area includes very young children with ASD.

Early Start Denver Model

A well-known intervention that targets joint attention behaviours in young children with ASD is the Early Start Denver Model (ESDM; Rogers & Dawson, 2010; Rogers et al., 2012; Waddington et al., 2016). ESDM curriculum covers motivation, initiation, joint attention, receptive and expressive language, imitation, and play skills. This intervention is often delivered by parents in the family home (Rogers & Dawson, 2010; Rogers et al., 2012; Waddington et al., 2016). A 2015 systematic review evaluated 12 studies with ESDM as the primary intervention. Reviewed studies were a mix of single-case research and randomized-control trials. A total of 209 young children with ASD were included (Waddington et al., 2016). Five studies included parent-implemented ESDM consisting of weekly parent education as well as coaching and feedback on ESDM techniques. Results of the systematic review support that ESDM intervention led to positive outcomes in spontaneous language, verbalizations, imitation, social orienting, and/or joint attention (Waddington et al., 2016). All included studies reported some positive outcomes for child participants, staff, and/or trained parents.

ESDM Canada: Who Are They and What Do They Do?

Michaela Jelen (University of Alberta), Janet Harder, and Mary McKenna (private practice)

The Early Start Denver Model (ESDM) Canada is comprised of three certified ESDM Trainers, each with a strong commitment to deliver evidence-informed practices to support children and families living with ASD. Each team member has spent years working with children with ASD and achieving clinical and training competency in the ESDM model. Drawing on professional backgrounds in speech-language pathology, educational psychology, and behaviour analysis, the model continuously evolves, ensuring that services meet the needs of both professionals and families, while also striving to evaluate and contribute to ongoing research in early intervention and ASD. ESDM Canada provides and participates in:

1. ESDM training: for professionals to learn and work toward clinical competency in the ESDM approach to intervention. It includes an intensive workshop where professionals work directly with a child and parent using evidence-based ESDM practices. Upon workshop completion, participants are invited to further advance their knowledge and work through the standardized ESDM certification process with individualized support from their trainer.
2. Parent coaching: all ESDM Canada team members are trained and experienced in providing parent-coaching services to caregivers supporting children who are demonstrating social-communication delays. ESDM Canada supports caregivers, both face-to-face and via online video conferencing technology, to use evidence-informed practices to support their child's development. Through the coaching process, parents are supported in making sense of the evidence-based strategies as they relate specifically to their unique child and family circumstances, within a collaborative and reflective coaching process.
3. Research: ESDM Canada participates in research evaluating the implementation and effectiveness of early intervention, professional training, and coaching practices. From 2017 to 2020, ESDM Canada led the clinical team for the Parent and Child Early Coaching Research Project, conducted out of the University of British Columbia. It trained and supported 39 parent-coaches in parent-coaching practices in communities across BC. This project will help with the understanding of how to implement evidence-based practice in varied community settings, both rural and urban.

The ESDM is an early intervention model developed by Drs. Sally Rogers and Geraldine Dawson. It is a relationship-based approach to intervention with children aged 0–60 months with diagnosed or suspected ASD. The ESDM utilizes data-based decision-making and merges behavioural, relationship-based, and developmentally focused practices into one intervention program. The model emphasizes child individualization while maintaining fidelity within the standardized model. This model can be delivered with a clinician and child, through coaching to caregivers, or as a group intervention within inclusive settings. ESDM has a solid research base demonstrating positive outcomes for toddlers (e.g., Rogers et al., 2012) and children with ASD (e.g., Vivanti et al., 2013), their parents (e.g., Vismara, McCormick, & Wagner, 2016), and community providers (e.g., Vismara et al., 2013).

Read about It. Think about It. Write about It.

- There are many different approaches to comprehensive behavioural intervention packages and EIBI. Choose two interventions and compare and contrast the approaches.
- If you were a parent of a child with ASD and had to choose a comprehensive behavioural package, which approach might appeal to you the most?

Modelling

Modelling is an established intervention to increase communication and interpersonal skills in children and youth with ASD between 3 and 18 years old (NAC, 2015). Modelling is an important intervention for practitioners to use as it focuses on imitation skills, one of the core difficulties observed in young children with ASD (Dawson & Rogers, 2010). Because of this issue, EIBI programs use considerable focused programming to address this important area. Examples of beginner-level imitation programs are motor imitation with an object (e.g., roll a car, place a block in a cup), as well as imitation of actions (e.g., wave, raise arms up, and blow a kiss). Emphasis is placed on motor imitation as skills in this area are strongly correlated with future language skills (Kleeberger & Mirenda, 2010). Modelling involves the learner observing a demonstration of a target behaviour and performing the same behaviour (NAC, 2015). Modelling is an effective strategy to teach a range of simple and complex actions. Simple actions are single motor responses, like those included in beginner EIBI imitation programs. A complex action is a sequence of smaller actions linked together to form a complex behaviour. For example, playing a board game is a complex behaviour made up of many simple motor movements.

Modelling can be implemented in a few ways. A modelled response delivered directly in front of the learner is called live or *in vivo* modelling, which is the type of modelling used in beginner motor imitation programs. With live modelling, typically one therapist and one learner sit facing one other. The therapist presents a clear instruction like *copy me* and demonstrates the target behaviour. If necessary, the therapist provides additional prompts to assist the child in this imitation. After the child imitates a response, a reinforcer is provided. The ultimate goal of imitation training is generalized imitation, where the learner copies new actions in many locations and with a wide variety of people (Kleeberger & Mirenda, 2010).

Another type of modelling is video modelling. This strategy involves learners imitating target behaviours after observing a video recording of a model demonstrating the behaviour (Boudreau & D'Entremont, 2010; Kleeberger & Mirenda, 2010). Several advantages are associated with this teaching method, such as cost effectiveness, time efficiency, and portability (Boudreau & D'Entremont, 2010). Practitioners can record models performing behaviours and learners can review these recordings as often as necessary. Practitioners can edit and replace demonstrations, ensuring the best possible version of the target behaviours are used for teaching (Boudreau & D'Entremont, 2010). Advances in portable technology like smartphones and tablets allow for video-recorded demonstrations of behaviour to be viewed directly in the setting where behaviours should be performed. Learners can watch recorded demonstrations of models demonstrating how to pack a backpack in the classroom—the very setting where the target behaviour is expected. Additionally, a video recording of a target behaviour is a permanent product. Instructors can re-use recordings with other learners (Boudreau & D'Entremont, 2010). Video modelling may also be more effective for teaching as this format reduces the amount of interpersonal interaction required for learning. During live modelling, learners must maintain attention on the demonstrator the whole time the skill is being modelled. Sustaining such attention can be a challenge for many learners with ASD, whereas watching videos allows observers to pause and replay target behaviours. Because of these many benefits, video modelling has been used to teach a variety of skills to a broad group of individuals with ASD. Video modelling has been effective in teaching self-help, social skills, perspective-taking, academics, and play skills (Kleeberger & Mirenda, 2010).

A 2010 study carried out in Fredericton, New Brunswick, assessed whether toy-based play skills learned through video modelling would generalize to novel toys and settings, as well as whether learned skills would be maintained after the video model was removed (Boudreau & D'Entremont, 2010). Two preschool boys with ASD viewed short video clips of adult models playing with veterinary and construction toy materials. Each video included modelled actions (e.g., give a puppy a needle, drive a dump truck) as well as corresponding scripted phrases (e.g., "puppy sick," "vroom, vroom, beep, beep"). The video modelling intervention consisted of each participant viewing the video demonstration, followed by a 10-minute play session with the same toy materials. In approximately 20 sessions, both participants acquired all modelled responses and scripted phrases, as well as demonstrating novel, unmodelled actions and phrases. Both participants maintained these skills for a short period of time following the last intervention session (Boudreau & D'Entremont, 2010).

Naturalistic Teaching Strategies

Naturalistic teaching strategies (NTS) are a group of intervention practices for young children with ASD. After reviewing 32 studies, authors of the NAC document determined this set of interventions as established for increasing communication and interpersonal skills in children zero to nine years old (NAC, 2015). Across Canada, several variations of NTS are provided: Social ABCs, Project ImPACT (Improving Parents as Communication Teachers), JASPER (Joint Attention Symbolic Play Engagement and Regulation), the aforementioned Early Start Denver Model, and incidental teaching are all naturalistic interventions. Each of these naturalistic approaches has subtle, procedural differences that make them unique. More important is the set of strategies and techniques common to all naturalistic teaching approaches.

Features of Naturalistic Teaching Strategies

1. Learning takes place in natural settings like homes, parks, or childcare centres. NTS can be implemented anytime during a daily routine (Ingersoll & Dvortcsak, 2010). Discrete trial teaching and verbal behaviour instruction often take place in a clinical setting, with the child and interventionist sitting at a table. NTS do not require specific seating arrangements or settings for learning.
2. Interactions are child-led. Developmental approaches to learning teach parents or others to recognize and respond to child initiations, like staring at—or reaching for—an item (Ingersoll & Dvortcsak, 2010). In behavioural-based teaching, the adults set up the teaching environment and deliver the instructions to begin learning opportunities. Whether involved adults or children initiate learning opportunities is one of the fundamental differences between behavioural and naturalistic teaching methods (Ingersoll & Dvortcsak, 2010).
3. Positive affect is prioritized. There is considerable empirical evidence supporting a relationship between parental interaction styles and social communication development in children (Brian et al., 2016; Dawson & Rogers, 2010; Ingersoll & Dvortscak, 2010). NTS prioritize parental strategies that lead to positive parent-child interactions. Naturalistic approaches teach parents to follow their children's leads, display pleasant facial expressions, and teach communication partners to respond to all communication attempts (Ingersoll & Dvortcsak, 2010). These are effective parenting practices to improve social engagement.

Intervention methods that use a naturalistic approach teach a common set of skills. As these practices are primarily implemented with very young children with ASD, the skills targeted are early learner skills. NTS teach:

1. Social engagement: Social engagement includes teaching joint attention behaviours (e.g., giving, showing, and pointing). It is important for young children with ASD to improve social engagement, which is foundational for more advanced behaviours such as imitation, play, and language (Ingersoll & Dvortscak, 2010).
2. Language: NTS emphasize teaching language as this is a noteworthy area of difficulty in young children with ASD. NTS prioritize teaching spontaneous (child-initiated) communication. NTS address nonverbal communication such as gestures, eye contact, and pointing, as well as spoken words.
3. Imitation: NTS focus on teaching imitation, as this is a necessary prerequisite to learn more complex skills such as self-help and leisure activities. Imitation is also a teaching strategy used in modelling interventions, so it is beneficial for young children to learn to imitate modelled actions. NTS teaches imitation through social routines: patty-cake, peek-a-boo, and songs with actions are common social routines used in naturalistic teaching. These types of activities encourage young children to pay attention to others' facial expressions (Ingersoll & Dvortcsak, 2010).
4. Play skills: NTS use everyday, regularly occurring routines as learning opportunities. Much of a young child's day is dedicated to play; therefore, learning functional, appropriate play skills is important to teach. Play skills are also closely related to complex skills such as language and motor development (Ingersoll & Dvortcsak, 2010).

Social ABCs

Social ABCs is a manualized, ABA-based, parent-delivered, naturalistic intervention for toddlers with ASD. The Social ABCs curriculum teaches parents to create functional language opportunities with their child. Verbal communication is prioritized as this area is often reported as a primary parent concern (Brian, Smith, Zwaigenbaum, Roberts, & Bryson, 2016). Parents are also taught to

> **generalization**: when a behaviour is demonstrated in a different learning environment without re-teaching. There are two types: (a) response generalization, where the responses are untrained and functionally equivalent; and (b) stimulus generalization, where the responses occur in a setting different than the instructional setting (Cooper et al., 2020).

express positive emotions. This skill is prioritized as it is a prerequisite for more advanced emotional recognition skills (Brian et al., 2016). A pilot study across two Canadian treatment sites—IWK Health Centre in Halifax, Nova Scotia, and the Hospital for Sick Children in Toronto, Ontario—evaluated the practicality and acceptability of Social ABCs' curricula and intervention methods (Brian et al., 2016). Twenty toddlers received approximately 8.5 months of intervention. Parents received coaching on how to show positive emotions, enhance communication, and manage behavioural challenges (Brian et al., 2016). Following intervention with Social ABCs, children increased the rate of initiations and vocalizations and showed increased responsiveness to adult cues (Brian et al., 2016). Following training, parents provided more opportunities for language and increased the number of child-directed smiles. Parents rated this intervention as favourable, acceptable, and helpful (Brian et al., 2016).

There are several benefits associated with using NTS. These practices lead to increased skill generalization, less reliance on adult prompting, and increased spontaneous demonstration of skills (UCLA Jane & Terry Semel Institute for Neuroscience & Human Behavior, 2019).

Project ImPACT

Melissa Lavallee, Clinical Supervisor, Surrey Place, Toronto, Ontario

Surrey Place provides specialized clinical services to children and adults living with developmental disabilities, autism spectrum disorder (ASD), and visual impairments in Toronto. To help our clients reach their full potential, we offer a variety of groups and workshops for clients, families, and caregivers, including Project ImPACT.

Project ImPACT (**Im**proving **P**arents **a**s **C**ommunication **T**eachers), developed by Brooke Ingersoll, PhD, and Anne Dvortcsak, MS, CCC-SLP, is a parent-training curriculum that focuses on improving social communication in young children with autism by teaching parents how to maximize teaching opportunities for their child. Surrey Place participated in an intensive research project and training program with the creators of the program throughout 2015. Staff were trained to fidelity on both the use of the ImPACT strategies with children and on coaching families in the use of the strategies.

With the increasing support for naturalistic developmental behavioural interventions, parents and professionals are looking toward programs that focus on the core deficits of ASD and include strong caregiver participation. Project ImPACT supports parents in identifying the current language and play skills of their child(ren) and setting goals to improve the variability and complexity of those skills following a developmental progression. Using a naturalistic approach, the techniques in Project ImPACT help parents recognize and then capitalize on their child's motivation to promote engagement and social reciprocity during everyday routines and play opportunities. Behavioural techniques like prompting, fading, and reinforcement are used to build new skills in the areas of language, imitation, and play that can be maintained in naturally occurring, socially reinforcing contexts.

This training package is geared toward parents of newly diagnosed children up to the age of about six years. The program is typically delivered over 12 weeks with weekly sessions alternating between parent-directed workshops and individual coaching sessions with the parent and child. During workshops, parents and trainers discuss key concepts, watch videos of each technique, and role play. This meeting time can serve as a great forum for parents to troubleshoot specific challenges with the support of other parents. During the alternating weekly coaching sessions, the trainer models the techniques specific to the goals for the child directly with that child; parents then have an opportunity to practise these techniques with guidance from the trainer followed by continued practice at home.

At Surrey Place, we have expanded our delivery of this service to support more families at all quadrant sites in the city. We offer 12-week courses and a more intensive 6-week course that has parents attend the workshop at the beginning of the week, followed by a coaching session later that same week. It is rewarding to watch parents and children connect over bubbles and ball play, to watch a child search for parental reactions or to seek out the next silly face, and to see a child begin to connect language to those interactions.

Parent Training

Participating in parent training is a meaningful way for family members and/or caregivers to be involved in an individual's learning. The initial NAC publication reviewed a narrow range of parent-training literature, only including studies that trained parents to take on a therapist role (NAC, 2009). Phase 2 (NAC, 2015) includes a broader range of parent involvement activities, after reviewing 11 articles evaluating parent training spanning a variety of methods such as group-based education and caregiver support groups. This intervention is labelled established for children 0–18 for increasing interpersonal and play skills as well as reducing restrictive and repetitive behaviour (NAC, 2015).

Kelly Alves, professor at Seneca College in King City, Ontario, and Kimberly Maich, professor at Memorial University in Newfoundland and Labrador, published a paper reporting on parent perspectives of a group-based education curriculum (Alves & Maich, 2019). Analysis of focus-group data indicates parents support hands-on coaching and opportunities to hear directly from other parents (Alves & Maich, 2019). Direct parent-to-parent conversation was also reported as important by participants in a fathers-only support group (Elfert & Mirenda, 2015). Through this research from the University of British Columbia, participants shared that hearing the experiences of others in similar circumstances was the most helpful aspect of the group (Elfert & Mirenda, 2015). It is evident that parent training serves an important role in the treatment and education for ASD.

Parent Training

Courtney Vibert, Manager of Parent Education, Surrey Place, Toronto, Ontario

As a constant support in their child's lives, families need to feel confident and equipped to handle new situations as they arise without the direct support of a clinician, especially as behavioural treatment is often short term in nature. In addition, with often long waitlists for services, the considerable amount of time and cost involved in delivering direct behavioural interventions, and the availability of services in remote areas, parent training and involvement has become a necessary component of treatment. Parent education has many benefits for both the family and child. A literature review by Preece and Trajkovski (2017) found a range of positive impacts of parent education programs, including reductions in stress and anxiety, improved coping, enhanced parent-child interaction and communication, better understanding of ASD, efficacy and confidence in strategy use, and improved parental quality of life. Some studies have also begun to show the social benefits of attending parent education, as it provides an opportunity for families to connect with others who are going through similar experiences. Multiple studies have also demonstrated that parents can learn a variety of complex skills (e.g., environmental arrangement, visual strategies, behavioural principles) through a range of methods of training delivery (e.g., manuals, lectures, live modelling, video modelling, parent-child coaching; Matson, Mahan, & Matson, 2009; Suppo & Floyd, 2012). At Surrey Place, in Toronto, we provide specialized clinical services to children and adults living with developmental disabilities, autism spectrum disorder, and visual impairments. Within our Autism Services program, we offer a wide range of clinical, ABA-based treatment programs, as well as parent-training programs that are offered in combination with direct treatment or as a standalone education service for families. As research has shown multiple methods of training delivery can be effective for caregivers, we aim to offer a variety of program options that can meet the unique needs and learning styles of families.

Improved outcomes for children and youth with ASD depend, to a large degree, on the involvement of caregivers in learning the strategies being taught to their children and incorporating these techniques into their home routines. Given this, many of our ABA treatment programs have parent training opportunities built into them. For example, if a child attends a language group two times per week in order to build communication skills, families are offered a parent-training package alongside the treatment program. Caregivers attend three interactive workshops where they learn about language development, strategies to elicit communication, and prompting and reinforcement strategies. They also participate in a guided observation of a child session to view the therapists modelling the use of the techniques. Finally, caregivers have a one-on-one training session within the child treatment program in order to receive coaching and feedback on their use of the strategies.

Surrey Place also offers standalone group caregiver workshops on a wide range of topics, including toilet training, sleep, emotional regulation, social skills, mealtime routines, supporting transitions, and others. Caregivers attend these interactive educational sessions to learn about relevant research, improve their understanding of ASD and resources available to them, and to gain knowledge and confidence in using behavioural strategies with their children. After attending a two-hour workshop, caregivers receive an individualized follow-up session to help them plan to apply their learning to their own families and home or community environments.

Parent training is a vital service component that can contribute toward positive outcomes and quality of life for both children and families. Many families at Surrey Place have reported that they have gained more confidence in their ability to teach new skills and work through challenging behaviours at home when equipped with the knowledge and resources gained though our parent training programs.

Peer-Training Package

Peer-training packages teach typically developing students the skills needed to interact with peers who have ASD (Zagona & Mastergeorge, 2018). This intervention method begins with selecting appropriate peers. Suitable peers are same-age, socially competent, willing, and available to participate (NAC, 2015).

Peers are trained to initiate interactions, prompt learners with ASD, and deliver reinforcement (Brain & Mirenda, 2019; NAC, 2015; Zagona & Mastergeorge, 2018). After training, peers and students with ASD participate in a structured, adult-supported play interaction. The adult prompts peers to use the skills described in the training session. The adult models responses and delivers feedback and reinforcement to the trained peers (Brain & Mirenda, 2019; NAC, 2015; Zagona & Mastergeorge, 2018). Peer training, often referred to

> **peer-mediated social skills interventions:** a social communication teaching strategy where peers are taught skills to enhance interactions between peers and children with disabilities. Peers are taught the skills to interact with children with disabilities and practise them. They are then prompted by the adults in natural settings to use these skills to engage with, include, and promote skills in the children with disabilities or other social communication difficulties (Goldstein, Schneider, & Thiemann, 2007).

as peer-mediated interventions, are implemented in inclusive classrooms or as part of a specific social skills programs (Brain & Mirenda, 2019; Hundert, Rowe, & Harrison, 2014; Zagona & Mastergeorge, 2018) because these types of settings provide ongoing social interaction opportunities (Zagona & Mastergeorge, 2018). It is recommended that training settings include familiar and interesting materials and activities to increase student motivation (Brain & Mirenda, 2019; NAC, 2015; Zagona & Mastergeorge, 2018). The NAC (2015) document includes a review of three studies evaluating peer training and determined that this intervention method is established for children and adolescents aged 3 to 14 years. Peer-mediated interventions are used to address social and interpersonal difficulties (NAC, 2015). An empirical review of 17 studies listed responding to others, social reciprocity, and initiations as common behaviours modified through peer-mediated interventions (Zagona & Mastergeorge, 2018).

Hundert and colleagues (2014) of Hamilton, Ontario, carried out a non-concurrent, multiple-baseline investigation that included three children with ASD attending kindergarten. At the time of the study, all three participants did not demonstrate peer interaction during free play. The initial intervention was an individualized, eight-step social script listing appropriate play behaviours where participants watched a brief video demonstration of two children playing as per the script (Hundert et al., 2014). This intervention did not lead to any change in peer interaction. A second condition called peer buddies was subsequently added to increase initiations with all kindergarten children (Hundert et al., 2014). Peer buddies training included a 20-minute, interactive, class presentation where students observed adults modelling how to initiate, respond to, and maintain play (Hundert et al., 2014). Researchers summarized the play rules with a slogan similar to the procedures outlined by Laushey and Heflin (2000): "stay with, play with, and talk to your buddy" (Hundert et al., 2014, p. 209). When peer buddies were combined with social scripting, all participants increased the percentage of time engaged in interactive play in both training and generalization settings (Hundert et al., 2014), whereas generalization of interactive play did not happen when *only* social script training was provided. Peer buddies specifically included initiation as part of the intervention, lending support that this is a meaningful skill to include when teaching peers (Brain & Mirenda, 2019; Hundert et al., 2014; Zagona & Mastergeorge, 2018). Practitioners interested in improving social and communication skills in students with ASD should consider peer-mediated interventions, as they are low cost and rated favourably by teachers, peers, and students with ASD (Brain & Mirenda, 2019; Hundert et al., 2014; Zagona & Mastergeorge, 2018). Another example of peer-mediated interventions occurring in the Ontario context is the Camps on TRACKS project (see Chapter 10).

Pivotal Response Treatment

Pivotal response treatment, also referred to as pivotal response training (PRT), is an ABA-based teaching method that specifically targets *pivotal* areas of development such as motivation, initiation, self-management, and generalized responding

(Cadogan & McCrimmon, 2015; Koegel, Koegel, & Brookman, 2003; NAC, 2015). PRT emphasizes these important skills areas because they are foundational and contribute to development in other areas like cognitive, play, and social and motor skills (Koegel & Koegel, 2006). A systematic review of PRT authored by Cadogan and McCrimmon (2015), from the Faculty of Education at the University of Calgary in Alberta, reports that this intervention qualifies as naturalistic as it is often implemented by trained caregivers during familiar, child-initiated interactions. Authors of NAC reviewed 14 studies including PRT as the primary intervention. This naturalistic teaching method is established for increasing both communication and interpersonal skills in children with ASD up to nine years old (NAC, 2015).

Pivotal Skills

PRT uses specific teaching techniques to target foundational, pivotal skills. By gaining skills in pivotal areas of motivation, responding to multiple cues, self-management, and initiations, learners can improve in other areas.

1. Motivation: PRT incorporates motivating items and activities into teaching. Learning opportunities begin with an informal preference assessment. One way to quickly assess preference is to hold up two items (e.g., a book and a stuffed animal) and provide an opportunity for children to choose. Allowing the learner to select toys and materials increases motivation to learn and creates a balanced learning environment (Cadogan & McCrimmon, 2015; Koegel et al., 2003; NAC, 2015; Dunlap et al., 2010).
2. Responding to multiple cues: Individuals with ASD often have difficulty generalizing learned skills. PRT addresses this by teaching learners to respond to multiple cues. A variety of instructions and materials are used to reduce the likelihood that learners may become over-selective to certain features of items or specific situations. A PRT approach to teaching the vocal term *open* would incorporate multiple scenarios (cues) to practise this word. The therapist or caregiver could set up scenarios such as holding a closed jar of bubbles in front of the child, standing in front of the door to go outside, giving the child a closed marker, or holding a closed container of snacks. These multiple examples show the child the range of situations in which the vocal phrase *open* can be used. Providing multiple cues increases generalization.
3. Initiations: Initiating is a common problem area often observed in individuals with ASD (APA, 2013b; Ingersoll & Dvortcsak; 2010, Rogers & Dawson, 2010). Naturalistic teaching methods such as PRT prioritize teaching initiating and create many opportunities for learners to show and share materials (Koegel & Koegel, 2006; Koegel et al., 2003; Dunlap et al., 2010). PRT incorporates interesting, developmentally appropriate materials like pop-up books and puppets to create motivating interactions that set the stage for learners to point, reach toward, and ask questions about items (Dunlap et al., 2010).

Pivotal Response Treatment in Nova Scotia

In Nova Scotia, PRT is the provincially funded, early-intervention program available to young children with ASD. PRT is a year-long intervention that begins with one week of intensive, in-home parent coaching (Smith, Flanagan, Garon, & Bryson, 2015). The first six months of intervention includes daily, therapist-delivered teaching. During the final six months, direct services are gradually reduced from ten hours to six hours per week (Smith et al., 2015). In collaboration with family members, individualized treatment goals focusing on communication, initiations, and self-management skills are selected.

A 2015 prospective study assessed the effectiveness of PRT (Smith et al., 2015). This investigation included 118 toddlers diagnosed with ASD living in three regions of Nova Scotia: Halifax, Cape Breton, and Other Mainland. Researchers collected detailed, initial assessment data measuring expressive language, receptive language, and cognitive skills. Following one year of PRT, all groups made noteworthy improvements. Children in a low-IQ group made significant improvements in parent-reported communication and adaptive skills. Participants in moderate- and high-IQ groups made significant gains in communication, social skills, daily living, and adaptive skills. Additionally, children in the high-IQ group demonstrated reduced maladaptive behaviour. This study demonstrates that one year of PRT led to favourable outcomes for a wide range of young children with ASD (Smith et al., 2015).

Read about It. Think about It. Write about It.

- Write down three pivotal skills you think are important for any child to learn. Are these skills easy to teach or complex? Do they involve multiple components?
- Do you agree with the approach of teaching pivotal skills?

Self-management

The goal of self-management is to increase independence and decrease reliance on adults (Cadogan & McCrimmon, 2015; Koegel et al., 2003; Dunlap et al., 2010). Self-management is a very important social and interpersonal skill that involves regulating, self-monitoring, and assessing behaviour (NAC, 2015). This broad skill develops over time. Early self-management skills are individualized to age and developmental level and begin with children correctly identifying appropriate and inappropriate behaviour. An example is an adult saying, "Show me how you wait nicely." The child then demonstrates calm, quiet waiting. The child is demonstrating self-regulation by adjusting behaviour to match the adult's request (NAC, 2015; Dunlap et al., 2010).

Multidisciplinary Approach to Emotional Regulation in Alberta

Rebecca Wattman, Instructor Therapist, Skills4Life, Hutton House, London, Ontario

New Heights School and Learning Services is a private, specialized school for children and youth with autism and similar learning disabilities in Calgary, Alberta. The school provides education to students from Junior Kindergarten through to Grade 12. I worked there for eight years, and the last five years, I was the educational assistant in the Grade 1 to 3 class. Emotional regulation was a large part of the teaching throughout all aspects of the curriculum. From my personal experience, a multidisciplinary approach to emotional regulation was a key element in the teaching of this skill set.

The multidisciplinary team consisted of a teacher, educational assistant (EA), occupational therapist (OT), speech and language pathologist (SLP), psychologist, family counsellor, the principal, and the vice-principal.

Effectively teaching emotional regulation consisted of several different aspects that were integrated to maintain consistency with language and responses, repetition and practice in a variety of settings, and a collaborative team approach to increasing the capacity of the students in regulating themselves and their emotions.

The OT, SLP, and psychologist each taught a weekly class in the classroom to target emotional and self-regulation. The OT used the Zones of Regulation and would teach different regulation strategies for each colour on the emotions chart. The program focuses on providing different options for each colour and teaching the different strategies in hands-on, practical, and natural teaching opportunities. The SLP would teach the language surrounding the different emotions and recognizing these emotions in others and the students themselves through role play and other activities. The psychologist would further teach recognizing emotions and how to help work with the emotions in a positive way. The Social Thinking Superflex program was integrated with the zones by all disciplines to help label emotions and teach students how to use their Superflex powers to defeat them and self-regulate. This was more from a cognitive-behavioural perspective in understanding how to accept, overcome, and change different emotions. Although these were taught in different classes, the language and strategies were consistent and incorporated into each class. The three disciplines had each taken the program and the core concepts and come together to bring their own discipline-specific spin on the program. Use of the strategies would occur over all sessions and build on each other. This provided students opportunities to practise these new learned skills throughout all classes, even when formal teaching was not being presented. Students would check in with their emotions and how their body felt throughout the day and be given support from educators to effectively use the strategies that worked for them. Further, the family counsellor would help integrate these strategies into the student's home to continue to provide opportunities to use new skills and assist in the regulation in the student's home.

Although there were targeted classes, the classroom teacher and EA also used these strategies in all aspects of teaching, including recess and unstructured times. Regulation throughout the day was an important piece in achieving success with the students' learning of self-regulation and academic learning. With the younger students, we would begin with prompting them to identify emotions and work through strategies, with the end goal of them being able to self-regulate and use the strategies in appropriate and effective ways. The team was constantly in communication with one another to discuss what was going well, and what areas may require further teaching or a more targeted effort.

The OT, SLP, psychologist, and family counsellor were the same therapists for the entire school. This helped to generalize the skills learned in early elementary to the higher grades as they progressed in their educational career and further built on their skills with the same language, adapting to age-appropriate methods of identifying emotions. For example, in the Grade 1 to 3 class, it was a basic, four-colour emotions chart (red for angry or frustrated; yellow for excited or silly; green for ready to learn; and blue for sad or tired); more complex emotions were added in the Grade 4 to 6 class (jealousy, boredom, fear, etc.). The multidisciplinary team enabled us to work collaboratively for the success of the students, and their families, in an effective and tiered approach throughout their educational journey.

Social Skills Package

Social skills is a broad term describing the range of skills and abilities a learner needs to meaningfully participate in social environments like home, school, and community (NAC, 2015). Social skills package interventions are an effective strategy to address the wide range of social challenges associated with a diagnosis of ASD. These interventions can be delivered in an individualized setting, through peer-mediated interactions, or in adult-directed small groups (NAC, 2015). Social skill interventions include behavioural teaching methods such as prompting and reinforcement to target eye contact, initiations, and maintaining conversations (Bellini, 2016; NAC, 2015). After reviewing 21 articles, the NAC considered this intervention established for increasing communication, interpersonal, learning readiness, and play skills (NAC, 2009, 2015; Wong et al., 2014).

Social skills package interventions are effective for adolescents 13 to 18 years old (NAC, 2015). This can be a complicated time for friendships and social interactions. During the teenage years, friendships begin to shift from play-based to talk-based (Waugh & Peskin, 2015). The skills required to successfully navigate teen social interactions are much more sophisticated than the skills needed during childhood interactions. During this time, teens need to be able to initiate conversations, coordinate and arrange plans outside of the classroom, and be emotionally available to peers (Bellini,

2016; Waugh & Peskin, 2015). These are likely areas of difficulty for teens with ASD. Social skills appear to be a challenge for all individuals with ASD; even individuals with advanced verbal skills, refined adaptive skills, and little to no interfering behaviour experience negative implications because of underdeveloped social skills (Bellini, 2016; McVey et al., 2017; Waugh & Peskin, 2015). Individuals with this profile may have had some success during childhood social situations where there was an increased focus on play skills but may struggle to navigate the fast-paced interactions during teen and early adulthood years (Bellini, 2016; Waugh & Peskin, 2015).

Why Teach Social Skills?

It is very important that practitioners address social issues prior to and during adolescence. Peer acceptance during late childhood and early teenage years is one of the most influential predictors of mental health in typically and atypically developing adults (Waugh & Peskin, 2015). Educators should be mindful of this likely trajectory and prioritize teaching skills that will increase the likelihood of peer acceptance and friendships. Friendships play a valuable role in social and emotional development. Friendships also provide a variety of experiences to practise managing emotions, cooperation, and problem solving. Studies assessing friendships consistently demonstrate that individuals with ASD experience friendships differently than typically developing peers. Individuals with ASD have fewer stable, reciprocal friendships and spend less time socializing outside the classroom (Waugh & Peskin, 2015). In typical development, social circles expand during the teen years; however, for most teens with ASD, the opposite is true, and social circles remain the same or shrink (Waugh & Peskin, 2015). There are many unfortunate and possible outcomes for individuals with ASD with poorly developed social skills. Typical teens may comment that teens with ASD appear insensitive, self-centred, and socially disinterested (Waugh & Peskin, 2015). This contradicts the claim by many teens with ASD that friendships are important and having a meaningful friend is a common social goal (Bellini, 2016; McVey et al., 2017; Waugh & Peskin, 2015). There are practical reasons for educators to teach social skills. Research supports that underdeveloped social skills can compromise physical health (Waugh & Peskin, 2015). Individuals with ASD may not readily demonstrate the social skills required to initiate a phone call to arrange a doctor's appointment, sit appropriately in crowded waiting rooms, or engage in conversation exchanges to report health complications or symptoms (Waugh & Peskin, 2015).

Assessing Social Skills

All well-designed interventions should begin with a comprehensive assessment of the learner's current abilities. Assessment is the first step of treatment, as this process provides meaningful information about strengths and areas of need. When conducting a social skills assessment, it is necessary for evaluators to determine why students fail to demonstrate social behaviours (Bellini, 2016). Two main reasons for the absence of

Bellini's Autism Social Skills Profile-2

Never N | Sometimes S | Often O | Very Often V

Component Skill	How Often?	With Prompting?	Scoring			
			SER	SPA	DSB	Total
Invites peers to join him/her in activities	N S O V 1 2 3 4					
Joins in activities with peers	N S O V 1 2 3 4					
Takes turns during games and activities	N S O V 1 2 3 4					
Interacts with peers during unstructured activities	N S O V 1 2 3 4					
Asks questions about a broad range of topics	N S O V 1 2 3 4					
Asks questions to request information about a person	N S O V 1 2 3 4					
Engages in one-on-one social interactions with peers	N S O V 1 2 3 4					
Interacts with groups of peers	N S O V 1 2 3 4					
Maintains the "give and take" of conversations	N S O V 1 2 3 4					
Talks about or acknowledges the interests of others	N S O V 1 2 3 4					
Exhibits poor timing with his/her social initiations	N S O V 4 3 2 1					
Page 2 scoring summary			SER	SPA	DSB	Total

Figure 3.15: Sample Social Skills Assessment

Source: Bellini, 2016, p. 256.

social behaviours are *skill acquisition deficits* and *performance deficits* (Bellini, 2016). Skill acquisition deficits implies that students have not learned the specific social skills. This type of deficit is addressed through behavioural interventions such as prompting, modelling, and reinforcement (Bellini, 2016). Performance deficits imply that learners can perform the social skills but fail to do so; perhaps this problem is due to lack of motivation, anxiety, or sensory reasons (Bellini, 2016). A performance deficit can also occur because the student had a negative experience during a past social interaction.

Performance deficits pose a significant barrier to social skill development in teens with ASD, especially female teens (Bellini, 2016; McVey et al., 2017). During the teenage years, typical female relationships are complicated and challenging to navigate as they include subtle forms of aggression, manipulation, and rumour spreading (McVey et al., 2017). Female teens with ASD struggle with these advanced emotional concepts and have greater difficulty developing and maintaining friendships than male teens (McVey et al., 2017). During childhood, females with ASD learn social skills more quickly than males but experience higher frequency of social rejection and are more likely to withdraw from social interaction opportunities (McVey et al., 2017). This lends support to performance, rather than skill acquisition, being the primary barrier for female teens with ASD.

Program for the Evaluation and Enrichment of Relational Skills (PEERS)

PEERS is a parent-assisted social skills program for adolescents and young adults with ASD (Laugeson & Frankel, 2010; McVey et al., 2017; Schiltz et al., 2018). This group-based intervention teaches teens skills necessary to make and maintain friendships (Laugeson & Frankel, 2010; McVey et al., 2017; Schiltz et al., 2018). There is an extensive body of research supporting the effectiveness of this intervention across a wide range of demographics. The PEERS curriculum has been translated and delivered in Korean, Chinese, Hebrew, and Dutch (Semel Institute for Neuroscience and Human Behaviour, 2020). There is empirical support that, following participation in PEERS, participants experience reduced symptoms in depression and anxiety (Schiltz et al., 2018). Researchers in Montreal, Quebec, examined the effectiveness of a modified PEERS with a cohort of adolescents with ASD. Service delivery was modified to two sessions per week for seven weeks (Marchica & D'Amico, 2016). Participants were 13- to 17-year-old adolescents. Results show that following seven weeks of PEERS, participants achieved statistically significant improvements in overall social skills and a decrease in problematic behaviour and levels of conflict. Participants also improved in the mean number of arranged get-togethers (Marchica & D'Amico, 2016). This study contributes to the extensive body of research empirically supporting PEERS as effective for increasing social behaviours in Canadian adolescents.

Skills targeted through PEERS include the following:

- Conversation skills
  - Trading information
  - Two-way conversation
  - Electronic communication
- Choosing suitable friends
- Appropriate use of humour
- Entering and exiting conversation
- Planning a get-together
- Being a good sport
- How to deal with rejection
  - Teasing
  - Bullying
- Managing disagreements
- Managing rumours and gossip (Laugeson & Frankel, 2010)

Read about It. Think about It. Write about It.

- How important is teaching social skills to individuals with ASD?
- Some advocate for accepting persons with ASD and their social uniqueness. Would teaching social skills contradict this view?
- How interconnected do you think communication and social skills are? Are there some social skills that are not dependent on communication?

Story-based Interventions

Story-based interventions are written descriptions outlining expected behaviours in social or academic situations (NAC, 2009, 2015). Story-based interventions are designed to increase interpersonal, self-regulation, and communication skills and have been identified as established for children, adolescents, and young adults (under age 22) by the NAC. Typically, they identify a target behaviour and involve a written description of the situations under which specific behaviours are expected. Most stories try to increase perspective-taking skills and are written from the first- or third-person perspective. The most well-known story-based intervention is Social Stories, developed by Carol Gray (NAC, 2015).

> **perspective-taking**: also called theory of mind, the ability to infer another person's mental state, then take that information to make sense of their behaviour and predict what the person will do next (Peters & Thompson, 2018).

Social Stories

Janette Seymour, Professor, Behavioural Sciences Program, Seneca College, Ontario

Social Stories was developed by Carol Gray in 1991. The goal for this intervention strategy was to address deficits in theory of mind, joint attention, perspective-taking, central coherence, and executive function through teaching social understanding. "Other methods of influence—persuasion, bribery, or charismatic appeals—are push strategies. Story is a pull strategy. If your story is good enough, people—of their own free will—come to the conclusion they can trust you and the message you bring" (Simmons, 2006).

A social story is a process and product that accurately describes a situation, skill, or concept according to specific criteria that guide the development of the social story to ensure the characteristic patient and supportive quality of every story (Gray, 2010). Each story has an individualized format, voice, and content that is descriptive, meaningful, and physically, socially, and emotionally safe for the audience, resulting in an overall patient and supportive quality (Gray, 2010). The format clarifies the content and enhances the meaning for each specific audience. This means the content of the story is based on information related to the specific situation, skill, or concept and to the specific audience. The content of each story should be literally accurate. For example, the statement "I go to school every day" is not literally accurate since students do not attend school on weekends, holidays, or during the summer. Stories should be written in a supportive and reassuring voice from the first- or third-person perspective that gently suggest possible actions, responses, or behaviours. Phrases that are judgmental or authoritarian are prohibited. For example, the verbs *should* and *must* and the directives *can't, shouldn't, don't* are to be avoided (Gray, 2010).

The social story consists of specific types of sentences designed to address the relevant "Wh" questions by describing context (where); time-related information (when); relevant people (who); important cues (what); basic activities, behaviours, or statements (how); and the reasons or rationale behind them (why). See Table 3.4.

Social stories are written according to a specific ratio suggesting that for every coaching statement there should be two or more descriptive, perspective, or affirmative statements. Stories should engage and interest the audience and need to be written at a language-level similar to or below the audience's comprehension level. Stories can include specific areas of interest or fascination and can be presented in a variety of formats, such as songs and cartoons, or pre-recorded in order to enhance audience engagement. Stories should be introduced in a positive manner and in a relaxed setting and never used as a consequence for behaviour. They need to be reviewed regularly but the specific schedule depends on the audience. The impact of the story should be monitored to correct errors and assess the impact (Gray, 2010).

Table 3.4: Types of Sentences in Social Stories

Descriptive Sentences (De)	Describes a situation occurrence in detail like who, what, where, and why for a child to analyze and understand the situation
Directive Sentences (Di)	Describes appropriate social response for that situation
Perspective Sentences (P)	Describes one of the responses or emotional feelings of the child
Affirmative Sentences (A)	Refers to a law, ethical rule, or morally accepted opinion
Cooperative Sentences (Co)	Describes how other individuals offer aid in a given situation
Control Sentences (Cn)	The strategies response created by the child that helps control the situation

Source: Gray, 2010.

Learning to Ride the Bus

Janette Seymour

Note: The following is an example of a social story. This story was written for an adolescent to increase their understanding of the social "rules" related to personal space and using public transportation.

My name is Sam. Most days I take the bus to school. Sometimes I take the bus to other places like the mall, the movies or the gym.

Lots of other people take the bus. They take the bus to go to work or to school or to other places.

Sometimes the bus is almost empty and there are many empty seats.

I can choose where I sit. Sometimes the bus is full and there are no empty seats. I can stand and hold a nearby pole. Sometimes the bus is crowded and there are no seats and many people standing.

If the bus is very crowded, I will try to find a place to stand where I can hold a nearby pole. Sometimes this means that people will be standing very close to me. They may even bump up against me. This is what happens when the bus is crowded.

I will try to remember to take a deep breath and count to 10 silently in my head. It is important to share the space when the bus is crowded.

When I get off the bus, I will have more space. Riding the bus means I can go to lots of different places.

Read about It. Think about It. Write about It.

- What is your initial impression of social stories? Do you think they would be helpful for all people on the autism spectrum?
- What characteristics are important to assess before implementing social stories with an individual?

SPOTLIGHTS ACROSS CANADA

Research: British Columbia

Brain and Mirenda (2019), researchers from the University of British Columbia, in Vancouver, investigated whether low-intensity, peer-mediated intervention increased engagement and communication in middle-school children with ASD. In the article *Effectiveness of Low-Intensity Peer-Mediated Intervention for Middle School Students with Autism Spectrum Disorder*, participants included classroom teachers, three students with ASD, and peer coaches. The study was implemented in the lunchroom at three private middle schools in Western Canada (Brain & Mirenda, 2019). Interesting, age-appropriate materials such as sports equipment, climbing structures, and swings were available. Each student with ASD was partnered with two to four peer coaches, who were selected based on a strong social profile and previous interest in socializing with the student with ASD. Target behaviours measured included engagement and communicative acts, high fives, smiles, and gestures. Peer coaching was delivered across two sessions and trained peers to initiate, respond to participant-initiated activities, and prompt communicative acts, as well as praise and compliment the student with ASD (Brain & Mirenda, 2019). Researchers collected 30-second partial interval data during a 10-minute observation. During baseline, no occurrences of peer interaction were observed. Results show that following peer coaching, all three participants significantly increased the percentage of time engaged with peer coaches and the number of intervals including communicative acts. When asked, all peer coaches and student teachers rated the peer-training experience positively (Brain & Mirenda, 2019).

Atlantic Provinces

JASPER Program for Young Children with Autism—Newfoundland and Labrador

JASPER (Joint Attention Symbolic Play Engagement Regulation) is a play-based, naturalistic treatment model focused on teaching young children with ASD foundational social communication skills such as joint attention, imitation, and play (Kasari,

Freeman, & Paparella, 2006). This intervention is currently available to children under eight with ASD living in Newfoundland and Labrador (Grandy, 2018).

In 2016, the researcher who developed JASPER, Dr. Connie Kasari, partnered with Eastern Health in Newfoundland and Labrador to train clinicians, educators, and practitioners in the JASPER model (Grandy, 2018). With an initial cohort of 12 trained practitioners, Newfoundland and Labrador was the first province to adopt the JASPER program. To date, there are more than 50 trained personnel providing JASPER to children in this province. JASPER is intended to be a short-term treatment including 24 sessions provided once or twice per week (Grandy, 2018). Sessions include common toys such as dolls, cars, and animal toys to teach attending, sharing, and showing interest (Grandy, 2018).

Jan Young Guerra, Eastern Health's Manager of Direct Home and Autism Services, described the positive impact JASPER has had:

> The opportunity for Eastern Health families to implement JASPER has meant children with autism in the province have the opportunity to access the latest and very best evidence-based treatment. The children are making tremendous gains in the shortest time period that I have ever known in my 30 years of working in this field. The clinicians [and] parents report seeing the children learn and acquire skills right before their eyes. (Grandy, 2018)

Eastern Health has recently introduced virtual monitoring using Web-based programs that enable clinicians to observe practitioners and parents implementing JASPER in remote areas of the province (Canadian Healthcare Technology, 2018).

Described in the recent Autism Action Plan, the Government of Newfoundland and Labrador is continuing to invest in JASPER as an ASD intervention available to young children in that province (Government of Newfoundland & Labrador, 2019).

A LOOK BACK

Chapter 3, "Social Communication–based Interventions," focused on:

- An overview of social communication as part of the DSM-5 (American Psychiatric Association, 2013b) and some of the characteristics for ASD
- Effective, evidence-based, social communication strategies including cognitive behaviour intervention packages, behaviour treatment, modelling, natural teaching strategies, parent-training packages, peer-training packages, pivotal response treatment, self-management, social skills packages, and story-based interventions

ADDITIONAL RESOURCES

Connectability

https://connectability.ca/en/

This comprehensive website includes a wide range of resources, tip sheets, and visuals that could support children, youth, and/or adults with an intellectual disability. This website includes ideas for creative arts activities, resources related to employment and transition to adulthood, as well as information on financial planning.

Words Matter: A Collaborative Language and Communication Guide in the Autism Field

https://autismcanada.org/wp-content/uploads/2015/04/AC_LanguageDocument-2016-1.pdf

This brief document provides meaningful information on what it means to use person-first language. This document provides examples of undesirable phrases and terms to avoid when discussing ASD, as well as several well-written examples of preferred language that is sensitive to context.

Speech Therapy Centres of Canada

https://www.speechtherapycentres.com/social-communication-difficulties/

A speech language pathologist is often involved in treatment programs for individuals with ASD. This website provides a brief overview of the role a speech pathologist has in the assessment and treatment of social communication disorders. This website includes a brief list of social communication skills that individuals with ASD often find difficult. Additionally, this website includes informational blog posts on a wide variety of speech-therapy related topics.

PECS Canada

https://pecs-canada.com/

Pyramid Educational Consultants are the sole source for resources and training related to the evidence-based picture exchange communication system (PECS). This website provides information on online and in-class professional development opportunities. This website also provides readers with a link to the most recent research assessing various aspects of the PECS program.

ESDM Canada

http://www.esdmcanada.ca/home.html

The Early Start Denver Model is an evidence-based intervention for young children with ASD. The team of clinicians at ESDM Canada provide online and in-person training to parents and professionals. This website describes a variety of information sessions and training options. Staff at ESDM Canada have partnered with researchers from the University of British Columbia and the University of Alberta, investigating best practices for parent coaching. The most recent results of this investigation (PACE project) are posted on this site.

Social Stories

https://autismcanada.org/living-with-autism/treatments/non-medical/communication/social-stories/

Social stories can be a useful tool to provide information. These stories, written from the individual's perspective can help prepare for transitions, explain routines, or social expectations. This website provides the reader with a brief summary of social stories, defines the various types of sentences to be included, and provides an example. This is a valuable website for anyone considering writing a social story.

Visual Schedule Builder

https://autismawarenesscentre.com/visual-supports-best-way-use/

Autism Awareness Centre, Inc., hosts conferences across Canada on a wide range of ASD-topics. This website includes information on upcoming training events, as well as a very detailed book and resource list. Resources are listed by most recent release date and include products suitable for professionals, parents, individuals with ASD, and their siblings.

CHAPTER 4

Behaviour-based Interventions

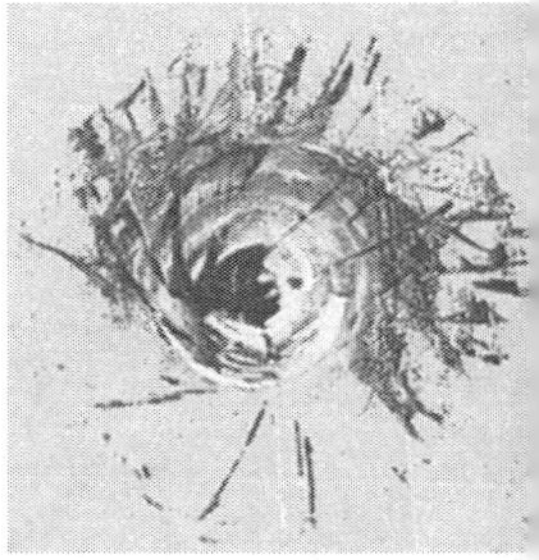

LEARNING OBJECTIVES

- List challenging behaviours that are commonly seen in individuals with ASD, including the repetitive and restricted patterns of behaviour that are a component of the DSM-5 diagnosis for ASD.
- Identify behavioural interventions that are used to address common behavioural issues in ASD, including antecedent-based interventions, task interspersal, task analysis, chaining, prompting, prompt fading, time delay, positive reinforcement, negative reinforcement, extinction, differential reinforcement, and behavioural skills training.
- Increase familiarity with behavioural interventions and research completed across Canada with individuals with ASD.

This chapter focuses on established behavioural interventions that address several of the challenging behaviours associated with a diagnosis of autism spectrum disorder (ASD). Behavioural interventions can be applied individually or in combination to reduce the frequency, intensity, and intrusiveness of these behaviours. The chapter reviews some common characteristics of this category of behaviours, discusses effective assessment practices, and provides an overview of antecedent and consequence-based interventions.

TYPES OF BEHAVIOUR

Restricted, Repetitive Behaviour

Restricted, repetitive, and non-functional behaviour are umbrella terms broadly categorizing two areas of behaviour commonly associated with ASD: repetitive sensorimotor behaviours and insistence on sameness (American Psychiatric Association, 2013b). A recent comparative review from Queen's University in Kingston, Ontario, described the variability in form, frequency, and intensity of repetitive behaviours in individuals with ASD. This variability poses difficulty for assessors when trying to quantify restricted and repetitive behaviours (Jiujias, Kelley, & Hall, 2017). Restricted and repetitive behaviours are an early red flag of atypical development, with signs of over-focusing on objects appearing by 12 months of age (Jiujas et al., 2017). The severity of these behaviours is often linked to cognitive ability and age. A younger learner in the lower IQ range is more likely to display repetitive sensorimotor behaviour (e.g., tapping objects, rocking, hand flapping). An older, more cognitively able student is more likely to demonstrate restricted topics of interest, repetitive-question asking, and insistence on sameness (Jiujas et al., 2015; Scahill et al., 2015). Engaging in repetitive behaviour and/or talking about restricted areas of interest is a preferred activity for many individuals with ASD. Some may become upset if prevented from performing these actions or if redirected to another conversation topic. Research supports that repetitive behaviours change over the lifespan. The frequency and intensity of motor movements lessen as individuals with ASD age. However, this is not true for insistence on sameness. Attachment to routines and restricted areas of interest are reported to become more severe over time (Jiujas et al., 2017).

repetitive sensorimotor behaviours: stereotypic and repetitive movements that include the body (e.g., hand flapping or rocking) or objects (e.g., turning the wheels on a car or flipping pages in a book; Jiujias et al., 2017).

insistence on sameness: adherence to well-established routines (e.g., tucking in all dining room chairs), as well as restricted areas of interest. Restricted interests are intense preoccupations with an object or topic. Common examples of restricted interests include elevators, numbers on bus routes, and licence plates. Such preoccupation with restricted interests is atypical in focus and intensity (Scahill et al., 2015).

Self-injurious Behaviour

Self-injurious behaviour is a form of repetitive, motor behaviour that is self-directed and can cause damage to skin and tissue (Dimian et al., 2017; McLean et al., 2016). Common topographies of self-injurious behaviour include head-hitting, head-banging, skin-picking, pinching, and self-biting (Dimian et al., 2017). Estimates of self-injurious behaviour vary widely based on the selected sample. Some researchers estimate its prevalence from 2 to 24%, with other estimates as high as 55 to 60% (Dimian et al., 2017). Bishop and colleagues, as described in Dimian and colleagues (2017), sampled 830 children with ASD and reported that 20 to 58% presented with self-injurious behaviour. Children between 6 and 11 years old with significant cognitive delays were most likely to engage in self-injurious behaviour. Self-injurious behaviours are frequently targeted for reduction as these behaviours have the potential to negatively impact the quality of life of the individual with ASD and their family. The implications of self-injurious/challenging behaviour can include:

- Risk of injury
- Social stigmatization
- Barrier to learning
- Less involvement in classroom routines
- Receiving less instructional time (McLean et al., 2016)

Challenging Behaviour

Some of the behaviours that individuals with ASD demonstrate can be described as problematic or challenging. Challenging behaviours are actions that can potentially harm the individual with ASD or others (McLean et al., 2016). They can include physical aggression, verbal aggression, property destruction, tantrums, and noncompliance (McLean et al., 2016; Zaidman-Zait et al., 2014). Managing even one challenging behaviour can be a major source of stress for parents, family members, and educators. Repeatedly coping with challenging behaviour is linked to staff burnout, job dissatisfaction, and higher levels of parent- and staff-reported anxiety (McLean et al., 2016). Baker and Blacher (2015) studied youth with ASD, intellectual disabilities (ID) and typically developing youth to determine whether IQ was a protective factor for symptoms of disruptive behaviour (attention deficit hyperactivity disorder, oppositional defiant disorder, and conduct disorder). Using the *Child Behavior Checklist* and two *Diagnostic Interview Schedule for Children* scales, researchers found that youth with ASD scored higher (indicating more problems) on all measures when compared with typically developing youth. They also found that in youth with ASD, IQ was *not* a protective factor for disruptive behaviour, indicating that IQ did not differentiate youth with ASD. However, it is also important to note that there was *not* a significant difference between youth with ASD and youth with ID for disruptive behaviours.

Zaidman-Zait and many noteworthy researchers across several Canadian universities carried out a longitudinal study examining the relationship between parental stress and different types of challenging behaviour in young children with ASD. Results of the study show a bidirectional relationship between parental stress and the presentation of child behaviours such as aggression, tantrums, and noncompliance, aligning with other results (Dimian et al., 2017; McLean et al., 2016; Zaidman-Zait et al., 2014). Parents report challenging behaviour, more than any other symptom of ASD, as contributing to family distress (Zaidman-Zait et al., 2014).

Challenging behaviour can occur for many reasons. In behavioural terms, the reason a behaviour occurs is called a *function*. Prior to developing a plan to reduce problematic, self-injurious, or repetitive and restrictive behaviour, educators should collect information to determine *why* these behaviours are happening (the function). McLean and colleagues (2016), affiliated with Autism in Education, Atlantic Provinces Special Education Authority (APSEA) out of Halifax, Nova Scotia, published an information paper titled *Teaching Essential Skills to Prevent the Development of Challenging Behaviour in Learners with Autism Spectrum Disorder.* This paper describes several forms of challenging behaviours, the implications and risk factors associated with these behaviours, as well as prevention and intervention strategies. It also includes a well-organized summary of common functions of challenging behaviour:

> Challenging behaviours function to get something that the individual wants (attention; access to a preferred item, activity, or situation; a pleasant sensation) or to escape or avoid something that the individual does not want (aversive tasks, activities, items, situations; non-preferred people; unpleasant sensations). (McLean et al., 2016)

Read about It. Think about It. Write about It.

- Given the different types of behaviour identified in this chapter (repetitive and restricted, challenging, and self-injurious behaviour), what do you generally think of when you hear the term *behaviour*? Did it encompass all of these areas?
- Ask three people who have had exposure to ASD, but just have general knowledge of the disability, if challenging behaviours are part of the ASD diagnosis. What did you discover? Were you surprised with the results? Why or why not?

FUNCTIONAL BEHAVIOUR ASSESSMENT

A foundational principle of applied behaviour analysis (ABA) is that behaviour has a purpose (Miltenberger, 2016). In behavioural terms, the purpose of (or reason for) a behaviour is called a function (Martin & Pear, 2015; Miltenberger, 2016). Broadly, target behaviour occurs for two main functions: to gain something (e.g., attention, items, sensory input) or to remove something (e.g., escape tasks, demands, or activities; Martin & Pear, 2015; Miltenberger, 2016). Gathering information on the antecedents and consequences of a problematic behaviour is called *functional behaviour assessment.* Functional behaviour assessment (FBA) is a foundational component to planning successful interventions for a range of problematic behaviours, including those with repetitive and restricted patterns. Within FBA, there are multiple assessment methods available to choose from (see Figure 4.1).

function of behaviour: the reason, or purpose, for a behaviour, determined through observation and data collection. The function of a behaviour can be either to gain access to something or to escape something. The four most common functions of behaviour include (a) escape, (b) attention, (c) sensory, and (d) tangible.

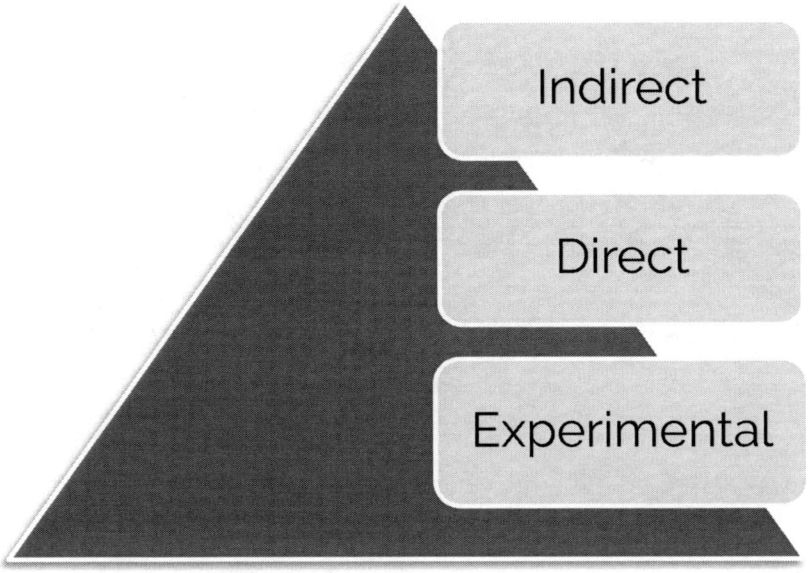

Figure 4.1: Types of Functional Behaviour Assessment
Source: Authors.

Indirect

Indirect functional behaviour assessment methods rely on parents, siblings, teachers, and/or the individual with ASD to fill out questionnaires, surveys, or rating scales regarding the problematic behaviour (Martin & Pear, 2014; Miltenberger, 2016). Another form of indirect behavioural assessment includes structured interviews (see Figure 4.2). Those familiar with the individual with ASD and the problematic behaviour can answer questions related to what happens before and after the behaviour (Martin & Pear, 2014; Miltenberger, 2016). Clinicians and educators often select indirect behaviour assessment tools as they are quick and easy to administer (Miltenberger, 2016). Practitioners need to be aware of some disadvantages associated with

functional assessment interview: an indirect assessment that is semi-structured. It assists with obtaining information from informants that help lead to the function of the behaviour. The interview is set up to provide information about the setting events, antecedents, behaviours, and consequences, as well as the four primary functions.

functional assessment questionnaires: questionnaires that have multiple options for the respondents to choose from when completing it about a certain target behaviour. Forms are then scored to provide some hypothesized functions of the behaviour based on the responses.

FAST

Functional Analysis Screening Tool

Client:______________________________ Date:____________

Informant:_________________ Interviewer:_________________

To the Interviewer: The FAST identifies factors that may influence problem behaviors. Use it only for screening as part of a comprehensive functional analysis of the behavior. Administer the FAST to several individuals who interact with the client frequently. Then use the results to guide direct observation in several different situations to verify suspected behavioral functions and to identify other factors that may influence the problem behavior.

To the Informant: Complete the sections below. Then read each question carefully and answer it by circling "Yes" or "No." If you are uncertain about an answer, circle "N/A."

Informant-Client Relationship

1. Indicate your relationship to the person: ___Parent ___Instructor ___Therapist/Residential Staff ________________(Other)
2. How long have you known the person? ____Years ____Months
3. Do you interact with the person daily? ____Yes ____No
4. In what situations do you usually interact with the person?
   ___ Meals ___ Academic training
   ___ Leisure ___ Work or vocational training
   ___ Self-care ____________________(Other)

Problem Behavior Information

1. Problem behavior (check and describe):
   __ Aggression ________________
   __ Self-Injury ________________
   __ Stereotypy ________________
   __ Property destruction ________________
   __ Other ________________
2. Frequency: __Hourly __Daily __Weekly __Less often
3. Severity: __Mild: Disruptive but little risk to property or health
   __Moderate: Property damage or minor injury
   __Severe: Significant threat to health or safety
4. Situations in which the problem behavior is <u>most</u> likely to occur:
   Days/Times________________
   Settings/Activities ________________
   Persons present ________________
5. Situations in which the problem behavior is <u>least</u> likely to occur:
   Days/Times________________
   Settings/Activities ________________
   Persons present ________________
6. What is usually happening to the person right <u>before</u> the problem behavior occurs?________________
7. What usually happens to the person right <u>after</u> the problem behavior occurs?________________
8. Current treatments________________

1. Does the problem behavior occur when the person is not receiving attention or when caregivers are paying attention to someone else?	Yes No N/A
2. Does the problem behavior occur when the person's requests for preferred items or activities are denied or when these are taken away?	Yes No N/A
3. When the problem behavior occurs, do caregivers usually try to calm the person down or involve the person in preferred activities?	Yes No N/A
4. Is the person usually well behaved when (s)he is getting lots of attention or when preferred activities are freely available?	Yes No N/A
5. Does the person usually fuss or resist when (s)he is asked to perform a task or to participate in activities?	Yes No N/A
6. Does the problem behavior occur when the person is asked to perform a task or to participate in activities?	Yes No N/A
7. If the problem behavior occurs while tasks are being presented, is the person usually given a "break" from tasks?	Yes No N/A
8. Is the person usually well behaved when (s)he is not required to do anything?	Yes No N/A
9. Does the problem behavior occur even when no one is nearby or watching?	Yes No N/A
10. Does the person engage in the problem behavior even when leisure activities are available?	Yes No N/A
11. Does the problem behavior appear to be a form of "self-stimulation?"	Yes No N/A
12. Is the problem behavior <u>less</u> likely to occur when sensory stimulating activities are presented?	Yes No N/A
13. Is the problem behavior cyclical, occurring for several days and then stopping?	Yes No N/A
14. Does the person have recurring painful conditions such as ear infections or allergies? If so, list:____________	Yes No N/A
15. Is the problem behavior <u>more</u> likely to occur when the person is ill?	Yes No N/A
16. If the person is experiencing physical problems, and these are treated, does the problem behavior usually go away?	Yes No N/A

Scoring Summary

Circle the number of each question that was answered "Yes" and enter the number of items that were circled in the "Total" column.

Items Circled "Yes"	Total	Potential Source of Reinforcement
1 2 3 4	____	Social (attention/preferred items)
5 6 7 8	____	Social (escape from tasks/activities)
9 10 11 12	____	Automatic (sensory stimulation)
13 14 15 16	____	Automatic (pain attenuation)

Figure 4.2: Functional Assessment Screening Tool (FAST)

Source: Iwata, B. A., DeLeon, I. G., & Roscoe, E. M. (2013). Reliability and validity of the Functional Analysis Screening Tool. *Journal of Applied Behavior Analysis, 46*, 271–284. (reproduced with permission by author)

these measures. The responses individuals provide to indirect assessments are based on past experiences of the problematic behaviour. Because of this, answers can be biased and inaccurate.

Direct

A direct functional behaviour assessment involves an observer recording moment-by-moment data on antecedents and consequences connected to the problematic behaviour (Martin & Pear, 2014; Miltenberger, 2016). A common method of direct behaviour assessment is ABC recording (see Figure 4.3). This recording method requires the observer to be present in the setting where the target behaviour occurs. When the individual demonstrates the problematic or challenging *behaviour*, the observer writes down what happened right before (*antecedent*) and what happened immediately after (*consequence*). Direct functional behaviour assessment can also be completed through video observation. A treatment session, or lesson, is recorded to be watched later. The observer reviews the video and records instances of the target behaviour, as well as antecedents and consequences. During direct functional behaviour assessment, observers record antecedents and consequences as they are observed. This approach, when and where possible, leads to more accurate results than indirect assessment methods (Martin & Pear, 2014; Miltenberger, 2016).

> **ABC data collection**: a type of direct observation method to help determine the function of a *behaviour* partially informed by what is observed occurring immediately before (*antecedent*) or immediately afterwards (*consequence*).

Experimental

Practitioners can also determine the function of behaviour by conducting a scientific experiment called a functional analysis, another type of FBA. A functional analysis is a systematic approach to determine the antecedents and consequences contributing to problematic behaviour (Miltenberger, 2016). During a functional analysis, antecedents and consequences are intentionally manipulated to identify scenarios that cause the behaviour to happen (Martin & Pear, 2014; Miltenberger, 2016). This differs from ABC data collection, where the observer records events as they occur—naturally. It is essential that individuals planning to implement interventions with a goal of reducing behaviour conduct a functional behaviour assessment prior to intervention. Interventions selected should be based on the function of behaviour.

ABC Data Observation Sheet

Name: ______________ Setting: ______________

Start Time: ______________ End Time: ______________

Antecedent What Happened Before the Behaviour?	**Behaviour** What Did the Behaviour Look Like?	**Consequence** What Happened After the Behaviour?
Possible Antecedents: ☐ Given Task/Activity ☐ Told "No" ☐ Attention to Self/Others ☐ Busy, Loud Environment ☐ Left Alone ☐ Presence of Person	Possible Behaviours: ☐ Refusal ☐ Aggression ☐ Crying/Whining ☐ Screaming ☐ Running/Eloping ☐ Hitting Self/Others	Possible Consequences: ☐ Adult Attention ☐ Peer Attention (+ or -) ☐ Reprimand ☐ Leave Area/Task ☐ Loss of Privilege ☐ Access/Removal of Item

Figure 4.3: ABC Data Collection Sheet

Source: Authors.

BEHAVIOURAL INTERVENTIONS

Behavioural interventions are a broad class of behaviour change strategies largely informed by ABA. These interventions can be separated into antecedent and consequence events. Often, these practices are implemented and evaluated in combination (e.g., task analysis plus reinforcement), but for ease of organization, this chapter will describe antecedent and consequence-based behavioural interventions separately.

Read about It. Think about It. Write about It.

- Look for three resources to complete a functional assessment. What did you notice about the ease of finding the materials? Are they easy to understand?
- There is controversy over completing a conventional functional analysis as conditions are set up to make target behaviours happen. What are your first impressions of this practice? If you have a person who has severe levels of challenging behaviours, do the benefits outweigh the risks?
- How would you make the decision to conduct a functional analysis?

ANTECEDENT-BASED INTERVENTIONS

Antecedent-based interventions are behavioural practices delivered or present prior to a behaviour (i.e., pre-behaviour; Martin & Pear, 2015). Antecedents can include many possibilities: who is present in the learning environment, the type of work task or learning materials, the amount of attention available, and the instruction provided are all examples of antecedents. Modifying antecedents is an effective strategy to reduce problematic behaviour and increase desired behaviour. Some ways antecedents can be manipulated are to adapt learning materials, change the way instructions are presented, or alter seating arrangements. Because antecedents are proactive and may prevent problem behaviours from occurring, they are often emphasized in program planning (Miltenberger, 2016). Antecedent manipulations that improve the learning environment—such as providing opportunities for choice, making social attention readily available, and adjusting how much work is presented at a time—are effective behavioural practices for reducing repetitive behaviour and increasing prosocial behaviours like compliance and work completion (Hansen & Wadsworth, 2015; Kern & Clemens, 2007).

The initial publication from the National Autism Center (2009) reviewed 99 articles evaluating the effectiveness of a wide range of antecedent-based strategies. Labelled in the initial NAC document as *antecedent package* (see Figure 4.4), this group of practices met the criteria as an established practice for individuals with ASD between 3 and 21 years old (NAC, 2009). Interventions included within the antecedent package category increased skills in communication, interpersonal and personal responsibility, and self-regulation, as well as decreased problem behaviour (NAC, 2009).

antecedent interventions: modifying what occurs before the target behaviour, usually involving the situation, which will make the occurrence of the target behaviour less likely to occur in the first place (NAC, 2015).

Antecedent Package {99 studies} Evidence Level} Established

These interventions involve the modification of situational events that typically precede the occurrence of a target behavior. These alterations are made to increase the likelihood of success or reduce the likelihood of problems occurring. Treatments falling into this category reflect research representing the fields of applied behavior analysis (ABA), behavioral psychology, and positive behavior supports.

Examples include but are not restricted to: behavior chain interruption (for increasing behaviors); behavioral momentum; choice; contriving motivational operations; cueing and prompting/prompt fading procedures; environmental enrichment; environmental modification of task demands, social comments, adult presence, intertrial interval, seating, familiarity with stimuli; errorless learning; errorless compliance; habit reversal; incorporating echolalia, special interests, thematic activities, or ritualistic/obsessional activities into tasks; maintenance interspersal; noncontingent access; noncontingent reinforcement; priming; stimulus variation; and time delay.

Skills Increased

Academic	Communication	Higher Cognitive Functions	Interpersonal	Learning Readiness	Motor	Personal Responsibility	Placement	Play	Self-Regulation
	X		X	X		X		X	X

Behaviors Decreased

Problem Behaviors	RRN	SER	General Symptoms
X		X	

Ages

0-2	3-5	6-9	10-14	15-18	19-21
	X	X	X	X	

Diagnostic Classification

Autistic Disorder	Asperger's Syndrome	PDD-NOS
X		

Figure 4.4: Antecedent Package

Source: NAC, 2009, p. 44.

The most recent publication from the NAC (2015) combined antecedent- and consequence-based interventions into the broad term *behavioural interventions*. This publication reviewed 155 articles assessing behavioural interventions and describes this set of strategies as established for increasing a wide range of skills and decreasing several types of problematic behaviour.

Task Interspersal

Interspersing familiar tasks with unknown tasks is an antecedent strategy often included in educational programming for individuals with ASD (Kern & Clemens, 2007; Rapp & Gunby, 2016).

Rapp and Gunby reviewed four published studies and one dissertation comparing task interspersal to massed-trial teaching (Rapp & Gunby, 2016). The reviewed publications included 20 participants primarily diagnosed with ASD. Results of this review support that task interspersal is an effective antecedent practice for increasing

> **task interspersal**: giving a pre-determined number of known targets before adding in an unknown target. Common ratios of known to unknown are 3:1 or 4:1. For example, asking a student to perform three mastered skills before asking the current teaching target (Rapp & Gunby, 2016).

response maintenance and reducing escape-maintained behaviour. Task interspersal reduces problem behaviour and increases the student's compliance to follow instructions. Educators who modify task difficulty by adjusting the ratio of easy to hard tasks reduce the likelihood that students will demonstrate problem behaviour as a means of escape.

massed-trial teaching: the presentation of several back-to-back trials of unknown material. A trial is made up of an instruction, the learner's response, and then reinforcement for the correct answer or error correction for an incorrect answer (Rapp & Gunby, 2016).

Task Analysis

Task analysis is an antecedent strategy that breaks a complex action down into smaller, simpler responses (Martin & Pear, 2015; Miltenberger, 2016). Many of the daily living, play, and interpersonal skills individuals with ASD may need to learn are complex actions made up of smaller component responses (see Figure 4.5 for a sample of a task analysis for washing a dish). It is possible that individuals are unable to initially demonstrate some of these skills because the amount of task presented at one time is too much (Miltenberger, 2016). A task analysis lists the smaller, easier to perform actions as a way of modifying how a task is presented.

Writing a Task Analysis

The first step to writing a task analysis is to determine all the component responses included within the complex action. It is not recommended that practitioners write task analysis from memory, which might mean that necessary components are overlooked (Martin & Pear, 2015).

- Observe a skilled person perform the task;
- Ask a person who performs the task often with an expert on the task;
- Complete the task yourself. (Miltenberger, 2016)

If a task analysis is completed by observing a competent person perform the task sequence, the observed individual should be similar in age to the individual requiring the task analysis (Miltenberger, 2016). This approach helps the task analysis reflect the relevant, age-appropriate sequence of responses the individual should demonstrate. For example, if developing a task analysis for a 13-year-old describing the steps for making lunch, the behaviour of someone of similar age should be observed—not a famous chef on a televised cooking show.

The most accurate method for developing a task analysis is to perform the complex action and simultaneously record each step (Martin & Pear, 2015; Miltenberger, 2016).

WORK EXPERIENCE PROGRAM

ADAPTIVE LIVING SKILLS—WASHING A DISH

Objective: The student will initiate and complete each step in the following sequence.									
Reinforcement: Immediate social praise after each correct step.									
Criteria: 3 consecutive sessions without prompting									
DATE:									
CONTENT: P = prompt D = directive ✓ = independence									
1. Turn on water faucet.									
2. Grab sponge and dish soap.									
3. Squirt dish soap on sponge and wet sponge.									
4. Move sponge in circular motion on front of plate.									
5. Move sponge in circular motion on back of plate.									
6. Put down sponge.									
7. Hold plate underneath water to rinse.									
8. Set clean plate down.									
9. Turn off water.									
10. Grab towel and dry off front of plate.									
11. Dry off back of plate.									
12. Place plate in cabinet.									
CORRECT / TOTAL:									
COMMENTS:									

Figure 4.5: Task Analysis for Washing a Dish

Source: Authors.

However, practitioners should be aware it is common practice for a task analysis to be revised after teaching begins. As a student learns the skill, behaviours can be combined, or, if needed, steps can be broken down further into smaller responses to assist with progress (Martin & Pear, 2015; Miltenberger, 2016).

Chaining

The end product of a task analysis is a list of component behaviours sequenced in the order performed. Once a practitioner has sequenced this list, the next task is choosing

Table 4.1: Chaining Methods

Type	Example
Backward Chaining	• Last component response taught first • One behaviour taught at a time • Uses additional prompting and fading procedures
Forward Chaining	• First component response taught first • One behaviour taught at a time • Uses additional prompting and fading procedures
Total Task Presentation	• Task analysis taught as a single unit • Several behaviours taught at a time • Uses additional prompting and fading procedures

Source: Miltenberger, 2016.

a chaining procedure to teach the steps (Martin & Pear, 2015; Miltenberger, 2016). Backward chaining, forward chaining, and total task presentation are three behavioural interventions available to teach a task analysis (Martin & Pear, 2015; Miltenberger, 2016). The difference between these methods is the order in which steps are taught. All chaining methods are similar in that additional antecedents, like prompting and fading, are used along with chaining to teach a complex action (Martin & Pear, 2015; Miltenberger, 2016).

Prompting

Many educators, practitioners, and parents know to reward appropriate behaviour when it occurs, but what happens if the behaviour doesn't occur in the first place? How can a reward be provided if behaviour doesn't happen? This situation can be remedied by providing a prompt.

> **prompt**: assistance provided to the learner as an antecedent strategy between the instruction and the behaviour to increase the likelihood that the desired behaviour will occur (Miltenberger, 2016).

Prompts are an efficient and effective way to help learners perform desired tasks (see Figure 4.6 for prompting strategies). Once a task is demonstrated, reinforcement can be provided (Kearney, 2008; Martin & Pear, 2015; Miltenberger, 2016). For many learners with ASD, prompts are necessary because the natural S^D (the event or instruction) is not sufficient to get the behaviour to happen. Prompts can be categorized as response prompts or stimulus prompts (Cooper, Heron, & Heward, 2020; Miltenberger, 2016).

PROMPTING

Prompt: a stimulus that increases the likelihood of a person providing the desired response (Alberto & Troutman, 2013).

Six Common Types of Prompts

Physical **Verbal** **Model** **Gestural** **Visual** **Positional**

1. **Physical**: Physically guiding the person to perform the new skill
2. **Verbal**: Verbally stating information to the person to aid them in performing the new skill
3. **Model**: Demonstrating the new skill
4. **Gestural**: Pointing (or other gestures) that lead the person to perform the new skill
5. **Visual**: Using visuals to guide the person to perform the new skill
6. **Positional**: Placing materials in order

Figure 4.6: Types of Prompts
Source: Alberto & Troutman, 2013.

Response prompts involve another person providing assistance. Physical guidance, pointing, and demonstrating a skill are examples of response prompts (Miltenberger 2016). *Stimulus prompts* involve enhancing features of the learning materials to assist with correct responding (Miltenberger, 2016). *Within-stimulus prompts* make learning materials bigger or bolder. *Extra-stimulus prompts* are additional cues like arrows or underlining to help learners perform correctly. *Positional prompts* are a less-intrusive form of prompting used in educational and clinical settings (Leaf et al., 2016); the correct item is positioned closer to the student, while other items remain further away (Leaf et al., 2016; Martin & Pear, 2015). It is more likely that the closer item would be selected.

Not all prompts are equal. Prompts such as physical guidance are much more intrusive than gestures or modelling. Physical guidance is a form of prompting that has a lot of involvement from another person. Parents, clinicians, and educators need to be aware when teaching a skill using verbal prompting. Often, verbal prompting can look similar to repeating the instruction. Some individuals with ASD quickly become reliant

Table 4.2: Response and Stimulus Prompts

Type	Example
Response Prompt	• Physical, verbal, modelling, gestures • Involves another person
Stimulus Prompt	• Positional, within stimulus, extra stimulus • Modifies and/or enhances learning materials

Source: Miltenberger, 2016.

on hearing the instruction more than once before completing the task. This can lead to challenges when attempting to fade verbal prompts. Educators should aim to use the least intrusive, most effective prompt. That means selecting the lowest level of prompting that leads the student to perform the correct response. Figure 4.7 shows a hierarchy of prompts listed from most to least intrusive.

Prompt Fading

As mentioned, when a new skill is first taught, it is typically necessary to provide additional prompts to help the student reliably perform the desired target behaviour. Once the learner begins to demonstrate the new skill, prompts can be removed. This is known as *prompt fading.*

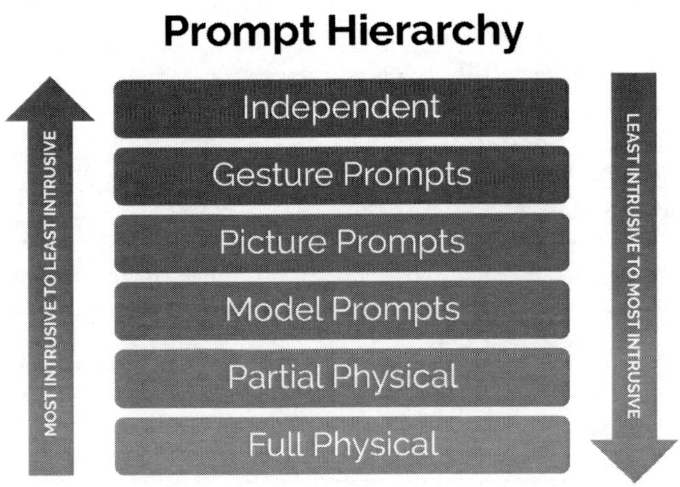

Figure 4.7: Most to Least Intrusive Prompts

Source: Miltenberger, 2016.

The end goal of teaching is the independent, correct performance of these new skills. Therefore, it is important that educators tasked with teaching individuals with ASD develop a plan to fade prompts from the outset of teaching. It is important to fade prompts as soon as possible to avoid prompt dependency.

> **prompt fading**: the practice of gradually removing prompts so the behaviour can be performed independently (Kearney, 2008; Martin & Pear; 2015; Miltenberger, 2016).

> **prompt dependency**: a situation in which students will not attempt to respond unless prompts are provided or can only respond correctly when prompts are provided (Leaf et al., 2016).

Several prompt-fading strategies are available for practitioners to choose from: most-to-least prompt fading; least-to-most prompt fading (see Table 4.3); and time delay (Leaf et al., 2016; Martin & Pear, 2015; Miltenberger 2016). When most-to-least prompting is in use, instructors begin teaching with the most intrusive prompts (e.g., full physical guidance). This level of assistance almost guarantees a correct response (Leaf et al., 2016).

Most-to-least prompt fading, least-to-most prompt fading, and time delay are all effective for achieving independent, correct responses. Therapists, clinicians, and educators are often concerned with the most efficient practices for teaching new skills (Cengher et al., 2016). Studies evaluating efficiency of teaching across the three prompt-fading procedures recommend most-to-least prompting with time delay as the most efficient teaching practice for students with ASD (Cengher et al., 2016).

> **efficiency of teaching**: ensuring teaching is provided in the most optimal fashion possible. Efficiency can be measured by the length of time needed to learn a new skill, the number of errors, and/or the amount of resources required (Cengher et al., 2016).

Table 4.3: Types of Prompt Fading

Prompt Fading Type	Description
Most to Least	Begin teaching with physical guidance, moving to visual cues, then verbal cues, and ending with the natural S^D
Least to Most	Begin teaching with least amount of prompt, increase level of prompting following error or no response
Time Delay	Inserting a gradually increasing amount of time after the instruction but before a prompt

Source: Cooper, Heron, & Heward, 2007.

Table 4.4: Types of Fading through Time Delay

Type	Description
Constant	Inserting a fixed amount of time after the instruction but before a prompt
Progressive	Inserting a gradually increasing amount of time after the instruction but before a prompt

Source: Miltenberger, 2016.

Time Delay

When fading prompts using time delay, instructors increase the time between delivering the instruction and providing the prompt (Malott & Shane, 2014). During initial teaching opportunities, the instruction and the prompt are delivered simultaneously (e.g., zero seconds apart). After several teaching presentations with a zero-second prompt delay, the instructor adds in a brief pause after the instruction. This is the time delay. This brief pause provides an opportunity for the student to demonstrate the target behaviour more independently, prior to the prompt. If the student performs the behaviour, prompts are no longer required. If the student does not perform the behaviour, the instructor continues to prompt and attempt time delay following additional learning opportunities.

Read about It. Think about It. Write about It.

- Looking at the number of antecedent strategies presented, what are the benefits of using these approaches? What are the downfalls?
- Although antecedent strategies are often seen as the least intrusive strategies, what are some downfalls of using prompts? What can you do to protect yourself from these issues?

CONSEQUENCE-BASED INTERVENTIONS

Positive Reinforcement

Positive reinforcement is an effective behavioural intervention to use when teaching new skills. Positive reinforcement involves immediately delivering an event (e.g., praise statements, high fives, edible treats, or preferred activities) after an individual has demonstrated a desired behaviour. As a result of positive reinforcement, the individual is more likely to demonstrate the reinforced behaviour in the future (Malott & Shane, 2015; Martin & Pear, 2015; Miltenberger, 2016).

Reinforcer is the term used to describe the items or events provided following a behaviour that increase the likelihood the behaviour will occur again (Martin & Pear, 2015;

Miltenberger, 2016). Reinforcers are individualized and vary from person to person. For positive reinforcement to be an effective behaviour change procedure, therapists, teachers, and parents need to figure out what is reinforcing for the student. There are several ways to determine what could serve as a reinforcer. Educators could ask the student, or people familiar with the student, questions about preferred items and activities. Another way to find out information on possible reinforcing items and/or activities is to have people complete a questionnaire or checklist (see Table 4.5). There are pre-established surveys and checklists available to help determine potential reinforcers (Malott & Shane, 2015; Martin & Pear, 2015; Miltenberger, 2016).

Educators can also determine reinforcers by performing a direct assessment, called a preference assessment. A preference assessment involves identifying potential reinforcers (perhaps through an indirect questionnaire or survey), presenting items to the student in a structured manner (e.g., two or more at a time), and recording data on the item approached or selected (Miltenberger, 2016; see Figure 4.9).

REINFORCEMENT

Reinforcement: a behaviour is followed by the presentation or removal of a stimulus that increases the likelihood that the behaviour will occur again (Alberto & Troutman, 2013).

Reinforcer: a stimulus presented or removed after a behaviour that increases the likelihood that the behaviour will occur again (Alberto & Troutman, 2013).

Reinforcement practices need to be:

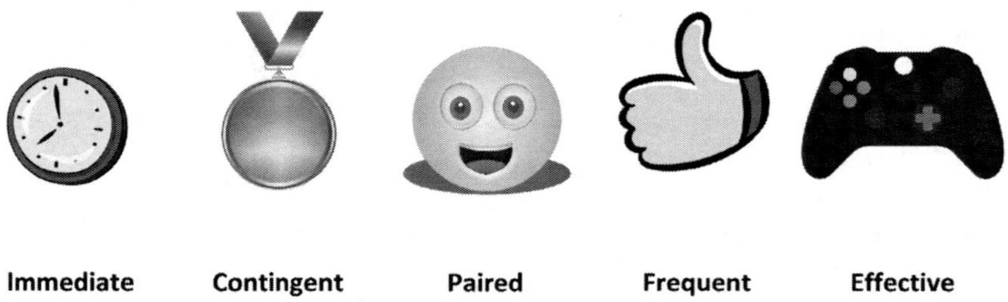

1. **Immediate:** The reinforcer must be presented immediately after the behaviour.
2. **Contingent**: Only give the reinforcer when the behaviour is observed.
3. **Paired**: Pair the reinforcer with another reinforcer (e.g., praise).
4. **Frequent**: Present the reinforcer frequently when learning the new skill (Homme, Csanyi, Gonzales, & Rechs, 1970).
5. **Effective**: Use the simplest system.

Figure 4.8: Positive Reinforcement

Source: Authors.

Table 4.5: Sample Reinforcer Inventory

Item	Highly Preferred	Somewhat Preferred	Not Preferred	Available Now or Access in Future? (Circle One)	
Food: Specify ________________				Now	Future
Drink: Specify ________________				Now	Future
TV Shows: Specify ________________				Now	Future
Movies: Specify ________________				Now	Future
Sensory Items: Specify ________________				Now	Future
Board Games				Now	Future
Video Games				Now	Future
Computer/Tablet				Now	Future
Music				Now	Future
Displaying Work				Now	Future
Time with Peers/Adults				Now	Future
Scents				Now	Future
Running/Throwing/ Jumping				Now	Future
Recess				Now	Future
Books/Puzzles				Now	Future
Excursions				Now	Future
Tokens (e.g., Points)				Now	Future
Certificates				Now	Future
Painting/Drawing/Crafts				Now	Future
Grades				Now	Future
Sports				Now	Future

Source: Authors.

Negative Reinforcement

Another application of reinforcement is *negative reinforcement*. Practitioners often mistakenly associate negative reinforcement with behaviour reduction, possibly incorrectly associating the word *negative* with *less* (Kearney, 2008).

preference assessment: a direct assessment to determine which among several potential reinforcers are preferred by an individual, in order to find an effective reinforcer for that individual (Martin & Pear, 2015).

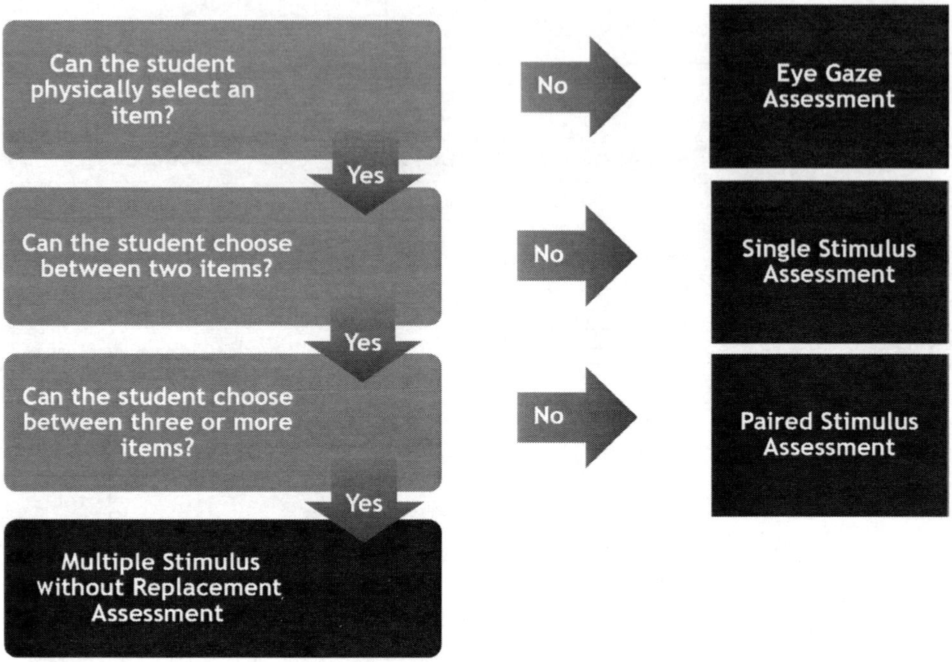

Figure 4.9: Types of Preference Assessments
Source: Cannella-Malone, Sabielny, Jimenez, & Miller, 2013.

Table 4.6: Types of Reinforcement

Type	Description	Future Behaviour Change
Positive Reinforcement	The delivery of a reinforcer immediately following a target behaviour	Target behaviour increases
Negative Reinforcement	The removal or lessening of an aversive immediately following a target behaviour	Target behaviour increases

Source: Cooper, Heron, & Heward, 2020.

Read about It. Think about It. Write about It.

- Write one example of positive reinforcement and one example of negative reinforcement. Remember: they both increase behaviour.
- When have you heard the term *negative reinforcement* used but *punishment* was intended?

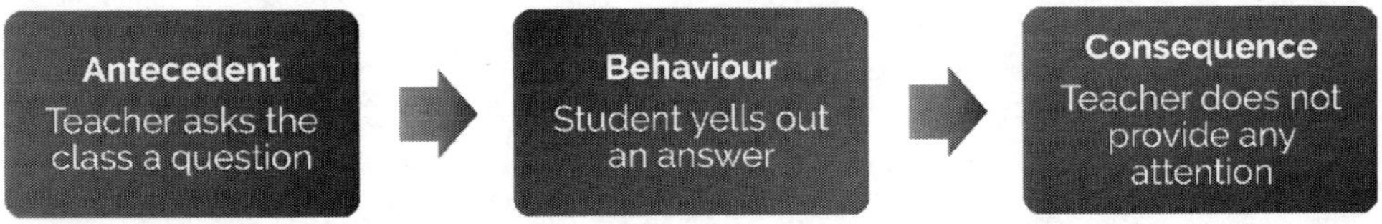

Figure 4.10: Extinction for Behaviour Maintained by Attention

Source: Authors.

In behavioural terms, the word *negative* means *removal* of a stimulus or event (Cooper et al., 2020). Like positive reinforcement, negative reinforcement increases behaviour. Unlike positive reinforcement, which involves adding an item or event after a behaviour, negative reinforcement increases behaviour by removing an unpleasant (aversive) event (Malott & Shane, 2015; Martin & Pear, 2015; Miltenberger, 2016).

Extinction

Extinction is a consequence event that reduces the frequency of a behaviour by withholding the item or event that previously reinforced the behaviour (Martin & Pear, 2015).

extinction: the removal of reinforcement for a previously reinforced target behaviour. As a result of the complete removal of reinforcement, the behaviour reduces in the future (Cooper et al., 2020).

extinction burst: an immediate increase in the target behaviour (the frequency) after reinforcement has been removed. The existing reinforcement could have been positive, negative, or automatic (Cooper et al., 2020).

In this example, the teacher determines that *yelling out answers* needs to be reduced. The teacher no longer provides attention for this behaviour. The teacher has placed the behaviour of yelling out answers on extinction.

Defining extinction is often easier than implementing it. There are a few important considerations for educators to be aware of prior to selecting extinction as a behaviour reduction strategy. Practitioners should anticipate that the behaviour placed on extinction may temporarily increase in frequency, intensity, or duration. Essentially, things may get worse before they get better. The temporary increase in behaviour because of no longer receiving reinforcement is called an *extinction burst.* In the above example, it is possible that the student will yell out many answers, talking louder as a strategy to get the teacher to provide attention. See Figure 4.11 for hypothetical data of a behaviour placed on extinction. Following the implementation of extinction, the target behaviour increases in frequency before gradually reducing.

Another side effect of extinction is *spontaneous recovery.* This is the possibility of an extinguished behaviour spontaneously reappearing after initially decreasing (Kearney,

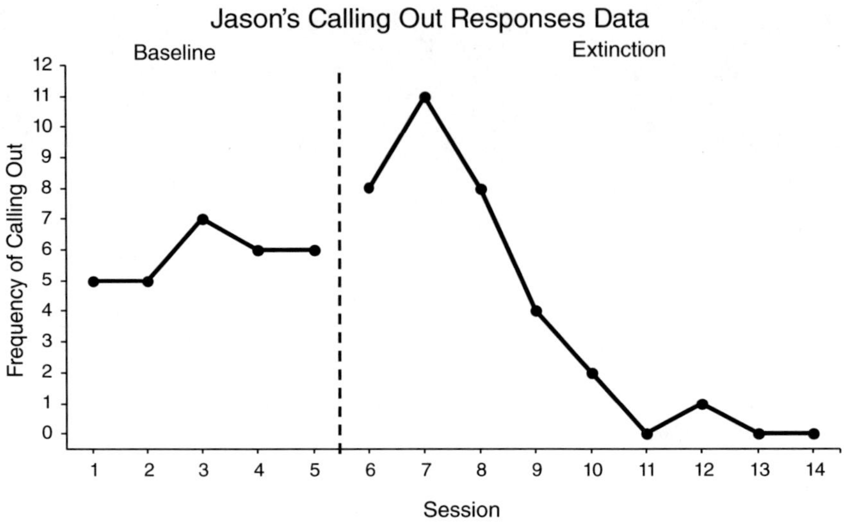

Figure 4.11: Hypothetical Extinction Graph

Source: Authors.

2008; Martin & Pear, 2015). Extinction is most effective when combined with positive reinforcement. This means behavioural interventions are being applied to two behaviours. The behaviour targeted for reduction is placed on extinction while a suitable replacement behaviour receives reinforcement. The behavioural intervention that combines extinction and reinforcement is called *differential reinforcement* (Martin & Pear, 2015; Miltenberger, 2016).

Differential Reinforcement

Differential reinforcement is a type of behavioural intervention that involves reinforcing one behaviour, or a set of behaviours, while withholding reinforcement (extinguishing) for another behaviour (Cooper et al., 2020). Table 4.7 describes variations of differential reinforcement that parents, clinicians, and educators can use when trying to reduce challenging behaviour: differential reinforcement of *alternative* behaviour (DRA), differential reinforcement of *incompatible* behaviour, and differential reinforcement of *other* behaviour (Cooper et al., 2020; Miltenberger, 2016).

Neil, Vause, Jaksic, and Feldman (2017), from the Centre of Applied Disability Studies and the Department of Child and Youth Studies at Brock University in St. Catharines, Ontario, included DRA in a treatment package to reduce obsessive-compulsive behaviours in an 11-year-old youth with ASD. They determined that obsessive-compulsive behaviours were maintained by adult attention. Using differential reinforcement, therapists withheld attention following obsessive behaviours and provided attention for using coping strategies and replacement behaviours (Neil et al., 2017). Following intervention, obsessive behaviours reduced to zero occurrences.

Table 4.7: Common Types and Examples of Differential Reinforcement

Type	Definition
Differential Reinforcement of Alternative Behaviour (DRA)	• Reinforcing a desired alternative behaviour (e.g., raising hand to answer a question) • Withholding reinforcement for a problem behaviour (e.g., calling out answers)
Differential Reinforcement of Incompatible Behaviour (DRI)	• Reinforcing a desired behaviour that cannot happen simultaneously with the problem behaviour (e.g., playing with toys as intended) • Withholding reinforcement for a problem behaviour (e.g., lining up toys)
Differential Reinforcement of Other Behaviour (DRO)	• Reinforcing the absence of a problem behaviour (e.g., receiving reinforcement following an interval of time that did not include calling out answers or lining up toys)

Source: Cooper, Heron, & Heward, 2007.

Tanner and Andreone (2015), clinicians from CBI-Monarch House in Burnaby, British Columbia, demonstrated the effectiveness of differential reinforcement paired with graduated exposure to decrease food refusal and expand the number of foods a three-and-a-half-year-old child with ASD would consume. Clinicians used a 12-step food exposure hierarchy to guide intervention. Correct responses were differentially reinforced with tokens, whereas inappropriate responses (e.g., spitting out food, pushing food away) were placed on extinction (Tanner & Andreone, 2015). The intervention was highly effective, as the participant expanded his food repertoire from 4 to 50 different foods (Tanner & Andreone, 2015).

BEHAVIOURAL SKILLS TRAINING

Behavioural skills training is an ABA-based teaching method that combines antecedent and consequence interventions to teach a wide range of academic, adaptive, and daily living skills (Jull & Mirenda, 2016; Miltenberger, 2016). Behavioural skills training is comprised of four main components: verbal and/or written instructions, modelling, rehearsal, and feedback (McLean et al., 2016; Miltenberger, 2016). Instructions and modelling constitute antecedent practices, rehearsal is the opportunity for the individual to demonstrate the target skill, and feedback is the consequent-based intervention.

Behavioural skill training involves:

1. Describing the target behaviour appropriate to level of understanding of the person training;
2. Modelling the target behaviour;
3. Providing opportunities to practise the target behaviour (may be in-vivo);
4. Delivering reinforcement and feedback as needed; and
5. Observing performance of target behaviour in a real-life situation. (McLean et al., 2016)

Behavioural skills training is an effective intervention to teach service workers how to best engage with students with ASD. Researchers from Brock and York Universities conducted a three-hour behavioural skills training intervention to teach graduate students to implement cognitive behaviour therapy to improve emotional regulation in children with ASD (Hassan, Thomson, Khan, Riosa, & Weiss, 2017). Following training, six of seven graduate students gained skills in accurate delivery of cognitive behaviour therapy, and all participants rated behavioural skills training more favourably than self-directed learning.

Read about It. Think about It. Write about It.

- Think of a skill you would like another person to implement with a person with ASD you support. Write a task analysis of all the steps (written instructions) that you use to support the person in a certain situation.

SPOTLIGHTS ACROSS CANADA

Research: British Columbia

Stephanie Jull, working out of Canucks Autism Network in Vancouver, British Columbia, and Pat Mirenda, professor and researcher at the University of British Columbia, carried out a community-based study utilizing behavioural skills training to teach recreational swimming instructors to incorporate behavioural teaching practices when coaching young children with ASD. The article titled "Effects of a Staff Training Program on Community Instructors' Ability to Teach Swimming Skills to Children with Autism" included six instructors across two indoor pools in recreational facilities in Western Canada. Instructors were exposed to the four components of behavioural skills training—instructions, modelling, rehearsal, and feedback—through a three-hour didactic workshop and in-pool coaching (Jull & Mirenda, 2016). During in-class training, coaches received instructions and modelling on how to build rapport; use a visual schedule; and deliver *learning loops*, an instructional sequence similar to a discrete trial (Jull & Mirenda, 2016, p. 33). Individualized, in-pool coaching provided an opportunity for swim instructors to practise and receive feedback delivering learning loops. Following intervention, all coaches increased rapport-building skills and demonstrated proficiency using a visual schedule. There was variability across coaches on the accurate delivery of a learning loop: some coaches provided clear instructions but failed to deliver praise; other coaches delivered clear instructions and praise but were inconsistent with providing an effective prompt. Swimming skills improved across all eight children receiving coaching, with 18 to 100% of the skills assessed improving by at least one level. Social validity data were provided by coaches and parents of enrolled children. Swim instructors strongly agreed to statements about the training process. One instructor commented that this form of training should be mandatory for all coaches. Parental comments overwhelmingly supported the swim coaching and hoped similar training could be connected to other recreation programs like gymnastics and skating. This article demonstrates that behavioural skills training is a well-received intervention that yields meaningful results in a community-based setting.

Research: Ontario

Sarah Dunkel-Jackson, Kara Kenney, Shannon Borch, and Cheryl Neely Neveu, from Seneca College, Kinark Child and Family Services, and Peel District School Board in Ontario, published a case report evaluating trial-based functional analysis in a school-based setting. The article titled *Intervention Evaluation of Trial-based Functional Analyses in School* describes Liam, a pseudonym for a nine-year-old student with ASD who engages in high rates of swearing and headbanging (Dunkel-Jackson et al., 2018).

In traditional functional analysis methodology, a student is placed through repeated test conditions to determine the variables maintaining problematic behaviour. Condition sessions can range from 5 to 15 minutes and take place in highly controlled treatment rooms. The time and setting constraints make it difficult to implement traditional functional analysis in a school setting. Authors of this case report mitigated many of the barriers associated with traditional functional analysis. The trial-based functional analysis was carried out in various locations within the student's school: gymnasium, library, classroom, and hallway (Dunkel-Jackson et al., 2018). Additionally, the authors used a trial-based method that terminates a session following the first occurrence of the target behaviour, therefore reducing the amount of time the student is exposed to the experimental condition. Analysis of the trial-based data determined Liam engaged in headbanging and swearing to escape independent work tasks and social interaction, as well as to gain access to preferred items. Authors used this data to develop a function-based intervention that included demand-fading. This study demonstrates that high-quality behavioural experiments can be carried out in school settings.

Research: Nova Scotia and New Brunswick

The Preschool Autism Treatment Impact (PATI) is a repeated measure study carrying out comparative research on outcomes and costs attached to various early interventions for ASD (Smith et al., 2019). With this objective, PATI released a paper comparing the effectiveness of two publicly funded behaviour intervention and service-delivery models in New Brunswick (NB) and Nova Scotia (NS; Smith et al., 2019). In NB, children receive a maximum of 20 hours per week of comprehensive early intensive behaviour intervention (EIBI) provided by private contractors through the Department of Education and Childhood Development. In NS, children receive a maximum of 15 hours of pivotal response training-based intervention provided through healthcare teams. As part of this parallel observation study, 591 families were included: 298 children from NB and 221 children from NS. At the beginning of intervention and one year following, parent-reported data were obtained through several measures such as *Vineland Adaptive Behavior Scales* (2nd edition) and *Social Responsiveness Scale* (2nd edition). Results show notable differences between groups prior to service start (Smith et al., 2019). On average, children enrolled in the NB EIBI program were one year younger and reported lower severe symptoms of ASD and higher adaptive skills than children enrolled in the NS program. Both groups reported similar family demographics (e.g., marital status, education level, and primary language spoken in the home). Researchers commented that the difference in age at treatment onset could be a result of differing diagnostic practices. The number of direct service hours provided across intervention methods was another noteworthy difference. In NB, approximately 1,000 service hours were delivered, compared to approximately 550 hours in NS. Despite the significant differences in age at service start, initial skill set, and intensity of service, both groups demonstrated comparable gains following one year of service. This study begins to quantify cost of service-delivery with treatment outcomes.

A LOOK BACK

Chapter 4, "Behaviour-based Interventions," focused on:

- A review of common challenging behaviours that individuals with ASD face, including the diagnostic criteria of repetitive and restricted patterns of behaviours.
- An overview of common behavioural assessment procedures used for challenging behaviours in the field of applied behaviour analysis and often with persons with ASD.
- Common intervention strategies for addressing challenging and repetitive/restricted patterns of behaviour, including common antecedent and consequence-based interventions.

ADDITIONAL RESOURCES

Parent's Guide to Applied Behaviour Analysis

https://www.autismspeaks.org/tool-kit/atnair-p-parents-guide-applied-behavior-analysis

This guide, written for parents of children with ASD, provides a comprehensive overview of applied behaviour analysis. This document assists parents to recognize features of a well-designed and delivered ABA program.

Autism Canada—Behavioural Interventions

https://autismcanada.org/living-with-autism/treatments/non-medical/

On this website, Autism Canada lists a range of medical and non-medical interventions available to enhance the emotional and social well-being of individuals with ASD. Autism Canada recommends a multidisciplinary approach to treating ASD.

Identifying Applied Behavior Analysis Interventions

https://bc-aba.org/wp-content/uploads/2017/12/APBAwhitepaperABAinterventions.pdf

This document, authored by members of the Association of Professional Behavior Analysts, outlines defining features of ABA, as well as dispelling some common myths about this scientific approach to learning.

Evidence-based Practices for the Treatment of Challenging Behaviour in Intellectual and Developmental Disabilities

http://www.ontaba.org/pdf/ONTABA_OSETT-CB_Final_Report_Jan_2019.pdf

This website links to the report authored by the Scientific Expert Task Force for the treatment of challenging behaviour. This is an informative read for stakeholders interested in scientific evidence supporting interventions for behaviour reduction.

Teaching Essential Skills to Prevent the Development of Challenging Behaviour in Learners with Autism Spectrum Disorder

https://autismineducation.ca/assets/files/info-papers/teach-skills-prevent-challenging-behaviour.pdf

This information paper, written by members of Autism in Education, describes functions of challenging behaviour. Authors provide a summary of research conducted by Dr. Hanley that discusses teaching instruction following and friendship skills as a proactive means of preventing challenging behaviour.

Association for Professional Behavior Analysts

https://www.apbahome.net

The Association for Professional Behavior Analysts is a nonprofit organization that works with all levels of government to advance behaviour analysis. This website lists upcoming conferences and information on how to become a member.

Behavior Analyst Certification Board (BACB)

https://www.bacb.com/

The BACB oversees the professional credentialling requirements for certification in ABA. This website provides extensive information on the requirements needed to meet the various levels of certification available. Practitioners can search the online registry to find a BACB certificant.

CHAPTER 5

The Sensory Domain

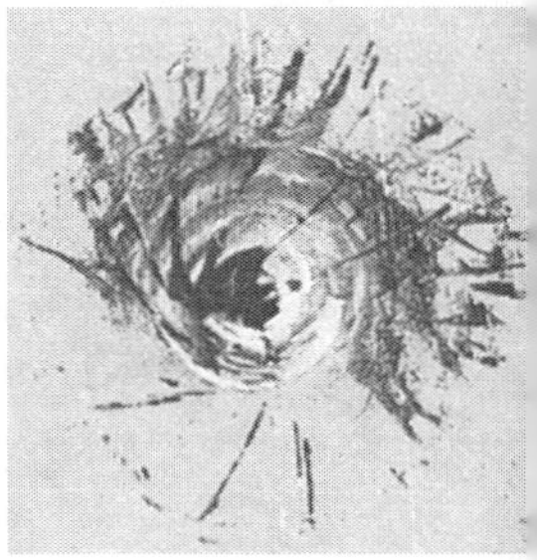

LEARNING OBJECTIVES

- Review historical mentions of sensory features in early identifications of ASD and various sensory theories and frameworks.
- Identify three main classification systems that examine how to organize various sensory features.
- Recognize the main sensory characteristics and how these may be demonstrated in persons with ASD.
- Explore research that examines sensory intensity as it relates to different characteristics in ASD and the prevalence of sensory issues compared to the general population.
- Increase familiarity with common sensory interventions often utilized for persons with ASD.

This chapter explores literature related to the sensory needs, issues, and impacts for persons with autism spectrum disorder (ASD). Although the mention of sensory hyper- and hyporeactivity to certain sensory stimuli is not new—it was mentioned in early definitions by Kanner and Asperger (see Chapter 1)—the recognition of its impact and influence in ASD was more formally recognized in 2013 in the fifth edition of the *Diagnostic and Statistical Manual for Mental Disorders* (DSM-5). The DSM-5 mentions sensory hyper- and hyporeactivity as a diagnostic subcategory under repetitive and restricted patterns of behaviour. In addition to the DSM-5, this chapter examines two additional classification systems that group sensory symptoms. This chapter also explores the recent research examining sensory features in ASD and relating the intensity of sensory features within the general population among persons with ASD. An in-depth examination of various senses is provided to help the reader better understand the multifaceted and complex sensory components in the human body and how these can affect persons with ASD. Lastly, this chapter looks at the different types of sensory assessments and interventions that are suggested, even though the literature is still in its infancy in this area. None of the suggested interventions have been found to be an evidence-based intervention (EBI) for ASD as of yet in the major reviews published; this area is still an emerging one in the field of ASD. However, given its inclusion in the DSM-5, it is important to be aware of the field.

HISTORY OF SENSORY FEATURES

As noted throughout, ASD is described as a complex neurodevelopmental disorder (APA, 2013b). An array of possible symptoms are included in the diagnosis of the disorder; the DSM-5 adds unusual responses to sensory information (APA, 2013b). However, sensory differences were recognized in the earliest descriptions of individuals with autistic disorder and Asperger's disorder (APA, 1994).

Kanner's Cases

Kanner (1943) described 11 separate cases—3 females and 8 males—with varying degrees of sensory features. Kanner described hyporeactivity, hyperreactivity, and unusual sensory interests in all of the case studies in his 1943 paper *Autistic Disturbances of Affective Contact.*

Several of Kanner's patients showed mixed responses to sensory information. Examples included failure to orient to their names, failure to notice people entering or leaving the room, having dramatic responses to loud or unexpected noises, having fear or dislike for innocuous objects or activities. Kanner reported that Donald T. (see Chapter 1) did not appear to be aware of individuals within his environment: "He does not observe the fact that anyone comes or goes and never seems glad to see father or mother or any playmates," and he displayed an unusual interest in objects. He "developed a mania for spinning blocks and pans and other round objects" and showed unusual responses to everyday activities enjoyed by typically developing children (e.g., fear of tricycles). Kanner also described several cases of sensory seeking and unusual focused behaviours: "turn[ing] the lights on and off" (p. 226); "pull[ing] blinds up and down"; and "tear[ing] cardboard boxes into small pieces and play[ing] for hours" (p. 232).

Asperger's Cases

Hans Asperger introduced his case studies on *autistic psychopathy* around the same time as Kanner (Asperger, 1944, 1968, 1979, as cited in Wing, 1981). Wing introduced the more neutral term *Asperger's syndrome.* In her article "Asperger's Syndrome: A Clinical Account," Wing described six sample cases of individuals described by Asperger. This article introduced the idea that individuals diagnosed with autistic psychopathy as described by Asperger also had a variety of sensory features. Some examples included:

> **hyperreactivity**: a high level of sensory sensitivity and high ability to detect sensory signals that then causes the person to react atypically (Ide, Yaguchi, Sano, Fukatsu, & Wada, 2019).

- "afraid of climbing" (p. 127)
- "ignored the other children and carried on with his unusual preoccupations" (p. 127)
- "Rarely initiated any activity, but waited to be told what to do ... he used to rock himself when unoccupied" (p. 126)
- "He was clumsy in gait, and slow on tests of manual dexterity ..." (p. 128)
- "He was described by his teacher as 'showing no initiative'" (p. 128)

Read about It. Think about It. Write about It.

- Given Kanner and Asperger's accounts of some sensory features of ASD in their initial descriptions, how much would you describe as sensory and how much is repetitive and restricted patterns of behaviour? Does it make sense that the sensory component of ASD, as listed in the DSM-5, falls under repetitive and restricted patterns of behaviour?

From its earliest introduction, it is clear that individuals with varied iterations of ASD have had difficulty processing sensory information, including complex combinations of hyperreactivity, hyporeactivity, and unusual sensory interests.

hyporeactivity: an under-arousal to sensory input and inability to accurately detect sensory signals from the environment that causes the person to respond in unusual ways.

SENSORY FEATURES IN THE DIAGNOSTIC AND STATISTICAL MANUALS

The DSM-5 (APA, 2013b) includes the terms *hyporeactivity*, *hyperreactivity*, and *unusual sensory responses*. Previously, sensory differences were included in the DSM-III (American Psychiatric Association, 1980) with this criterion: "[b]izarre response to various aspects of the environment, e.g., resistance to change, peculiar interests, in or attachments to animate or inanimate objects" (p. 90). The DSM-III also suggested "[h]yper and hyposensitivity to sensory stimuli, e.g., hyperacusis," found under the diagnostic criteria for childhood onset pervasive developmental disorder (p. 91). The subsequent *Diagnostic and Statistical Manual of Mental Disorders* (DSM-IV; American Psychiatric Association, 1994) did not include atypical sensory responses, but they reappeared in the DSM-5 (American Psychiatric Association, 2013).

Sensory processing disorders and sensory integration dysfunction are not yet recognized as distinct disorders by the American Psychiatric Association (Miller, 2012). However, most clinicians and researchers recognize that sensory features in children with and without ASD do, in fact, exist. Research is unclear as to whether atypical sensory processing features should be standalone diagnoses, as they can co-occur with a variety of developmental and mental disorders (e.g., learning disabilities, attention deficit hyperactivity disorders, schizophrenia, and Tourette's disorder; Owen et al., 2013). Pfeiffer, May-Benson, and Bodison (2018) reported that a substantial number of children with and without disabilities have difficulties with sensory processing dysfunction, with estimates between 5 and 55% of children without an additional diagnosis having problems in one or more areas of sensory integration. A recent study reported that sensory challenges were the "most common co-occurring challenges/diagnoses" for 58% of the 719 children and youth whose parents responded to its survey questions (McLaughlin & Schneider, 2019).

> **sensory processing disorders / sensory integration dysfunction**: impairments in some or all of the sensory systems where someone is unable to receive the stimulus, transfer it to a neural impulse, and consciously experience that stimulus in a typical manner (Ahn, Miller, Milberger, & McIntosh, 2004).

SENSORY THEORIES AND SENSORY FRAMEWORKS

Sensory Integration Theory

Anna Jean Ayres, an occupational therapist and clinical psychologist, is credited with developing *sensory integration theory*. Ayres brought together knowledge from occupational therapy and psychology to create her theory to describe the relationship between neural pathways of the brain and their impact on learning and behaviour. She introduced her theory to explain the outward symptoms of sensory processing within the central nervous system expressed through the individual's behaviour (Pollark, 2009; Smith Roley, Mailloux, Miller-Kuhaneck, & Glennon, 2007). Ayres's work, however, is not necessarily specific to ASD. Most of her literature and theory were developed based on her work with children with learning disabilities (Ayres, 1972). There are three main components of sensory integration theory. First, the theory describes typical sensory behaviour. Second, it describes sensory integration dysfunction. Finally, its purpose was to guide interventions (Smith Roley et al., 2007).

Smith Roley and colleagues (2007) stated that, using Ayres's theory, sensory systems do not develop independently of one another. Rather, processing skills such as auditory and visual are dependent on foundational systems (e.g., tactile, pressure, temperature, muscle, joint, and body awareness). Sensory information is not processed in isolation but through multiple systems. According to Ayres (2005), unusual responses to sensory information are thought to be the result of a dysfunction involving registration, modulation, discrimination, internal organization, and integration of sensory information.

> The brain locates, sorts, and orders sensations—somewhat as a traffic officer directs moving cars. When sensations flow in a well-organized or integrated manner, the

> brain can use those sensations to form perceptions, behaviors, and learning. When the flow of sensation is disorganized, life can be like a rush hour traffic jam. (Ayres, 2005, p. 5)

Sensory Integration Therapy

It is this *rush hour traffic jam* that is supposed to improve with the introduction of *sensory integration therapy*. There are several components to Ayres's approach, including the assumption that integration therapy can provide individuals with the necessary sensory stimuli to integrate information. Then individuals would be able to access information from their other senses. The actual activities are reported to regulate affective behaviours and allow individuals optimal alertness and attentional skills so that learning opportunities can be utilized (Ayres, 1972). They varied among children and were dependent upon the results of a group of assessments, including an assessment of sensory functioning.

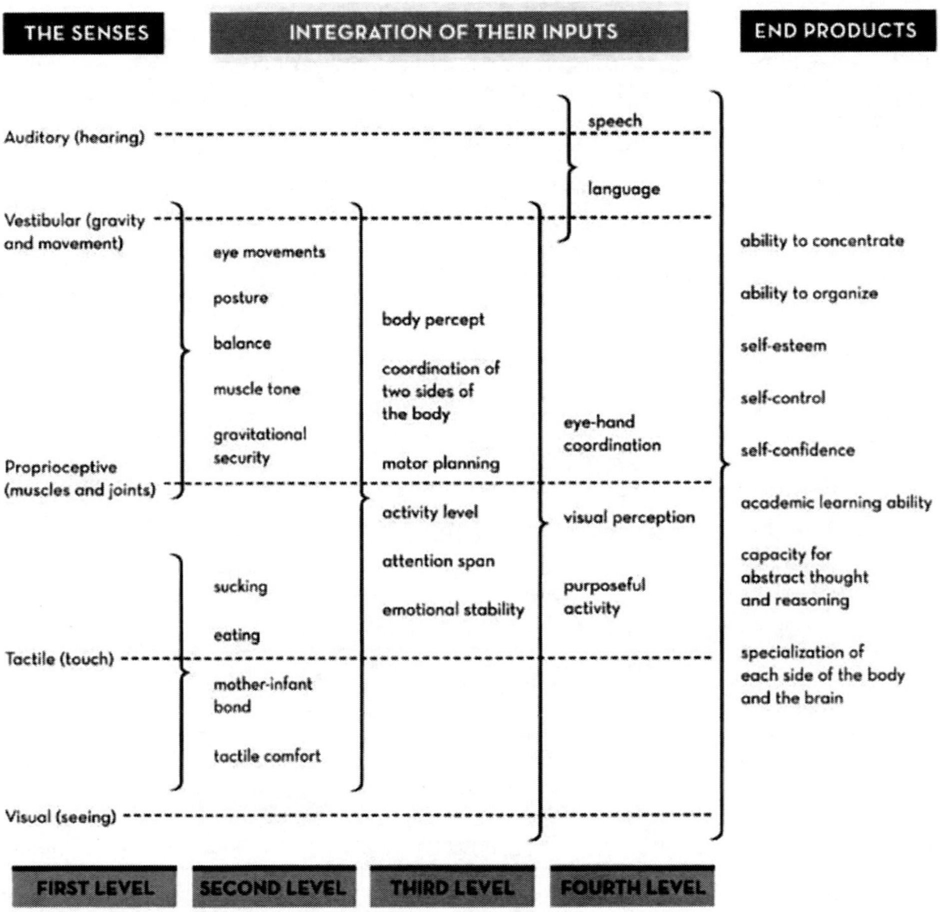

Figure 5.1: The Senses, Integration of Their Inputs, and End Products
Source: Ayres, 2005.

Ayres proposed that motor development follows a sequence that is both influenced and dependent on sensory input (Ayres, 1961, as cited in Smith Roley et al., 2007) and is a postural model to understand children's motor development. She indicated that to sit up required input from the vestibular and proprioceptive systems. She highlighted postural control as essential for a child to begin to engage in higher-order academic and cognitive skills. She proposed that tactile, vestibular, proprioceptive, and visual systems provide the foundations of reading and writing skills.

Sensory Processing

Sensory processing is a term used to describe how information gained through the various sensory modalities is used and processed through the central nervous system. As well, this term is used to describe responses to that sensory information (Acevedo, Aron, Pospos, & Jessen, 2018; Schauder & Bennetto, 2016). Our sensory system is made up of seven systems or modalities (see p. 189).

The term *modulation* refers to the ability to use and respond appropriately to sensory information while remaining at a level of alertness sufficient to be able to participate in daily and learning activities (Hyche & Maertz, 2014). The American Psychiatric Association (2013b) does not recognize the use of the term *sensory processing disorders*; however, it does use the terms *hyporeactive*, *hyperreactive*, and *unusual interest* (p. 50) as possible diagnostic criteria under ASD. Interestingly, efforts were being made toward including sensory processing disorders in the DSM-5; however, the final decision-making noted insufficient evidence to determine that it should stand alone (Miller, 2012).

Table 5.1: DSM-5 Terminology around Sensory Features

DSM-5 Hyporeactive	DSM-5 Hyperreactive	DSM-5 Unusual Sensory Interest
Hyposensitivity	Hypersensivity	Sensory seeking
Hyporesponsivity	Hyperresponsivity	Sensory orienting
High threshold	Low threshold	Sensory interests
Under-responsivity	Over-responsivity	Sensory craving
	Sensory defensive	
	Sensory avoiding	

Source: Authors.

Read about It. Think about It. Write about It.

- Would you agree that sensory processing disorders and sensory integration dysfunction are not separate disorders as stated in the DSM-5? Why or why not?
- Given that ASD has a sensory component in its diagnosis and standalone diagnoses for sensory disorders are not recognized, do you think ASD may be overdiagnosed for those with more prevalent sensory difficulties? Why or why not?

Hyporeactive is a term that indicates an atypical response to sensory stimulation. Those who are hyporeactive require *more* sensory input for a response to occur. For example, young children with ASD may not respond to their names. They may need information from multiple modalities to respond (e.g., tactile, visual, and/or auditory). They also may not notice people entering or leaving their immediate environment (Germani et al., 2014; Lane, Young, Baker, & Angley, 2010; Watts, Rodgers, & Riby, 2016). *Hyperreactive* is also a term that indicates an atypical response to sensory stimulation. However, children who exhibit a hyperreactive response require *very little* sensory information to create a response. For example, a light touch may be perceived as painful, or they may experience a typical voice volume as loud and painful (Germani et al., 2014; Lane et al., 2010).

CLASSIFICATION SYSTEMS

There are a variety of classification systems, models, or theoretical frameworks for understanding sensory features in individuals. The three mostly commonly recognized are:

- *Diagnostic Manual for Infancy and Early Childhood* (Interdisciplinary Council on Developmental and Learning Disorders [ICDLD]; Miller et al., 2005)
- Dunn's Model (Dunn, 1997)
- Diagnostic and Statistical Manual (DSM-5; APA, 2013b)

Interdisciplinary Council on Developmental and Learning Disorders

The *Diagnostic Manual for Infancy and Early Childhood* (Miller et al., 2005) includes three types of sensory processing difficulties, developed using Ayres's (2005) sensory integration dysfunction theory, as shown in Figure 5.2.

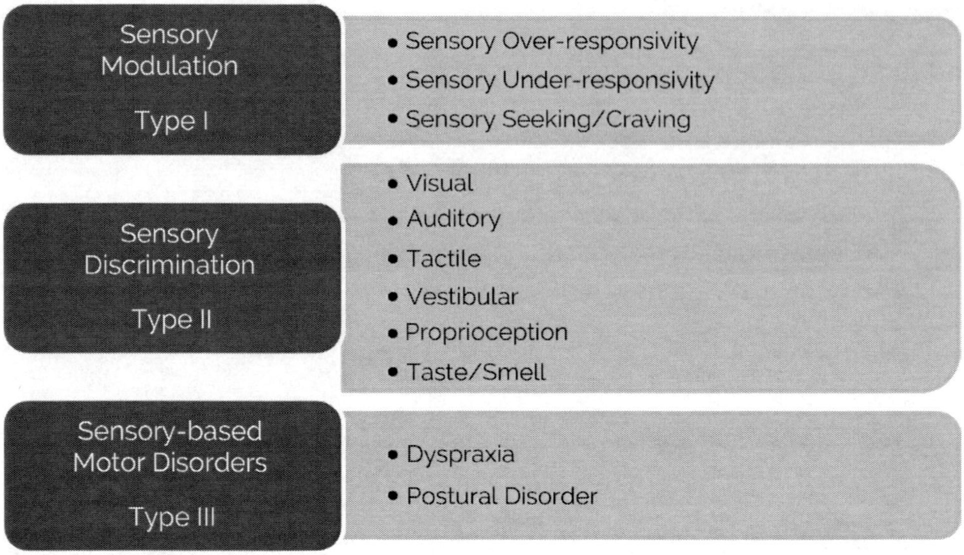

Figure 5.2: Types of Sensory Processing Difficulties

Source: Miller et al., 2005.

Type I: Sensory Modulation

Sensory modulation is when difficulties modulating sensory input taken from the environment are encountered, and individuals lack the ability to respond appropriately to sensory stimuli and remain at the optimum level of functioning to participate in daily activities. In this model, modulation difficulties can present as sensory over-responsivity, sensory under-responsivity, and as sensory-seeking behaviour (Hyche & Maertz, 2014; Miller et al., 2005; Reebye & Stalker, 2008). Over-responsivity is associated with either fearfulness or stubbornness, whereas under-responsivity is associated with self-absorption and seeking sensory information.

> **sensory-seeking behaviour**: engagement in sensory behaviours that appears atypical (such as rocking or hand flapping), which may be a result of trying to gain sensory self-stimulation from engaging in these behaviours (Liss, Saulnier, Fein, & Kinsbourne, 2006).

Type II: Sensory Discrimination

Sensory discrimination problems happen when individuals have difficulty perceiving and understanding sensory information taken from their environments, then assigning meaning to this information. They may also have difficulties understanding the characteristics of sensory information; for example, discriminating light touch from deep touch. They often have difficulty interpreting the specific qualities of the sensory information and discriminating similarities and differences (Hyche & Maertz, 2014; Miller et al., 2005; Reebye & Stalker, 2008). Individuals with sensory discrimination challenges have problems identifying, recognizing, discriminating, and assigning meaning. While problems may occur across all areas of sensory processing, sensory discrimination challenges most commonly occur within the tactile, vestibular, or proprioceptive sensory systems (Hyche & Maertz, 2014; Miller et al., 2005; Reebye & Stalker, 2008).

sensory discrimination: differentiating between various intensities of sensory inputs and individual levels of sensitivity to particular sensory inputs.

Type III: Sensory-based Motor Disorders

These disorders occur when individuals have difficulty processing environmental information and then following through with motor responses. Sensory-based motor challenges are subdivided further into two subtypes: dyspraxia and poor postural ability. Dyspraxia simply means an inability to plan and sequence motor movements (either gross or fine motor). Such individuals often appear awkward, poorly coordinated, and may display difficulty with daily activities such as using a pencil for handwriting, handling eating utensils, dressing (e.g., zipping zippers and fastening buttons), and navigating elevators or escalators. Poor postural ability generally presents as inappropriate or inadequate muscle control (either hypo- or hyper-), inadequate control of movements, and poor trunk stability. Such individuals may experience difficulty maintaining their posture when standing and sitting and do not self-adjust when necessary (Hyche & Maertz, 2014; Miller et al., 2005). Sometimes these individuals walk with a wide gait, are slumped in their seats, or have their heads on their desks.

Dunn's Model

Winnie Dunn (1997, 2001) offered another model of conceptualizing sensory processing features, also based on Ayres's sensory integration theory. Dunn suggested four subtypes: poor registration, sensitivity to sensory stimuli, sensation seeking, and sensation avoiding. Both the neurological threshold (high to low) and the behavioural responses (accordance to counteract) are thought to be on continua.

neurological threshold: sensory input required for the brain to register that sensory information (Brown, Tollefson, Dunn, Cromwell, & Filion, 2001).

accordance: behaviour consistent with the related neurological threshold (Brown et al., 2001).

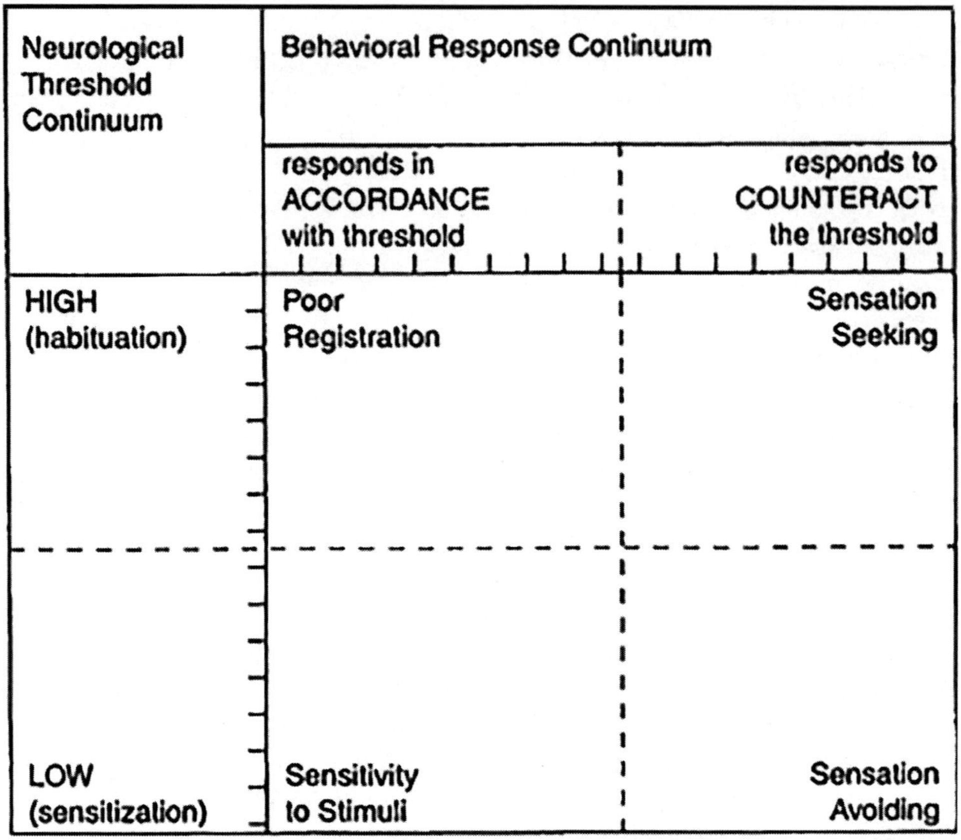

Figure 5.3: Dunn's Proposed Model of Sensory Processing: Relationships between Behavioural Responses and Neurological Thresholds
Source: Dunn, 1997.

> **counteract**: responding contrary to the sensory threshold (Brown et al., 2001).

In her 2001 Eleanor Clarke Slagle lecture, Dunn (2001) indicated that individuals have different degrees or thresholds for noticing, responding to, and becoming irritated by sensory information. These thresholds then determine the choices that everyone makes in day-to-day life. Both experiences and thresholds are reflected in moods, temperament, and how lives and environments are organized for each individual (Dunn, 2001). The anchor points of the Dunn model are as follows:

1. Those with high sensory threshold require a significant degree of sensory information for a response and are considered to have a low sensory registration. They do not seem to notice sensory information easily; for example, they may require multisensory input to respond to their name and/or

they may not notice that their clothing is twisted. Dunn refers to those individuals with a low sensory registration and a passive response pattern as *low registration*.

2. Those with low sensory registration may have an active response pattern, meaning that they seek out or crave sensory information. Dunn refers to those who have low registration but an active response pattern as *sensation seeking*.
3. Individuals who are sensory hyperreactive require minimal sensory information for a behavioural response. These individuals seem to notice everything and can be easily distracted by information within their environments. However, these individuals may have a passive response style. Dunn calls this pattern with a high registration and passive response style *sensory sensitivity*.
4. Individuals who are sensory hyperreactive and have an active response pattern, such as covering their ears to avoid auditory information or wearing sunglasses to reduce light, attempt to avoid sensory information from their environment. Dunn refers to individuals who have a high registration and an active response pattern as *sensory avoiding* (Dunn, 2001).

Dunn's model is important because the most commonly used self-and-other report-rating scales (*Infant/Toddler Sensory Profile* [Dunn, 2002]; *Sensory Profile*, Second Edition; *Short Form Sensory Profile*, Second Edition [Dunn, 2014]; *Adolescent/Adult Sensory Profile* [Brown & Dunn, 2002]) all use Dunn's model.

FEATURES OF SENSORY ISSUES IN ASD

Processing Difficulties and ASD

Pfeiffer and colleagues (2018) stated that children with and without disabilities have difficulties with processing sensory information (i.e., 10 to 55% of children without disabilities; 40 to 88% with various diagnoses). When the literature specific to ASD is examined, this rate increases to between 69 and 95% (Baranek, David, Poe, Stone, & Watson, 2006; Crane, Goddard, & Pring, 2009; Green, Chandler, Charman, Simonoff, & Baird, 2016; Tomchek & Dunn, 2007).

Various studies have examined the presence (or absence) of specific

sympathetic nervous system: part of the autonomic nervous system that is activated in fight or flight situations or when reacting to stress (Panju, Brian, Dupuis, Anagnostou, & Kushki, 2015).

vestibular: the ability to orient in typical day-to-day functions; a major component of understanding sensory information (Kern et al., 2006).

subtypes of sensory features along with an ASD diagnosis. Schoen, Miller, Brett-Green, and Neilson (2009) compared individuals with ASD and children with sensory modulation disorders (SMD) around how their sympathetic nervous systems responded to a series of sensory challenges. Results suggested children with ASD diagnoses "had lower baseline arousal and lower reactivity" (p. 9). Participants also displayed greater under-responsivity in both the vestibular and proprioception modalities than the comparison group (children with SMD). However, these authors also found that children with ASD were more likely to be overresponsive to the taste/smell modality.

> **proprioception**: the human sense of understanding where the parts of the body and their movements are in space (Fuentes, Mostofsky, & Bastian, 2011).

Domain-specific Findings

Affective

Lane and colleagues (2010) studied a group of young children diagnosed with ASD to examine patterns of sensory differences and potential relationships to adaptive functioning. These authors suggested three subtypes: sensory-based inattention seeking; sensory modulations and movement sensitivity; and sensory modulation with taste/smell sensitivity. They further suggested that those with taste/smell sensitivity also experienced the most significant problems with adaptive functioning. As well, taste/smell sensitivities, auditory filtering, and movement sensitivity were associated with more maladaptive behaviour. Ben-Sasson and colleagues (2008) assessed toddlers with ASD to look at patterns of sensory differences and the impact on affective domains (e.g., anxiety). These researchers found three sensory clusters: relatively low-frequency sensory responses; mixed sensory features combining under-responsivity and over-responsivity; and high frequency, showing sensory behaviour across all areas of sensory functioning. Results suggested that parents of children in the mixed and high-frequency groups reported more difficulty in the affective domains.

> **adaptive functioning**: skills that are used when coping with demands in the everyday environment; they are essential for independent living and self-care (Liss et al., 2001).

One study examined high-risk (i.e., those with an older sibling diagnosed with ASD) and low-risk infants (i.e., those with no family history of ASD). They found that infants subsequently diagnosed with ASD were more likely to have difficulty with auditory processing and hyporeactivity (Germani et al., 2014). Green and colleagues (2016) studied children from 10 to 14 years with and without ASD but also with special educational needs. They found that 92% of the children with ASD had sensory differences, but so did 67% of the special education needs group. They also concluded that sensory differences were also more likely to be associated with emotional problems (Goodman, 1997, as cited in Green et al., 2016).

Behavioural

Some authors have proposed that hyporeactivity may distinguish young children with ASD from others who are typically developing or have other neurodevelopmental disorders. Two review articles by DeBoth and Reynolds (2017) and Watts and colleagues (2016) examined the research evidence examining subtypes within individuals with ASD. The DeBoth and Reynolds review suggested that the findings were mixed and stated that, while there was some evidence to support sensory differences as a cause for challenging behaviour, the evidence is still emerging. These authors suggested that, rather than relying on sensory modulation to explain atypical behaviour, clinicians need to consider other causes.

Unusual sensory interests is a term used in the DSM-5 to indicate children who seek out sensory information. They are considered the "movers and shakers and touchers and tappers" (Hyche & Maertz, 2014, p. 14). Children who are seeking sensory information may engage in repetitive behaviours, such as turning lights on and off repeatedly, or they may insist that the volume on the television needs to be louder than typical. Some children with unusual sensory interest will appear similar to children diagnosed with attention deficit hyperactivity disorder.

Cognitive

Watts and colleagues (2016) found that there has been some evidence of hyporeactivity in individuals with ASD, but they noted significant variability across studies. Some of this variability was age- and design-related, including quality of the relevant research studies. Studies that used young children reported patterns of hyporeactivity when compared with other clinical populations; however, studies of children in older age groups showed mixed results (Joosten & Bundy, 2010; Kirby, White, & Baranek, 2015). The results of Watt and colleagues' systematic review suggested an association between individuals with ASD who have below average cognitive functioning and show patterns of hyporeactivity. However, they also noted insufficient studies to determine if individuals with ASD and average cognitive functioning also have similar sensory features.

Severity and Age

There is mixed evidence regarding the severity of ASD symptoms and level of sensory responses when the general population is compared to those with ASD (Lane et al., 2014; Watts et al., 2016). Robertson and Simmons (2013) compared scores on Baron-Cohen and colleagues' (2001) Autism Spectrum Quotient (AQ) and the Glasgow Sensory Questionnaire (GSQ) to determine if individuals with more autistic traits on the AQ would have greater sensory differences on the GSQ. The results suggested that in the general population "atypical sensory processing (including both hyper and hyposensitivity) as measured by our sensory questionnaire, was more common in individuals with higher levels of autistic traits" (p. 780). Crane and colleagues (2009) studied adults diagnosed with ASD and their patterns of sensory differences, then compared them to a group of adults from the general population. These authors concluded that adults with ASD reported greater sensory differences when compared to the general population. Mayer (2017) also compared adults with ASD with individuals from the general population, and she reported no significant differences between adults with ASD and neurotypicals. Recognition that individuals with ASD experience sensory difficulties when compared with typically developing peers has been extensively reported (Baranek, 2002).

> **neurotypical**: a person who thinks, behaves, and perceives in manners that are considered by the majority of the population as *normal*. It is also defined as not having ASD or another intellectual and/or developmental disability (Rudy, 2019).

Some studies suggested that unusual sensory responses diminish with age (Kern et al., 2006). Other research reports that sensory features in ASD are common throughout the lifespan but are not well understood (Baranek, Little, Parham, Ausderau, & Sabatos-DeVito, 2014)—or well accepted. There is limited research investigating sensory features in adults with ASD (Crane et al., 2009). Most research has focused on infants, preschoolers, and school-aged children.

Read about It. Think about It. Write about It.

- Examining the current research presented about sensory characteristics in persons with ASD, do you think there is enough information to identify sensory patterns, commonalities, and trends?
- Why do you think the research around sensory needs and ASD is not as conclusive at this point compared to other topics and issues?

SENSORY MODALITIES

Within the sensory domains, children can be hyporeactive in one or more modalities and hyperreactive in another or multiple modalities. Alternatively, children can have mixed reactions. For example, a child may be hyperreactive to noise in the classroom and simultaneously may be hyporeactive to verbal input from the teacher or other students. These features can be confusing to the adults involved in their care. Some children may react negatively to the sound of a pencil on paper, and it may interfere with learning, but the same child may not respond to individuals within their environment and may require multiple modalities to be used in order to obtain a response.

SENSORY DOMAINS

In recent years, increased attention has been given to sensory features in individuals with ASD in an attempt to understand how these individuals experience their world and to determine whether individuals with ASD have unique profiles of sensory features. The latter has yet to be established (Acevedo et al., 2018; Kirby et al., 2015; Masataka, 2017; Mayer, 2017; Perez Repetto, Jasmin, Fombonne, Gisel, & Couture, 2017; Schauder & Bennetto, 2016; Watts et al., 2016). Each of the primary sources of sensory input, how each individual experiences this input through the central nervous system, and the potential impact (if any) on each person need consideration. The seven sensory domains are as follows:

1. Auditory (Sound)
2. Visual (Sight)
3. Tactile (Touch)
4. Olfactory (Smell)
5. Gustatory (Taste/Texture)
6. Vestibular (Balance)
7. Proprioception (Body Awareness/Muscle and Joints)

Auditory (Sound)

The auditory sensory system allows individuals to be aware of sound—auditory information—in the environment (Heflin & Alaimo, 2007; Hyche & Maertz, 2014; Reebye & Stalker, 2008). The sensory response to auditory information for children with ASD may be typical, hyporeactive, hyperreactive, or it may appear as an unusual level of interest. Children may also have a varied response when they experience certain sounds as difficult or painful (hyperactive); they may not register or respond to other sounds (hyporeactive); and/or they may seek out certain sounds (unusual interests). Haesen, Boets, and Wagemans (2011) found pitch processing in individuals with ASD is generally the same as typically developing individuals; however, some studies suggested that they may experience more difficulty orienting their attention to speech sounds versus other nonspeech sounds (e.g., clicks, tones; Ceponiene et al., 2003).

Children who have hyperreactive responses to auditory information can be bothered by what most would see as innocuous noise. They may be startled easily by unexpected noises or find them painful (e.g., fire drills and public address system announcements). On the other hand, children who are hyporeactive to auditory information may not respond to what seems like everyday auditory input and may require multiple sources to even respond. In classrooms, children may not respond to teacher instructions unless their attention is first gained. Sometimes, educators interpret such behaviour as deliberate or defiant; in fact, instructions did not register (Hyche & Maertz, 2014).

Visual (Sight)

The visual modality allows for the perception of visual information through structures in the eyes. Information gained this way allows the brain to navigate environments; understand objects, space, and distance; and know where it is in relationship to others and objects (Heflin & Alaimo, 2007). It works closely with other systems to provide sensory information.

Visual issues in individuals with ASD may be linked to differences in the central nervous system and the visual systems (Coulter, 2009). Coulter (2009) found that such visual differences were common in related literature. She suggested that, along with actual *problems* with the visual system (e.g., nearsighted or farsighted, the eyes' ability to work together to see a single vision, the ability of the eye muscles to work together to allow different gazes, the ability to distinguish objects from their background), individuals with ASD may have difficulties with a number of vision-based *skills*. These may include problems with visual spatial skills, motion processing, spatial awareness, photosensitivity, hyperreactivity to colour, problems with visual closure, gaze aversion, lateral vision (using peripheral vision to process visual information), as well as difficulty processing faces. Other significant individual differences can exist, such as heightened visual ability (hyperreactivity) or significant difficulties processing visual information. Hyperreactivity to visual stimuli may mean a reaction to sunlight or distress from flashing lights or to certain colours. Other examples include difficulty focusing on learning tasks in environments with fluorescent bulbs (photosensitivity) or finding the contrast between black ink and white paper unbearable during reading, making learning difficult (hyperreactivity). Some individuals with hypersensitivity to colour may also limit food choices based on the colour of the food or choose to play with toys of a certain colour (Coulter, 2009).

A common symptom often associated with ASD is the use of lateral vision or attempting to look at—and process—visual information through the corners of the eyes. Coulter reported that one reason for using lateral vision is that some individuals have difficulty processing visual information with both eyes at the same time. For individuals with inter-hemispheric integration problems—left and right hemispheres of the brain not working well together—the use of lateral vision allows the individual to process visual information through one hemisphere of the brain allowing for faster and more efficient processing. However, individuals with ASD may also use lateral vision in an attempt to control the amount of visual information they receive (Coulter, 2009; Heflin & Alaimo, 2007).

Those who are hyporeactive to visual information may not respond to bright or flashing lights, may be bothered by direct sunlight, or may react to spinning or other stimulating information (Heflin & Alaimo, 2007; Hyche & Maertz, 2014; Reebye & Stalker, 2008). Those who have unusual sensory interest may seek out visual stimulation such as bright lights or flashing objects or they may flick their fingers in front of their eyes. Coulter (2009) reported that some individuals with ASD who experience poor visual spatial skills may use hand flapping or finger flicking in front of the eyes to provide the central nervous system with information about where their bodies are in space.

Tactile (Touch)

The tactile modality allows individuals to feel both light and deep touch. It is the largest sensory system in the body and includes the skin and all the nerves at the surface of the skin that provide input to the brain. The tactile system discriminates between where our bodies end and the rest of the environment begins (Hyche & Maertz, 2014; Reebye & Stalker, 2008). The tactile system allows for sensing touch, pain, or pressure to the body, and to perceive the environment while reacting appropriately (e.g., pulling away from a hot surface; Heflin & Alaimo, 2007).

Individuals with atypical responses in this area may withdraw from light touch (hyperreactive), have difficulty engaging in activities that involve getting their hands dirty (e.g., finger-painting or playing with playdough), or experience being bumped or touched by others as painful. At home, parents may find their children in significant distress about certain fabrics, tags on clothing, or the ridge on the top of some socks. As well, there may be difficulty with grooming, including bathing or showering, hair washing, and changing clothes. Teachers may find that these children avoid messy activities or situations where they may be accidently bumped or touched by others (Hyche & Maertz, 2014; Reebye & Stalker, 2008).

Children with tactile differences may not sense pain from touching a hot surface, which may result in injury (hyporeactive). They may not notice if their clothing is too tight, twisted, or that their shoes are on the wrong feet (Heflin & Alaimo, 2007). Children who are hyporeactive may also engage in activities that provide sensory information, bump into objects, or constantly touch objects around them. They may run their hands along the walls at school to provide tactile information, pick their skin, or even bang their heads (Alberta Learning, 2003).

Olfactory (Smell)

The olfactory sensory system allows individuals to perceive smells from their environment. The olfactory modality is one area of sensory processing with limited research. Therefore, it is challenging to figure out difficulties for individuals with ASD

(Tonacci et al., 2017). Individuals with olfactory differences may be hyporeactive, hyperreactive, have unusual sensory interests, or they may have a mixed presentation (Ashwin, Chapman, Howells, Rhydderch, & Baron-Cohen, 2014). Individuals with hyperreactivity to smell may react with distress to what seem like innocuous smells, such as the smell of shampoo or deodorant. Children with hyperreactivity to smells may move away from certain people, may gag at the smell of certain foods or garbage in classroom garbage cans. They may react to the smell of markers, chalk, paint, or books. Individuals who are hyperreactive may choose to participate in activities based on the smells in the immediate environment (Cermak, Curtin, & Bandini, 2010; Hyche & Maertz, 2014). Individuals with ASD may also react to odours at greater distances than their typically developing peers (Ashwin et al., 2014). This level of sensitivity can make it difficult for others to determine sources of distress.

Children who are hyporeactive may be unresponsive and not notice strong smells in their environment. Children who have unusual sensory interests may seek out strong and what typical individuals would perceive as offensive smells. As an example, fecal smearing, called *scatolia*, is found in the medical literature. Sensory-seeking behaviour can be one factor in scatolia (Reynolds, 2017). Reynolds (2017) indicated that many families who experience this challenging behaviour may need and seek information but often do not raise the problem with involved professionals due to feelings of embarrassment.

Gustatory (Taste/Texture)

The gustatory system allows for the experience of taste through receptors on the tongue. Individuals with atypical gustatory reactions may be hyperreactive, hyporeactive, have unusual interests in the tastes and textures of food, or have a mixed presentation (Boudjarane, Grandgeorge, Marianowski, Misery, & Lemonnier, 2017; Hyche & Maertz, 2014; Reebye & Stalker, 2008). Those with hyperreactivity may gag at the taste or texture of certain food or may refuse to eat foods with specific textures (e.g., mushy or crunchy), certain tastes (e.g., spicy, salty, sweet, sour, or savoury), or respond negatively to the temperature of food (Chikazoe, Lee, Kriegestorte, & Anderson, 2019). They are more likely to refuse to try new foods. Significant health implications can occur as hyperreactivity to food may result in extreme dietary restrictions (Cermak et al., 2010). These children may also experience difficulty with oral hygiene, perhaps because of the texture of the toothbrush or the strong flavour of mint-based toothpaste (Cermak et al., 2010).

Children with hyporeactivity, on the other hand, may not distinguish taste and might consume things that can be dangerous as they do not react to bad tastes. For example, they may consume spoiled food or drinks without recognition that the food tastes bad. They may consume foods that are extremely hot without difficulty but cause physical damage (Cermak et al., 2010; Hyche & Maertz, 2014; Reebye & Stalker, 2008). Children who have unusual interest in the gustatory modality may lick or chew objects; they may appear to be constantly hungry or wanting food. They may also crave certain types of food such as extremely crunchy food or even non-food items, known as pica (Cermak et al., 2010).

> **pica**: the eating of non-nutritive objects in a compulsive manner that often leads to medical complications and health issues (Rose, Porcerelli, & Neale, 2000).

Vestibular (Balance)

The vestibular system allows the feeling of movement and the changes in position from information provided through the inner ear. It can be activated by self-driven actions as well as by the external world (Cullen, 2012). Additionally, the vestibular system provides information about balance, helps coordinate movement, tells direction, and enables individuals to remain upright (Cullen et al., 2009). It uses information from other sensory systems, such as the visual and proprioception, in an integrated manner for movement, body positioning, and posture. Problems with the vestibular system, on the other hand, can result in gaze instability and postural imbalance (Bhojne & Chilnis, 2002).

Individuals with hyperreactivity to vestibular stimuli may fear movement or may experience problems orienting themselves. They may have difficulty walking on certain floors (e.g., carpets, mats, grass); avoid elevators or escalators; or appear to hold their heads in rigid positions (Hyche & Maertz, 2014). Individuals with hyperreactivity to vestibular input may become nauseated easily on car trips, experience difficulty engaging in activities that require them to put their heads in certain positions (e.g., head tilting for hair washing), become disoriented easily, and avoid or refuse to participate in activities that require changes in speed or direction (e.g., playing tag in gym class; Government of British Columbia, 2000; Hyche & Maertz, 2014).

Children who are hyporeactive may appear to be slow or lethargic, may take longer to move, or may appear to be able to move at one speed—regardless of the circumstances. They may be able to tolerate a significant amount of vestibular stimulation such as twirling, rocking, or spinning with seemingly little or no reaction (Bhojne & Chilnis, 2002). Children may have unusual sensory interests, appear to crave movement, or they may appear to be in constant motion, such as rocking and twirling.

Proprioception (Body Awareness/Muscle and Joints)

Proprioception allows for an awareness of the body in space or the body in relation to the environment. Information related to proprioception is provided via the muscle and joints and allows, for example, the feeling of pressure when carrying heavy objects. Children who experience proprioceptive difficulties may not make use of their other senses (e.g., vision) to judge where their bodies are in relation to their environments (Blanche, Reinoso, Chang, & Bodison, 2012).

Children who are hyporeactive to proprioceptive sensory information may push others too hard without realizing it, may tire easily, and may also press really hard on their pen or pencil during writing tasks (Hyche & Maertz, 2014). They may not be able to hold their body or adjust their position for optimal learning as would typically developing individuals. They may seem to have difficulty performing fine and gross motor tasks such as climbing, riding bikes, throwing balls, and/or holding pencils and writing. Individuals who are hyperreactive may appear clumsy and uncoordinated, may avoid participating in sports, and may prefer sedentary activities (Hyche & Maertz, 2014). Those who have unusual sensory interests may appear to walk hard, push hard, appear rough when playing, and may walk on their toes (this latter action increases proprioceptive feedback; Heflin & Alaimo, 2007).

Read about It. Think about It. Write about It.

- Record all the senses that were presented above. Describe any sensory hyper- or hyporeactivity that *you* have to any of these areas. Are your reactions similar or dissimilar to the characteristics described for a person with ASD? Why or why not?
- When reading about common hyper- and hyporeactivity across the senses, think about a person with ASD you have worked with. Did they have atypical responses in all the areas or just some? How did this differ from your list written above?

SENSORY BEHAVIOURS AND VARIED ENVIRONMENTS

Individuals with ASD may experience more difficulty processing sensory information in unfamiliar environments and may exhibit a preference for their home environments. This is likely because they are more comfortable and the environment may be much more predictable than other spaces. Fernández-Andrés, Pastor-Cerezuela, Sanz-Cervera, and Tárraga-Minguez (2015) studied children with and without ASD to see how they process sensory information across the home and school environments; they found that children with ASD showed the greatest levels of dysfunction when assessed and compared with typically developing peers across both environments: "[a] high percentage of the ASD group obtained scores in the *Some Problems* to *Definite Dysfunction* ranges" (p. 209). They also found that the greatest area of difficulty for this group related to processing auditory information, followed by tactile sensory processing difficulties across both environments. However, teachers rated greater dysfunction than parents for both social participation and praxis.

In 2017, Sanz-Cervera, Pastor-Cerezuela, González-Sala, Tárraga-Minguez, and Fernández-Andrés compared children with ASD, attention deficit hyperactivity disorder (ADHD), and ASD comorbid with ADHD, and typically developing children aged five to eight across home and school environments using parent and teacher ratings. In terms of sensory issues, children with both ASD and ADHD were the most affected at school, while the children with ASD alone and ADHD alone had comparable scores at home. At school, children with ASD and both ASD and ADHD together showed the most challenges related to auditory issues and social participation.

> **praxis**: the individual's ability to use cognition to direct motor control. It includes three components: first, the ability to conceptualize an idea that allows purposeful interaction with their environment; second, the cognitive ability to know what to do with an object; and third, being able to anticipate a plan of action (Ayres, Mailloux, & Wendler, 1987).

ASSESSMENT OF SENSORY MODALITIES

The assessment of sensory processing disorders typically follows a team-based approach (Schaaf & Lane, 2015). Generally, sensory measures have been developed by occupational therapists. Therefore, the assessment and intervention of sensory-based features should be led by an occupational therapist in conjunction with other professionals, such as psychologists, school counsellors, and educators. Schaaf and Blanche (2011) stated, "the gold standard for assessment of sensory integration includes the use of the *Sensory Integration and Praxis Tests* (Ayres, 1989) combined with standardized parent and/or teacher report of the impact on daily functioning" (p. 1437). Assessments of sensory features in ASD should be comprehensive, involve those who know the relevant students, and consist of multiple measures.

> **occupational therapist**: a university-educated, regulated health professional that delivers the services of occupational therapy, which is a type of healthcare that helps individuals overcome issues that interfere with doing things deemed individually important (Canadian Association of Occupational Therapists, 2016).

A variety of sensory measures have been developed and standardized for use for school-aged children and adolescents. Here are some of the commonly used measures; this list may not be exhaustive. The most common assessment measures are parent ratings, teacher ratings, and self-report. At this time, students must be 11 or older to be eligible to rate their own sensory features.

Miller-Kuhaneck and Kelleher (2018) are in the process of developing a sensory tool that will allow teachers to examine their students, as well as help their school

Table 5.2: Assessment Tools for Sensory Modalities

Assessment Tool	Type of Tool	Age Range	ASD Normed?
Sensory Profile, Second Edition (SP2) (Dunn, 2014)	Parent/caregiver/ teacher rating	3 years to 14 years, 11 months	Yes
Sensory Profile Adolescent/Adult (Brown & Dunn, 2002)	Self/parent/ caregiver rating	11 years and older	Yes
Sensory Processing Measure Sensory Processing Measure—Preschool (Glennon, Miller-Kuhaneck, Henry, Parham, & Ecker, 2007, 2010)	Parent/teacher/ caregiver rating	2 to 5 years (Preschool version) 5 to 12 years (Grades K–6)	No
Sensory Integration and Praxis Test (SIPT) (Ayres, 1989)	Standardized individual performance test	4 years to 8–11 years	No
Classroom Sensory Assessment (Miller-Kuhaneck & Kelleher, 2018)	Teacher use	School-aged children	Expected in 2020
Sensory Processing Scales (Schoen, Miller, & Sullivan, 2014)	Parent/caregiver rating	Children and adults	No

Source: Authors.

promote environments that make teachers aware of the sensory features of their classroom and to promote awareness of sensory experiences in general. Given our focus on inclusive environments in most school settings, it is increasingly critical that we consider the learning environment and how it impacts learning from multiple perspectives—including sensory perspectives.

SENSORY INTERVENTIONS

Although it is established that characteristics of sensory processing issues are seen in children with ASD, *how* to intervene continues to be controversial given the current dearth of evidence-based interventions; these approaches do not yet have sufficient evidence to qualify as EBIs. Teachers and other educational personnel may be pressured by families to use certain types of interventions; this is also true in relation to children with ASD who experience sensory-based issues. Understanding that students who experience difficulty processing sensory information may also experience significant difficulties learning is critical for educators, caregivers, and families (Autism in Education Partnership, 2018).

Multiple reviews of sensory-based interventions exist (e.g., Baranek, 2002; Barton, Reichow, Schnitz, Smith, & Sherlock, 2015; Case-Smith et al., 2014; May-Benson & Koomar, 2010; Schaaf & Blanche, 2011). While most have suggested gains, overall, the results have not provided sufficient evidence for the widespread use of sensory-based interventions and the resources that are required for their implementation. The *National Standards Project—Phase 2* (NAC, 2015) also provided a large-scale review of research interventions specific for individuals with ASD and suggested that sensory intervention approaches continue to be in the unestablished category (see Chapter 2). Barton and colleagues (2015) carried out a systematic review of sensory-based interventions with children with disabilities and found the evidence to be inconclusive. However, this type of intervention continues to grow in popularity. Sensory-based interventions are widely used with children who have developmental disabilities. In their review, 30 studies were identified, which included more than 800 children over more than 30 years and multiple treatment groups. The findings suggested "limited support, at best, for sensory-based treatments for children with disabilities" (Barton et al., 2015, p. 78).

Pollark (2009), a Canadian occupational therapist from the CanChild Centre for Childhood Disabilities at McMaster University in Hamilton, Ontario, also supported the conclusion of the reviews. She stated, "to date the evidence of [sensory integration therapy's] effectiveness is weak at best" (p. 8). She further commented that occupational therapists need to ensure they use evidence-based interventions. She indicated a commitment to an approach just because it was developed by an occupational therapist may mean children are not receiving interventions that may be more beneficial. Law (2006) further recommended that the focus should be on understanding each individual child, their sensory differences, and structuring their home and school environments to minimize sensory reactions.

While it seems to make sense to provide children with sensory-based interventions, given that most do not pose a safety risk and sensory intervention may even be pleasurable (Autism in Education Partnership, 2018), these approaches need to be used with caution. It is critical to understand the relationship between the environment and related behaviour. If sensory-based interventions are used without caution, clinicians, educators, and parents may inadvertently increase problem behaviour (see functional behaviour assessment on p. 150).

Sensory Rooms

There are many schools across the country that have developed sensory spaces for children diagnosed with ASD. There is no clear evidence that sensory integration therapy remediates the underlying sensory system dysfunction. However, there is some evidence for the use of sensory spaces and sensory-based strategies for individuals with sensory differences (Pollark, 2009). In their research summary, *Autism Services in Ontario: Impacts on Family and Child Well-Being* (2019), McLaughlin and Schneider recommended that "safe and compassionate strategies for calming and self-regulation, such as sensory rooms and breaks, should be developed in consultation with autistic people and experts" (p. 14).

The assessment of sensory differences can provide valuable information and may help explain specific behaviours and guide interventions (Fernández-Andrés et al., 2015; Pollark, 2009). Around ASD, it is also important to focus on evaluating the environments—and modifying them—to ensure full participation in daily activities. For example, reducing the noise level for a student who has auditory hyperreactivity or using incandescent lighting for a student who has visual hyperreactivity (as opposed to fluorescent lighting) may be helpful modifications that allow participation. As well, sensory activities may be embedded into daily routines so that inappropriate behaviours are not accidently reinforced: "delivering the sensory activity as a consequence of the learner demonstrating desired behaviour, instead of problem behaviour, may increase desired behaviour in the future" (Autism in Education Partnership, 2018; see functional behaviour assessment on p. 150).

The Sensory Space at Pierre Elliott Trudeau Elementary School, Vancouver, BC

Pearl Chow, Occupational Therapist, Vancouver Coastal Health

Pierre Elliott Trudeau Elementary School is a Kindergarten to Grade 7 school in Vancouver, British Columbia. Its lineage dates back to 1885, with the current building opening in 2003 to a vibrant and committed community of learners. The school has long promoted inclusive sensory considerations in the classroom. Teachers, educational support staff, and administrators recognized more could be done for students with different learning profiles: students with physical and cognitive differences; those with learning difficulties; and children with ASD. The school began consulting with an occupational therapist from the Vancouver Paediatric Team and a dedicated multisensory space as an adjunct to learning was created.

Committed school staff, in collaboration with occupational therapists, began to research and explore options. They visited a local *Snoezelen* room. The occupational therapist provided expertise in prescribing specialized equipment. The school staff approached the parent advisory committee for support, they held fundraisers including a walk-a-thon, and they explored grant applications. The approval and support from the school district was gained to fund the major equipment while the school bought complementary sensory tools. By 2008, the room began to take shape, and, over the years, the school has continued to fundraise and solicit donations from local businesses to maintain and enhance the room.

> ***Snoezelen* room**: officially called Snoezelen Multi-Sensory Environments, they are described as relaxing environments that function to reduce stress and agitation but are also available to please the sensory processes and are stated to assist in facilitating communication (Snoezelen, 2019).

This multisensory room was designed to modify sensory experiences for those with ASD and other special needs to help them better cope with the world around them. Many children with ASD struggle with sound, light, touch, temperature, and more; they react too much or not enough to senses within and around them. The room is meant to create safe experiences for a wide range of calming and stimulating activities often in a fundamental, graded way. Children can explore and learn to use their senses to hone physical skills with improved focus and become less overwhelmed. The room can vary in set up to reduce anxiety or stimulate and encourage communication. Opportunities to play also support development of social skills. The learning done in the multisensory room promotes regulation in real-life experiences.

A full spectrum of sensory experiences is part of this room. The occupational therapist provided input on the types of sensory equipment to address not only sound, light, touch, smell considerations but also addressed the primary and powerful vestibular and proprioceptive senses. In total, five ceiling anchors were installed to give the most flexibility in use of suspended equipment. A horizontal linear glider can act as zip line or swing as children learn to propel themselves. Other swings can be climbed on, sat in, or crawled through and set up for slow rocking or fast, erratic movement. A path is available to challenge balance and a climbing wall can be adjusted for just the right level challenge.

A soft floor of thick, martial art foam is underfoot. The school set up a lighted bubble tube and mirror in a cushioned corner. Fibre optic lights can be explored with the hands. Students can rest in a vibrating chair with or without a kaleidoscope of slow-moving coloured circles projected on the ceiling. Overhead lighting filters through blue and white cloud covers. Donated audiovisual equipment creates different moods. A tire encased in plastic wrap requires lots of cooperation and energy to push and roll.

The schedule of the multisensory room is well-subscribed, with children often going at regular and predictable times. At any given time, you may find one student who needs to rock in a swing with lights dimmed or a small group working on a math lesson on the floor interspersed with turns riding a glider or walking the balance path. Sometimes, two children might wrangle the tire on its side and bang on it like a drum.

The staff at Trudeau Elementary have valued this room from its inception and clearly post its philosophy for all to see. It continues to inspire both staff and students to keep it clean, safe, and ready for use. This space is not meant to be used as a reward or break time; rather, it is a tool to complement learning, especially for those who need supports to better handle sensory experiences. Advocacy for its importance continues as the multisensory room is considered a non-enrolling classroom (not occupied all day by one set of learners), and therefore is not recognized in capacity calculations set by the BC Ministry of Education for elementary schools. It takes a dedicated, invested, and caring school staff to champion the value of a multisensory space and continue to speak up on its positive impact on students, especially those with ASD.

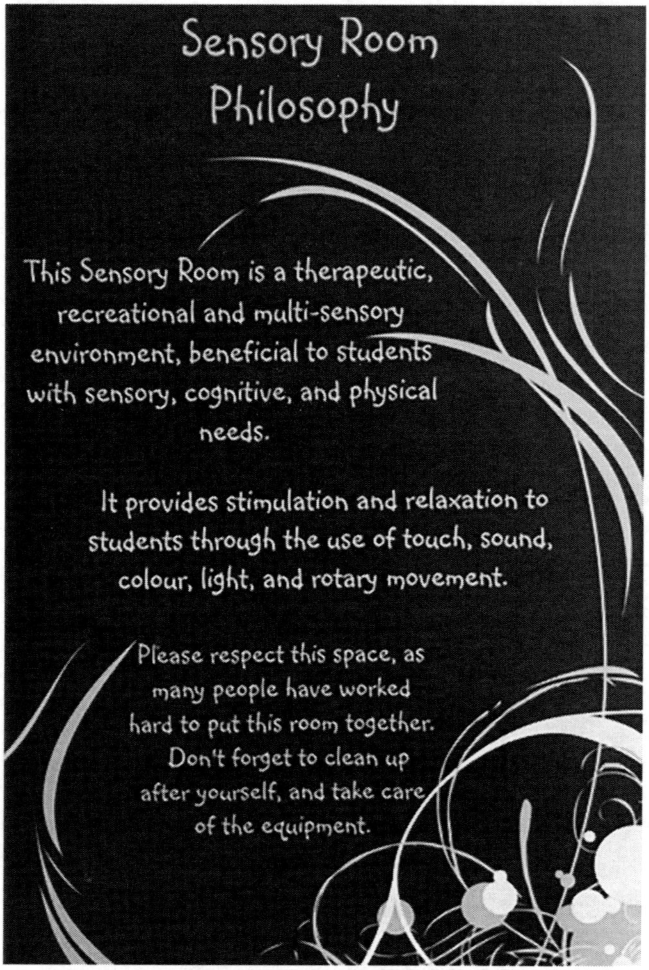

Figure 5.4: Pierre Elliott Trudeau Elementary School's Sensory Room Philosophy

Source: Pearl Chow.

Figure 5.5: The Climbing Wall in Pierre Elliott Trudeau Elementary School's Sensory Room
Source: Pearl Chow.

Often, other schools and districts request to tour and learn from Trudeau in setting up their alternative learning spaces. For 10 years, Trudeau Elementary addressed the sensory needs of students who all attended inclusive classes. In 2018 to 2019, the school also became home to a district classroom dedicated to children with ASD. The room belongs to all learners in the school for multisensory tools to relax, explore, stimulate, and learn.

Best Practices in School Environments

What are the best practices for children diagnosed with ASD and experiencing sensory-based problems within the school environment?

1. The best approaches are those based in behavioural strategies, as these strategies have the strongest scientific evidence.
2. Atypical sensory responses can be best explained by understanding the relationship between the environment and behaviour. Behaviours are learned through the interaction between the environment and are maintained by their consequences (see Chapter 4 for discussions about behavioural strategies as an EBI).

SPOTLIGHTS ACROSS CANADA

Research: Mutiple Jurisdictions

Germani and colleagues (2014), a group of researchers from Alberta, Ontario, and Nova Scotia, conducted longitudinal studies on high-risk infants (those with an older sibling diagnosed with ASD). These researchers investigated sensory processing difficulties in high-risk infants and compared them with low-risk infants (those with no family history of ASD). They found that high-risk infants who received a diagnosis of ASD during the course of their study had higher scores on auditory processing and on the low registration (hyporeactive) on the *Infant and Toddler Sensory Profile* (Dunn, 2002) when compared with high-risk infants who did not receive a diagnosis and low-risk infants.

Research: Mutiple Jurisdictions

In a separate study, Perez Repetto and colleagues (2017) were involved in a pan-Canadian research study, *Pathways for Better Outcomes*. These Quebec-based researchers followed a subsample of children diagnosed with ASD. Using a standardized measure, the *Sensory Profile*, these researchers examined sensory behaviour at two points in time: at diagnosis and again two years later. Results suggested that the sensory profile of children remained relatively stable over time. Dugas, Simard, Fombonne, and Couture (2018), who were also involved in the pan-Canadian study, compared children with ASD scores on the *Sensory Profile* and the *Sensory Processing Measure*. Results suggested some agreement between the two measures; however, many children with ASD have significant eating problems, and these authors suggested the need for better tools to determine olfactory and gustatory problems in children with ASD. They recommended that occupational therapists collect information about sensory processing through multiple measures and through observation and interviews.

Research: Mutiple Jurisdictions

Peverill and colleagues (2019) at the Autism Research Centre, Dalhousie University, Halifax, Nova Scotia, along with researchers from four other centres in Canada (Montreal, Quebec; Hamilton, Ontario; Edmonton, Alberta; and Greater Vancouver, British Columbia) conducted a longitudinal study investigating preschool feeding problems in children with ASD. Using a variety of measures, they sought to investigate the trajectory of feeding problems in a cohort of children over four time periods, to determine the variables that would predict feeding problems in the children who participated in the study. The researchers suggested that there were four groups, including: a group without feeding difficulty that remained stable over time, a group with some difficulty (but subclinical) with feeding problems that declined over time, a group with significant feeding difficulties (at a clinical level) that declined over time, and a group of children (8.3% of their sample) with severe and stable feeding problems. These authors suggested that there is a relationship between adaptive functioning, behavioural difficulties (internalizing and externalizing), and increased feeding problems. They found a positive relationship between feeding problems and internalization behaviour across all four groups in the study. As well, externalizing behaviours were found to be a predicator for feeding problems only in Group Four, the severe and stable feeding problems group. The authors concluded that it is important to consider feeding issues; however, these issues should be considered as "part of a wider regulatory problem (i.e., externalizing/internalizing behaviour, sleep disturbances, etc.), rather than ASD-specific symptoms" (p. 8).

Research: Quebec

Nadon, Ehrmann Feldman, Dunn, and Gisel (2011), a group of researchers from Quebec, investigated the link between sensory processing and eating problems in children ages three to ten with ASD. These researchers studied children's eating behaviour along with their sensory profiles. Children who obtained a *definite difference* score on tactile sensitivity showed unusual food preferences, including texture, colour, and temperature. They reported that children showing tactile defensiveness (hyperreactivity) may be less likely to explore food and show more food selectivity.

Research: Ontario

Black and colleagues (2017) in Ontario are studying how sensory hypersensitivity (DSM-5 hyperreactive) in children with ASD is linked with both anxiety and insistence on sameness (I/S). These authors studied children with ASD and a group of typically developing peers. These authors found that individuals with hypersensitivity and ASD were more likely to have specific phobias, separation anxiety, and insistence on sameness when compared with typically developing peers. These authors stated, "our data clearly suggests that different subscales of anxiety have distinct relationships with I/S and hypersensitivity" (p. 2466). They did not find a relationship between hypersensitivity and social anxiety.

A LOOK BACK

Chapter 5, "The Sensory Domain," focused on:

- The early mentions of sensory difficulties in persons with ASD and the progression to inclusion into the DSM-5
- Common classification models of organizing sensory features
- Review of the senses and linkages to hyper- and hyporeactivity in persons with ASD
- Early research and common interventions for sensory difficulties

ADDITIONAL RESOURCES

Reynolds, K. (2017). *What to Do about Smearing: A Practical Guide for Parents and Caregivers of People with Autism, Developmental and Intellectual Disabilities*. London, UK: Jessica Kingsley Publishers.

This book is a practical guide to interventions for smearing that is easy to read and geared toward parents but also provides useful strategies for caregivers.

Sensory Audit for School and Classrooms

http://www.aettraininghubs.org.uk/wp-content/uploads/2012/05/37.1-Sensory-audit-tool-for-environments.pdf

This weblink provides a useful tool for educators interested in assessing sensory aspects of their classroom. This checklist highlights some visual, auditory, and olfactory scenarios that may impact student learning.

"The Most Autism-Friendly Town in Canada"

https://www.todaysparent.com/the-most-autism-friendly-town-in-canada/

This enjoyable article profiles Channel-Port aux Basques, Newfoundland, known as the first autism-friendly town in Canada. It describes several ways that businesses and local governments support residents with ASD.

Canadian Association of Occupational Therapists Position Statement on ASD and Occupational Therapy

https://www.caot.ca/document/3656/autism.pdf

This position statement written by the Canadian Association of Occupational Therapists (CAOT) discusses this profession and its involvement with ASD.

Miller-Kuhaneck, H., & Watling, R. (2010). ***Autism: A Comprehensive Occupational Therapy Approach*****. Bethesda, MD: AOTA.**

This book provides a comprehensive overview of ASD and its history as well as information regarding the theories and causes of ASD. It emphasizes various sensory techniques and discusses leisure, self-care, self-management, and sensory processing, as well as diagnostic criteria, communication, and motor skills.

Canadian Association of Occupational Therapists Occupational Therapy in Autism—Webinar

https://www.caot.ca/client/product2/156/item.html

This website directs users to an archived webinar on Occupational Therapy in Autism.

Rogers Arena—Autism Aware Facility, Vancouver, BC

https://rogersarena.com/fan-services/autism-aware-facility/

Rogers Arena in Vancouver, BC, is the first NHL stadium able to offer resources and supports to individuals with ASD during hockey games or concerts. This website lists the various resources available to fans with ASD or sensory sensitivity.

Sensory Differences and Autism Spectrum Disorder

http://www.gov.pe.ca/photos/original/eecd_autismeng2.pdf

This document provides detailed support for the use of behavioural-based interventions to address sensory differences in individuals with ASD.

Sensory Processing Problems in Children and Youth

https://www.ementalhealth.ca/Canada/Sensory-Processing-Problems/index.php?m=article&ID=8890

This useful website provides a comprehensive overview of sensory problems in children and youth, with detailed descriptions on various sensory sensitivities.

SECTION III

Autism Spectrum Disorder across the Lifespan

The first two sections of this book examined the definition and history of autism spectrum disorder (ASD), then focused on current effective interventions to support persons with ASD. Section III focuses on critical issues that occur across the lifespan and how different provinces and territories have structured policy and supports for persons with ASD. Since services from infancy to adulthood are created and offered provincially in Canada, examples of supports and how certain services are delivered provincially will be focused on. By dividing the chapters across the lifespan, critical issues that large numbers of persons and families supporting a person with ASD will face at different life stages are covered more in-depth. Chapter 6 looks at the early years and highlights the red flags for ASD in early childhood and the supports in inclusive daycares and intensive treatment options. Chapter 7 examines the education system and supports it provides to students with ASD across Canada. Chapter 8 looks at adulthood and common barriers and services offered to adults with ASD. Lastly, Chapter 9 looks at the family perspective from receiving a diagnosis, accepting the diagnosis, accessing resources, and advocating.

CHAPTER 6

The Early Years

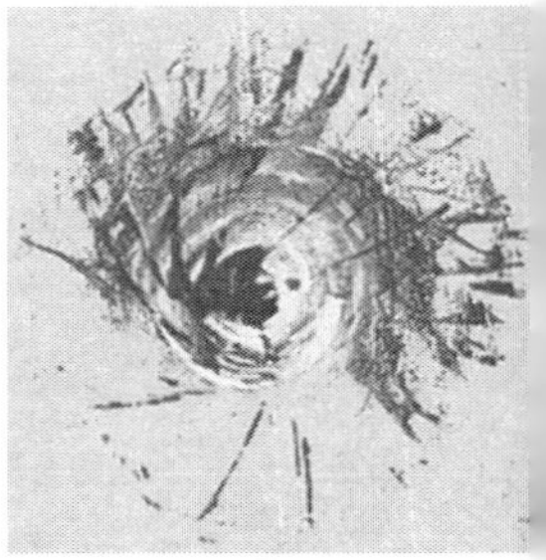

LEARNING OBJECTIVES

- Describe early screening for infants and preschoolers with ASD, as well as red flags that are noted and often provided to childcare providers.
- Review inclusive practices and training for early year professionals around identifying and supporting children with ASD.
- Summarize intensive therapy for young children with ASD.
- Discuss sample highlights of early years programs, interventions, and models across Canada.

This chapter highlights many experiences in the early years—prior to formal school entry—for children, families, and services providers when identifying, diagnosing, and supporting children with autism spectrum disorder (ASD). Since approximately half of ASD diagnoses occur in these early years, many of the early years professionals in Canada's early childhood education and care are trained in identifying red flags and helping families identify resources for diagnosis. This chapter identifies early ASD screening, checklists for identification, and red flags for both parents and childcare providers. It then focuses on the number of children with ASD who are included in childcare and preschool, common supports, and support documents that may accompany them to help them learn new skills and be included. A brief overview of intensive interventions that are often offered for young children with ASD is included. Lastly, different programs, supports, and resources across Canadian jurisdictions are highlighted.

OVERVIEW

Around half of ASD diagnoses in Canada occur prior to the onset of formal K–12 public schooling. More specifically, 56% occur prior to age six (Public Health Agency of Canada, 2018c). This means that many children with ASD are diagnosed when they are either receiving education and care within childcare settings or are in the preschool years. Waitlists for services aside, young children diagnosed with ASD are likely to receive intervention services along with childcare services (if the latter are in place).

Volden and colleagues (2015) reviewed service provision for 414 preschool children with ASD using a cross-Canada sample and found that some type of specialized service was typically in place within a few months of a formal diagnosis. By school entry, close to 95% of children were receiving at least some service; however, service provision varied both by jurisdiction and population density.

According to Dudley and Emrey (2014), the impact of ASD is incalculable in many ways, with the exception of considering what it costs for a family to raise children with ASD into adulthood. More specifically:

> If that child is severely impacted and requires constant and lifelong supports, then the value of caregiver time required to support that individual is approximately $5.5 million higher than that for someone without autism. An autism diagnosis of a high-needs child at age two represents the equivalent of telling the family that they must make an immediate lump-sum investment on that day of $1.6 million, invested at a five-per-cent return, to pay for the lifetime costs of care and support their loved one will require. And that amount does not even account for added professional services, such as speech therapists, psychologists, and occupational therapists, or additional out-of-pocket expenses that may be required, such as special equipment or diets. (p. 1)

SCREENING

Even though early intervention is an important component of success for young children with ASD, wide-scale screening for ASD in young children in order to obtain diagnoses and services is not a common practice. Laurie Mawlam, Executive Director of Autism Canada, wrote the popular media article entitled "Why Universal Screening for Autism Is a Good Idea" (2016) that cited high prevalence rate, benefits of early diagnosis—and early intervention—as well as better outcomes in foundational areas such as social communication. From a North American lens, Letto and Bornstein (2018) examined the area of systematic preschool screening from Canadian and American perspectives. They found only three studies related to screening for ASD in young children; however, they also found that these studies had

> **ASD screening**: often called or combined with a developmental screening, where a short checklist is completed to compare the child's development to common developmental milestones. A brief, ASD-specific screening may be completed when there are risk factors or specific ASD behaviours are being observed (see the section on M-CHAT-R as an example). Completed for most young children at regular time points from 6 to 24 months when visiting the family physician, and referrals for ASD-specific screeners may be made (CDC, 2018).

substantial risks of bias. Overall, they reported that such research is inconclusive. They also noted that there is not yet sufficient evidence to demonstrate that systematic screening tools related to ASD are either more helpful or more harmful. The Canadian Task Force on Preventative Health Care (2016) released specific guidelines recommending *against* such screening:

> The task force recommends against screening for developmental delay using standardized tools in children aged 1 to 4 years with no apparent signs of developmental delay and whose parents and clinicians have no concerns about development. Thus, this recommendation applies to children for whom there is no concern about failure to sequentially acquire age-appropriate developmental milestones for gross and fine motor, social, emotional, language and cognitive domains. Milestone ages should be based on the oldest age by which the skill should have been achieved. The recommendation does not apply to children who present with signs suggestive of possible developmental delay, those whose parents express concern that could indicate developmental delay or those whose development is being closely monitored because of identified risk factors, such as premature birth or low birth weight. (p. 585)

Read about It. Think about It. Write about It.

- Have you ever experienced a developmental or ASD screening for a child? What was your initial impression? Do you think these are helpful or harmful? Why?
- List the potential benefits and drawbacks of early screening.

RED FLAGS

As noted, two essential keys to supporting young children with ASD are the intertwined practices of both early detection and early intervention. These practices typically lead to referrals for further assessment by medical, psychological, and/or behavioural services. In addition to being educated on potential interventions for young children with ASD, professionals supporting students in childcare centres are responsible for identifying concerns or red flags in young children who might not yet be

> **red flags**: key characteristics and behaviours that are commonly seen in ASD that children may begin to exhibit. These characteristics and behaviours have been demonstrated to be signs of ASD and are not always part of typical development. If there are a number of items on the list that educators, parents, or caregivers see, they are urged to seek additional support for ASD screening.

5. Does your child make unusual finger movements near his or her eyes? (**For Example**, does your child wiggle his or her fingers close to his or her eyes?) Pass Fail

5. Does ________ make unusual finger movements near his/her eyes?

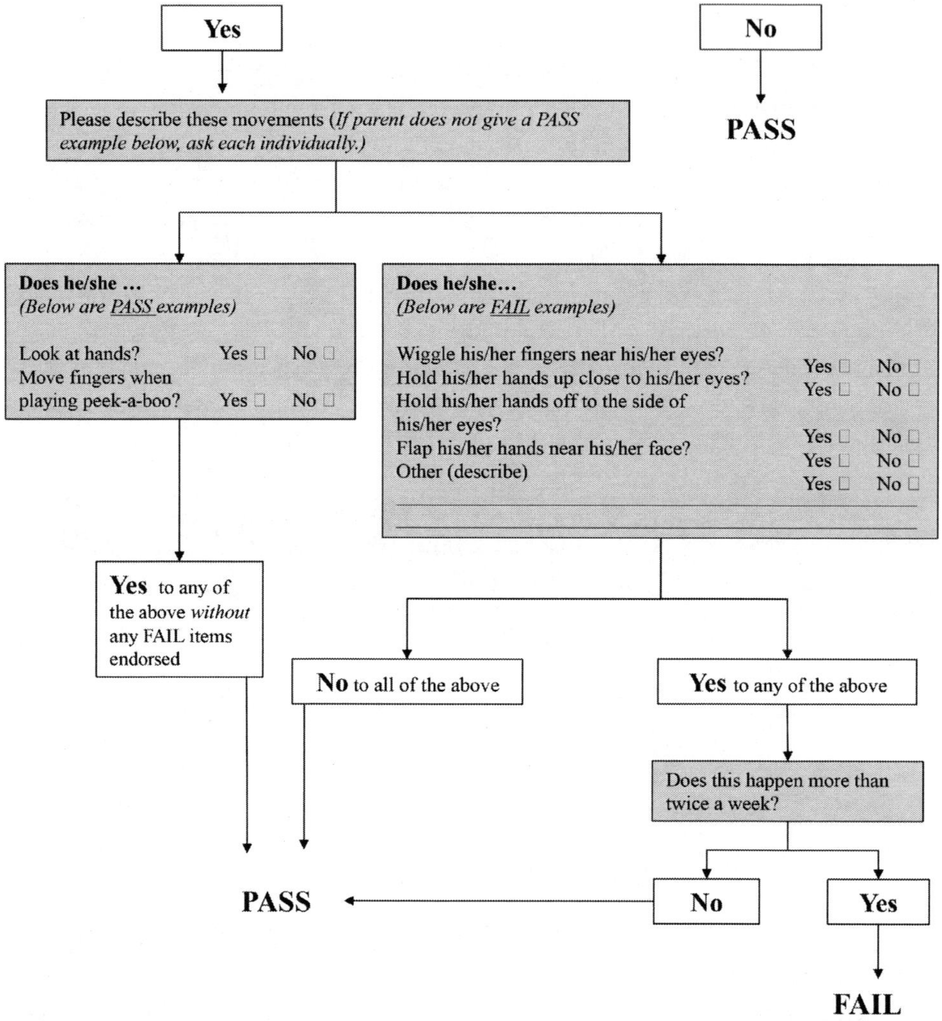

Figure 6.1: Sample Item from the *Modified Checklist for Autism in Toddlers, Revised* (M-CHAT-R) and the *Modified Checklist for Autism in Toddlers, Revised, with Follow-Up* (M-CHAT-R/F)

Source: Robins, Fein, & Barton, 2009a, 2009b.

diagnosed. They also document and communicate concerns related to foundational skills like imitation, joint attention, and peer interest (Barton & Harn, 2012). Being aware of easily accessible screening tools, such as the *Modified Checklist for Autism in Toddlers, Revised* (M-CHAT-R) or the *Modified Checklist for Autism in Toddlers, Revised, with Follow-Up* (M-CHAT-R/F), can be beneficial (Robins, Fein, & Barton, 2009a, 2009b).

Many less formal sources provide information outlining red flags in young children with ASD. The Government of Canada (2018d), for example, provides what they term the "signs and symptoms of ASD," categorized by age group. At any age, they note that behaviours such as "repeats words and phrases over and over" or "gets upset by minor changes in routine and surroundings" (para. 4) are reasons for assessment for ASD. More regionally, geographic areas may develop and share their own manuals related to red flags on a broad scale. Ontario's York Region (2009), for example, utilizes the *Red Flags: A Quick Reference Guide for Early Years Professionals in York Region*. In the area of ASD, 11 social concerns, 7 communication concerns, and 7 behavioural concerns are listed red flags, including "any loss of social skills at any age" (p. 7) and "prefers to play alone, decreased interest in other children" (p. 7). Autism Speaks Canada (2018c) provides an ages-and-stages list of red flags or signs of autism, with the caveat that "some children *without* autism have some of these symptoms, and not all children *with* autism show all of them" (para. 4).

Possible signs of autism in babies and toddlers:

- By 6 months, no social smiles or other warm, joyful expressions directed at people
- By 6 months, limited or no eye contact
- By 9 months, no sharing of vocal sounds, smiles or other nonverbal communication
- By 12 months, no babbling
- By 12 months, no use of gestures to communicate (e.g., pointing, reaching, waving, etc.)
- By 12 months, no response to name when called
- By 16 months, no words
- By 24 months, no meaningful, two-word phrases
- Any loss of any previously acquired speech, babbling or social skills

Possible signs of autism at any age:

- Avoids eye contact and prefers to be alone
- Struggles with understanding other people's feelings
- Remains nonverbal or has delayed language development
- Repeats words or phrases over and over (echolalia)
- Gets upset by minor changes in routine or surroundings

- Has highly restricted interests
- Performs repetitive behaviours such as flapping, rocking or spinning
- Has unusual and often intense reactions to sounds, smells, tastes, textures, lights and/or colors. (Autism Speaks Canada, 2018c, para. 5)

Montreal-based developmental pediatrician Munz suggests waiting until children are a year old to actually refer for formal assessment, but to watch for regression of skills and idiosyncratic behaviour (Yanofsky, 2018). More specifically, such notable behaviours can be described as:

> peculiar play—like lining up toy cars rather than driving them along the floor—a desire to be isolated or an acute sensitivity to loud noises or bright lights. Behaviours like hand flapping, toe walking, self-isolation and repetition of words or actions are also signs to look out for. (Yanofsky, 2018, para. 4)

Helpful audiovisual examples are also available through an online *ASD Video Glossary* hosted by Autism Navigator (Florida State University, 2018), which includes specific red flags videos depicting "a wide range of intensity, symptoms, and behaviours in children affected by ASD. The signs are as varied as the number of children affected. These signs can be subtle or, to the untrained eye, easy to miss" (Autism Speaks, 2009). Professionals in early childhood settings (e.g., teachers, early childhood educators) do not diagnose ASD. However, it can be helpful to be educated on how to talk to parents about possible signs and characteristics of ASD, should the occasion arise when ASD is suspected or the childcare centre believes that families should consider investigating developmental issues. Autism Speaks (2018) emphasizes that "if you suspect a developmental delay or autism, speak up! Your intervention can change a child's life." Yet caution and care in documenting and describing concerning characteristics and appropriate next steps are always essential to beneficial, respectful communication with parents.

Read about It. Think about It. Write about It.

- What strategies would you use to identify if the characteristic a child is showing is a red flag versus a child's unique personality? What steps can you put in place to accurately identify red flags before approaching family members?
- In many places across Canada, an issue to providing early intensive behaviour intervention to children with ASD is the lack of qualified professionals with knowledge in applied behaviour analysis. Is this problem an issue in your province or territory? If relevant, how has this issue changed in the past 10 years?

INCLUSION

Universal access to childcare is an important objective (Killoran, Tymon, & Frempong, 2007). For children with exceptionalities, this includes "the dire need to focus on our pre-school settings and the inclusion of young children with disabilities. Very few children are attending their community preschools. If we envision an inclusive community, young children must begin their school years with their peers" (Killoran et al., 2007, p. 92). Even so, the practice of inclusion varies across licensed childcare centres. Currently, "legislation and policy that make it illegal to exclude children with special needs are lacking" (Crowther, 2010, p. 44), and childcare centres are permitted to refuse children with special needs. One research team in Ontario, for example, found that 35% of preschools in the Toronto area excluded children who already had disability labels from attending (Killoran et al., 2007).

> **inclusive education**: where students are welcomed and attend their neighbourhood schools, are in regular classrooms, and are supported to learn and participate in all components of school life (Inclusive Education Canada, 2017).

When children with special needs can access such childcare settings, multiple issues remain, including the absence of proper funding, resources, facilities, and training. Some individual centres and geographic regions struggle with inclusion, and others are firmly committed to inclusion as an essential practice. It is typically recognized that "inclusive early education is not just about placement in a program, but also active participation in social interactions and the development of children's abilities and skills" (Underwood, 2013, p. 1).

Tools do exist to help examine inclusive practices specific to childcare centres. Many sites make use of the *SpeciaLink Early Childhood Inclusion Tool* (Irwin, 2009). This tool is not ASD-specific, but it does give a general sense of a centre's overall approach to inclusion, consisting of the *SpeciaLink Child Care Inclusion Practice Profile* and the *SpeciaLink Child Care Principles Scale* (Crowther, 2010).

> The SpeciaLink Early Childhood Inclusion Quality Scale is a tool for assessing inclusion quality in early childhood centres and for helping centres move toward higher quality inclusion. The Scale provides a picture of sustainable and evolving inclusion quality—an emerging issue as more children with special needs attend community-based centres and as inclusion pioneers leave their centres and a new generation of directors and early childhood educators take on the inclusion challenges. (SpeciaLink: The National Centre for Child Care Inclusion, 2009)

The inclusion of children with ASD in childcare settings appears difficult to count, track, and monitor on a wide scale. Perhaps surprisingly, most wide-scale reports on early childhood do not reference ASD, may not retain statistics around ASD for young children, may use only numbers for support services in general, or may use unique categories such as *neurological conditions*. Therefore, it is difficult to quantify inclusion for children with ASD in childcare settings from an overall Canadian perspective, or even provincially or territorially (Friendly et al., 2018; The Atkinson Centre for Society and Child Development, 2017).

Read about It. Think about It. Write about It.

- Ask three sources in your community about the level of inclusion of children with ASD in childcare settings in your region. Was this expected or surprising to you? Why or why not?

INDIVIDUAL PROGRAM PLANS

Children who are already diagnosed with ASD are likely to have some type of individualized program plan (IPP) to support education and care in the childcare context. In Alberta, such plans are referred to as early childhood services individualized program plans; in Saskatchewan, personal program plans; and Ontario, individual program plans. New Brunswick, as another example, has a plan specific to early childhood and ASD: the personalized learning plan.

> **individualized program plan (IPP)**: "an approach to providing services to individuals with special needs: the process involves developing a written plan based on the child's strengths, needs, and interests" in order to provide a plan for educating and supporting the child in an inclusive manner in the childcare environment (Allen et al., 2015, p. 279).

IPPs and their development also include:

- A supportive team made up of parents and a number of professionals (Allen et al., 2015);
- Intentional planning for the child's time in childcare and information sharing (Underwood, 2013);
- A process that includes problem identification, implementation of strategies, and adaptation of the program if changes are needed (Crowther, 2010);
- Staff and funding (Underwood, 2013);
- Direction and structure (Allen et al., 2015);
- A profile (Crowther, 2010);

- Access to multidisciplinary services (Underwood, 2013);
- An outline for implementation of the plan (Allen et al., 2015); and
- A method to evaluate the plans created and adapt (Allen et al., 2015).

The five components of an IPP are:

1. Observation and assessment
2. Identification of strengths, needs, and interests
3. Setting of goals and objectives
4. Creation of an implementation plan
5. Evaluation (Allen et al., 2015, p. 280)

INTENSIVE THERAPY

Likely the most commonly recognized and utilized intervention for young children with ASD is an intensive, discrete trial training (DTT) focused intervention typically termed early intensive behaviour intervention (EIBI), or some variation of this nomenclature (see Chapter 3). As with most other services related to ASD, such interventions are jurisdictionally provided, and not all jurisdictions provide ASD-specific funding. For example, British Columbia provides multiple choices for children and families, but Nunavut does not provide funding specifically directed toward ASD. A glance at the jurisdictional funding specific to young children with ASD, provided by Autism Canada (2017a), makes this intensive, therapeutic focus quite evident. Recent research found that "early intervention has been recognized as the best indicator for optimal outcome" (p. 16). Due to such conclusions, multiple Canadian jurisdictions have increased governmental funding for this intervention. Volden and colleagues (2015) found that behavioural services were provided to young children soon after their diagnoses (28%), with almost 58% receiving treatment by the one-year mark.

Refer to Table 6.1 for a jurisdiction-by-jurisdiction overview of funding for preschool-aged children with ASD.

> **early intervention**: services provided to young babies and children who have disabilities and their families. The types of services are broad (e.g., physical therapy, occupational therapy, speech therapy, and behavioural therapy), but intervention at a young age can help children overcome challenges and impact their future learning (CDC, 2018).

Table 6.1: Funding for Preschool-aged Children with ASD

Jurisdiction	Program	Ministry	Eligibility	Funding
AB	Family Support for Children with Disabilities	Children's Services	N/A	Funding per child based on assessed need
BC	Autism Funding under Age 6	Children and Family Development	Children under 6	$22,000 per year per child
MB	Applied Behavioural Analysis (ABA) Program	Family Services and Housing Health Education	Preschool and school-aged children	Up to a maximum of $6,000 per year for the home-based portion of the ABA program for school-aged children
NB	Services for Children with Autism Spectrum Disorders	Education and Early Childhood Development	Preschool children diagnosed with ASD	Up to $33,000 per year per child
NL	Direct Home Services Program	Health and Community Services	Preschool children and infants with significant behavioural delays	Information not available
NS	Early Intensive Behaviour Intervention Treatment (Pivotal Response Therapy)	Health	All preschool children are eligible; due to limited capacity, priority is given first to age 5, then 4	Current funding supports approximately 50% of preschool children with ASD
NT	Autism Program	Health and Social Services, Education, Culture and Employment, NWT Disabilities Council	Preschool and school-aged children	Information not available

Jurisdiction	Program	Ministry	Eligibility	Funding
NU	Services to Children with Disabilities	Health and Social Services; NGO funded by Health and Social Services	Children up to 19 (anyone affected by autism including families, educators, employers, etc. No specific program for children with autism at present)	No specified maximum; YT and NT overall budget is $460,000 for direct interventions and $79,000 to Autism Yukon
ON	Ontario Autism Program	Children and Youth Services	Age 17 or under	Funding per child based on assessed need
PE	Autism Early Intervention Program—Preschool Children	Education, Early Learning and Culture	Preschool children	$200 per week per child; also covers materials for therapy including $300 for start-up and $100 per month thereafter
QC	Autism Action Plan	Health and Social Services	Preschool children	Information not available
SK	Autism Early Childhood Therapy Program (AECTP)	Health Learning Community Resources and Development	Children 3–5	Information not available
YT	Services to Children with Disabilities	Health and Social Services; NGO funded by Health and Social Services	Children up to 19 (anyone affected by autism including families, educators, employers, etc. No specific program for children with autism at present)	No specified maximum; YT and NT overall budget is $460,000 for direct interventions and $79,000 to Autism Yukon

Source: Autism Canada, 2017.

SPOTLIGHTS ACROSS CANADA

Research: Manitoba

In many areas of Canada, healthcare, social services, and education are responding to increasing numbers of children diagnosed with ASD (Ouellette-Kuntz et al., 2014). Between 2010 and 2014, 3,079 Manitobian children aged 0 to 14 had an ASD diagnosis, yet:

> At present, there is little information regarding the extent of treatment of core symptoms for children with ASD in Manitoba, or the additional mental disorders that they may experience. However, anecdotal evidence suggests that many children in Manitoba must wait to access the services and treatments that may help them to achieve their full potential. (Ouellette-Kuntz et al., 2014, p. 1)

In Manitoba, ABA-based EIBI is available to children throughout three years of preschool as well as three years of transition-to-school support; however, a lack of skilled providers and accessibility issues result in the program being expensive and difficult to implement. Children diagnosed with ASD usually receive special education funding and qualify for behaviour programming. Children with ASD, in this study, were more likely to be diagnosed with other psychiatric conditions (e.g., anxiety disorders) and were more likely to be taking psychotropic medications related to a complex set of variables.

> **psychiatric disorder**: also called mental illness, a health condition involving "changes in emotion, thinking or behaviour" (or a combination) that affect functioning in social, familial, and school activities, and relationships (APA, 2018, para. 1).

Initiative: Saskatchewan

Saskatchewan's Early Childhood Intervention Program (ECIP) is funded by the Government of Saskatchewan, Ministry of Education. ECIP provides in-home support services to families with children aged zero to six years experiencing a developmental delay or at risk to develop a delay, including those with ASD.

Saskatchewan Early Childhood Intervention Program, Ministry of Education

Merla Parker, Early Childhood Intervention Program Consultant

The program is intended to support families by utilizing a strength-based approach to promote and build family capacity to parent children who experience developmental delays, bridge children and families to existing services and therapies within their communities, and assist with the transition to social and learning centres like childcare and school settings.

While Saskatchewan supports a program of early intensive behaviour intervention (EIBI) for young children who are diagnosed with ASD, the nature of that service places the majority of the focus on the individual child. Families and caregivers are involved and are encouraged to take an active role in the child's intervention program; however, direct and intensive interventions to build important skills and reduce challenging and interfering behaviours for children with ASD are delivered directly to the child. The Early Childhood Intervention Program (ECIP) takes a slightly different focus, supporting the family as a whole, providing a complementary service to families and bridging a gap in family support in the services currently available to children with ASD and their families.

The primary strengths of ECIP lie in the emphasis placed on the needs and priorities of the family as a whole. Parental input is sought out and welcomed, and parents are considered integral and equal partners. Early Childhood Intervention Program consultants collaborate with parents and families to identify priorities for intervention or supports that are most important and meaningful to the family and then support the family to work toward the goals that have been identified. For example, a family may indicate that it would be meaningful for the whole family if the child could learn the skills necessary to eat at the table so they could enjoy family dinners together. Parents are encouraged and empowered to address the concerns that are most important to them and would make the most significant impact on the family's quality of life.

The Early Childhood Intervention Program currently has 14 regions across Saskatchewan from which families may access support and resources. Families may self-refer to avail of the program, or they may be referred by family physicians, public health representatives, preschool educators, or other helping professionals who may be involved with the child and family. The program staff who provide support to families represent a wide range of training, experience, and educational backgrounds. Professionals who serve in this role include teachers, social workers, and those trained in early childhood development, among others.

Saskatchewan's Early Childhood Intervention Program may also provide opportunities for collaboration with multidisciplinary partner professionals, such as occupational therapists, speech-language pathologists, and autism interventionists representing other departments and organizations that may also be involved in supporting the child and family. ECIP consultants coach parents and caregivers to carry out program plans developed by one or more of these partner professionals, in addition to supporting the family with other identified priorities. Although opportunities for common training, case planning, and program development between Early Childhood Intervention Program staff and other supporting professionals are limited, when these opportunities can be facilitated, the value of the resulting communication and teamwork in supporting children with ASD and their families is recognized by everyone involved.

Research: Alberta

Maternal Employment Disruption

Hodgetts, McConnell, Zwaigenbaum, and Nicholas (2014) published a two-phase, mixed-methodology study entitled *The Impact of Autism Services on Mothers' Occupational Balance and Participation*. They reviewed literature around maternal responsibilities in parenting children with ASD—incorporating occupational and leisure outcomes. One outcome of such literature noted that "mothers also spend a significant amount of time finding, accessing, and retaining services; coordinating services between sectors; advocating for their children; and driving their children to appointments" (p. 82). The authors extended this issue and took a unique look at how services themselves impacted material workforce and leisure pursuit, what the disruptive characteristics were around these services, as well as those related to children and families. Utilizing both adapted standardized surveys ($n = 139$) and semi-structured interviews ($n = 19$), the authors used quantitative (e.g., confirmatory factor analysis) and then qualitative (grounded theory-based; coding and thematizing) methods to explain the related experiences of mothers of children, adolescents, or young adults with ASD in Alberta. The researchers found that 78% of surveyed mothers shared that "the professional supports and services for their child impacted their employment above and beyond the lived experience of parenting a child with autism" (p. 87). More specifically:

> Half of the mothers chose their job to specifically meet their child's service needs, almost one-third of the mothers decreased work hours and/or stopped working because of their child's service needs, and almost one-fifth of the mothers moved their family to a new geographical location to access services. (p. 87)

Only 6 of 18 interviewees were able to work full-time and only 9 part-time, as labelled under *Occupational Imbalance & Sacrifice*. Twelve mothers cited service provision needs (e.g., appointments, advocacy, time, organization) as the reason they worked fewer (or no) hours. Two themes emerged related to workforce participation from these interviewees: the disruption of both employment and discretionary time ("Something Had to Go," pp. 87–88) and lost workforce opportunities ("Lost Opportunity," p. 88). The following example describes such an impact:

> For one mother, service needs were so intense that she sold her lucrative personal business, in which she took a lot of pleasure and pride, after close friends repeatedly expressed worries over her and her son's wellbeing: "[My friends] said, 'You're going to drop one day and you're going to be no good to you or your son.'"

School entry did not solve these employment disruptions due to ongoing appointments, programs, transportation, and the need to accomplish tasks during the school day in order to be available consistently in after-school and evening hours. One mother reflected: "there is no way that it could all jive if I worked outside the home, because that is my job, to keep it all rolling" (p. 88). The authors found that "current child resources [are] largely dependent on maternal implementation. This dependence on mothers' care despite the personal costs on mothers is a detriment of current care delivery models for many families" (p. 90). Recommendations included being attentive to the demands placed on the family unit around service provision, and its related demands (e.g., therapeutic homework); attending to continuity of services; and providing both policy and practices supporting maternal occupation balance, overall "to encourage services that directly and indirectly support, rather than burden, mothers of children with autism" (p. 91).

Source: Maich, Davies, & Sohrabi, 2019, pp. 123–125.

Funding: Ontario

One study of 354 Toronto-based preschool environments found that ASD was the most common diagnosis in enrolled children (Killoran et al., 2007). Yet parents report having difficulty finding childcare supports, perhaps due to rejection from a centre or centres, among other examples (Killoran et al., 2007). This type of difficulty with service provision might contribute to the finding that "many parents never get a break from their child as it is often extremely difficult to obtain suitable child care arrangements" (Factor, Perry, & Freeman, 1990, p. 139). One reason for this finding, however, is that families may have access to formal means of support, such as respite care (Factor et al., 1990) or licensed childcare for their children diagnosed with ASD. Issues of inclusion for students with special needs, including ASD, and issues of preparation for educators who will inevitably support students with ASD in either the childcare system or the school system—or both—have perhaps not yet caught up to the breadth and depth of change in recognizing early childhood educators as credentialled professionals. For example, one study found that up to 79% of centres perceived barriers: "the four greatest barriers were identified as physical, training, funding, and ratios" (Killoran et al., 2007, p. 91).

Although inclusion is a respected and desired element in childcare settings across Canada, Crowther (2010) describes its implementation as inconsistent, haphazard, and "lack[ing] appropriate guidelines, policies and proactive legislation that address ... the inclusion of children with special needs" (p. 40). Some centres are physically inaccessible (in one study, over 35% of centres in the region); some provide onsite clinical services for children with special needs, but others are associated only with off-site services for children with complex needs (Killoran et al., 2007). All provinces and territories, however, provide some level of funding eligibility for preschool-aged children when it comes to clinical service provision.

Initiative: Quebec

Setting an Example in Quebec: One Centre's Attempt to Raise Provincial Standards

Myra-Jade Lui, PhD, BCBA

In 2003, the Ministry of Health and Social Services of Quebec released its service offer for individuals with autism, *Un Geste Porteur d'Avenir* (*A Step Forward*). Since then, rehabilitation centres in the province have been tasked with offering children with autism a minimum of 20 weekly hours of intensive behavioural intervention until the age of 6. At that time, there were no board-certified behavior analysts in the province yet, and this mandate marked a time where behavioural professionals were in high demand both in the public and the private sector.

Fast-forward to 2012, almost a full decade from the launch of the service plan. Quebec researchers looked at how this mandate had been executed across the province and found vast differences across government-funded centres (Dionne, Paquet, Joly, & Rivard, 2011), reflecting the challenges associated with the execution of such a significant mandate.

It was during this time that the *Learning to Learn* program was created. Learning to Learn (LtL) is the CRDITED-Miriam IBI program offered to children under the age of six with a diagnosis of autism spectrum disorder. In 2010, it became the province's first government-funded, centre-based IBI program with an onsite BCBA. In 2018, this is still the case, with most government centres opting for less expensive community-based programs or non-intensive versions of centre-based programs. The commitment made to quality over quantity is a characteristic of the CRDITED-Miriam, and the LtL site has enabled students from different educational programs to complete much needed internships that will prepare them for the complex but rewarding work in autism intervention.

The interventions at LtL are developed by the clinical supervisor (BCBA) and clinical specialists and implemented by instructors who hold the official title of rehabilitation assistants. In Quebec, the role of an ABA/IBI instructor is not yet recognized under the ministry, and therefore these rehabilitation assistants are trained to carry out the responsibilities of applied behaviour analysis (ABA) therapists/instructors. At capacity, the program offers 20 hours of therapy to 15 children every week, with a clinical staff that includes 9 instructors (rehabilitation assistants), the clinical supervisor, and clinical specialists/senior therapist. With the 2017 provincial increases to autism services, the CRDITED-Miriam is working on growing the program to offer 23 children this service, staffed by 13 rehabilitation assistants and two clinical specialists.

Training takes place at the centre after an assessment is done to determine the instructors' baseline levels of theoretical knowledge. Training usually lasts anywhere from 30–90 hours, depending on the individual (and their assessment results), and the same assessment is done after the theoretical training component is completed. Training involves didactic teaching (theory), systematic observation (finding examples of the concepts learned during theoretical training), and hands-on application (being supported by other staff members) done in rotations until instructors demonstrate competence in all necessary skills. Clinical evaluations are done after six months of service and then on an as-needed basis.

As a centre-based program, there is virtually constant, onsite clinical supervision at LtL. In addition to the typical observation of instructors and clients that occurs on a daily basis, there are a number of measures that ensure that clinical supervision is done systematically. These measures include the use of fidelity checklists for complex interventions or for interventions that have not produced the desired behaviour change in a timely manner, as well as feedback notebooks for the staff. These notebooks contain both positive and corrective feedback for staff members when they are observed by a supervising staff member, as well as a section that allows the staff member to state how the supervising team can best help them achieve the aims listed in the corrective feedback section.

As behavior analyst board certification (BCBA/BCaBA) becomes a better-known qualification in Quebec, LtL has welcomed an increasing number of candidates who wish to complete their supervised experience in the centre. These supervised hours are offered to the candidates if they are full-time rehabilitation assistants in the LtL program, and as of 2017, the CRDITED-Miriam achieved status as the first approved site in Quebec for the hybrid master's program in applied behaviour analysis at the Florida Institute of Technology.

Initiative: Ontario

Although there is often no course of training specific to ASD for childcare centres, educators can take advantage of centre-based, community-based, local, provincial, national, and international opportunities for professional development. According to Crowther (2010), "one of the components of high-quality care is the amount of education and training early childhood educators receive" (p. 40). This education and training can take many forms, initiated either by individuals looking for additional learning opportunities or agencies offering training. One opportunity is an optional, ongoing initiative called Raising the Bar, designed to ensure that registered early childhood educators (RECEs) in Ontario (Ontario College of Early Childhood Educators, n.d.) receive additional training to promote standards in best practice (e.g., Affiliated Services for Children and Youth, 2020). This may come in the form of arrangements made by a single childcare centre to provide training to meet the needs of individual or small groups of RECEs;

a series of workshops presented collaboratively onsite (i.e., clinical and educational collaboration); or taking advantage of advertised courses (e.g., Toronto's Geneva Centre's training and certificate programs), conferences (e.g., Early Childhood Resource Teacher Network of Ontario), opportunities developed by professional agencies such as online webinars, or post-secondary programs (e.g., Autism and Behaviour Science Ontario Colleges graduate certificate). Allen and colleagues (2015) suggest that childcare centres supporting children with ASD should seek out training in "successful early intervention programs" (p. 213), such as ABA, DTT, pivotal response training (PRT), and incidental teaching. In addition, they should have the skills to build in structured routines, individualized programs, and validated instructional strategies.

Childcare centres also consider and plan for transitions to school-based services, a transition that is both stressful and apprehension-filled, yet also rife with potential opportunities (Atlantic Provinces Special Education Authority [APSEA], 2015): "as children make the transition from the family home, daycare, or preschool into school, they move into an environment of increased academic demands and more complex social situations, and their role expands to being a student" (p. 1). It is important for parents, families, and schools to

Table 6.2: Transition to School Timeline for Young Children with ASD

Timeframe	Activities
From 12 months to 6 months prior to school entry	• Provide families with as much information as possible about the transition process in general, including, o What to expect at each step in the process; o How individual transition meetings are arranged; o When individual transition meetings will take place; o How educational programs for children with ASD are developed and carried out in an inclusive school setting; o Supports available at school, board/district, department; o How families can prepare for the transition meeting. • Begin transition discussions, when possible and appropriate, between family, preschool service providers, and school team. • Be sure to obtain all necessary consents to share information. • Identify a transition contact person, and develop a transition timeline with benchmarks.

Timeframe	Activities
From 6 months prior to school entry to the beginning of school	• Invite the preschool providers to visit the child's prospective classroom at the new school and arrange for school personnel to visit the preschool/daycare, or observe via videotaped samples. • Arrange opportunities for the child and family to visit the new school; meet the new teacher and other staff; visit the playground, gym, and cafeteria; practice riding the bus, etc. • Organize transition meeting(s) for family, preschool service providers, and school team to identify the child's learning needs with respect to the curriculum; discuss any medical, behavioural, or communication concerns; determine any instructional supports, accommodations, and/or adaptations that may be required, and whether or not an individualized plan may be necessary to address the student's needs. • Discuss the strengths, challenges, and interests of the child in relation to educational program options and supports. • Determine any staff supports that may be required and plan for any necessary staff training. • Discuss referrals for services from professionals such as the board/district autism consultant as well as speech-language pathologist, occupational therapist, or physiotherapist who serve school-aged children where appropriate. • Identify and address any adjustments to the school and/or classroom environment that may be required to support the child's physical or developmental needs. • Develop a preliminary version of the child's schedule to ensure that everybody knows what to expect, that all necessary supports have been considered, and that the child is as prepared as possible for the new school and new routines.
Following school entry	• Create a plan for the method and frequency of ongoing communication with the family. • Discuss with families the possibility of peer sensitivity sessions for classmates to increase awareness and suggest friendship strategies. • Schedule review meetings to monitor progress and make any necessary adjustments to the student's program, schedule, or supports.

Source: Atlantic Provinces Special Education Authority (APSEA), 2015, p. 6.

plan proactively and communicate with sensitivity, understanding, and knowledge. Parents can also collaborate with both childcare and schools around varied transitional activities in each timeframe (see Table 6.2), from one year prior to school entry to school entry itself.

Read about It. Think about It. Write about It.

- Investigate a course or offering in your region for early childhood educators to gain additional knowledge to work with children with ASD. What did you discover?

Funding: New Brunswick

Children diagnosed with ASD prior to school entry in New Brunswick are eligible to receive 20 hours per week of EIBI. This service has been available to children with ASD and their families in New Brunswick since 2003; however, in 2016 the Department of Education and Early Childhood Development revised and updated the Autism Program Standards to ensure that the services and interventions provided to all children with ASD were equal and of the same quality. The Autism Program Standards clearly define the roles and responsibilities of the agency directors, clinical supervisors, and interventionists who provide EIBI services and specify that all interventions must be based on the best available research evidence. The standards emphasize that "each child will receive individualized instruction through programmed learning opportunities that will produce measurable and meaningful change and lessen their developmental delays while achieving pre-determined intervention goals" (p. 5). Families and professionals are provided with information about eligibility for EIBI services, guidelines regarding where the intervention may take place, details of the training required for staff providing the service, and suggestions for effective communication among families and agency teams collaborating to support preschool children with ASD (New Brunswick Department of Education and Early Childhood Development, 2016).

A LOOK BACK

Chapter 6, "The Early Years," focused on:

- Red flags and screening tools to help identify characteristic of children with ASD in the early years that may lead to further support and a diagnosis.
- An examination of supports for young children with ASD, including inclusion and support from childcare and intensive therapies.
- An overview of jurisdictional programs and highlights for supporting children with ASD in the early years.

ADDITIONAL RESOURCES

Affiliated Services for Children and Youth

https://ascy.ca/

Affiliated Services for Children and Youth is an integrated service provider in Hamilton, Ontario. This website includes resources relevant for parents and professionals on strategies to promote early communication, screening for hearing impairments, as well as resources for blind-low vision.

Early Autism Study

http://www.earlyautismstudy.org

A useful website for parents, educators, and practitioners providing detailed information on the Early Autism Study. Researchers from McMaster University in Hamilton, Ontario, aim to develop a screening tool for young children at risk for autism.

100-Day Tool Kit for Families of Newly Diagnosed Young Children: Autism Speaks Canada

https://www.autismspeaks.ca/science-services-resources/resources/tool-kits/100-day-tool-kit1/

From this website, individuals can request a copy of the 100-Day Kit. This is a comprehensive document with suggestions for parents on what steps to take during the first 100 days after receiving a diagnosis of ASD. Information included within this document is useful for early educators and service providers.

Provincial and Territorial Funding Programs for Autism Therapy

https://autismcanada.org/wp-content/uploads/2017/12/AC_ProgramsForAutismTherapy.pdf

This weblink provides a thorough breakdown of funding for ASD programs and therapy across provinces and territories.

Signs and Symptoms of Autism Spectrum Disorder (ASD): Government of Canada

https://www.canada.ca/en/public-health/services/diseases/autism-spectrum-disorder-asd/signs-symptoms-autism-spectrum-disorder-asd.html

This government website includes a comprehensive list of the early signs and symptoms of ASD, as well as a description of the assessment process. This is a useful resource for early educators, childcare personnel, and parents.

Early Signs: Autism Canada

https://autismcanada.org/wp-content/uploads/2015/11/AC_IsThisYourChild_2015.pdf

This PDF provides a succinct definition of ASD, a list of early warning signs, and a description of commonly implemented treatments and therapies. This would be a useful resource for childcare centres.

"A Qualitative Study of Autism Policy in Canada: Seeking Consensus on Children's Services"

https://childhealthpolicy.ca/wp-content/uploads/2015/06/Shepherd-Waddell-2015.pdf

This article provides parent, researcher, and policymaker insight on autism policy in Canada. This is an informative read for parents, educators, researchers, and clinicians interested in the complex nature of developing national approaches to ASD intervention.

Autism Spectrum Disorder among Children and Youth in Canada 2018

https://www.canada.ca/en/public-health/services/publications/diseases-conditions/autism-spectrum-disorder-children-youth-canada-2018.html

This 2018 report, "made in Canada," is the first national reporting of ASD prevalence rates in Canada. This comprehensive document provides provincial and territorial data as of 2015.

Autism in Education: An Atlantic Partnership

https://autismineducation.ca/

Autism in Education: An Atlantic Partnership is an interprovincial partnership that focuses on professional development, resource sharing, and training in Atlantic Canada. This website links to educational webinars, online tutorials, and comprehensive information papers on a range of ASD-related topics. This is a useful website for students, educators, parents, and clinicians.

M-CHAT-R/F

https://mchatscreen.com/ (Questionnaire)
https://mchatscreen.com/mchat-rf/scoring/ (Scoring)
https://mchatscreen.com/mchat-rf/ (Follow-up questionnaire for decision-making)

The M-CHAT-R/F is a 20-question two-stage parental-report screening instrument that is easy to score and available for free download. It is recommended for clinical practice, research, and educational purposes. The instrument is designed to screen toddlers ages 16 months to 30 months for symptoms of autism spectrum disorders. Any child with a positive score (medium-risk or high-risk range) is recommended for follow-up assessment.

"Quick and Easy Adaptations and Accommodations for Early Childhood Students"

https://files.eric.ed.gov/fulltext/EJ967485.pdf

This document provides a detailed rationale on the benefits of accommodating and adapting instructional material for young children with autism, behavioural disorders, or learning disabilities. Colourful pictures of modified tasks are included.

Talking to Parents about Autism Training Video

https://www.autismspeaks.ca/science-services-resources/resources/tool-kits/talking-to-parents-about-autism-kit/

This website provides information to early childhood educators on how best to initiate discussions with caregivers regarding a child's atypical development. A succinct one-page handout on developmental milestones is provided to assist with the discussion.

The State of Early Childhood Education and Care in Canada 2012

www.childcarecanada.org/sites/default/files/StateofECEC2012.pdf

This document, by the Moving Child Care Forward project, provides an overview of early childhood education and care across Canada as of 2012. This is a well-researched document intended to inform policy and highlight childcare challenges across Canada.

The SpeciaLink Early Childhood Inclusion Tool (The National Centre for Child Care Inclusion)

www.specialinkcanada.org/about/rating%20scales.html

SpeciaLink is a virtual resource committed to improving inclusion opportunities in education, recreation, and community. This website includes a wealth of information related to best practice for inclusive learning environments.

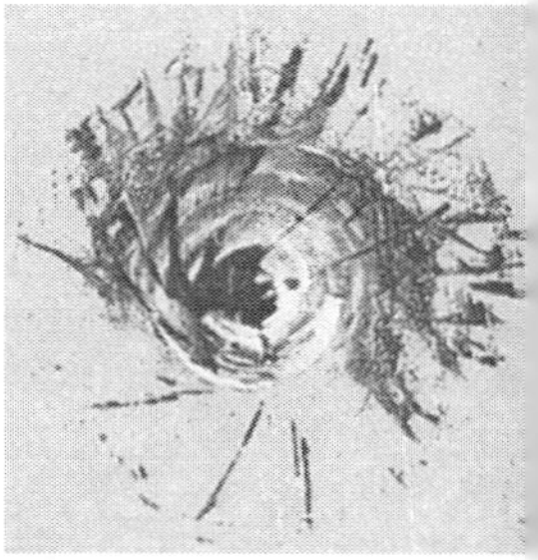

CHAPTER 7
The School Years

LEARNING OBJECTIVES

- Review different educational options for children and youth with ASD from inclusive settings to separate schools, with different options that combine various approaches.
- Distinguish between accommodations, modifications, and individualized courses to support children and youth with ASD with the individual education plan.
- Increase familiarity with some funding options for special education services.
- Highlight different experiences, programs, and structures to support children with ASD across Canada.

Students with autism spectrum disorder (ASD), their parents, and their educators have a range of options, practices, and services available in their jurisdictions, school boards, and schools, from fully inclusive settings in all jurisdictions to special, alternate settings in some. Such supports include the development of individual education plans (IEPs) with their processes and intricacies, and varied models of school-based services across the country. In this chapter, these topics—and more—are introduced using feature boxes and spotlights on Canadian regions to highlight unique contexts in meeting the educational needs of students with ASD.

INCLUSIVE PRACTICES IN CANADIAN SCHOOLS

In Canada, about half of the children diagnosed with ASD are formally diagnosed before or around the typical entrance into formal public schooling (56% by age 6), with almost 75% diagnosed by the age of 8, well within the school years (Philpott, Young, Maich, Penney, & Butler, 2019; Public Health Agency of Canada, 2018c). In recent decades, Canadian schools—some with a longer history than others—typically have moved toward inclusion (rather than segregation) in neighbourhood communities with same-aged peers for all students, including those with ASD (Ryan, 2009). Using proactive, flexible approaches such as universal design and differentiated instruction, inclusion means that the "classroom teacher [is] taking ownership of all students" (Bennett, 2009, p. 2). The number of students with ASD in school settings can be significant, depending on province, territory, school board, school, and classroom. In the clinical setting, a child, adolescent, or adult would typically encounter a lengthy, multidisciplinary, team-based process consisting of observation and formal assessment leading, potentially, to a diagnosis. A written outcome of this evaluation and any resulting diagnoses, including ASD, in a school-aged child is typically provided by a clinician, such as a psychologist, or a medical practitioner, such as a developmental pediatrician or a child psychiatrist. All these processes help students access services and allow most systems to then prioritize access to services. Categorical models do not necessarily mirror clinical language but retain similar features. However, not every jurisdiction categorizes exceptionalities following a clinical diagnosis of ASD. Canadian provinces and territories range from those where students must be categorized in the school system to obtain special education services (e.g., Newfoundland and Labrador) to those areas that meet needs without such additional steps (e.g., Nunavut; Maich, Hill, & Somma, 2018). The Canadian education system also includes federal funding for the Indigenous population in Canada (Maich & Sider, 2019b).

> To provide a distinctly Canadian perspective on special education in secondary schools, it is important to consider Canada's Indigenous population, those who originally inhabited the country. There are about 1.7 million Indigenous peoples in Canada of a total 2016 population of thirty-six million (Statistics Canada, 2017). About 44% of Indigenous peoples in Canada who have registered or treaty status live on reserves while the balance lives off-reserve (Statistics Canada, 2017). Students on reserve attend schools under federal governmental direction, unusual within Canada's typical provincial/territorial responsibility for education (see Normore, 2015). This arrangement is challenging, with approximately 30% lower funding for these schools—including students with SEN [special education needs] (Porter, 2016)—creating limited services for Indigenous students (e.g., educational assessments). High absentee rates, teacher recruitment, low literacy rates, and high drop-out rates further exacerbate the challenges faced by those students who have SEN (Normore, 2015).

Like the range of educational placements across the country from segregated to inclusive settings, students with ASD can be diagnosed *only* with ASD, but other students can be quite complex with multiple diagnoses and/or identifications. Penney (2013), for example, carried out a qualitative study of ASD and co-occurring anxiety and/or depression on a group of individuals from the age of 16 to 21 years in Newfoundland and Labrador. This study discovered that students with ASD, particularly ones with poor communication skills, remained underdiagnosed. In such cases, students have diverse education needs and possess distinct behavioural, cognitive, and communication capacities, which are usually overshadowed under an ASD umbrella. These students typically require individually designed educational plans to fulfil their academic and social needs, and careful planning and specialized training for teachers are required, as their awareness of ASD plays a fundamental role in student success. The study also emphasized the need for a vigilant program to support students diagnosed with ASD from potential future victimization and vulnerability to other related mental health issues. Many jurisdictions in Canada have developed manuals around supporting students with ASD and have included information about educating students with ASD in jurisdictional publications, policies, and processes developed around supporting students with exceptionalities. Some are specific to students with ASD—and others have broad emphases. Table 7.1 highlights jurisdictional teaching manuals and the subsequent examples depict some of these support documents.

Table 7.1: Teaching Manuals for (or Related to) Teaching Students with ASD

Jurisdiction	Title	Website
AB	*Teaching Students with Autism Spectrum Disorders* (2003)	https://education.alberta.ca/media/385138/teaching-students-with-asd-2003.pdf
BC	*Teaching Students with Autism: A Resource Guide for Schools* (2000)	http://www.bced.gov.bc.ca/specialed/docs/autism.pdf
	Parent Guide to Autism Spectrum Disorders (2017)	https://www2.gov.bc.ca/assets/gov/health/managing-your-health/autism/autism_handbook_parents_guide.pdf
MB	*Supporting Inclusive Schools: A Handbook for Developing and Implementing Programming for Students with Autism Spectrum Disorder* (2005)	https://www.edu.gov.mb.ca/k12/specedu/aut/pdf/ASD_Document.pdf
NB	*Strengthening Inclusion, Strengthening Schools. Report of the Review of Inclusive Education Programs and Practices in New Brunswick Schools* (2012)	http://www2.gnb.ca/content/dam/gnb/Departments/ed/pdf/K12/Inclusion/Inclusion.pdf
NL	*Programming for Individual Needs: Teaching Students with Autism Spectrum Disorders* (2003)	http://www.ed.gov.nl.ca/edu/k12/studentsupportservices/publications/TeachingStudentsAutism.pdf

(continued)

Table 7.1: *Continued*

Jurisdiction	Title	Website
NS	*Developing and Implementing Programming for Students with Autism Spectrum Disorder* (2012)	https://studentservices.ednet.ns.ca/sites/default/files/Developing%20and%20Implementing%20Programming%20for%20Students%20with%20ASD.pdf
NT	*NWT Ministerial Directive on Inclusive Schooling: Guidelines for Inclusive Schooling* (2016)	https://www.ece.gov.nt.ca/sites/www.ece.gov.nt.ca/files/resources/inclusiveschoolingmanualandguidelines-educatorversion-english.pdf
NU	*Reaching and Teaching All Students—A Model to Guide the Practice of Inclusive Education in Nunavut. Final Report of the External Review of Inclusive Education* (2015)	http://assembly.nu.ca/library/GNedocs/2015/002137-e.pdf
ON	*Effective Educational Practices for Students with Autism Spectrum Disorders* (2007)	http://www.edu.gov.on.ca/eng/general/elemsec/speced/autismSpecDis.pdf
PE	*Recommendations toward a Prince Edward Island Autism Action Plan: Another Piece of the Puzzle* (2009)	http://www.gov.pe.ca/photos/original/edu_autismplan1.pdf
QC	*Special Education: Issues of Inclusion and Integration in the Classroom* (2006)	http://www.education.gouv.qc.ca/fileadmin/site_web/documents/autres/organismes/CELA_avis-adaptation-scolaire_a.pdf
SK	*Teaching Students with Autism* (1999)	http://www.publications.gov.sk.ca/details.cfm?p=33260
YT	*Student Support Services Parent Handbook* (2015)	http://www.education.gov.yk.ca/pdf/schools/Parent_Handbook_2015.pdf

Source: Authors.

Manitoba has a handbook entitled *Supporting Inclusive Schools: A Handbook for Developing and Implementing Programming for Students with ASD* (Manitoba Education, Citizenship & Youth, 2005), providing an overview of supporting students with ASD in the school setting, including the steps to IEP development. In Manitoba, all students, including those with ASD, have a right to appropriate educational programming. Since ASD is a spectrum disorder, its symptoms and their severity range from mildly to severely disabling; as a result, programming for students with ASD may range from the provincial curricula to highly individualized programming. The Manitoba handbook states that students with ASD share similar symptoms of the disorder but display them in different manners, hence the need for tailored IEPs that are developed by a team, which includes specialists, teachers, administrators, parents, and perhaps the student with ASD. The IEP team needs to fully understand the difference in the needs of students with ASD in comparison with those of other students so that they can effectively design and implement an IEP. Students with ASD need structured routines; therefore, the team should first create a student profile by gathering information, sharing the data with the team and then using that data to create the student profile that includes the IEP. According to the manual, the team would then identify a case manager who in turn works with both the in-school team, which includes parents, school staff and students, and the supporting team of professionals. The next step would require the team to then focus on the direction of programming, planning, and designing specific outcomes for students with ASD. At the classroom level, teachers must put the IEP in action by first understanding the characteristics of students with ASD, such as strengths and needs, motivations and interests, structure, routine, predictability, and responsiveness to visual supports.

Another example is Saskatchewan's *Teaching Students with Autism: A Guide for Educators* (1999), which suggests 22 strategies for effective instructional approach and classroom management, 15 general strategies for communication development, and 10 guidelines and strategies for social skills training. Such suggestions are intended to be adjusted based on the specific and unique needs of each student, while targeting learning goals within individualized personal program plans.

Nova Scotia's *Developing and Implementing Programming for Students with Autism Spectrum Disorder* (Nova Scotia Department of Education, 2012) is another example of a provincial manual for students with ASD, developed to support program planning teams working with learners with ASD in Nova Scotia public schools. The resource guide provides an introduction to ASD and its associated characteristics and highlights research-supported strategies

universal design for learning (UDL): "a set of principles for curriculum development that give all individuals equal opportunities to learn. UDL provides a blueprint for creating instructional goals, methods, materials, and assessments that work for everyone—not a single, one-size-fits-all solution but rather flexible approaches that can be customized and adjusted for individual needs" (Center for Applied Special Technology, 2013, para. 1).

Table 7.2: Provincial and Territorial Education Acts and Related Special Education Services

Jurisdiction	Legislation and Policies
AB	*Education Act* (2012) Special Education Standards
BC	*School Act* (2006) Special Education Services
MB	*The Public Schools Act* (2017)
NB	*Education Act* (1997), S12.2 Student Services
NL	*Schools Act* (1997) Student Support Services
NS	*Education Act* (1995) Special Education Policy
NT	*Education Act* (1995) Ministerial Direction on Inclusive Schooling
NU	*Education Act* (2008) Consolidation of Inclusive Education Regulations (2011)
ON	*Education Act* (1990) Special Education Overview
PE	*Education Act* (2016) Special Education Needs
QC	*Education Act* (1988)
SK	*Education Act* (1995) Special Education
YT	*Education Act* (2002) Support for Students

Source: Authors.

for helping students with ASD develop important skills and reduce challenging and interfering behaviours. It also includes a comprehensive overview of best practices for developing and implementing educational programming for students with ASD based on individual strengths and needs, and it outlines a process for supporting individuals with ASD with transitions into school, from grade to grade and school to school, as well as from secondary school to community or post-secondary options.

> **differentiated instruction**: a method of individualized instruction to meet each student's needs (e.g., skill development). It can be described as a common-sense, flexible way of teaching diverse groups of students (Tomlinson, 1999, 2000).

In some jurisdictions, as noted, information on students with ASD is subsumed in other, related documents with wider emphases on inclusive or special education. Nunavut, for example, uses *Reaching and Teaching All Students—A Model to Guide the Practice of Inclusive Education in Nunavut* (Hall, 2015). Throughout this report, ASD is referenced in terms of examples of a "student-specific need" (p. 23) or "condition" (p. 3) related to funding, support services, multidisciplinary teams, legislation (e.g., education acts), assessments, and more.

It can be argued quite easily that physical and social inclusion are not yet wholly smoothly running, fully supported methods of instruction—or ways of being—in every and all schools across the country. Killoren and colleagues (2013) emphasize a not-yet-accomplished reality of one fully inclusive system:

> The reality is we have two clearly delineated streams, general and special education ... teachers are often constrained by legislation, terminology and board practices that do not fully embrace the shift towards a reconceptualization of schooling that supports inclusive learning environments for all children. Until legislation changes we must work within a system that has enough room for adaptations, yet few explicit requirements for accountability regarding inclusion. (p. 242)

Alternatives to inclusive settings remain in many jurisdictions, though major initiatives are also underway to emphasize fully inclusive environments for all students—including those with ASD.

Inclusion for Students with ASD

Dr. Sheila Bennett, Faculty of Education, Brock University

Inclusion for students with ASD is an ever-changing and somewhat idiosyncratic landscape. Advances have been made on educational approaches to working with students with ASD, and advocacy across many fronts is clearly evident. While not an absolute rule, in general, service delivery approaches that rely on a more clinically based model, associated with what would have been considered a *medical model* approach (see Chapter 9) focused on fixing, tend to choose a more segregationist route. In contrast, those educational settings that blend clinical and educational approaches within a *social model*, focused on examining the environment and collaboratively adjusting all the participants to create a space in which students with ASD can engage successfully, choose a more inclusive model of service delivery. It is worth aspiring to a rights-based model of schooling that assumes that each student has a place in a classroom, in a school, and in a community and demands that environments are created with accessible curriculum for everyone. We have believed for too long that special services require special places. Denying access for students with ASD to the larger school community as equals and denying access for students in the regular class to develop meaningful relationships with a more diverse population is equally devastating on both sides. A well-developed curriculum, best practices in clinical approaches, supports where necessary, and a robust educational experience is the right of every student. This can only be accomplished when we insist on excellence for all students, including those with ASD, in an inclusive setting. Access to friendships, the larger community, and the building of social capital does not need to be the price paid for services supposedly rendered.

> **inclusion**: school-based inclusion can be defined as children with disabilities "being educated alongside their typically developing peers" (Boer, Pijl, Minnaert, & Post, 2014, p. 572), where students with disabilities have access to participate in all aspects of their school community.

Read about It. Think about It. Write about It.

- Reflect on your experience or lack of experience being included with children with disabilities and ASD throughout your school career. How does that differ from inclusion in the school system or systems currently in your region?

ALTERNATE SETTINGS

Although inclusion is the standard setting for students—including students with ASD—in many of our public school systems, some self-contained or alternative settings persist. These settings focus on the needs of students with ASD in environments with low teacher-to-student ratios. They may be educationally focused, clinically focused, take place in in-patient hospital settings, or even private, for-pay environments supported by a range of sources, including parent-paid tuition. Alternate settings may serve as collaborative facilities to congregate students with ASD, when students struggle with maintaining placement in inclusive school environments and need a more goal-oriented treatment approach. Some alternate models offer greater flexibility in combining academic teaching with onsite, clinical supports in a school-type environment. Such schools may combine academic instruction with a more clinical or intense approach (e.g., applied behaviour analysis) and have multidisciplinary educators and clinicians on staff. W. Ross Macdonald school is a segregated, specialized setting where students with visual impairments live onsite during the school week, including a group of students who are also diagnosed with ASD.

W. Ross Macdonald School

Jennifer McMillan

Figure 7.1: Jennifer McMillan
Source: Barb Rogelstad.

Jennifer McMillan, Ontario certified teacher at W. Ross Macdonald School in Brantford, first began her teaching career supporting students who were both deaf and blind, moving on to teaching students who were blind or visually impaired in a setting unique in Canada. Along the way, she noticed a great quantity of students with multiple and complex needs in her school environment, including students with autism spectrum disorder in addition to their sensory impairments. To support her own professional learning, and with encouragement from her school leadership, she signed up for what was—at the time—a brand-new additional qualifications (AQ) course focused on supporting students with ASD. Here is an excerpt from one of the papers she wrote:

> The majority of programs that are intended for children who fall within the diagnosis of Autism Spectrum depend heavily on visual support mechanisms. This presents several major challenges when teaching a student who is diagnosed with both Autism Spectrum Disorder (ASD), as well as a Visual Impairment (VI). A number of strategies need to be implemented in order to effectively teach students with Autism Spectrum Disorder. When another diagnosis besides Autism is present, such as a Visual Impairment, it is imperative to adapt using strategies suggested within both fields. It is also very important to recognize that each student is unique and there is no standard method that is guaranteed to yield success with every child ... although development in children with Autism Spectrum

Disorder and Visual Impairment presents many obstacles, hope exists that by implementing adapted strategies and effective education practices, students will be enabled to achieve to their highest potential. It is important to have an understanding of both disabilities and their implications on the student and ability to learn.

With this professional learning in hand, she was assigned to a small classroom of students diagnosed with both ASD and serious vision issues and taught this class for five years. As far as Jennifer knows, although it was not officially labelled as such, it was the only one of its kind in the province. Perhaps unsurprisingly, she found very little research on the topic.

ASD and VI: students with both ASD and visual impairment (VI) also include those with "low vision (i.e., visual acuity of 20/70 to 20/200 in the better eye with correction) and those who are legally blind (i.e., acuity below 20/200 or visual field is restricted to no more than 20 degrees in the better eye with correction)" (Li, 2009, p. 22).

To prepare for her students, she read books and consulted with resource and board-level specialists through the ministry's Provincial Schools Branch and the Autism Spectrum Disorder School Support Program consultants from McMaster Children's Hospital—all of whom were a "huge support"—and found that her background areas of specialization were a significant help. For example, she found that concrete, tactile materials like a calendar, a first-then board, and a daily schedule, all made with small objects that students could touch, were very helpful.

Day to day, Jennifer reported, "I tried to stay as close to routine as I could." Her class took advantage of in-school educational and multidisciplinary services like the indoor sensory-based swimming pool, music class, rhythm band, music therapy, and physiotherapy. Jennifer also utilized the physio room every morning, both to meet the proprioceptive needs of students (e.g., riding bikes, treadmill, swings, large balls) and to provide a large indoor activity that allowed for whole-body movement and exploration. "This kept the rest of the day in focus and allowed them to concentrate on academic tasks," she noted. For academic tasks and skills building, she used a structured teaching classroom approach and task boxes created using resources like *Tasks Galore* (Fennell, Hearsey, & Eckenrode, 2013) and *How Do I Teach This Kid? Visual Work Tasks for Beginning Learners on the Autism Spectrum* (Henry, 2005), in addition to support of an educational assistant, working individually with students in 5- to 15-minute intervals.

Jennifer describes one of the challenges of teaching such a unique group of individuals as the lack of research and programs available, which encouraged her to "be very creative in my teaching and think outside the box a lot," making dollar stores one of her go-to resources. One of the innovations Jennifer used was a unique program

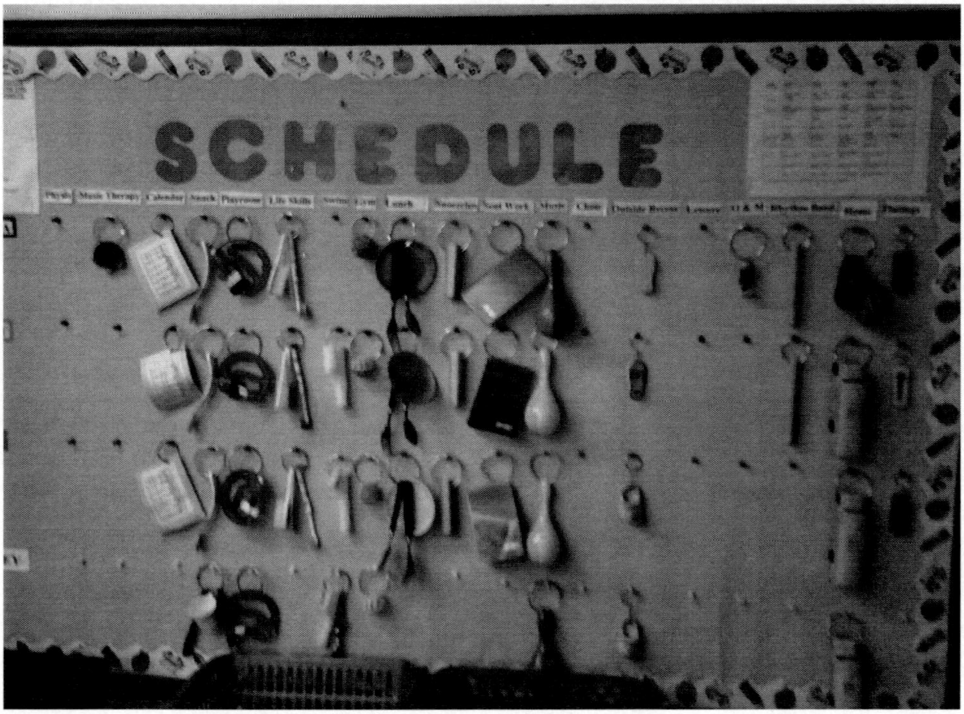

Figure 7.2: Tactile Calendar
Source: Jennifer McMillan.

that links together music keys on the piano with letters of the alphabet for teaching written language to musically strong students. One of the many benefits that Jennifer emphasized is that "my students taught me patience, how to be creative, and reinforced the concept that every student can learn. It might take a full year to reach a particular goal, but when they reach that—no matter how big or how small—they can do it. One small thing is still worth doing."

It is important to keep in mind that not every province and territory in Canada has equal access to such services—including alternate school placements and their supports—nor does every area in each jurisdiction. Nor do they necessarily value such settings. School-aged children can often continue to obtain funding for therapy, but this funding is also inconsistent depending on the province or territory where children and their families reside.

Even with funding in place, obtaining support for students with ASD in areas such as rural, northern, and/or isolated settings can be a complex process, even within a school system.

Table 7.3: Funding for School-aged Children

Jurisdiction	Program	Ministry	Eligibility	Funding
AB	PDD (Persons with Developmental Disabilities)	Community and Social Services	IQ < 70—Severe impact on daily living skills in 6 of 24 defined areas; onset < 18 years old	Funds are allocated to agencies to pay for required staff supports based on individual need
BC	Autism Funding Ages 6–18	Children and Family Development	Children aged 6 to 18	$6,000 per year per child
MB	Special Needs Funding	Education	School-aged children	$9,500–$21,130 per year
NB	Family Supports for Children with Disabilities	Social Development	Age 18 or under with a severe, lifelong disability	Social work and financial resources based on individual need
NL	Autism Services: Grade 3 and Below	Health and Community Services	Children from 18 to 96 months (until age 8 or Grade 3)	The program funds 30 hours per week for 2 years
NS	Direct Family Support for Children	Community Services	Dependent child aged 19 or below (family is eligible)	Maximum of $2,200 per month
NT	Autism Program	Health and Social Services, Education, Culture and Employment, NWT Disabilities Council	Preschool and school-aged children	Information not available

Jurisdiction	Program	Ministry	Eligibility	Funding
NU	Services to Children with Disabilities	Health and Social Services; NGO funded by Health and Social Services	Children up to 19 (anyone affected by autism including families, educators, employers, etc. No specific program for children with autism at present)	No specified maximum; YT and NT overall budget is $460,000 for direct interventions and $79,000 to Autism Yukon
ON	Ontario Autism Program	Children and Youth Services	Age 17 or under	Funding per individual based on assessed need
PE	Autism Early Intervention Program—School-Aged Children	Education, Early Learning and Culture	School-aged children	$6,600 per school-aged child
QC	Autism Action Plan	Health and Social Services	Various programs for school-aged children	Information not available
SK	Cognitive Disabilities Strategy (CDS)	Health	Children up to age 22	Up to $1,200 per child per month under CDS; the "Learning" component provides between $6,300 and $12,610 per child per year

(continued)

Table 7.3: *Continued*

Jurisdiction	Program	Ministry	Eligibility	Funding
YT	Services to Children with Disabilities	Health and Social Services; NGO funded by Health and Social Services	Children up to 19 (anyone affected by autism including families, educators, employers, etc. No specific program for children with autism at present)	No specified maximum; YT and NT overall budget is $460,000 for direct interventions and $79,000 to Autism Yukon

Source: Autism Canada, 2017.

INDIVIDUAL EDUCATION PLANS

Individual plans for exceptional students—including those with ASD—are jurisdictionally controlled and are often known by the term individual education plans (IEPs), though the exact terminology for such documents moves and shifts across the country, with additional options in some jurisdictions for interdisciplinary plans versus school-based plans (see Table 7.4).

IEPs are typically thought of as both legal documents in school settings and working documents that are changed and updated as the needs and characteristics of students change during their time in the K–12 school system. Some fairly universal principles for IEP development do exist, such as developing individualized skills-based programs in areas of need or deficit such as communication, social, behaviour, sensory, adaptive, and academic domains, as well as communication logs and transition plans (Wilczynski, Menousek, Hunter, & Mudgal, 2007), yet each province, territory, board, and/or district may choose to utilize different templates and/or software programs to create such plans.

Nova Scotia is a province whose individual plans—called individual program plans or IPPs—have undergone recent, systemic change following a provincial review. Some students with ASD and diverse needs may require specific adaptations or adjustments to their educational program in order to address their individual learning needs. For students in Nova Scotia for whom this is the case, an IPP may be developed to address areas such as academic programming, social skills, life skills, or enrichment (Nova Scotia

Table 7.4: Individual Education Plans across Canada

Jurisdiction	Name	Subtypes
AB	Individualized Program Plan	A) Learning disabilities, mild cognitive disabilities, and/or working 1–3 years below grade level B) Moderate or severe cognitive disabilities requiring individual goals C) Gifted and require additional challenges
BC	Individual Education Plan	
MB	Individual Education Plan	
NB	Personalized Learning Plan	
NL	Individual Education Plan	
NS	Individual Program Plan	
NT	Individual Education Plan	
NU	Individual Student Support Plan	Outlined in the *Education Act*
ON	Individual Education Plan	
PE	Individual Education Plan	
QC	Individualized Education Plan	
SK	Inclusion and Intervention Plan	A) Classroom-based, school wide B) Targeted/group C) Intensive individual
YT	Individualized Education Plan	

Source: Authors.

Department of Education, 2016, p. 4). The IPP process is intended to be a collaborative decision-making and planning process involving a team that includes the student's parents/guardians, school administration and teachers, partner professionals, if applicable, and the student themself, to the extent that they are able to participate. In 2015, Nova Scotia's minister of education conducted a comprehensive providence-wide review of IPPs to determine "if students were being put on plans for the right reasons and at the right time in their learning" (Government of Nova Scotia, 2016, p. 1). Results of the review showed that, for 87% of students on IPPs, there was evidence to support the need for the development of the IPP, and for 82% of students, the IPP was developed at the appropriate time in learners' educational experiences. However, the review highlighted a number of questions and challenges, including the appropriateness of IPPs for a significant percentage of African Nova Scotian students and students of Indigenous heritage; inconsistent transition planning processes; and questions about the tools being used to monitor and report student progress. The review resulted in a number of recommendations for the Department of Education and Early Childhood Development, as well as specific recommendations for school boards to improve the IPP process and increase consistency and effectiveness across the province. One of the recommendations resulting from this review was to update Nova Scotia's *Program Planning Guide for Parents and Guardians* in order "to support students, parents/guardians and educators in enhancing their understanding and to help ensure meaningful parental involvement in the program planning process" (Government of Nova Scotia, 2016, p. 14). The guide outlines the purpose of the IPP planning team, clarifies team member roles and responsibilities, provides parents and guardians with a comprehensive step-by-step overview of the IPP process, and explains how to deal with problems or issues of concern that may arise during the process. Parents are also provided with sample documents that they may see during the IPP process, an information organizer to help them prepare and know what to expect at each stage of the process, and a list of additional resources that they may wish to consult for further information.

Few publicly accessible examples of Ontario-based IEPs exist, with the exception of those samples available on EduGains (2015). These sample IEPs include some that are specific to students with ASD and are offered in French and English. Features that appear to be used frequently to enhance the flexibility and individualization for students with ASD in educational planning are accommodations, modifications, and especially the development of alternate courses.

individual education plan (IEP): a legal, working document listing accommodations and modifications that incorporates recommendations from the committee who recommends the child. It includes expectations, programs, services to provide, strengths and needs, and goals. It is also known as the special education plan (SEP), individualized program plan (IPP), student support plan (SSP), for example, in different parts of the country (Centre for ADHD Awareness, Canada, 2017).

Accommodations

Accommodations are examples of differentiation in areas such as instruction, environment, and assessment, which may overlap with examples of strong pedagogy already in use by skilled teachers of inclusive classrooms. However, when documented in an IEP, it is typically assumed that students have an essential and intense need for these accommodations, such as scribing for assessments, compared with most students in the classroom. For students with ASD who do not need more complex supports such as modifications or alternate courses, classroom accommodations are the most important component of such individualized programming. When accommodations are recorded in an IEP, they are typically assumed relevant across all subject areas and the educational experience, unless otherwise indicated. An issue to consider is the quantity versus quality of accommodations. For example, is it better to inclusively list all the accommodations a student may need, or prioritize three to five esssential accommodations in each area that educators are more likely to retain, emphasize, and fulfill?

> **accommodations**: "supports or services that are not provided to the general student population but that are required by individual students with special needs to help them achieve learning expectations and demonstrate learning" (Ontario Ministry of Education, 2004, p. 6). These may be referred to by other similar terms, such as adaptations (Government of Nova Scotia, 2016).

Modifications

Typically, if students are unable to meet the standards of the provincial curriculum at grade level, courses can be modified, or, in the case of a student with ASD or other exceptionalities, changed. This decision is one that should be taken seriously by the student's school team, as changes to the provincial curriculum have multiple implications for high-school streaming, diploma completion, and post-secondary options. Is it better to achieve a *low* evaluation with a grade-level curriculum or to achieve a *high* evaluation on a modified curriculum? Curricula can also be modified for students who are gifted and have ASD, allowing them to study subjects above grade level, though not all jurisdictions, boards, or schools support such adaptations. The important tools in developing

> **modification**: "changes made in the age-appropriate grade-level expectations for a subject or course in order to meet a student's learning needs. These changes may involve developing expectations that reflect knowledge and skills required in the curriculum for a different grade level and/or increasing or decreasing the number and/or complexity of the regular grade-level curriculum expectations" (Ontario Ministry of Education, 2004, pp. 25–26).

Table 7.5: Understanding Special Education in the Context of Nova Scotia's Public School Program

Public School Programs (PSP) is a document outlining the goals, policies and framework of public education in Nova Scotia.

1. Learning Outcomes define what all students are expected to know and be able to do. All students are entitled to differentiated instruction and culturally responsive teaching to help them achieve the outcomes.	2. Adaptations are strategies and/or resources to accommodate the learning needs of an individual student. Adaptations do not change the public school outcomes. They are planned, implemented, and evaluated to enable the student to achieve the outcomes.	3. An Individual Program Plan (IPP) is developed for a student who cannot meet the curriculum outcomes of the public school program, or for whom the outcomes do not apply. The IPP replaces some or all of the outcomes from the public school program with individualized outcomes.

Source: Government of Nova Scotia, 2016, Figure 1, p. 3.

a modified curriculum are the provincial curriculum, the classroom teacher's long-term plan, report cards, past IEP, and formal assessments. Alternatives to developing modified courses include modifying existing courses at grade level by, for example, decreasing the number or complexity of grade-level outcomes expected to be achieved. Each individual outcome from the curriculum can also be revised to meet needs. It is important to note that, in some jurisdictions, individual plans are only written for students who are not able to attain provincial/territorial standards, such as Nova Scotia (see Table 7.5).

Alternative Courses

Alternative (or alternate) courses are a third component of many IEPs that can be individualized for any student, including those with ASD. This component stands out as a creative way to individualize curriculum. Alternative courses can be utilized in *addition* to the courses of the provincial curriculum, or *in place of* the provincial curriculum. Provincially approved courses might be replaced if the student's skills are below those goal areas where a K–12 provincial curriculum exists, for example, if the student's math skills are below the goal areas in the kindergarten program or if the goals are not suitable for that child's needs. This type of program—like modifying courses—is a serious step that should be carefully discussed on an individual basis by the IEP team if it means replacing a government-developed program.

Alternative courses are typically built on more formal, norms-referenced or criterion-referenced assessments that make each student's skills and next steps evident. An example of such assessments might be the *Woodcock Johnson Test of Education Achievement*, depending on the practices of the individual board or school, or the *Assessment of Basic Language and Learning Skills* (ABLLS) or *Verbal Behavior Milestones Assessment and Placement Program* (VB-MAPP) from the clinical field. As with modified courses, three to five learning expectations are typically prioritized per term and written in a measurable manner, often referred to as "'SMART' goals: Specific, Measurable, Attainable, Routines-based, and Tied to a functional priority" (Jung, 2007, p. 54). Other commonly utilized tools for building alternative courses can be task analyses of basic life skills. The number of alternative courses used in place of the typical program of studies would depend on the individual skills profile, strengths, needs, and assessments of each student.

Alternative courses, as noted, can also be used to supplement the provincial curriculum in an area of need that extends beyond the academic focus areas of the typical program of studies. For example, a student with ASD may need a course developed in communication, social, behavioural, and sensory skills (Wilczynski et al., 2007) or in areas such as use of assistive technology, learning about ASD, and whatever topics are deemed needful by that student's team. Although these courses remain assessment-driven and have a similar structure (i.e., three to five learning expectations are prioritized per term), few formalized resources are available for their development. In these cases, educators need to seek out professional and academic resources, such as books, articles, and manuals, to support these individualized courses; no comprehensive database exists to provide a comprehensive foundation, in turn, for alternative courses.

Alternative Courses Development Example: Social Skills

Part of the diagnostic criteria for students with ASD is significant difficulty with social communication skills (American Psychiatric Association, 2013b). This area is problematic because it is a predictor of long-term, life success (Division of Behavioural and Social Sciences and Education of the National Research Council, 2001). Many students with ASD may not pick up and absorb social skills from examples of adult or peer social skills via simple, day-to-day modelling in everyday social settings. Even though such skills are foundational, they are rarely integrated into provincial academic curricula (Maich, Hall, & Sider, 2013; Maich, 2010). It is quite common, then, for students with ASD to need individual program development and direct instruction in social skills, and this instruction is best encapsulated in the writing of an alternative course, which provides goals, objectives, instructional strategies, and assessment methods.

> Because children with ASD do have built-in difficulties in social skills, ignoring this area of instruction can leave them with a great disadvantage over time. Ideally, social skills teaching should be assessment-based, individualized, and intensive ... even better: social skills teaching should happen in the inclusive classroom for authentic practice with their peers. (Maich et al., 2013)

The first requirement in writing such a course is the presence of an assessment related to social skills. If the student does not have one already in place, there are some informal checklists that are widely accessible and can be administered by professionals with various training backgrounds. Some examples are found in *Building Social Relationships 2* (Bellini, 2016) and *Social Skills Solutions* (McKinnon & Krempa, 2002). Both resources have easy-to-use checklists or rating scales, which help to provide a baseline and next steps for building an alternative course in social skills.

Reflections on Writing IEPs for Students with ASD

Monique Somma, Faculty of Education, Brock University

IEPs for students with ASD can vary as much as the characteristics of ASD itself. When developing an IEP for any student, I ask, "How can I modify the curriculum or provide accommodations to meet the learning needs of the student, while at the same time incorporating measurable goals into the overall goals of the class?" This is easier said than done and takes a lot of pre-planning, authentic attempts, and trial and error to understand where the student is at and what level of support is needed. One of the biggest challenges is deciding what strategies will best benefit the student. For example, when implementing an expectation for a student to play a turn-taking card game with a peer, I did not realize that the organization of the cards would pose a challenge for this student. I had to reconsider the plan and adjust the strategies to best meet his learning needs by creating a card placeholder. This change in strategy allowed the student the appropriate level of support in order to be successful socially. Developing curriculum-derived or alternative program expectations for the IEP that include classmates allows the student with ASD to meet his expectations and develop relationships at the same time. By carefully selecting curriculum-derived expectations that align with the expectations of the class, we create a greater sense of belonging for the student—for example, having the class work on designing a board game where they are working through several curriculum expectations while at the same time incorporating IEP expectations for language, math, and social skills for the student with ASD. Another method is to parallel the IEP expectations in the lesson or activity; for example, using project-based learning tasks with various outcomes allows all students to work on a similar assignment with various options for the final product, providing necessary choice and alternatives for a student with ASD. Nonetheless, developing IEPs that have just the right amount of challenge and are appropriate for each student requires collaboration among those who know the student best—including the student! The IEP expectations are the most important things that I want the student to learn but are by no means the only skills that the student will attain in a term. I need to select a few big expectations to focus on each term, for which I can monitor and track progress. As a working document, the IEP is designed to be tweaked and changed as the term goes on. If I make edits to an IEP 10 times over the course of the term, it doesn't mean that my IEP was poorly written; it means that I am taking the time to really get to know the student and adjust my teaching to better meet his needs.

Read about It. Think about It. Write about It.

- What are individual plans called in your province or territory? Research the regulations around their use in school systems in your area.

CONTINUING EDUCATION FOR TEACHERS

For teachers in specialized settings and educators supporting inclusive classrooms, ongoing professional development about students with ASD is a necessary requirement for meeting professional standards. Opportunities for professional learning can be employer-initiated (e.g., mandatory or optional workshops) but are often teacher-driven in the search for excellence. Teachers can continue to learn in traditional ways through collaboration, conversations, and reading relevant literature, like Lane's (2016) recommendations for supporting students with ASD in Newfoundland and Labrador's professional publication, *The Bulletin*. Here, Lane (2016) noted that there are so many effective strategies prescribed for the learning of ASD that personnel working with students with ASD can become overwhelmed. The individual differences in ASD made it a challenge to pick the best-suited activity for individual students; however, despite individual differences, there are some fairly common areas of concern, preference, and strength which can function as a beginning point for classroom accommodations. For example, some learners process visual information more accurately than verbal directions (we can provide visuals). Some students might have difficulty in understanding the whole as a sum of its parts (we can break tasks down into manageable parts). Some have difficulty with focusing attention, maintaining it, or shifting it (we can support transitions and provide routines). Some have difficulty with time management (we can use checklists) or organization (we can provide colour-coding, desk organizers, and to-do lists). Over time, educators and other school personnel can develop a set of strategies in their toolboxes to help each student reach their individual potential.

Professional development is also available in more systematic, group-based, structured learning, such as certificates, diplomas, and degrees. Regardless of its origins, professional development is widely available from school boards, ministry initiatives, and union-funded workshops as well as community-based learning. But we are not there yet; calls continue to exist for further professional development for school personnel.

> Educators need more training in exceptionalities, particularly ASD, to meet the needs of an inclusive classroom. Additional training should occur throughout degree programs and should reflect evolving 'best practice'. Educators consistently express that they feel ill-equipped to teach and support students with exceptionalities, even those who hold positions that exist for that purpose (i.e. Instructional Resource Teacher). Pre-service training around inclusive practices and exceptionalities should be required for all teacher education programs in the province.
>
> Additionally, a comprehensive in-service action plan should be made to provide updated professional development to all educators. Increasing resources is only part of the equation; any additional personnel must be knowledgeable and competent in scaffolding students and providing supports effectively and efficiently.
>
> A consensus throughout the province has been reached—the current model is not work[ing]; it is failing our students and educators. ASNL is at the forefront of advocating for change and will do so relentlessly until needs are met. Educators need more training, quality training, more support and more resources. Students need better trained professionals, more support and more resources. We are no longer asking, "What?"; we are asking "How?" (Government of Saskatchewan, 1999, p. 20)

Here are some innovative program highlights from across the country.

The Atlantic Interprovincial Autism in Education (AIE) Partnership is an initiative of the Atlantic Provinces Special Education Authority, an organization more commonly known in Atlantic Canada as APSEA. APSEA was established in 1975 as a cooperative agency of the provincial Departments of Education of New Brunswick, Newfoundland and Labrador, Nova Scotia, and Prince Edward Island to provide educational programs and services for children and youth from birth to age 21 who are deaf, hard of hearing, deafblind, blind, or visually impaired.

Autism spectrum disorder was not part APSEA's mandate or work until 2010. At that time, APSEA's executive and board of directors determined that the interprovincial partnership that characterized APSEA had the potential to provide a valuable model to support professional learning for educational personnel working with learners with ASD across the Atlantic region. Unlike APSEA's programs for children and youth with sensory impairments, which see itinerant teachers providing direct services to children and youth—in addition to resources, support, and coaching for families and school teams—the work of the AIE Partnership involves indirect services in the form of professional learning and resources for educational personnel. A unique aspect of the AIE Partnership, in addition to its interprovincial nature, is that the majority of the resources developed by the AIE Partnership are available in both English and French.

Due to the wide geographical region served by the AIE Partnership, the work of sharing information, research, and resources on topics and issues of collective interest or concern across the four Atlantic provinces requires creative and innovative approaches. The AIE website serves as an online resource library for educational personnel, partner professionals, families, caregivers, and individuals with ASD across the Atlantic region and beyond. The website features AIE Information Papers and Research Snapshots, which provide summaries of research related to empirically supported interventions and approaches for ASD, along with considerations and implications for professional practice. In addition, AIE hosts an annual webinar series, recruiting national and international experts in the field of evidence-based interventions for individuals with ASD to share their expertise using videoconference technology. An annual face-to-face professional learning symposium has also helped facilitate the development of an Atlantic community of practice and has served as a networking and collaborative learning opportunity for provincial and school board/district ASD specialists, partner professionals, post-secondary faculty and students, and families and caregivers of individuals with ASD.

Provincial Autism Training Framework

In collaboration with experts in the field, the New Brunswick Department of Education and Early Childhood Development (EECD) delivers a provincial Autism Training Framework to prepare both preschool and educational personnel to meet the learning and behavioural needs of learners with autism spectrum disorder (ASD). All professional learning in the Autism Training Framework is based upon principles of applied behaviour analysis, an evidence-based approach for learners with ASD.

The Autism Training Framework is made up of three levels of professional learning for preschool and educational personnel.

Level 1
ASD & Behavioural Interventions
online introductory training
customized for both preschool and educational contexts
Level 2
Learning for Teaching
online learning and on-the-job coaching in advanced concepts and practices
customized for intensive behavioural interventions in a preschool intervention program and for individualized programming in a school-based setting
Level 3
Continuing Education
ongoing education and coaching in emerging research and evidence-based interventions

A team of learning specialists and provincial autism coordinators in the Anglophone and Francophone sectors, from Early Childhood to grade 12, collaborate in the development and implementation of this training initiative. This collaboration promotes consistency in intervention approaches across the educational sectors, and facilitates a smooth transition from preschool into kindergarten.

Level 1 – ASD and Behavioural Interventions

This introductory level of training is designed for both preschool personnel (autism agencies) and all educational personnel (teachers, school administration, educational assistants, speech-language pathologists, school psychologists, etc.). This on-line training allows participants to gain a better understanding of strengths and needs of students with Autism Spectrum Disorder (ASD), as well as evidence-based teaching practices and interventions.

Level 2 – Learning for Teaching

This **advanced training program** is designed for Behaviour Consultants, Clinical Supervisors (preschool agencies), Education Support Teachers–Resource (school-based), and Education Support Teachers–Autism (district-based). Level 2 training helps professionals assess, develop, and implement interventions in key areas to address the unique needs of learners with ASD:

Through on-line training, on-the-job coaching, workshops, and a library of materials and resources, participants learn to

- Determine learners' strengths and needs using assessment tools for program planning
- Implement evidence-based strategies for teaching essential skills to learners with ASD
- Provide on-the-job coaching and support for agency personnel and school-based staff who are working directly with learners with ASD using a structured process

Level 3 – Continuing Education

In order to maintain skills and knowledge of best practices, professional learning opportunities are offered on an on-going basis. Examples of professional learning opportunities include workshops, consultation with a Provincial Autism Coordinator, and support in obtaining advanced certification in applied behaviour analysis.

New Brunswick is very proud of the work that they are accomplishing in providing high quality and comprehensive training that will allow children and youth with ASD in the province to develop essential skills for success.

Source: Government of New Brunswick, 2017.

Two comprehensive online professional learning programs are also among the resources and supports offered by the AIE Partnership to educational personnel across Atlantic Canada. *ASD and Behavioural Interventions: An Introduction for School Personnel* was developed in collaboration with the New Brunswick Department of Education and Early Childhood Development's e-learning team. This professional learning series consists of 10 online modules on topics such as the impact of ASD on learning, evidence-based practice, and supporting communication and social skills. Following the success of *ASD and Behavioural Interventions,* and based on feedback from participants who completed the training, the AIE Partnership also created an online video and resource library entitled *Take Flight: Equipping Educators and Empowering Learners with ASD to Soar.* Through the ongoing expansion of professional learning opportunities and sharing of resources and research, the AIE Partnership seeks to support the development of knowledge and skills related to ASD and evidence-based practice for educational personnel across the Atlantic region.

In an article in the Newfoundland and Labrador Teacher's Association *The Bulletin*, Paulette Jackman (2016) provided a brief review of *ASD and Behavioural Interventions: An Introduction for School Personnel*, which commenced on April 2, 2015. The program is comprised of 10 e-learning modules of 40 hours of instruction, available in both English and French. The program covers all the important aspects of strategies, ethical issues, real life videos, examples from school life, self-assessment, and goals. After successful completion of all the modules and a quiz at the end of every module, participants are awarded a certificate endorsed by the Minister of Education and Early Childhood Development. Over 400 participants had completed the training from Newfoundland and Labrador at that time; the number increased to around 1,200 in 2019 (P. Jackman, personal communication, May 24, 2019). The program is offered two times in a year.

continuing education: a time-limited program provided after initial knowledge received during teacher education to update, broaden, and develop skills and professional understanding to respond to practical issues in the classroom (Musset, 2010).

Continuing education for professional teachers, as noted—like that for clinicians and other educators—varies across Canada. Another example is through Alberta's University of Calgary. Within the Werklund School of Education at the University of Calgary, a unique program option for teachers enrolled in the Master of Education's interdisciplinary route is called Educating Students with an Autism Spectrum Disorder. This specialization consists of four courses offered fully online: Understanding ASD, ASD across Childhood, Frameworks and Evidence for Intervention with ASD, and Educating Children with ASD. It is described as follows:

> Designed with a developmental framework, this program provides targeted instruction on the primary and associated features of these clinical conditions, the developmental challenges of these conditions across childhood and adolescence, exposure to "best-practice" intervention approaches for children with ASD, and application of all of these topics to the classroom environment to enhance teachers' capacity to work with and educate students with ASD. Instructors are experts from the field with specialized knowledge and experience in each topic area. (University of Calgary, n.d.)

Figure 7.3: Autism in Education English Logo and Autism in Education French Logo

Source: Atlantic Provinces Special Education Authority (APSEA), 2020.

Its rationale is one of bridging the gap between need and services for children with ASD in provincial, inclusive school settings:

> The prevalence of autism spectrum disorders (ASD) is on the rise, and teachers are increasingly being called upon to educate children in this population. However, few teachers have received formal training or are aware of the primary characteristics of autism spectrum disorders and how the behaviours that these children present with can affect their learning. (University of Calgary, n.d.)

Dr. Adam McCrimmon's article "Inclusive Education in Canada: Issues in Teacher Preparation" (2015) addresses the very issue of why such a program is needed, citing the mismatch between the inclusive education models offered across Canada and the inadequacy of specialized, related preparation for professional teacher certification: "inclusion after years of separated education has brought challenges to Canadian classrooms, particularly regarding teacher competencies and capabilities to meet the learning needs of a broader student population" (p. 235). He notes that bachelor of education programs across Canada—even at large universities—offer few related courses. They do not offer a systematic approach to "definitions and/or descriptions of childhood disabilities in conjunction with mentored experience with research-informed effective classroom-based intervention practices" (p. 235), again underscoring the discrepancy between preparation and practice when it comes to school-based inclusion.

In another jurisdictional example, continuing education for Ontario Certified Teachers (OCTs) is regulated by the provincial professional regulatory body, the Ontario College of Teachers. One of the formal, documented means of obtaining additional knowledge, skills, and teaching credentials is through additional qualifications (AQ) courses, a province-wide initiative that is well-recognized provincially and an expected credential for many teaching positions in a range of roles. One agency that develops and delivers these AQs is the Elementary Teachers' Federation of Ontario (ETFO).

Teaching Students with Communication Needs: Autism Spectrum Disorder

Krista Walford, Retired Executive Staff Officer, ETFO-AQ

ETFO began development of this course in 2016 to assist teachers with the increased number of students identified with ASD over the last decade. Offered in 2017, the course enrolment continues to rapidly increase. The course is designed to expose participants to:

- the basic foundations for understanding Autism Spectrum Disorder from past to present;
- a range of strategies for classroom success, including decreasing problem behaviours, using visual strategies, and focusing on evidence-based pedagogy leading to student success; and
- the processes of exceptional student identification and IEP development, including transition plans.

This course is offered online four times each year (fall, winter, spring, and summer). The course is accessible to any teacher with Internet access. Feedback from participants is incredibly positive. For more information, please visit http://etfo-aq.ca.

Figure 7.4: Krista Walford, Retired Executive Staff Officer, ETFO-AQ

Source: Krista Walford.

ETFO-AQ Participant Testimonial

Carolyn Matson

At the time, with the rates of autism reported to be 1 in 68 children, I knew that it was important for me to be prepared for a future student with Autism Spectrum Disorder. I was interested to learn some theory as well as practical, evidence-based instructional strategies. After some self-directed learning and attending an autism conference I was keen to learn more.

I have taken Additional Qualifications courses through ETFO before so I was very excited when I heard that they are now offering a course to address my professional needs! Teaching Students with Communication Needs (ASD) was exactly what I was looking for.

This Additional Qualifications course is taught online and it has the perfect blend of historical background, theory, and practical strategies for immediate implementation in the classroom. Although the course is geared to teaching students with ASD, the educational strategies work well for a wide variety of learners. This online course linked me to practical print and electronic resources, data banks, informative videos, and it has also allowed me to be a part of a learning community of dedicated educators committed to serving all students.

During the course, I learned about applied behavioural analysis, using visuals to support learning, evidence-based treatments, and instructional strategies and writing IEPs for students with ASD. I feel more prepared to teach students with autism. I have resources at my fingertips, and I now know the reasons why I should choose a certain strategy for a particular student or situation.

Teaching Students with Communication Needs (ASD) has opened my mind and heart to the unique gifts that our students with ASD present to us. It has provided me with knowledge that will serve me well in my role as classroom teacher and as an instructor of Additional Qualifications Kindergarten Part 1 (online). I highly recommend this course!

Read about It. Think about It. Write about It.

- What are your next steps for your own professional development in the field of ASD?

Many other additional resources exist provincially, nationally, and internationally to enhance knowledge, skills, and resources available for supporting students with ASD in school settings. Within schools, this includes resources in the school community, such as classroom teachers and school administrators with training and experience in ASD, onsite resource teachers with expertise in ASD, and educational assistants, who provide additional support to classroom teachers and school communities and are valued members of school communities.

SPOTLIGHTS ACROSS CANADA

Research: Alberta

In 2012, McCrimmon, Altomore, Matchullis, and Jitlina examined school-based practices for what was, at the time, known as Asperger syndrome. They examined each jurisdiction's educational policies, including processes such as identification in the school systems and noted that the Canadian system is rife with geopolitical inconsistencies around school-based services for students with Asperger syndrome. McCrimmon and colleagues (2012) recommended enhanced pre-service teacher training, as well as improved education for teachers on topics such as best practices; modifications to the diagnostic-specific provision of supports existing in most jurisdictions toward identification that is needs-based; providing more criteria and guidelines around identification and diagnosis; enhanced screening and monitoring of domains beyond academic (e.g., social-emotional-behavioural); and a greater focus on topics that are typically considered to lie outside the academic curricula (e.g., social skills).

Initiative: Quebec

Quebec's Lester B. Pearson School Board (LBPSB) for ASD works under Ministère de l'Éducation, Enseignement supérieur (MEES) as a team to provide support to students with ASD in inclusive schools. English school boards receive assistance in various ways, including resources, training, coaching, and direct interventions. The MEES runs six centres of excellence to help inclusion of students with exceptional needs, including ASD, and the LBPSB operates a Twitter account and a dedicated website to disseminate related information. Its website provides multiple effective classroom strategies under the definition of ASD, supported by a team of 9 professionals that has produced 40 newsletters since 2002 (also available for review). The library tab has links to various webpages with introductions to several books that explore issues related to exceptionalities, as well as links to audiovisual recommendations. The materials tab has a range of links to suggested books and periodicals, communication books, community links, conference hosting, and curriculum-based activities (e.g., language arts, math, science and the body, matching and sorting), as well as intervention resources on topics such as data collection, protocols and procedures, social scripts, visual starter kits, visual schedules, and visual supports. The online resources tab provides links to webpages with bilingual materials, information on language and communication, language arts material, material resources, math material, and visual support activities. The family fund tab provides links to a financial support program available to children with disabilities.

Initiative: Nova Scotia

The Nova Scotia Department of Education and Early Childhood Development used a wide lens and identified a need to examine its policies and practices related to inclusive education in 2017. To that end, the government created a Commission on Inclusive Education and tasked the group with reviewing current policies and practices and interviewing educators, educational partners, families, community organizations, and stakeholders to determine what was working well and what changes would support a more effective and inclusive education system in Nova Scotia. In March 2018, the Commission released its final report, calling for a new model around inclusive education (Njie, Shea, & Williams, 2018) that includes increased funding, more specialized training and supports, and improved partnerships and collaboration between school, home, and community. The Commission's report also includes a number of recommendations focused specifically on learners with ASD, noting limited access to specially trained ASD and behaviour specialists and inconsistency in the application of supports and interventions. To address some of these challenges, the report calls for the creation of "new autism education guidelines as part of a provincial autism strategy for Nova Scotia schools" (p. 7).

A LOOK BACK

Chapter 7, "The School Years," focused on:

- Description of various school placement options for children with ASD
- Definitions and examples of methods to support individuals with ASD in the school system with individual education plans (IEPs)
- Examples of various school supports across Canada

ADDITIONAL RESOURCES

Atlantic Provinces Special Education Authority (APSEA)

http://apsea.ca

This website provides comprehensive information for parents and professionals on low-incidence sensory impairments such as deaf, blind, or low vision. The resources included are useful for individuals with ASD and other developmental disabilities.

Autism in Education Partnership

http://autismineducation.ca

The Autism in Education Partnership is an interprovincial collaboration affiliated with the Atlantic Provinces Special Education Authority (APSEA). This website includes links to information papers, webinars and online tutorials, as well as video presentations.

IEP Guide: Autism Speaks Canada

https://www.autismspeaks.ca/science-services-resources/resources/tool-kits/individualized-education-program-iep-guide-1/

From this link parents and/or professionals can request access to download a guide with information on writing IEPs for students with ASD.

PALS Autism School

http://palsautismschool.ca/site/

PALS Autism School, operating out of British Columbia, provides scientifically based programming for school-aged students (5–18) as well as adults (19+). This website includes a description of services as well as links to informational websites.

Canada Student Grant for Services and Equipment for Students with Permanent Disabilities

https://www.canada.ca/en/services/benefits/education/student-aid/grants-loans/disabilities-service-equipment.html

This website provides details on the federal grant program for students with permanent disabilities. Information on eligibility and services is provided.

Councils of Ministries of Education

https://www.cmec.ca/en/

The Council of Ministers Education, Canada, is an inter-ministerial group discussing educational related policy and projects. This website provides up-to-date information on educational indicators and statistics.

100-Day Kit for Families of Newly Diagnosed School Age Children: Autism Speaks Canada

https://www.autismspeaks.ca/science-services-resources/resources/tool-kits/100-day-kit-for-school-aged-children1/

From this website, parents can request access to a helpful resource from Autism Speaks. The 100-Day Kit for School Age Children provides information applicable to parents and professionals on planning for the 100 days following a diagnosis.

Community Care Access Centre

http://healthcareathome.ca/hnhb/en

This website provides a wealth of health-related information for patients and caregivers. Home and Community Care provides resources on accessing a family doctor and accessing home and school health care.

ConnectABILITY

http://connectability.ca/visuals-engine/

This interactive website allows users to create visual supports. Templates are available for visual schedules, reinforcement systems, and story boards.

W. Ross Macdonald School

https://pdsbnet.ca/en/schools/w-ross-macdonald/

W. Ross Macdonald is a unique school in Brantford, Ontario. This is alternative education placement for blind, low-vision, and deaf-blind students. This website includes a virtual tour of the learning setting, information on professional development, and useful resources for educators and parents.

EduGains ASD Resources

http://www.beta.edugains.ca/newsite/SpecialEducation/autism_spectrum_disorder.html

EduGains is a website that links to a variety of Ontario Ministry of Education documents. This specific link includes resources related to special education for students from kindergarten to Grade 12.

EduGains IEP Samples

http://www.beta.edugains.ca/newsite/SpecialEducation/transitions.html

Developing IEPs is a critical skill for educators. This website provides several samples applicable for students of varying ages and abilities.

Provincial Outreach Program for Autism and Related Disorders (POPARD)

https://www.autismoutreach.ca/

POPARD provides professional development and support across public schools in British Columbia. This website includes links to useful articles, handouts, resources, and online training modules for educators.

Ontario IEP Samples

www.ontariodirectors.ca/IEP-PEI/en.html

This website provides several samples of draft IEP reports. Educators are encouraged to refer to these templates as a starting point when developing an IEP for a student.

"Learning People Skills"

https://www.edcan.ca/articles/learning-people-skills/

This article highlights the impact an individual with ASD may experience because of social deficits. Authors discuss accessible assessment tools and tips for developing objective, measurable goals.

A4: Assessing Achievement in Alternate Areas

www.thea4ideaplace.com

This website provides lesson plan ideas on a wide range of topic areas. Topics include numeracy, literacy, social, communication, and adaptive living skills.

CHAPTER 8

The Adult Years

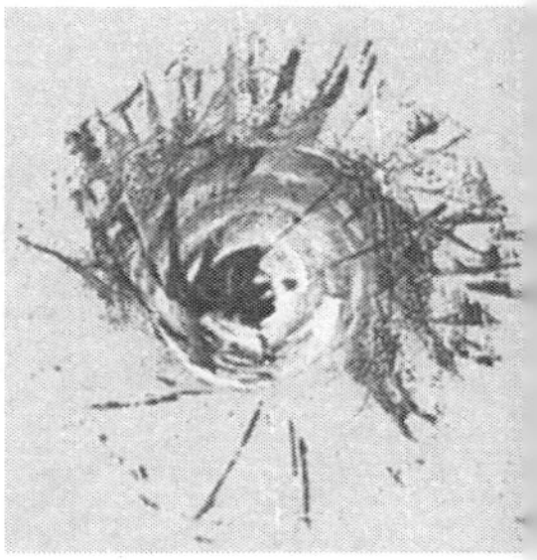

LEARNING OBJECTIVES

- Review common issues and triumphs faced by autistic adults who transition from adolescence or are diagnosed for the first time.
- Describe common trends in autistic adults around daily life skills, comorbid mental health issues, and social interactions, employment, and access to services.
- Become familiar with areas for autistic adults to be integrated into community settings, including: (1) post-secondary options, (2) employment opportunities, (3) recreation and leisure, (4) financial support, and (5) housing.

Note: Apart from lengthy sourced materials, this chapter is written in identity-first language, including authored feature boxes. See the preface for an explanation and literature support for this choice.

Transitioning into adulthood can be a very difficult time for many autistic individuals—even more so than their non-disabled peers. Often, they are leaving the structured setting of the school system to navigate a world of post-secondary education, recreation, housing, and financial support. In many cases, autistic individuals do not fit into the traditional supports for either developmentally disabled adults or supports for mental health issues. Their skills and intellect may not be a match for other services, and they may be manipulated or taken advantage of in other settings, with insufficient supports to meet their varying strengths and needs—especially in the area of social skills. This chapter reviews some of these areas of strengths and needs and examines various supports and strategies that have been found to be successful for adults transitioning into various parts of adult life, including post-secondary education, employment, recreation and leisure, housing, and financial supports. Looking at different programs and services across Canada highlights the differences in levels and types of (or lack of) supports available for autistic adults.

AUTISTIC ADULTS

Services for autistic adults are often inconsistent and less available than those provided for the under-18 sector, with little information about interventions that are effective (Dudley & Emery, 2014). More specifically, "service research does not reflect the heterogeneity of impairment, the demographic, or the range of services needed to help adults function with purpose in their communities" (p. 9). Unlike services for children, there may be none or few systematic, jurisdictionally funded services designed specifically for adults with autism spectrum disorder (ASD). Rather, funding may be focused on the diagnostic category of developmental disabilities, according to legislated practices. See Figure 8.1 for more information on funding.

> **IQ 70**: intelligence tests provide an intellectual quotient (IQ) or an estimate of individual cognitive ability. Intelligence tests have a standard score of 100 with a standard deviation of 15. The cut-off score, IQ of 70 (or below), has been traditionally required for a diagnosis of an intellectual disability (ID) in the DSM or an intellectual developmental disorder (IDD) in the *International Classification of Diseases*. In the DSM-5, intellectual ability (cognitive reasoning, problem-solving, judgment, and learning), adaptive functioning (conceptual, practical, and social), and the onset of deficits in the developmental period are the three diagnostic criteria of intellectually disabled adults. A mild ID or IDD is characterized by intelligence and adaptive functioning scores between two and three standard deviations below the population mean (standard score of 100 on standardized measures). However, to limit overreliance on the IQ scores for a diagnosis of ID and subsequent service provision, the DSM-5 allows clinicians to make clinical judgments on the severity level of the ID based on the individual adaptive functioning scores. The diagnosis of an ID now requires deficits in mental functioning that impact general, everyday functioning, as well as the three adaptive domains (APA, 2013b; World Health Organization, 2018).

Though many autistic adults have intellectual disabilities, others do not. Individuals tacitly described as *higher functioning* (commonly thought of as a misnomer) were typically diagnosed with Asperger's syndrome in the revised fourth edition of the *Diagnostic and Statistical Manual of Mental Disorders* (DSM-IV-TR; APA, 2000) until 2013: "Up to 50% of [autistic adults] do not have an intellectual disability (ID), yet their needs for support are as great as those with ASD and ID" (Autism Ontario, 2008, p. 13). In the current DSM-5, the sole diagnosis is autism spectrum disorder, rated on three levels of severity (APA, 2013b), rather than varied diagnoses such as Asperger's disorder. Funding to support daily living skills for autistic adults who do not also have an ID is difficult to obtain, which is an ongoing issue in the ASD community.

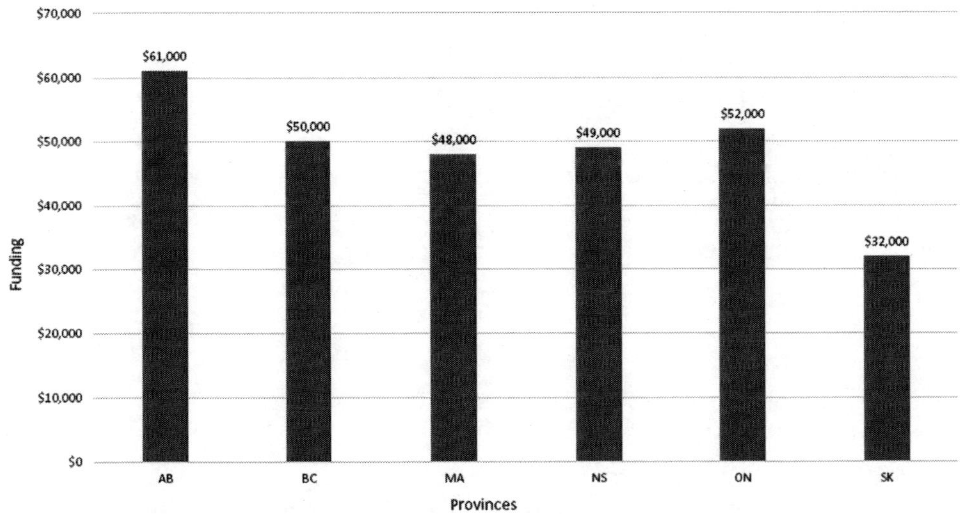

Figure 8.1: Average Funding per Individual (2010/2011)
Source: Dudley & Emery, 2014, p. 21.

Services

Another area where frequent advocacy is often necessary is in adult services; for example, "[we] had to fight for every single penny our son receives in support of his dignity, independence, integration, and equality of opportunity" (Stoddart et al., 2013, p. 35). Some autistic adults indicated that although they met the criteria in other ways, their cognitive ability did not, disqualifying them from additional funding and services (Stoddart et al., 2013). This issue leaves many individuals paying for their own services, despite lower incomes.

> **Asperger's disorder**: in the DSM-IV-TR (APA, 2000), Asperger's disorder was diagnosed through a qualitative impairment in social interaction and repetitive and restricted patterns of behaviour, having significant impact on everyday functioning, without a language delay before two years old, and no cognitive delays. It has since been removed from the DSM-5 as a separate diagnosis and thought to be subsumed within the term autism spectrum disorder (APA, 2013).

> **intellectual disability (ID)**: refers to a diagnosis made where significant difficulties in intellectual and adaptive functioning are demonstrated, as well as evidence of learning at a much slower rate than peers (Province of British Columbia, 2019).

Few wide-scale reports exist that focus solely on autistic adults, including service provision. In 2014, however, Weiss, Whelan, McMorris, Caroll, and the Canadian Autism Spectrum Disorder Alliance (CASDA) released a national needs assessment of more than 5,000 participants from all provinces and territories in Canada, targeted not only for families and professionals but autistic adults as well. It is described as "the largest survey of stakeholders across Canada to date" (p. 3). Those self-advocates who took part in this community-based research noted accessing around six services on average in the pathways of their lives (which varied in affordability) and, like other groups, identified insufficient services. Some gaps relevant for autistic adults included social, life, and employment skills (Weiss et al., 2014). More specifically, both self-advocates (who are not formally diagnosed) and autistic adults each identified their top five areas of service need. For autistic adults:

- Employment or day programs (60%)
- Social skills programs (49%)
- Life skills training (37%)
- Recreational programs (37%)
- Post-secondary education programs (34%; Weiss et al., 2014, p. 7)

For self-advocates:

- Mental health treatment (45%)
- Employment services (41%)
- Social skills (40%)
- Post-secondary education (37%)
- Housing/residential options (32%; Weiss et al., 2014, p. 7)

Read about It. Think about It. Write about It.

- Highlight the main skills you feel may need to be targeted for autistic adults in Canada. What services are needed to support these individuals?

Not quite a decade earlier, *Forgotten: Ontario Adults with Autism and Adults with Asperger's* was released by Autism Ontario (2008). At that time, the number of autistic adults was thought to be around 50,000. The National Epidemiologic Database for the Study of Autism in Canada has estimated that 1 in 94 children has ASD in Canada (Ouellette-Kuntz et al., 2014); now, the most comparable number is 1 in 66 (Public Health Agency of Canada, 2018a). Between 2008's *Forgotten* and 2014's *National Needs Assessment Survey*, another look at autistic adults in Ontario was undertaken, focusing on complex needs and systems that are unprepared for them. In 2013, an online survey was administered to 480 autistic adults, their parents, and service providers, dependent on the functioning level of individuals and their ability to self-report or have others report on their behalf (Stoddart et al., 2013). Of those involved, 72.5% were male, 27.5% female; 86.5% single, 9.0% married, and 2.3% separated or divorced (Stoddart et al.,

2013, p. 15). The wage of adults with ASD over 20 was low, with 32% earning below $10,000 and 73.2% earning less than $30,000. This puts many autistic adults below poverty levels (see Figure 8.2; Poverty Free Ontario, 2015; Stoddart et al., 2013). It is not surprising that Weiss and colleagues (2014) also found that caregivers of autistic adults cited difficulties affording relevant services as one of the top four service barriers; another pervasive barrier was age. Similarly, self-advocates with ASD noted affordability as the most common barrier to service provision. Only 64% of this first group received jurisdictional funding, yet 28% noted that even this funding was insufficient. For self-advocates, these numbers were 36% and 21% respectively.

Canadian provinces and territories have been planning for the present and future of autistic adults. For example, the Government of Manitoba's *Thrive* plan (2013), described as "a five-year plan for helping [autistic Manitobans] and their families," is an example of such proactive planning. *Thrive* emphasizes that the transition from high school to university, college, or work is a hard choice for young adults, which can be even more challenging for disabled young people, such as autistic youth. This plan can help these individuals move forward by providing various supports and services such as a strong learning environment from kindergarten through to graduation, support for young people making important decisions about their futures, programs and services to help autistic young people succeed in school and in the workplace, and providing smooth transitions from high school to appropriate adult supports and services (e.g., the workforce or post-secondary education). Various supports and services are available through the following: appropriate learning

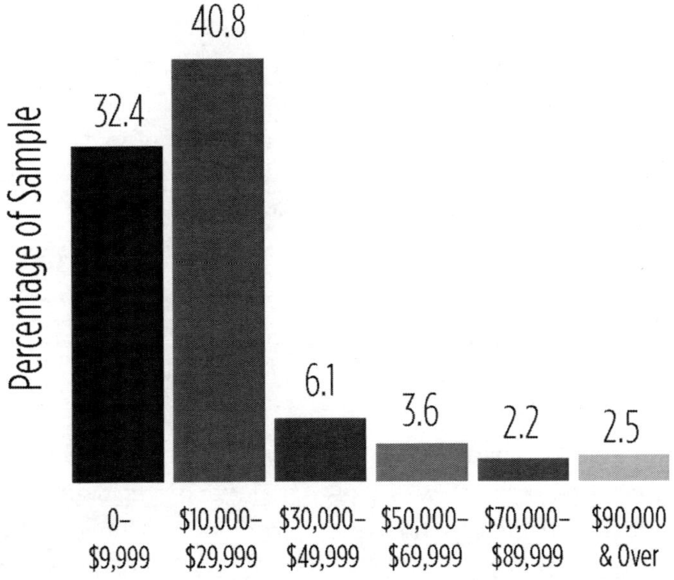

Figure 8.2: Annual Income for Adults 20 and Older with ASD (n = 315)
Source: Stoddart et al., 2013, p. 16.

opportunities in high school; scholarship programs for autistic young adults who want to continue their education; autistic youth receiving help with future planning; independent living skills programs (e.g., managing a budget, grocery shopping, cooking, cleaning, etc.) for autistic youth; transition plans in place when needed; and tutoring for autistic young adults who go to university or college.

Many autistic adults transition from childhood and adolescence with a diagnosis of ASD already in place, but some receive their first diagnoses in adulthood (Burke, 2005). With recognition of the importance of early diagnosis and intervention, researchers in one study examined the factors that influenced the age at diagnosis for autistic children in Nova Scotia. Investigators reviewed medical information from more than 120,000 children born in Nova Scotia between 1990 and 2002 and discovered that 884 of those children had received a diagnosis of ASD. The average age at diagnosis for those children was 4.6 years; however, this age of diagnosis ranged from 1.3 years to 15.7 years. Researchers discovered that the diagnostic age was influenced by a number of factors, including the area of the province in which the child was born, the age of the child's mother, and whether the child had been previously diagnosed with attention deficit hyperactivity disorder (ADHD; Frenette et al., 2011).

Clearly, some diagnoses exceed the age range found in this Nova Scotia-based study. Such a diagnosis in adulthood can be a relief after many years of concerns about fitting in, layered with many failed or awkward attempts at interacting with others (Burke, 2005). Before Asperger's disorder was added to the DSM-IV in 1994, many such individuals were referred to as *quirky* or *strange* (see Chapter 1; APA, 1994; Stoddart, 2005). Although they may have functioned at average or above-average levels for academic tasks and other activities of daily living, they also may have struggled to feel like they were fitting in with a social group. Some suggest that celebrated figures such as Albert Einstein and Bill Gates may have autistic traits. Bill Gates, the founder of Microsoft, for example, is referenced in popular media as an example of someone with Asperger's syndrome: "He has often been seen rocking and tends to speak in monotones—both habits acknowledged to be symptoms" (CBC News, 2013, para. 14).

The Diagnosis Itself Was Therapeutic

Anonymous

At 24 years old, Elizabeth had been involved with mental health practitioners for a number of years. Although she was a very bright and articulate student, she had always found some aspects of school, such as getting her thoughts from inside her head onto paper, extremely difficult. She remembers thinking that if she just tried harder, she should be able to do the things that other students seemed to do so easily. By the time Elizabeth entered university to pursue her undergraduate degree, she had received various diagnoses, including an anxiety disorder and mood disorder.

She received some services and supports to help address the characteristics associated with those diagnoses, but she always felt that there was a missing piece.

During her undergraduate program, Elizabeth was working with a psychologist to help her with strategies to address her stress and anxiety. Elizabeth recalls that, during one session, the psychologist began to explain that Elizabeth reminded her, in a number of ways, of a client with whom she had previously worked in another region. She explained that the client had been diagnosed with ASD, and she told Elizabeth, "I think you might have autism." Elizabeth was taken aback, as she was only familiar with two individuals with ASD, and both were quite significantly impacted by the challenges associated with ASD. However, after being referred to another psychologist, one who had more experience and expertise in diagnosing ASD in adults, and having the diagnosis confirmed, Elizabeth explains that the pieces started to come together.

"The diagnosis itself was therapeutic," she says, and having the knowledge that she had ASD allowed her to move forward in a number of ways. Whereas she had always thought that she simply was not trying hard enough, she now understood that her challenges were the result of how her brain worked and that there was a reason she found some tasks so difficult. Simply trying harder was not the answer. Understanding her strengths and challenges within the context of ASD made it easier for Elizabeth to understand how to work through situations she found difficult and how to use her strengths to mitigate some of the areas of difficulty. Once she understood how ASD affected her, she could begin to advocate for the supports and accommodations she required in order to be successful.

Elizabeth explains that she "made it 24 years before anyone thought, *Oh, you may have ASD*," and she knows that she is not alone in being an undiagnosed adult. Many professionals still do not understand autism in older individuals, and as a result, many remain undiagnosed. Elizabeth sees this as an unfortunate situation, as she asserts, "It can make it so much easier to be able to access services and to understand your own strengths and challenges when you have the correct diagnosis."

Although services and supports for adults diagnosed with ASD are still limited, advocacy efforts are increasing in this area, and there is an increasing awareness of the importance of such services. Some organizations and agencies, such as the Autism Society of Newfoundland and Labrador, offer programs and supports for young adults with ASD. Programs such as pre-employment and career services, life skills development, adult leisure opportunities, and community access activities provide adults with ASD the opportunity to participate in activities and learning experiences that address their individual strengths, interests, and needs.

As a professional who now works with individuals with diverse needs and their families, Elizabeth feels that her own experience and diagnosis provide her with a unique perspective on how families may be feeling and give her a better appreciation for what they may be going through. As Elizabeth explains, "As hard as it was to hear 'I think you might have autism,' it has changed my life."

Advocacy for autistic adults continues to be an ongoing concern (Allen, 2014; Autism Ontario, 2008; Stoddart et al., 2013; Weiss et al., 2014). Difficulties can originate from a lack of funding, especially to those who are so-called higher functioning, and include a lack of specialized services that meet the needs of autistic adults, all entangled with many potential comorbid mental health needs (Allen, 2014; Autism Ontario, 2008). Multiple, Canada-wide advocacy and information groups exist, and every province and territory in Canada has some formal, related information and/or advocacy groups to disseminate information specific to ASD. Autistic adults—like many others—may gather in less formal groups in less formal settings, such as online conversation, in order to provide support and advocacy for one another in ways that are more difficult to capture.

Table 8.1: Provincial and Territorial Advocacy and Information

Province/ Territory	Office Most Responsible for Disability Issues	Ministry in Which Disability Office Resides	Website
AB	Office of the Advocate for Person with Disabilities	Ministry of Community and Social Services	https://www.alberta.ca/family-social-caregiver-supports.aspx
BC	Accessibility Secretariat	Ministry of Social Development and Poverty Reduction	https://www2.gov.bc.ca/gov/content/family-social-supports/services-for-people-with-disabilities
MB	Disabilities Issues Office	Ministry of Families	https://www.gov.mb.ca/dio/
NB	Premier's Council on Disabilities	Premier's Council on Disabilities	https://www2.gnb.ca/content/gnb/en/departments/pcsdp.html
NL	Disability Policy Office	Department of Children, Seniors and Social Development	https://www.cssd.gov.nl.ca/disabilities/index.html
NS	Disability Support Program	Department of Community Services	https://novascotia.ca/coms/disabilities/index.html
NT	Services for Persons with Disabilities	Department of Health and Social Services	https://www.hss.gov.nt.ca/en/services/services-persons-disabilities

Table 8.1: *Continued*

Province/ Territory	Office Most Responsible for Disability Issues	Ministry in Which Disability Office Resides	Website
NU	–	–	https://www.gov.nu.ca/family-services/information/social-assistance-sa
ON	Accessibility Office	Ministry of Seniors and Accessibility	https://www.ontario.ca/page/ministry-seniors-accessibility
PE	Accessibility Support Office	Ministry of Social Development and Housing	https://www.princeedwardisland.ca/en/information/family-and-human-services/accessability-supports
QC	Office de personnes handicappe	Ministry of Health and Social Services	https://www.ophq.gouv.qc.ca/
SK	Office of Disability Issues	Ministry of Social Services	https://www.saskatchewan.ca/government/government-structure/boards-commissions-and-agencies/office-of-disability-issues
YT	Disability Services	Social Supports, Health and Social Services	http://www.hss.gov.yk.ca/disabilites.php
Canada	Accessibility Standards Canada	Employment, Workforce Development and Disability Inclusion	https://www.canada.ca/en/accessibility-standards-canada.html

Source: McColl & Jones, 2020, Tables 1 & 2.

Read about It. Think about It. Write about It.

- Brainstorm some challenges that autistic adults may face when transitioning from adolescence to adulthood. How do you think the systems of support in Canada help or hinder such transitions?

Dudley and Emery (2014) developed three profiles of autistic adolescents and adults and created *Needs Maps* of Persons A, B, and C. Each of these profiles represent varied lifespan characteristics, including descriptions of cognitive, communication, sensory, behavioural, restricted and repetitive interests, social, and daily living skills. Person A is a profile with this overall description: "a severely affected [autistic individual] with IQ 70 or less (age equivalent of 3–6 years) and who is non-verbal. He struggles with sensory issues and social interaction" (p. 33). Keep in mind that the Weiss and colleagues report found only 22% of self-advocates reporting concurrent intellectual disabilities. Refer to Figure 8.3 for a full needs map of Person A.

NEEDS MAPS

PERSON A

Person A represents a severely affected individual with autism spectrum disorder (ASD) with IQ 70 or less (age equivalent of 3–6 years) and who is non-verbal. He struggles with sensory issues and social interaction.

LIFESPAN CHARACTERISTICS

Cognitive: IQ is untestable due to his cognitive challenges, estimated age equivalent is 3–6 years. Over time and with support is beginning to match letters and recognize numbers. He is unaware of danger (prone to wander and would be unaware if lost). All doors at home have unique lock systems installed that prevent him from opening doors and gates. He can roam inside the house but must be checked every hour as to his activities (razors, stove, sharp objects, and open doors to outside all pose potential hazards).

Communication: Non-verbal, uses pictures in a limited way to communicate. Can locate exact picture for items (nouns) but cannot communicate concepts (sick, tired, angry).

Sensory: Touch: seeks out deep pressure (squeezing, hugs). Auditory: has low tolerance for noise levels and copes by plugging ears.

Behavioural: Behavioural issues include: yelling, occasional mild self-abuse (hitting head), non-compliant behaviours (refusing to stand up, refusing to walk). Behaviours occur when Person A is hungry, sick or unable to communicate his needs. Behavioural strategies work well to manage challenging behaviours.

Repetitive and Restricted Interests: Rigid attachment to certain objects requires constant work to enhance his ability to relinquish these objects without behaviours arising.

Social: Limited eye contact, uninterested in social contact but will observe others, likes to be around people but no concept of stranger danger.

Daily Living Skills: Requires hands-on assistance to complete skills such as brushing teeth, bathing, meal preparation, grocery shopping and cooking.

NOTE: *The trajectory for ASD development is unknown. With appropriate programs and supports, Person A could maintain the skills he has gained and continue to learn and move towards independence. Without appropriate supports in place, it is possible that this individual could regress and lose skills, becoming increasingly dependent on others with challenging behaviours that will restrict his ability to participate in employment, community integration, recreation and leisure, thus lowering his quality of life.*

Figure 8.3: Needs Map of Person A

Source: Dudley & Emery, 2014, pp. 33–36.

NEEDS MAP: PERSON A

<table>
<tr><th>Life-Stage and Supportive-Care Needs Above a Neurotypical Individual</th><th>Annual Hours</th><th>Activities of Supportive Caregiver</th><th>Gaps</th></tr>
<tr><td>Life Stage 1: Ages 14–17
DAYTIME HOURS AND NEEDS

DAY PREP HOURS: 6:30 am–8:30 am
Two hours, 365 days of the year = 730 hours of supportive care needed every year, although the actual time may vary on a weekend, but the tasks will not vary aside from school-related prep.
Supportive-Care Needs: Prompt A out of bed (schedules, sounds, light). He does not understand concepts of time and date; without this communicative understanding he may be uncooperative, or resistant to getting ready for the day. Choose and get weather-appropriate clothing/assist with dressing, get food, oversee eating breakfast, assist with daily grooming and assist with tooth-brushing for him, remind to sit on toilet. On school days, pack lunch for school; organize school bag and clothing. Care provided with a behavioural, communication framework – i.e., using pictures to communicate next steps, managing any behaviours that arise.</td><td>Day Prep 730 hrs</td><td rowspan="5">SELF CARE
Assistance with daily living tasks from hands-on doing for the individual to partial assistance to do a variety of tasks (bathing, wash hair, brushing teeth, orientate clothing, reminding about toilet, changing soiled clothing, assistance with cutting foods).

HOME-LIVING TASKS
Grocery shopping, cooking, additional laundry tasks due to soiled clothing, he requires full assistance with all tasks, partial direction and full supervision with completing tasks.

SERVICE CO-ORDINATION MANAGEMENT
If funded for professional supports or respite there is a co-ordinating function. Co-ordination duties include to hire, train, oversee programs for aides, co-ordinate with behavioural or speech experts, hire, train respite services, oversee payroll, organize team meetings, meet with funding co-ordinator twice a year to confirm care needs. Staff turnover, staff maintenance.

PERSONAL ORGANIZING TASKS
Organize all outings, social, recreational events, camps, paperwork needed. Financial-management tasks: finances, banking, and long-term financial planning.

HEALTH AND SAFETY MANAGEMENT
Extraordinary or ASD-specific-related dental and medical care, such as extra dental needs, medication administration, prescription filling, co-ordination of appointments for both physical health and mental health issues such as depression and anxiety, or physical health issues such as increase in seizure disorders. Home-safety monitoring.

COMMUNITY LIVING/EMPLOYMENT/RECREATION
Co-ordinate and oversee community involvement and volunteer or employment opportunities. Locate job opportunities; work with agencies, job coaching, job maintenance, troubleshooting.

TRANSPORTATION
Provide or co-ordinate safe transportation. Requires driving or assistance on public transit. Cannot walk independently.

ADVOCACY
Advocacy if services lacking and/or advocacy to maintain supports (attending meetings, planning, advocating, problem solving). Arranging employment supports and placements. Reviewing new treatment information and implementing therapies that may be beneficial (this could include dietary changes, alternative health strategies or new medications).</td><td rowspan="5">· Transition supports.

· Reliable and qualified respite workers.

· Longer-term and after-school respite workers (especially where difficult behaviours exist).

· Funding for behavioural psychologists and speech funding.

· Kinship care: Ability to pay for kinship care (siblings or relatives if appropriate and able).</td></tr>
<tr><td>TRANSIT HOURS: 8:30 am–9 am and 3:30 pm–4 pm
Travel to and from destinations at 0.5 hours each way = one hour x 365 days of the year.
Supportive-Care Needs: Assuming that each day of the year he will have the opportunity to go out to a destination at least once a day (e.g., school, summer program, recreation, community outing). Safe transport can only be accomplished via supervised walking, supervised public transit, special needs busing or caregiver drives. In transit, caregiver must understand behavioural, communication, social and sensory challenges. In this situation the caregiver drives Person A to school as special-needs busing is not working out.</td><td>Transit 365 hrs</td></tr>
<tr><td>SCHOOL DAYS HOURS: 9 am–3:30 pm
School year of 190 days x 6.5 hours a day = 1,235 hours when care is provided by the education system.</td><td>School Hours 1,235 hrs</td></tr>
<tr><td>SUMMER DAYS HOURS: 9 am–3:30 pm
30 summer days x 6.5 hours a day = 225 hours.</td><td>Summer Hours 195 hrs</td></tr>
<tr><td>DAYS OFF HOURS: 9 am–3:30 pm
(holidays, weekends, PD days, non-summer days).
145 days off at 6.5 hours a day = 1,087.5 hours.
Supportive-Care Needs: A neurotypical 14-year-old could by this age hold a job, or stay at home alone for the day and so requires little or no daytime care over summer or PD days. Person A continues to need constant vigilance and structure to his day. Some communities offer summer camps but these are not always available, appropriate or free.</td><td>Days Off 942.5 hrs</td></tr>
</table>

Figure 8.3: *Continued*

NEEDS MAP: PERSON A (cont'd)

Life-Stage and Supportive-Care Needs Above a Neurotypical Individual	Annual Hours	Activities of Supportive Caregiver	Gaps
EVENING HOURS AND NEEDS **EVENING HOURS: 4 pm–9:30 pm** 5.5 hours of care x 365 days a year = 2,007.5 hours. **Supportive-Care Needs:** Care provided is a combination of vigilance mixed with tasks of daily living, teaching skills and knowledge of behavioural management and communication techniques. Mealtime needs still require meals prepared and to oversee eating (holds fork, stays on task, cut food for him). Cleaning up after meal with direction of steps. Teaching skills and oversee skills needed around mealtime (load dishwasher). Vigilance is a care task (e.g., check on activities every 30 minutes), can never be left alone. Also reminding re: toileting, appropriate behaviour, working on behavioural challenges (dealing with issues as they arise, and working on developmental strategies to enhance independence). Later evening could be considered more "down time": watching TV, video games, transport to evening activity when needed and supervise activity (bowling, ski, swim), but still requires supervision or hands-on assistance to participate in activities. Bedtime preparations are to assist with bathing (reminding, supervising and competing tasks that are not independent), partial assistance with hair washing, brushing teeth, toileting, prepare room (sheets clean, drapes drawn for darkness, no dangerous items in room).	**Evening Hours** 2,007.5 hrs	SOCIAL/COMMUNICATIONS/BEHAVIOUR/SENSORY Teaching social skills. Examples of this for Person A will be to provide supports and teaching that increase: orienting to his name, continued eye contact to request and engage, tolerating noise, asking (via iPad) to leave room when in need of quiet time, understanding concepts of quiet and loud in public places, learning appropriate ways to ask for items, maintaining greetings with a wave, appropriate and inappropriate touching and, for puberty, teaching public and private places. SOME KEY TASKS SPECIFIC TO THIS LIFE STAGE Transition planning and co-ordination to move from youth programs and school system into adult programs. This requires paperwork filled in for all transition to adult programs, funding, and guardianship. Moving into adulthood means leaving the school system, which provided a structured day. Adult programs may be unavailable or inappropriate or unwilling to take highly behavioural individuals, leaving him with no well-structured daytime opportunities. Puberty issues, sexuality and relationships become a key focus at this age. Strategies to teach public and private locations regarding sexuality are essential for Person A. Increased anger, non-compliance, or violence issue may arise due to hormonal changes at puberty. CAREGIVER REQUIREMENTS: Behavioural-management skills (if behaviours are present), in particular if non-compliant behaviour arises, knowledge and ability to implement unique communication techniques, social-skills teaching, co-ordination and advocacy skills, willingness to provide hands-on care when needed. Meal preparation, assistance with laundry. Male aide is helpful for community outings when individuals are unable to use public toilets independently. Skills to oversee all executive-functioning tasks (managing programs, planning activities, banking and advocacy). **ANNUAL VALUE OF CAREGIVER TIME = $131,893**	
NIGHT HOURS AND NEEDS **NIGHT HOURS: 9:30 pm–6:30 am** Nine hours x 365 days a year = 3,285 hours **Supportive-Care Needs:** Occasional waking (2–3 times a week for 1–3 hours at a time), not toilet trained at night. Checking at these times to help with toileting or check safety. Person A can never be left alone at night; he may open doors, wander outside or pose a risk to others (e.g., inadvertently turn on gas elements, turn on electrical devices). CALCULATIONS (does not include school hours as provided by public system) DAY/EVENING COST: 4,240 hours x $21.43/hour = $90,863.20 NIGHT COSTS: 3,285 x $12.49/hour= $41,029.70 $90,863.2 + $41,029.7 = $131,892.90	**Night Hours** 3,285 hrs		

Figure 8.3: *Continued*

NEEDS MAP: PERSON A (cont'd)

Life-Stage and Supportive-Care Needs Above a Neurotypical Individual	Annual Hours	Activities of Supportive Caregiver	Gaps
Life Stage 2: Ages 18–64 **SUPPORTIVE-CARE NEEDS IN LIFE STAGE 2** Key needs after the end of school are to continue to be in an environment that he can maintain the skills he has and continue to learn and grow. Person A will likely still need constant, 24-hour supervision and assistance with daily living and complete care for executive-functioning tasks. School has finished, but there is still a need for structured programming, behavioural and communication supports. Hours covered by the education system are now filled by day programs, where they exist, and if they are appropriate and available. Often the appropriate trained staff and quality structured programs for adults with ASD are difficult to find. Assumption: Quality program and staff exist to replace school days. To simplify calculations we replace school-day hours with adult day-program hours available. CALCULATIONS (add previous hours supplemented by school system) Previous day and evening and night costs = $131,892.90 Add school hours now in need of adult supports (1,235 hours x $21.43) = $26,466 **Total: $131,893 + $26,466 = $158,359**	**Add in School Hours** Add in hours previously covered by school: 1,235 hrs	SOME KEY TASKS SPECIFIC TO LIFE STAGE 2: The key tasks remain the same as noted above in the 14–18 category. Lifespan-specific tasks can replace the transition-planning tasks with tasks that focus on estate planning, housing, employment or volunteer and community integration. It could be argued that estate planning should begin at a much younger age, yet in reality, it is likely that many families do not consider this until later in life. CAREGIVER REQUIREMENTS: As above, with emphasis on estate planning, housing, advocacy and provided structured/appropriate day programs. **ANNUAL VALUE OF CAREGIVER TIME = $158,359**	· Reliable, qualified, available respite and aid workers. · Respite longer-term in or out of home (more than a few days). · Structured, quality adult day programs. · Vocational, community opportunities. · Funds for behavioural therapists, speech, OT. · Availability of professional supports (e.g., psychiatrists). · Housing options (available, quality). · Lack of primary-care physicians trained in health issues that impact adults with complex developmental disabilities.

Figure 8.3: *Continued*

Independence in Daily Life Skills

When one group of Canadian autistic adults was asked about the amount of help needed with services, more than 64% required assistance with finding and using services, 59% required help with finances, 58% required assistance with household repairs, 54% required assistance in arranging appointments (52% with attending appointments) and 50% with shopping, groceries, and doing mail (Stoddart et al., 2013). These results demonstrate the consistent need for help with services, which gives an even stronger message considering that the largest group of respondents for the study were described as having Asperger's disorder or high-functioning autism (50%; Stoddart et al., 2013). In addition, few resided on their own with no supports (13.6%), whereas the majority lived with their parents (59.8%; Stoddart et al., 2013). For adults, a huge part of the approach involves choice. See the feature box below for an example of helping individuals to participate in their daily planning in an adult residential context.

Promoting Active Choice and Participation in Adults with ASD in a Residential Setting

Christina Cicci, Central West Specialized Developmental Services

As a behaviour therapist assistant working in an adult residential environment, one of the biggest challenges I frequently experience is participation. Specifically, participation in an activity whether the activity is preferred, non-preferred, or completely novel. How do we motivate adults to participate in tasks that benefit their home environment, such as completing laundry? What about routines that benefit their personal health, such as hygiene or exercise? Even participating in leisure activities that would be considered fun or relaxing to most can be difficult for some individuals, especially if it involves a new setting, new people, or the anticipation of challenging situations. Using a schedule that primes an individual about upcoming expectations, splitting a long or complex task into simpler steps with frequent breaks, or providing opportunities to access reinforcement for participating in non-preferred tasks are strategies that can be successfully implemented in the adult residential setting. The following cases highlight two different interventions I have used to increase participation.

In the first case, an autistic woman in her twenties living in a group home was refusing to participate in outings she typically enjoyed, such as going to the local park for lunch or joining her peers for a movie night. This individual was typically extremely rigid about her daily routine and tolerance of unexpected events was very low. However, a higher likelihood of successful participation was observed any time she learned about an event in advance. As a result, we designed a schedule that would give her the details of her daily activities and outings prior to preparing to leave the house, allowing her time to process the plans for the day and to ask further questions about the activities if she so wished. Due to staff-to-individual ratios that are often higher than 1:1, ease of intervention delivery in an adult residential setting is essential. Since this individual was able to read, the details on the schedule were written out in text instead of using pictures, allowing staff to easily change or update the schedule as necessary without needing a picture icon for every new change or event. As a result of implementing this schedule, her rates of participation in outings increased to those observed prior to her beginning to refuse participation. She spends quality time with her peers and has opportunities to expand her experiences in the community!

In the second case, a developmentally disabled man in his forties living in a group home required an intervention to help motivate him to participate in activities within his house, including doing his laundry and completing physical exercises. Since this individual was able to communicate a clear list of preferred items that he loved, we designed a token system for earning these items during specific intervals. Developed in collaboration with the individual, staff, and clinical team, a visual choice board of numerous tasks he could complete to earn tokens was provided to him alongside a visual menu of each preferred item with its corresponding token price (the number of tokens he needed to exchange to receive the item). Ensuring the entire program was represented visually, establishing a set plan with the individual for which tasks to include and which reinforcers to offer, and building in multiple opportunities for choice meant the program was easy for staff to implement and allowed the individual to exercise a large amount of control over his day, all while increasing participation. Even while completing his least preferred tasks, frequent reminders about how many tokens he had earned and the amazing items for which he could exchange them would result in expressions of excitement toward getting closer to his end goal.

It is paramount that we recognize the importance of supporting and motivating individuals to participate in their own lives, regardless of age or the environments in which they live. Interventions developed with unique needs in mind can be extremely effective in increasing participation and, with careful attention paid to design and delivery, these interventions can be implemented with success in any setting.

Even so, parents of autistic adult offspring still worry about their adult children when or if they are not able and involved—or living. Dudley and Nakane (2017) prepared a discussion paper for the Autism Society Alberta (see Spotlights for further details). They suggest that in such families, the "care dynamic is inverted" (p. 5) and

> **choice**: a promoted concept in disabilities studies where a person has control over their support and various options in order to enhance their personal welfare, not simply consumer choices that are dictated by policies (Rabiee, 2012).

eventually becomes unsustainable, and that lifelong caregiving itself can lead to ill health. Financial supports, housing, community, care—and the quality of these—create layers of concern in aging parents.

Mental Health Concerns

Consistent with related literature in other geographical contexts, a diagnosis of ASD was found to be comorbid with other mental health concerns in Canadian adults. Complex diagnoses can impact not only autistic adults but also their families and support systems: "Families with an individual who had these complicating issues felt more stress, especially where they found a lack of services, complexity of systems, and a lack of professional support to help them learn skills to maintain the involvement of their relative" (Dudley & Emery, 2014, p. 6). One example of such comorbidity or dual diagnosis is depressive disorders. Canadian researchers Hudson, Hall, and Harkness (2019) carried out a meta-analysis and concluded that the percentage of adults, adolescents, and children with "unipolar depressive disorders" (p. 165) currently appears to be around 12.3%. In autistic adults, this disorder is three to four times as prevalent than in non-autistic adults (Hudson et al., 2019). Buck and colleagues (2014) found that 52.7% of autistic adults were likely to have an anxiety disorder in their lifetime, which is a prominent comorbid psychiatric disorder, followed by depression (Stoddart et al., 2013). In addition, 31% of autistic adults in this research felt they had an undiagnosed psychiatric condition. Some of these individuals even needed emergency room services for behavioural, psychiatric, or psychological services (Stoddart et al., 2013). Psychiatric diagnoses are more common when an intellectual disability and ASD are both present, with up to one of every two autistic individuals affected by such complexities, as reported by Canadian researchers (Lunsky, Garcin, Morin, Cobico, & Bradley, 2007). Although some regions in Canada have expertise in these complex adults, such services are not mandated, and related expertise is piecemeal and typically associated with university-based clinical expertise in urban centres (Lunsky et al., 2007). See Figure 8.4 for a full breakdown of comorbid psychiatric conditions. In Weiss and colleagues' (2014) needs assessment, healthcare issues described by participating healthcare workers included anxiety, depression, and sleep problems (77%, 66%, and 49%, respectively, and rising over time).

> **comorbidity**: the co-occurrence of more than one health condition, disease, or diagnosis (Valderas, Starfield, Sibbald, Salisbury, & Roland, 2009).

> **dual diagnosis**: refers to the diagnosis of both an intellectual disorder and a psychiatric diagnosis, co-existing for the same person (Werner & Stawski, 2012).

Social Interactions and Employment

Since one of the characteristic elements of a diagnosis of ASD is social interaction, it is not surprising that the difficulties with socialization stood out. In fact, 38.4%

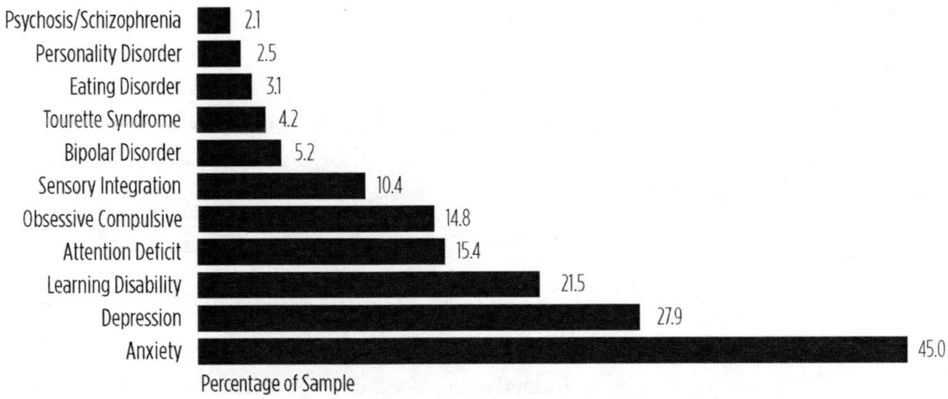

Figure 8.4: Comorbid Mental Health Concerns in Adults with ASD

Source: Stoddart et al., 2013, p. 22.

of participants in one Canadian study reported socializing less than once per month (Stoddart et al., 2013). This information continues to highlight the difficulties autistic adults have in social relationships, with the majority of them indicating they did not have a best friend and many feeling it was hard to maintain friendships (Stoddart et al., 2013). It is often the case that friendships can end because of social mistakes that autistic adults may make, potentially becoming overly dependent on one friend, or the fact that the other person finds the autistic adult annoying. Many individuals reported family as the primary means of socialization, turned to online avenues for socialization, and felt that there were few social activities and programs available (Stoddart et al., 2013). Very few of the respondents were employed, and a sizable number of participants engaged in recreation in the community for their daily activities, yet many indicated that their primary daily activities included watching TV, playing on the computer, or staying home with their caregivers (Stoddart et al., 2013).

TRANSITIONING FROM ADOLESCENCE

Transition into adulthood is an important milestone for most youth, who are becoming more independent and embarking into the employment and educational worlds for their future careers.

> All individuals moving towards adulthood must navigate numerous transitions. Some of these transitions include puberty, the end of publicly funded school, consideration of career and employment opportunities, further education at post-secondary institutions, relationship development and possibly moving away from the family home. (Dudley & Emery, 2014, p. 14)

Transitions can become daunting when ASD is in the mix. First, funding sources change to different programs; different methods for accessing funding are used; and often there is much more onus on the individual to advocate for the needed services. With these changes come new worlds to navigate. As difficult as this is for most young adults, navigation becomes that much more complex with additional services for and with a disability. Given that transitions are difficult for autistic individuals in general, transitions to new settings in adulthood can cause substantial anxiety and stress (Alcorn MacKay, 2010; APA, 2013b). One Canadian research project using a policy lens with parents, policymakers, and researchers found that this unique life transition was not represented optimistically—not an unusual finding in this study or beyond (Shepherd & Waddell, 2015). All participants, indeed, described transitioning from adolescence to adulthood with trepidation, even dread. Words and phrases used included "black hole," "criminal," "it's like the ship has sailed and you're on your own in the ocean," and "they just get nothing" (p. 3561). An east coast study (Audas, Ryan, Walsh, Wells, & Murphy, 2015) found a theme of insufficiency of support and care, particularly during this time of transition to very limited services in Newfoundland and Labrador.

One major theme found in another Canadian-based research project with parents of adolescents moving into adulthood was "preparing for 'the future'" (Ho, Fergus, & Perry, 2018, p. 15). This included parents providing more opportunities for choices and decisions as their adolescents moved into adulthood, emphasizing communication, collaboration, and trust. At this transition point, parents being interviewed noted that more hope was present, was "filled with small but achievable goals" (p. 19), and pointed toward a concrete future (Ho et al., 2018). This point of view is in contrast to the earlier study by Shepherd and Waddell (2015).

POST-SECONDARY OPTIONS

Just like any other students, autistic students can access numerous post-secondary options, including publicly funded college, university, apprenticeship programs, and private options. At each post-secondary institution, there should be an accessibility office, where supports to help disabled students access their programs and individual classes are provided. Supports for autistic students in post-secondary environments can include accommodations such as extra time for test writing, assistance with coaching on field placements, the hiring of note-takers for classes, or educational assistants to assist with tasks in the classroom for those with more substantial needs. Very little research is available in this area, and the inclusion of autistic students in post-secondary classrooms is still somewhat new for disability offices (Alcorn MacKay, 2010).

Attending post-secondary education can be challenging for autistic students because of a multitude of factors. First, navigating the huge number of buildings among noisy, crowded hallways, and little direction from educators can be overwhelming (Alcorn MacKay, 2010). Another difficulty is that such individuals may have trouble sustaining their interest in a course beyond their specific area of interest, making elective courses difficult to complete successfully (Alcorn MacKay, 2010). In addition, with the rigidity that comes with ASD, students studying in their areas of special interest have been known to challenge professors, add unsolicited information in the classroom (often uncalled for or without a raised hand), and get frustrated when the content does not match what was envisioned. In one of Canada's larger jurisdictions, it was estimated that approximately 1,100 students with ASD would attend post-secondary institutions from 2009 to 2011 (Alcorn MacKay, 2010). As the prevalence of ASD is rising, this number is likely to continue to increase.

Sometimes, community colleges can be a helpful place for autistic students to start because of the smaller class sizes, smaller campuses, and the ability of accessibility services to provide a more customized support system and accommodations (Adreon & Durocher, 2007). However, one difficulty is that smaller class sizes and hands-on approaches make the autistic student more visible, making it then more difficult for that person to blend into crowds (Adreon & Durocher, 2007). With the social challenges that these individuals face as part of the diagnosis, another potential area of struggle is group work, required more often in college classrooms (Alcorn MacKay, 2010; APA, 2013b).

> **accessibility office**: a department at a post-secondary institution that focuses on providing support to disabled students attending the school. The office typically provides a range of supports and can include assistance with assessment and/or diagnosis, determining accommodations, accessing needed accommodations (e.g., note-taker, test centre, technology), and advocacy.

Read about It. Think about It. Write about It.

- What was your transition like from high school to adulthood? How does this compare and contrast to the experiences described for autistic adults?
- Look up resources that target the transition for youth to adulthood for disabled persons. What options are available for transitioning into employment, post-secondary education, and/or recreation?

Accommodations

Traditionally, accommodations for those with specific learning disorders can also be accessed for individuals with ASD, such as test-taking in a quiet space, extra time for tests, special seating arrangements, and recorded lecture notes (Adreon & Durocher, 2007). To receive accommodations, an assessment must be completed or documentation must be provided identifying a specific disability (Alcorn MacKay, 2010); however, a recent court case may have repercussions that will change some of these expectations. Student Navi Dhonota initiated a human rights complaint with the Ontario Human Rights Commission, arguing that students should not be asked to disclose specifics of mental health diagnoses to receive supports.

York University Student Wins Mental-Health Fight

Effective immediately, Dhanota and hundreds of other students seeking supports at York won't have to label their illness to get help. The school still requires an assessment from a licensed doctor to confirm the student has a legitimate condition that may require faculty flexibility or other supports, but the focus is now on determining how the disability affects their learning. For example, some students may need to take tests at a particular time of day because medication makes them drowsy.

"From the very beginning, I knew I wanted all students to have this," said Dhanota, who is pursuing a PhD in critical disability studies. "Students across Canada should not have to disclose."

Dhanota is part of what researchers are calling a "tidal wave" of students seeking academic accommodations for mental-health issues. Without adequate help, researchers have shown members of this group are less likely to graduate than those in other disability classifications.

Source: Zlomislic, D. (2016). York University student wins mental health fight. *The Toronto Star.* Retrieved from https://www.thestar.com/news/gta/2016/01/12/york-university-student-wins-mental-health-fight.html

---

Accommodations that may provide additional assistance for an individual with ASD include the option to do group work individually, assistance in selecting courses, permission to attend additional sections of the same course, and scheduling flexibility (Adreon & Durocher, 2007). A negative aspect is that because some individuals are required to take fewer classes, their financial obligations can be higher due to increased tuition over multiple terms (Alcorn MacKay, 2010).

Taking Charge of Education

One significant difference between high school and post-secondary studies is that the students are required to take the lead in requesting assistance and leading their educational journeys, just as they are becoming more involved with other decisions of everyday life (Alcorn MacKay, 2010; Ho et al., 2018; Manett & Stoddart, 2012). This is done, in part, to recognize and acknowledge rights to autonomy and choice. In addition, because these students are adults, post-secondary institutions require written permission in order to talk to involved parents, sometimes preventing necessary additional communication that once occurred in high school (Manett & Stoddart, 2012). In ideal practice, accommodations must be arranged ahead of time in order to schedule classes and test-taking and provide professors and instructors with advance notice (Manett & Stoddart, 2012).

The difficulty with these practices, however well-intentioned they may be, is that taking charge, managing, organizing, and recognizing the need for assistance is sometimes difficult for autistic adults (Alcorn MacKay, 2010; Manett & Stoddart, 2012). Many autistic adults struggle with executive functioning, as well as the ability to plan and organize appointments and strategies that are needed for success (Stoddart et al., 2013). In addition, the struggle with change, social skills, and communication can make this process increasingly difficult (Manett & Stoddart, 2012). Lastly, autistic individuals may have difficulty with the introspection that would help them to realize that they are struggling, that they are behind, or even recognize the hidden curriculum of what they should be doing in the post-secondary classroom environment (Lombardo & Baron-Cohen, 2011; Manett & Stoddart, 2012).

In a review of services provided to autistic students in Ontario, Alcorn MacKay (2010) provided a summary of secondary and post-secondary school services, noting gaps in accommodations for students with ASD in the post-secondary education system. It was recommended that post-secondary staff should: 1) be trained as ASD coaches; 2) obtain professional development in ASD; 3) provide safe spaces; 4) create transition plans whenever possible; 5) create partnerships with parents for planning and executing the post-secondary journey; 6) provide supports to those completing psychological assessments for adults with ASD, to provide helpful learner-specific recommendations for the institution; and 7) continue research in this area.

The Bumps and Triumphs of Aidan's Journey to Adulthood

E. Sterling, Sooke, BC

Our son Aidan has been diagnosed with Asperger's since Grade 6, and largely his designation has brought us into contact with financial and people resources that were helpful. Aidan also received a gifted designation, as he has a high IQ, and so he was able to do well for most of his school years with little effort. It all came crashing down, however, in Grade 11, as he encountered classes that had higher demands (he had never really "studied" before), and he experienced his first broken heart. Aidan failed three out of four courses (which we withdrew him from) in one term and became clinically depressed. He began taking antidepressants and seeing a psychologist regularly, and we worked hard to modify the demands upon him at school.

I discovered later that this was the age at which I was supposed to be beginning some transition planning through his autism worker; I had only met with her once to learn about the government funding in British Columbia ($6,000 per year for school-aged kids) and to discuss what I could use it for. We had used the money for an autism counsellor, a tutor, and then another autism behavioural specialist—all with varied success.

Truthfully, as Aidan navigated the last two years of high school, my top priority with him was to help him get to graduation. I knew, despite his protestations, that he would be proud of himself for achieving it and would feel shame if he did not. So that last year and a half was a struggle: trying different classes, taking a couple of online courses to avoid certain teachers and to get to graduation on time, nagging and encouraging him to finish tasks on time ... plus taking him to the psychologist and watching his medications.

Once graduation was achieved, we wondered what to do next, so as to not lose momentum. We enrolled Aidan in driving school to give him another goal to pursue, and he enjoyed the classroom sessions as well as the in-car sessions with a very friendly and supportive teacher. At the same time, I began investigating the supports available to Aidan as an adult. The Canada Revenue Agency (CRA) had asked for us to reapply for the disability tax credit when Aidan turned 18, and when we reapplied, we were rejected, because Aidan's family physician had not put the right wording on the application form. So we appealed, and in the meantime, our tax refunds were up in the air. We also applied for disability supports from the government, knowing that, at least for the present, full-time work wasn't a likely outcome, as Aidan had struggled so much with deadlines and responsibility at school. The application process was an enormous undertaking. We first applied online in June 2016, waited six weeks for a phone interview, after which we had to fax information in (his psych assessment, and some financial information), and then went to a Service Canada location so that he could produce identification and they could certify it. In September, we finally received word that we had been "pre-approved" and now could receive the 28-*page* booklet/application form!

The booklet had sections to be filled out by a medical doctor (our family physician) and a specialist (our psychologist). I had learned, from the CRA debacle, that wording had to be very specific, so I photocopied the booklet and filled in the sections as they needed to be, and gave the copy to our doctor so that she could see what the expectation was. Fortunately, she found that very helpful and was glad to fill in the right information the first time! We had to pay for extra hours of the psychologist's time (not covered by extended health since it wasn't therapy) to assess him and fill out her part of the booklet. The application was completed in October, and he began receiving support in November. Since they don't pay retroactively, I was kicking myself for not starting the application process earlier, but I didn't know enough then to do so!

In October, we also became aware that there was a program (VITAL—Vocational Independence for Transition to Adult Life) in the city closest to us that was designed for older teens and young adults with autism to help them transition to independence. The autism funding, which didn't run out until Aidan's nineteenth birthday, could pay for at least the first five to six months of it. It all seemed quite ideal, except for the long commute by bus (over an hour each way). Aidan had a weekly appointment with a support worker and would also have the opportunity to get work-related certifications (Serving It Right, Food Safe, etc.). It was quickly apparent that Aidan was reluctant to attend the sessions, not because they weren't useful when he got there, but because he hated the commute, and one time fell asleep on the bus and got turned around in the city and ended up coming straight back home. Aidan was politely booted from the VITAL program in February, as he was not reliably attending sessions and was refusing to follow through with some of the requirements of the job-seeking program.

In the meantime, we also had a first meeting with someone from Community Living BC (CLBC), who would take over where the school-aged autism funding had left off. It took several months to get that appointment, but the service was good once we had it. Unfortunately, due to lack of funding, Aidan was assessed to receive only $233.33 per month for "community inclusion," which obviously would not go very far.

At the end of March 2017, Aidan let me know that he had been looking at apartments to rent, which was a complete surprise to me! I was happy he felt ready to try living independently, as I was worried that he would remain "stuck" in his teenage desire to live at home and avoid chores and other responsibilities. His sleep pattern was abysmal, as he preferred to be awake (and online) at night and sleep during the day, which obviously interfered with our lifestyle as a family of five. Moving out seemed a good solution for everyone. It felt like serendipity when I checked listings in our small town and saw a local listing for a bachelor suite that was a three-month rental only. When I spoke to the owner, she made it clear that she was testing out renting this space, and so the three months was a trial for everyone. That seemed perfect for Aidan, as we needed to see how he would do on his own before committing to a long-term rental.

Aidan moved out within the month, and we helped him get set up in this attic suite that was mostly furnished, rented out by a woman with experience working with youth at risk—a perfect match! We found a local support provider that could use CLBC's money and found an ideal candidate who lives only blocks from Aidan's new place. Because Aidan was now living outside of the home, we appealed to CLBC to increase his funding. Instead, due to budget cuts, his funding (and everyone else's) was cut, and his worker, who originally could see him once per week (for about two hours), was now only able to see him every two weeks.

Aidan has now been living in his own place for six months, and he loves it. His disability support just went up by $100 per month, thanks to our new government, but even before that, he received enough to pay his rent (including utilities), Internet, food, and other essentials. He occasionally gets fast food take-out but mostly lives on the cheap, which is good on a limited income. He is not the greatest at keeping himself or his space clean, so his support worker or I will check in every couple of weeks and help him catch up on dishes if he needs it. If he comes for a visit, I ask him to shower first, which otherwise he avoids. I have a key to his suite, which I have used on occasions that he has missed or almost missed an appointment—dentist, eye doctor, or with his support worker. It is frustrating that despite all of her attempts and mine, he will not use any of the techniques offered to keep on top of his schedule. His support worker was trying to help him enter the workforce on a part-time basis, but I think we have all come to realize that he is not ready for that yet.

I get worried and upset at times that Aidan is not yet working and seems uninterested in encountering the world beyond his online gaming friends and his family. But then I have to remind myself that he is washing his own clothes, making his own meals, and buying his own groceries, none of which he used to do when living at home. I have decided that transitioning to living on his own is a huge step that I need to acknowledge, and perhaps it is enough that he is getting used to being on his own—work can wait. I am happy that he is happy.

Manett and Stoddart (2012) have provided a range of suggestions for autistic students to make their transitions to post-secondary life easier. They suggest registering for any transitional or mentorship programs for the transition into college or university, as well as any social skills groups that may be offered at the institution. Many of these programs are available for any student entering college or university, with an ASD diagnosis, no diagnosis, or any diagnosis. Second, they recommend that students or parents connect with the disability office early, the year before enrolling, and again in the summer before the individual starts school. Bursaries are available for disabled students; more information can be found in the funding section of this chapter. It is also important to plan out a course load that is specific and manageable for the student to set the stage for success. Beginning with fewer classes while learning the ins and outs of post-secondary education can be helpful. Lastly, strategically plan a method of assistance for communicating with the disability office, peers, professors, and others involved in the student's education. Because it is more difficult for the student to understand social norms, having a mentor, coach, or someone to help read and review information before sending email, handing in assignments, or attending a meeting with a professor is helpful.

EMPLOYMENT OPPORTUNITIES

Employment is a significant area of concern for many autistic adults. For example, it appears that Canadian employment rates for autistic adolescents and adults (over 15 years old) are around 14.3%, compared to the typical working-age employment rate in

Canada of 73.6% (Nicholas et al., 2018). One jurisdiction cites that only 13.9% of autistic adults have full-time employment, and 6.9% have part-time employment in Ontario (Stoddart et al., 2013). In addition, many of these individuals are underemployed based on their skill set and education (Accardi & Duhaime, 2013). Overall, the employment rate of autistic adults, according to a cross-Canada group of researchers, "is unacceptably low" (Nicolas et al., 2018, p. 693). This is true even in the context of national legislation like the Government of Canada's *Employment Equity Act* (1996), although the purpose of the Act is to achieve equality in the workplace; nobody should be denied employment due to being a woman, Indigenous person, person with disabilities, or a member of a visible minority.

The fact remains that many individuals struggle to obtain and maintain employment due to difficulties in social skills, which emerge in the interview process and continue on in the navigation, understanding, and implementation of social rules in the workplace. Although individuals may have the skills required to do a given job, a lack of social skills may hinder those individuals from cooperating with others to successfully perform the job duties. See "Challenges in Employment for Autistic Adults."

> **employment coaches**: persons who support disabled people in an employment setting by providing training on their job responsibilities (Bennett, Brady, Scott, Dukes, & Frain, 2010).

Challenges in Employment for Autistic Adults

Challenges to Accessing Employment Faced by Youth and Adults with ASD:

- Preparing for and attending an interview—difficulties managing anxiety, reading social cues, communicating appropriate information
- Social interactions with colleagues, organizational skills, and sensory challenges
- The work activities required might not be perceived as challenging, rewarding, or meaningful
- Colleagues and bosses' misunderstanding of the individual's behaviours and challenges
- Lack of general awareness of the strengths that an individual with ASD can bring to the workplace
- Training that does not support the individual's specific needs related to ASD and other features

> **psycho-vocational assessment**: an evaluation of a person's skills and abilities that is related to employment outcomes (e.g., specific disabilities, literacy issues, characteristics that make certain job skills more successful/unsuccessful; Falvo, 2009).

- Difficulty with self-advocacy: sharing information about personal needs and accommodations

Recommendations for the Community:

- Increase employment support programs geared to individuals with ASD
- Increase training for frontline workers in generic employment agencies to better understand the strengths and needs of the ASD population
- Customize existing employment programs to better support the ASD population
- Educate employers to understand how to cultivate talents and preferences of those with ASD
- Educate employers to embrace neurodiversity and mental health more in an effort to create meaningful discussion and support for those with ASD
- Empower employers to consider non-traditional working arrangements that may reduce stress for individuals with ASD (e.g., working from home)
- Improve transitional services at the high school and post-secondary levels to ensure individuals are prepared to enter the workplace
- Increase research on vocational interventions specific to those with ASD to better understand and advocate for appropriate services
- Create opportunities for individuals with ASD who would like to pursue entrepreneurial activities (e.g., start-up costs, financial and management training, mentorship, and more)
- Increase employment coaching and support for individuals with ASD who have successfully entered the workforce but may be struggling in their current positions

Recommendations for the Individual and Family:

- Enrol in cooperative education opportunities in high school, volunteer in the community, and seek out summer employment to get experience in a variety of settings
- Enrol in programs that focus on employment, life skills, and social skills to prepare the individual for adult independence
- Connect the individual living with ASD to family and friends for informational interviews about specific jobs or careers and access online information to learn more about different jobs
- Engage the individual in job-shadowing opportunities
- Develop strong self-advocacy skills so that personal strengths and needs can be communicated to the employer in an effective manner
- Begin career planning discussions as early as possible in adolescence to ensure successful transition to the world of work

- Identify the individual's strengths, skills, interests, talents, and cognitive style
- Make use of psycho-vocational testing and assessment
- Don't just look for a job, but for a job that is "the right fit" for the individual
- When self-employment is viable, evaluate the individual's talents, whether he/she has a product or service that has the potential to be sold, strengthen the individual's entrepreneurial skills, and look for small business training and mentoring

Source: Accardi & Duhaime. (2013, updated 2020). Finding and keeping employment. Autism Ontario KnowledgeBase. Retrieved from http://autismontario.novosolutions.net/default.asp?id=153

Multiple supports and strategies for employment exist in various jurisdictions and regions across Canada, some specific to disabled adults, and others specific to autistic adults (Nicholas et al., 2018); however, such "vocational support strategies" are fairly rare (p. 696). One cross-Canada study found that, among various results, resources and services are often difficult to access as well as insufficient (only 41% of participants found resources sufficient; only 51.4% found vocational services sufficient; Nicholas et al., 2018). Participants tended not to disclose their diagnoses of ASD during employment searches; for example, "I certainly would never, ever, ever, ever have admitted that I had Asperger's or autism in my previous careers because I think it would have been a huge stigma. It would have prevented me from getting employment" (p. 699). Some participants noted, though, that during-employment disclosures could elicit understanding, acceptance, and support. Participants also reported the need for supportive working environments, such as a continuum of ongoing supports, family involvement, and collaborative service provision (Nicholas et al., 2018).

Types of Employment Supports

Here are some examples:

- help preparing for work
- help finding a job that is right for you
- help keeping a job
- job coaching
- on-the-job training
- help to move to the next level in your career
- software and mobility devices that can help you do your job

- interpreter or intervenor services
- transportation assistance
- assistive devices and training to use them
- tools and equipment you need for your job
- special clothing for your job
- specialized computer training
- other items you may need

Source: Ontario Ministry of Community and Social Services, 2018.

See the box "Job Development Strategies for Adults with ASD" for a list of various employment assistance strategies and for a model of optimal resource integration to support autistic adults in the workplace.

Job Development Strategies for Adults with ASD

Many individuals with ASD have characteristics that could make them attractive to potential employers, including punctuality, attention to detail, consistency, reliability, or good visual-spatial or mechanical skills. Whatever skills the person possesses, it is important to emphasize strengths and contributions (s)he could make to the business.

There are certain job development strategies that may be particularly useful and productive to prioritize when job searching with and for job seekers with ASD.

- Person-centred planning is vital in the job placement process and helps job developers identify both the strengths and support needs that a person with ASD brings to the job search. Several ICI publications on this topic can be downloaded for free from the Web:
    - *Starting with Me: A Guide to Person-Centered Planning for Job Seekers*
    - *More Than Just a Job: Person-Centered Career Planning*
- Career Exploration. Many individuals with ASD may have to go through an extensive career exploration process, especially those with limited employment exposure and experience. Intensive counseling to identify options; spending time getting to know the neighborhood/community; participating in workplace tours and informational interviews; and trying out real job activities will help job seekers to hone in on employment interests and goals. Employment staff may also have to provide some individuals with alternative ways of expressing their preferences such as the use of AAC devices or by pointing to pictures or symbols.
- Job Carving/Job Creation can be an effective approach. It often makes sense to take advantage of a person's unique set of skills and interests by

carving out or creating a job within an existing business. In doing so, job developers need to demonstrate to the employer that the job seeker can make their business more efficient or productive. For more information about how to go about this process, see the ICI publication:
  - *When Existing Jobs Don't Fit: A Guide to Job Creation*

> **job coach**: a hired person who assists others in preparing for a job site and attends that job site, as needed. This person also helps employees learn the skills required in a given job, provides feedback, and delivers additional training that may be needed to learn a particular job.

- Networking has been proven to speed up the job search! Building on the personal and professional business contacts of employment staff, the job seeker, family members, neighbors, and friends is a far more effective strategy for job development than making cold calls. This can often enhance that vital opportunity by providing a foot in the door to individuals with more significant barriers. For more information and tips about the how-tos of networking, see ICI publications:
  - *Networking: A Consumer Guide to an Effective Job Search*
  - *Making Networking Easier for Job Seekers: A Guide*
  - *Teaching Networking Skills: Paving a Way to Jobs and Careers* (manual)

Source: Kurtz, A., & Jordan, M. (2008). Institute brief: Supporting individuals with autism spectrum disorders: Quality employment practices (pp. 7–8, para. 8). Boston, MA: Institute for Community Inclusion at the University of Massachusetts Boston.

Read about It. Think about It. Write about It.

- Given the list of employment supports available, what supports do you think are the most helpful for autistic adults that you support?
- Do an online search to see if these employment services are offered in your community and inquire about how to enrol.
- Temple Grandin has contributed creative ideas for autistic adults to obtain employment. Look up these creative strategies and highlight how this may be applied to someone you support or have supported.

RECREATION AND LEISURE

Recreation and leisure services vary significantly between individuals. It is indicated, however, that such services are often a need, due to the inherent difficulty with social skills and making and keeping friends for autistic adults (Stoddart et al., 2013). In addition, the anxiety around attending various social groups can be overwhelming. Families have identified recreation supports as a necessity, as staying at home with family, watching TV, and being alone are isolating (Autism Ontario, 2008; Stoddart et al., 2013). A research study in central and southwestern Ontario demonstrated that there were some discrepancies relating to the quantity of services available. Professionals indicated more services were available than parents had stated, potentially demonstrating a disconnect between the advertising of the programs and the places where families sought programming information. This may also indicate a lack of fit between the programs and the disabled individuals (White & Weiss, 2010). Nonetheless, the importance of quality of life is crucial. García-Villamisar and Dattilo (2010) found that enrolling autistic adults in a one-year recreation program significantly decreased stress and increased quality of life indicators (e.g., satisfaction, independence, competence, and social interaction) as compared to a control group. These results highlight the importance of recreation and socialization.

Recreation programs for autistic adults can have various forms and target various skills. Many programs focus on improving social skills due to the difficulties that individuals face in such situations. There are numerous social program possibilities. First, there are those that are informal and work on social skills naturally, through group activities in the community (e.g., dancing, bowling, going out for dinner, etc.). In addition, there are those that focus on teaching social skills, such as PEERS, with a facilitator and participants. PEERS, designed for high-functioning autistic adolescents, is a parent-assisted program delivered over 14 weeks in 90-minute sessions (Laugeson, Frankel, Gantman, Dillon, & Mogil, 2012).

Agencies for developmentally disabled adults also may offer regular programming in the day and evening that varies from cooking classes and art classes to daily living skill programs. These are usually on a first-come, first-served basis, and some have waitlists. There are also recreation programs offered by local municipalities available to disabled individuals, either exclusively or in an inclusive setting. In fact, many autistic adults attend recreation activities available in their communities and bring a personal support worker for assistance when needed.

FINANCIAL SUPPORT

In addition to whatever provinces or territories may or may not provide, there are a number of tax benefits available to disabled Canadians or those who are caring for a disabled child. The disability tax credit (DTC) is available to help offset the extra costs of being disabled (Canada Revenue Agency [CRA], 2019a), and simplifying the application process is a current focus for the CRA (2019b). For example, in 2015, $7,766 was available to be claimed for an autistic individual, with an additional $4,530 for those under 18 and additional attendant care costs in other areas of tax claim (CRA, 2019a). If the disabled individual does not claim the amount, a caregiver may claim it. The Canadian DTC "is a non-refundable tax credit that helps [disabled persons] or their supporting persons reduce the amount of income tax they have to pay" (CRA, 2019a, para. 1). Because many disabled individuals incur expenses such as medical costs, transportation, specific equipment or technology related to their individual needs that would be higher than expenses required of Canadians who are not disabled, the DTC is intended to reduce this financial disparity. However, research by Dunn and Zwicker (2018) suggests that many Canadians who would qualify for the DTC are not benefiting from this opportunity. They indicate that, across Canada, only 40% of Canadians who could claim the disability tax credit are doing so, with 2014 rates ranging from a low of 35.2% in Ontario to a high of 72.9% on Prince Edward Island (Dunn & Zwicker, 2018, p. 11).

Other tax benefits include the working income tax benefit to assist those who are working but making low wages, which can be due in part to disability (CRA, 2019). Registered disability saving plans (RDSPs) are available for disabled individuals who have been approved for the DTC (Government of Canada, 2017). This saving plan allows families and the individual to save for the future with the government contributing, with the money growing while invested (Government of Canada, 2017); however, it only has around an 11% uptake (Dudley & Emery, 2014). Canada is the first country in the world to have created RDSPs as an invested savings plan that can be taken out at any time for whatever the individual or family chooses and does not affect disability payments (up to a certain amount) (Government of Canada, 2017).

In 2017, the Government of Canada introduced the new Canada caregiver credit (CCC), replacing three tax credits previously available to Canadians: the caregiver credit, the family caregiver credit, and the credit for infirm dependents age 18 or older (Government of Canada, 2018c). Canadians who are the primary caregivers for a family member "with a physical or mental impairment" may qualify for the new caregiver credit (Government of Canada, 2018c, para. 5). Family members who may be claimed under the new CCC include a spouse or common-law partner, a child or grandchild, parent, grandparent, uncle, aunt, niece, or nephew if they have been resident in Canada during that year and they rely on the claimant to "regularly and consistently provide them with some or all of the basic necessities of life, such as food, shelter, and clothing" (Government of Canada, 2018c, para. 7).

While the Government of Canada indicates that the new CCC will provide qualifying Canadians with tax credits that are equivalent to, or in some cases higher than, credits received under the previous system of three separate credits (Government of Canada, 2018c), a recent University of Calgary policy brief suggests that tax credits meant to benefit Canadians living with diverse needs, and those who care for them, may not be affording all the benefits they are intended to provide (Dunn & Zwicker, 2018).

Dunn and Zwicker (2018) recommended a number of actions the government might take and policy changes that could be implemented to support Canadians with disabilities and their caregivers to access the full range of tax benefits available to them. They suggest that improving efficiency of administration and making the processes to access benefits such as the DTC clearer and more transparent would increase access to such programs for prospective recipients. In addition, they emphasize that closer monitoring and evaluation of the program in order to gather accurate information on utilization rates would allow government to determine the effectiveness of the program and identify areas for improvement.

All about the RDSP

The registered disability savings plan (RDSP) is a Canada-wide registered matched savings plan for people with disabilities. Here are some basics:

- For every $1 put in an RDSP account, the federal government will match it (if your family income is below $95,259) with up to $3. This is the Canada disability savings grant.
- For people living on a low-income (less than $31,120), the federal government will invest $1000 each year for 20 years. This is the Canada disability savings bond.
- People living on an income between $31,120 and $47,630 can still receive a partial bond.
- Anyone can contribute to an RDSP—family, friends, and even neighbours. This gives people who want to help a way to do so!
- RDSPs offer some of the best returns on investment available. Your money will grow. It might even triple in size!
- The RDSP is exempt from most provincial disability and income assistance benefits. The government will not claw this money back. (To find out how your province treats the RDSP, go to www.disabilitysavings.gc.ca.)
- There are no restrictions on how RDSP withdrawals are spent.

Source: RDSP, 2020, para. 1.

Financial supports are also available for those attending post-secondary institutions. Such supports are typically provided by jurisdiction, just as education is a provincial/territorial responsibility, for the most part. However, some national funding is available. Financial support in the form of grants is available to support permanently disabled students, and exceptional needs for equipment and/or services can be accessed through the Canada Student Grant for Services and

> **independent living**: a philosophy that states disabled adults should live in their chosen communities, make choices and decisions in their lives, and participate in every part of their lives (Independent Living Canada, n.d.).

Equipment for Students with Permanent Disabilities (Government of Canada, 2019). The Repayment Assistance Plan for Borrowers with a Permanent Disability is another program that helps students with disabilities pay off their loans after finishing school. Eligibility is based on income and disability-related costs (DisabilityAwards.ca, n.d.). Additional awards for post-secondary autistic students may also be available through local agencies and within each individual post-secondary institution.

Read about It. Think about It. Write about It.

- Given the list of employment supports available, what supports do you think are the most helpful for autistic adults that you support?
- Do an online search to see if these employment services are offered in your community and inquire about how to enrol.

HOUSING

Housing is another area in high demand for autistic adults. The issue of housing for adults with ASD is important and ongoing, but it is not limited to adults with ASD. Jurisdictions may offer some type of supported housing, but it may not be a categorical approach. In other words, housing may be related to disability but not specifically to ASD. In any case, a range of options for autistic adults is needed, just as there are for nondisabled adults or other disability or diversity areas. One example is Nova Scotia's Independent Living Support (ILS), which provides financial assistance to pay for services for individuals who are semi-independent but still require support. Eligibility is determined through functional and financial assessments where an individual is determined to have unmet needs, and funding amounts are based on the assessed needs. This particular program is a person-directed, collaborative model designed "to promote independence, self-reliance, security and social inclusion by creating a flexible and responsive delivery system that incorporates the strengths of a participant, their personal and community resources, and approved ILS Service Providers" (Nova Scotia Independent Support, n.d.). Supports are used to maximize independence in daily life, help individuals build and maintain relationships and connections, maintain individual health and wellness, enable development and growth, and delay the need for relocation to a staffed—rather than independent—residential support option (Department of Community Service, Nova Scotia, 2009). Perhaps at the other end of a spectrum of adult housing supports is Manitoba's developmental centre (Province of Manitoba, n.d.). The Manitoba Developmental Centre (MDC) is an accredited residential option located in Portage la Prairie. MDC offers supervision, supportive care, and developmental programs for adults with intellectual disabilities. There are two areas of specialization at MDC: the Extended Care/Geriatric Program and the Habilitation/Specialty Program.

The Extended Care/Geriatric Program caters to individuals with complex medical conditions who require medical, nursing, and therapeutic care, and "the Program also provides convalescent care for medically fragile residents and rehabilitation care for elderly residents" (Province of Manitoba, n.d., para. 5). The Habilitation/Specialty Program caters to those with behavioural needs who may be a risk to themselves, to others, or to their environment and "provides specialized services for residents diagnosed with autism, residents who are deaf and/or blind, and for residents requiring support to fully participate in their activities of daily living" (Province of Manitoba, n.d., para. 6). MDC cares for approximately 160 individuals and works to help individuals transitioning into their communities; new admissions are only allowed on a short-term basis or by court order under the *Vulnerable Persons Living with a Mental Disability Act*.

Almost 60% of those partaking in Stoddart and colleagues' (2013) Ontario survey lived with family. Only 13.6% were living on their own with no supports, and some lived on their own with help from family (5.9%), with professional support (2.3%), and in group homes (8.4%; Stoddart et al., 2013). The 1950s saw the start of a movement away from institutions, where disabled individuals lived together and received specialized treatment within segregated settings (Davidson et al., 2001; Lamb & Bachrach, 2001). As institutions closed, individuals moved into the community to receive individualized services (Davidson et al., 2001; Lamb & Bachrach, 2001). In Ontario, for example, institutions began closing as early as 1977, with the final closure in 2009 (Autism Ontario, 2008); Alberta closed its last institutions closer to 2014 (Dudley & Emery, 2014). Such closings have also led to difficulties, as the subsequent systems have not been funded sufficiently or approached systematically, leading to fewer housing options for many, a lack of integration of services, and an abundance of individuals living with family members (Autism Ontario, 2008; Lamb & Bachrach, 2001). Dudley and Emery (2014) have reported that Quebec is working on an insurance plan that would provide lifelong supports.

Available housing options are on a wide spectrum depending on the needs of individuals and their capacity to live independently. These types can vary from living independently to living in group homes or nursing homes with constant care. Although many autistic adults have typical cognitive functioning, they may lack skills in adaptive areas that are required for everyday living. Thus, they often remain in family homes (Autism Ontario, 2008; Stoddart et al., 2013). A study based in Newfoundland and Labrador indicated that 75% of their autistic adult participants lived at home with family members (Memorial University of Newfoundland Health Research Unit, 2003). In 2010, Nova Scotia reported that "only 18 percent of [autistic individuals] become independent as adults" and that "over 40 percent of autistic adults continue to live with their parents" (Nova Scotia Department of Education, 2010, p. 54). In addition to the ILS option, Nova Scotia reported additional options as of 2019, citing the need for housing options that keep individuals in their communities while still granting them access to community supports such as skill-building programs, networking, and leisure

Table 8.2: Possible Housing Options

Independent Options • Own • Lease • Rent • Co-op	There are many options for individuals to live on their own like many other adults. However, this requires the individuals to have employment in order to support their house or to have families buy it, which is difficult with the financial pressures of having a child with a disability.
Supported Living	Supported living "offers services to individuals with disabilities who are able to live in a home or an apartment. The services, typically minimal in nature, are based on the individual's specific support needs and are provided by caregivers working under the direction of the individual" (Autism Speaks, 2011, p. 13).
Semi-Independent Living (SIL)	Twenty-four-hour supports are available for the individual, who lives either independently or with others. Support for independent living skills is provided by the staff at the residence.
Group Homes	A group of unrelated people live in the home with staff support 24/7. The home is owned by an agency that hires staff. Staff provide instruction and activities in the home and community.
Group Living / Ownership	Similar to a group home; however, the home is bought by a group of families who hire staff or contract an agency to hire staff.
Teaching Family Model (Foster Home Living)	A professional family has one or more person with a disability who lives in the home.
Farmstead Communities	A number of individuals live, usually on a farm, with residential supports.
Assisted Living	A care facility offers assistance with daily living skills and hygiene. It does not offer complex medical supports like a nursing home.
Nursing Homes	A care facility providing complex care to individuals. The difficulty is that these are designed for the geriatric population, and unfortunately younger people are often placed here with no other options.
Developmental Centre	Large centres for people with developmental disabilities living together.

Sources: Autism Ontario, 2008; Autism Speaks, 2011b; Ombudsman Ontario, 2014.

activities. According to the *Choosing Now* report, there are three additional housing options for adults with ASD (Autism Nova Scotia, 2019). Many autistic adults continue to live with their parents or guardians so they can access direct family support funds; however, this approach is not always possible or may be detrimental. Another popular option is the alternate family model, in which an individual is placed with two or more non-related people who can provide adequate support. Such placings are an imperfect alternative, as availability of spaces is limited and the problem of isolation is not immediately solved. The third option available is a licensed home providing special care, which includes a broad range of settings, most often with residential staffing support (even up to 24-hour professional supports), including rehabilitation and developmental programs for disabled adults.

Read about It. Think about It. Write about It.

- Research housing options that have been created across Canada. What are some of the strengths and weaknesses in each model?

There are other creative, affordable, and sustainable options for individuals with disabilities (Housing Study Group, 2013), but such examples are inconsistent across provinces, territories, cities, towns, and even individual families.

Celebrating Another Housing Option for Adults with Disabilities

Years ago, when our family's now 18-year-old son, Robert, was dually diagnosed with PDD-NOS and bipolar disorder, we came across a website with housing options that looked interesting, but immediately discarded it as impossible for us! For one thing, we were concerned that our son—who was then struggling in residential care at London's Child and Parent Resource Institute (CPRI)—would never be able to again live within our family unit; for another, I was apprehensive about the fit between this program and our city bylaws. Fast-forwarding to 2007, with the guidance of our realtor Karen Hobbs-Thomson of REMAX, my husband and I purchased a home with an "empty shell" in an outbuilding that was comprised of about 300 square feet, including a similarly tiny basement with full ceiling height. We purchased our home with the idea that this space could somehow be converted from its former use as the boiler room for commercial greenhouses into a transitional living area that fit well with our prediction that our son would want some freedom by age 18—but not too much!

Immediately after purchasing our home, we began researching the options and checking out various possibilities that would align with our municipal regulations in the City of Brantford. After struggling for some time, we approached Brantford

Housing, where Tom Hodgson enthusiastically reminded me of the Canadian Mortgage and Housing Corporation (CMHC) support for creative options in housing. Specifically, he kindly ordered and provided me with a copy of CMHC's "Residential Rehabilitation Assistance Program (RRAP): Secondary/Garden Suite" application package. Within RRAP, the use of a Secondary/Garden Suite is described as follows: "Canada Mortgage and Housing Corporation (CMHC) offers financial assistance for the creation of a Secondary or Garden Suite for a low-income senior or adult with a disability—making it possible for them to live independently in their community, close to family and friends" (CMHC, 2010, para. 1).

What Is a Secondary Suite or a Garden Suite?

A secondary suite, sometimes called an in-law suite, is a self-contained unit within an existing home or an addition to a home. This means there are full kitchen and bath facilities, as well as a separate entrance. A garden suite is a separate living unit that is not attached to the principal residence but built on the same property. Garden suites are sometimes referred to as "granny flats" because they were originally created to provide a home for an aging parent of a homeowner. Like a secondary suite, a garden suite is a self-contained unit. Regardless of which type of housing is chosen, secondary and garden suites must meet all applicable building code requirements, as well as local municipal planning and zoning regulations.

Who Can Apply?

You may be eligible to receive assistance if: you are a homeowner or private entrepreneur owning residential property that would accommodate an affordable, self-contained rental unit for a low-income senior (65 years of age or more) or adult with a disability; your property meets with the applicable zoning and building requirements; you consent to enter into an operating agreement that establishes the rent that can be charged during the term of the Agreement; you also agree that the household income of the occupant(s) of the newly created self-contained unit will be below a CMHC set level (adapted from CMHC 2018, paras. 1–6).

Our next step was to contact our city's planning department to see what proactive steps needed to be taken prior to the approval of a permit for this forgivable loan, described in detail above. During these lengthy and sometimes challenging processes, we were fortunate that our call for help came across the desk of Lucy Hives, a senior planner for the City of Brantford. Together, we researched various options; searched out paperwork, drawings, measurements, and plans; and reached various conclusions. First, we applied for a zoning change to allow the development of a fully self-contained unit on our property's outbuilding, currently zoned as a single-family dwelling space. Later, this option was discarded and we were requested to design

Figure 8.5: Robert's Apartment

and build a fully enclosed breezeway, which would join our main house together with our outbuilding. This joining together, along with full interior access to the unit for our son, would then allow us to obtain permit approval.

At this point, we were extremely privileged to have Rob Wilkie enter the scene, owner of Rob the Builder in Kitchener-Waterloo (robthebuilder@primus.ca). Rob was able to take our vision and the city's regulations and craft them into a plan that worked for all involved. With this breezeway fully excavated, built, and finished with a series of shoe racks, coat hooks, and other storage devices to create delight in any mother—of a child with ASD or not—the second phase of constructing the living area could begin.

Years of planning went into several nail-biting weeks of preparing lengthy, detailed, and precise responses to a range of questions, inquires, and regulations put in place to support this CMHC program, as we prepared a package to be forwarded for approval. After several series of follow-up questions, answers, and more documentation, we received the "go ahead" letter! This was a day of celebration in our home!

Together with the unwavering support and ready assistance of Anne De Rosse, also of the Housing Department in the City of Brantford, we successfully navigated the step-by-step process of construction, approvals, and reimbursement. As of the time of this writing, we are awaiting only the last piece of the approval on the completion of our extended living space from the Fire Marshall, the Electrical Safety Authority, CMHC, and the City of Brantford. We have been proud to be a part of Brantford's first use of this imaginative program.

This is what Tom Hodgson, RRAP Agent, very kindly had to say about the process:

> It was so exciting to receive the inquiry from Kimberly Maich with respect to CMHC's Secondary Suite program. I could tell after speaking with Kimberly for a short time that she was the perfect candidate for the program. The City of Brantford Housing Department had just recently taken over the administration

of the program so we were thrilled about the possibility of seeing an application come to fruition. After visiting Kimberly and seeing the finished project it was obviously a resounding success. Kimberly's son Robert will be able to live independently but will also be close enough to family and friends to receive necessary support. Thanks Kimberly for your patience, determination and unwavering positive attitude throughout the process.

Consider CMHC's programs as an option for your [offspring] who [is] not quite ready to face the world with complete independence but is ready to spread their wings slightly in the sight of their parents. Here are a few pieces of advice from one experience:

- Your work will be done on a very tight deadline—have your contractors ready, waiting, and prepared for a quick turn-around. For example, Rob Wilkie, our dedicated builder, often slept in the living area itself while working (quietly) into the wee hours of the morning.
- Be prepared to deal with many details and to gather and share information from a variety of sources. Be patient and persistent!
- Photocopy everything you submit. Keep your information organized every step of the way. A clear proposal is a more readily accepted proposal.
- Don't be afraid to use the courier for speedy delivery!
- Ensure all your approvals are in place as soon as possible. Pay for your permit up front. Even though you may not be reimbursed for its cost, you will be prepared to start work as soon as your forgivable loan is approved. For example, when we received our approval letter, our work was to begin "immediately," and we were given a specific completion date.
- Be certain that your contractors know that they will be waiting for reimbursement for their work and that the program does not include up-front costs.
- Plan to have extra funds on hand for unexpected costs, as well as preparation costs. For example, prior to applying for this program, we paid close to $20,000 to waterproof the basement area and to build the breezeway required by municipal regulations.
- Keep in mind that you have a responsibility to maintain CMHC standards for a long period of time to fulfill the requirements for loan reimbursement.
- Finally, celebrate this program, an exceptional option for our grown sons and daughters with ASD or other disabilities.

Source: Maich, 2012.

SPOTLIGHTS ACROSS CANADA

Initiative: Manitoba

Manitoba's *Thrive: A Five-Year Plan for Helping Manitobans with ASD and Their Families* (2013) provides adult services to individuals with ASD with their unique needs and challenges that can affect their abilities to problem solve and live independently. To address these challenges, autistic adults need extra support to live full, productive lives and realize their potential. *Thrive* can help these individuals move forward by providing more opportunities for autistic adults to develop life skills; gaining access to education and employment training programs; offering help for autistic adults to find and keep jobs; and providing assistance for young autistic adults to live independently. *Thrive* can help these individuals through the following: creating partnerships with the community to develop a life-skills networking group for autistic adults, creating ASD-specific services within existing educational and employment service programs, and through independent living services that help young autistic adults develop the skills they need to live on their own.

Research: Alberta

In 2017, Dudley and Nankane developed a discussion paper for the Autism Society Alberta. Descriptively entitled *Who Will Take Care of Our Kids (When We No Longer Can)? The Challenges Facing Adults with ASD and Their Aging Parents*, its focus is clear. Thirty-four respondents answered three questions focused on sustainable quality of life, gaps, and innovative/new models. The gaps noted were summarized in five points:

- The lack of quality housing, which has resulted in growing waitlists
- The life that people face when the individual turns 65
- The lack of caring, training and available staff
- The lack of public awareness of challenges faced by aging families, and
- The lack of mentorship for families and individuals to connect with those who have succeeded in creating a sustainable quality of life (Dudley & Nankane, 2017, p. 4)

Even though it was evident that parents of adult children were working within a system described as "fragmented, unintuitive, and difficult" (p. 5), some helpful key practices were found to help reach "sustainable, quality, life-long support" (p. 5):

- Creating a network of committed people for support
- Planning early
- Enhancing financial security through RDSP contributions and discretionary trusts

- Accessing home settings with high-level qualified agency staff who work in collaboration with families
- Ensuring communication through ongoing care and support plans

Possible innovations and/or new models that emerged in this discussion paper included roles for technology; specialized insurance; mentoring/guardianship plans and supports; practical, visual tool kits of information (e.g., housing models); a one-door model of both information and services; and housing initiatives. The discussion paper ends with: "this report attempts to convey a sense of hope that positive movement is occurring, while at the same time highlighting a sense of urgency that families are struggling and a better way forward must be created" (Dudley & Nankane, 2017, p. 29).

Policy: Newfoundland and Labrador

In 2019, Newfoundland and Labrador's Department of Health and Community Services released the three-phase Autism Action Plan (2019–2022) with short-term, medium-term, and long-term actionable items within six focus areas. This plan includes a number of items related to services for adults with ASD. In focus area one—related to assessment, diagnosis, awareness, and acceptance—implementation plans include "new standardized assessment tools for community supports that target individualized support needs for [developmentally disabled adults] including ASD" (p. 4) and "more diagnostic clinics for children and adults within each regional health authority" (p. 5). Focus area two emphasizes support, including support for families and for caregivers. In focus area two, "seamless service provision for adults with developmental disabilities through the creation of a new Supporting Abilities Program" is included. The third focus area emphasizes evidence-based strategies and includes "improved access to cognitive behavioural therapy and other evidence-based interventions for children and adults living with ASD and experiencing mental health concerns" (p. 7). Focus area five, which centres on community-based living, includes:

> Partnerships between the Government of Newfoundland and Labrador and community agencies, municipalities, Indigenous governments and organizations, and the private sector, to increase awareness and to develop a range of supports, including life skills networking groups and leisure groups for adults with ASD. (p. 9)

A LOOK BACK

Chapter 8, "The Adult Years," focused on:

- The transition to adulthood and various opportunities and barriers adults face

- Common issues and trends that adults with ASD are reporting
- The transition into various aspects of community life including post-secondary education, employment, recreation and leisure, housing, and financial supports.

ADDITIONAL RESOURCES

Canadian Caregiver Credit (Government of Canada)

https://www.canada.ca/en/revenue-agency/services/tax/individuals/topics/about-your-tax-return/tax-return/completing-a-tax-return/deductions-credits-expenses/canada-caregiver-amount.html

This website provides detailed information for the Canadian caregiver credit. This is a non-refundable tax credit for individuals supporting a spouse, partner, or dependent with a physical or mental impairment.

Disability Tax Credit (Government of Canada)

https://www.canada.ca/en/revenue-agency/services/tax/individuals/segments/tax-credits-deductions-persons-disabilities/disability-tax-credit.html

This website provides information on the disability tax credit. Information available includes eligibility and application process.

***Ending the Wait: An Action Agenda to Address the Housing Crisis Confronting Adults with Developmental Disabilities* (Housing Study Group)**

https://clmiss.ca/wp-content/uploads/2019/02/Ending_the_Wait_final_sep6.pdf

This document provides an overview and analysis of housing-related issues for adults with developmental disabilities. A summary of findings and recommendations for a three-year action plan are included.

***Forgotten: Ontario Adults with Autism and Adults with Asperger's* (Autism Ontario)**

https://www.autismontario.com/sites/default/files/2019-01/Forgotten%2BReport%2BAutism%2BOntario.pdf

This report, published in 2008, summarizes funding options and services available for adults with ASD. Recommendations for improvements are included.

Housing and Residential Supports Tool Kit (Autism Speaks)

www.autismspeaks.org/sites/default/files/housing_tool_kit_web2.pdf

This website provides an overview of housing options for adults with ASD. Users can access a template to assist with planning and preparing for alternative housing arrangements.

Thrive

http://www.gov.mb.ca/fs/thrive/

This website summarizes Manitoba's five-year plan to increase access to ASD-related information, resources, and services.

The Youth KIT (CanChild)

https://www.canchild.ca/system/tenon/assets/attachments/000/000/721/original/Youth_Kit_Online.pdf

The Youth Kit is a useful tool to assist teens transitioning to adulthood. This interactive document poses several questions and helps with goal setting and planning.

ASD Central for Adults: Autism Canada

https://www.facebook.com/groups/1710172265882835/

This website links to a social media site for adults with ASD. Interested members can request access to join the private group.

The Adult Autism Spectrum Quotient (AQ)

https://autismcanada.org/about-autism/diagnosis/screening-tools/adult/

This website links to an online screening tool for adults. The Adult Autism Spectrum Quotient includes a series of questions with Likert-scale responses.

Blueprint for a National Autism Spectrum Disorder Strategy

https://www.casda.ca/wp-content/uploads/2019/03/Blueprint-for-a-National-ASD-Strategy-1.pdf

This report, drafted by members of the Canadian Autism Spectrum Disorder Alliance, proposes an initial framework for a national autism strategy. This is an informative read for anyone impacted by autism.

Ontario Adult Autism Research and Support Network

http://www.ont-autism.uoguelph.ca/resources.shtml

The Ontario Adult Autism Research and Support Network (OAARSN) aims to share best practices for adults with ASD. This website links to adult-related resources and provides links to past newsletters and bulletins published by OAARSN.

Is It Autism and If So, What Next? A Guide for Adults

https://www.autismspeaks.ca/science-services-resources/resources/tool-kits/is-it-autism-and-if-so-what-next-a-guide-for-adults-1/

This tool kit was developed to assist adults who may have or have been recently diagnosed with ASD. This kit includes a description of ASD and tips on when to consult with professionals.

Repayment Assistance Plan—Permanent Disability Assistance

https://www.canada.ca/en/services/benefits/education/student-aid/grants-loans/repay/assistance/rap/permanent-disability.html

This website provides information on repayment assistance available to some students with a disability.

Transition Resource Guide for Students with Disabilities: ASD

https://www.transitionresourceguide.ca/disabilities/autism-spectrum-disorder-asd

This website provides useful information for students with ASD planning to transition to post-secondary education. This site includes planning tools, checklists, and resources for students, parents, and educators.

CHAPTER 9

Parents and Families

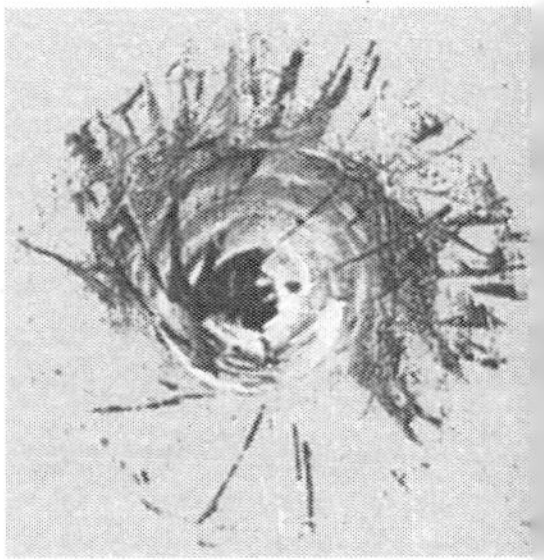

LEARNING OBJECTIVES

- Recall historical context of the perception of the parent of a child with ASD, including negative perspectives and new, more modern models for supporting families with children with ASD.
- List jurisdictional resources available to assist families.
- Recognize the importance of advocacy and developing advocacy skills for families to fight for the needs of their child.
- Review provincial and territorial highlights and examples of family supports and programs.

Like much of the commentary that impacted the history of autism spectrum disorder (ASD), how parents of children with ASD were viewed historically has been primarily negative. A common misconception early in ASD history was that the cause of ASD was a *refrigerator mother*, cold and nonconforming toward their children with ASD—causing them to be aloof and disengaged socially. Efforts to dispel these misconceptions have thankfully led to newer models that support families and the process of learning about their child. After reviewing this context and these new models, this chapter provides helpful resources for families and examines the Canadian context of supports and resources for families of children with ASD.

Like any other individual, every child, adolescent, and student with a disability comes with context. The child's parents and family or caregivers are part of such context, what Hobbs (1978) referred to as an ecosystem, with the child in the centre, surrounded by clusters, such as family, community, neighbourhood, and school. It is clear that the family has an important place in the life of the child; that the child has a place of priority in the family ecosystem; that the child-parent relationship is an evolving, multidirectional relationship, and that, if problems occur in the ecosystem of the child, the "efforts to help a child should address the system as a whole" (p. 757). However, current supportive, positive conceptions of children (at any age), family, and disability have not always existed—and have certainly not always been respected—in the fields of ASD, disability, and beyond.

HISTORICAL VIEWS OF PARENTS, FAMILIES, AND DISABILITIES

Phillip Ferguson (2002) states that how families react to children with disabilities is "inescapably embedded within a socio-historical context" (p. 124), providing a patterned framework that shifts with culture over time. According to Ferguson, the early 1800s to the early 1900s were infused with *blame*: parents were to blame for the burden of childhood disability, due to their own (likely) disability, (poor) socioeconomic status, (female) gender, (lack of) morality, or (lack of) work ethic. From approximately 1920 to 1980, however, this blame on parental problems shifted to *damage* in the family context: an outcome that was assumed to be intrinsic to disability and inevitable and fit with the dominance of the medical model in the field, which still influences current attitudes and behaviours. Ferguson categorized these into four conceptions encompassing behavioural and attitudinal parental reactions, as well as that seemingly inevitable damage (see Table 9.1).

> **medical model**: in the disability literature, this model emphasizes limitations, that the disability focuses on biology (impairment) and not social and environmental factors. It often portrays victimization and looks at solutions that focus on the person and not the community (Public Service Alliance of Canada, 2015).

> **social model**: in the disability culture, this model looks at disability as an issue created by societal, environmental, and attitudinal barriers. It suggests that solutions should focus on change in the social environment, and that disabilities are seen to be caused not by the disability itself, but by living in a society designed for the nondisabled (Public Service Alliance of Canada, 2015).

These are but some of the many models that tended to blame parents or assign negativity, in some way, to parenting a child with a disability. Others are specific to families raising a child with ASD, such as Bettelheim's so-called refrigerator mother (see Chapter 1); typically, they are aligned with a medical model of disability that focuses on ASD as a deficit-based issue that needs—along with the parents and families—to be fixed (Straus, 2013).

Table 9.1: Nature and Source of Parental Reactions

	Inherent Disruptions	Contextual Disruptions
Attitudinal	Psychodynamic approaches	Psychosocial approaches
Behavioural	Functionalist approaches	Interactionist approaches

Source: Ferguson, 2002.

Read about It. Think about It. Write about It.

- Examine the ways that services are offered to families with ASD in your region. Are some of the stereotypes or challenges listed above portrayed to parents in the way that enrolment in services happen, how services are delivered, or how parental roles are delineated?

CURRENT VIEWS OF PARENTS, FAMILIES, AND DISABILITIES

According to Ferguson (2002), the last two decades have brought with them "a dramatic evolution of our attitudes and supports for people with disabilities and their families" (p. 127). This change is evidenced by transformations in legislation and practices, as well as movement to framing within a positive, social model of disability that frames disability as "socially constructed rather than biologically given" (Straus, 2013, p. 462). Ferguson (2002) notes that more positive models have emerged throughout this period, such as *adapted*, *evolving*, and *supported* families. As well, the development of methods for measuring stress levels in order to determine appropriate family interventions have appeared in the literature (Weiss & Lunsky, 2011). Freedman, Kalb, Zablotsky, and Stuart (2012) help to dispel some popular media myths around households parenting children with ASD with findings that such families are at no higher risk for separation and divorce, even when examining severity of related symptoms. Their analysis of data from almost 78,000 parental interviews found "no association between a child having an ASD diagnosis and whether or not the child lives in a family consisting of two biological or adoptive parents" (p. 542). However, Bilaver and Havlicek's 2013 study of almost 10,000 children found that children with ASD are placed in foster care at twice the typical rate, that placement in care is four times as long, and that kinship placements are less common. Perhaps, then, children with ASD have a qualitatively different experience in foster care than is typical, especially when considering how even minor changes and transition can be challenging for children with ASD.

Parenting children with ASD is also still associated with challenges—even extraordinary ones—that may impact stress levels, mental health, well-being, and social relationships. Hickey, Dubois, and Hartley (2018) broke down the types of social exchanges that 368 parents encountered when raising a child with ASD, finding that fathers tend to experience more informal types of positive social exchanges and mothers more emotional positive social exchanges. The source for these exchanges are primarily spousal, but so were primarily negative social exchanges: a balanced level of emotional exchange. Overall, they noted that "mothers of children with ASD reported not only more positive but also more negative social exchanges with family, friends, and health professionals than fathers" (p. 475), reflecting childcare roles, employment roles, and service involvement roles in parenting children with ASD. In addition to findings related to depressive symptoms in parents of children with ASD, the following practical advice is provided:

> The most frequent types of positive social exchanges for all sources were informational (e.g., useful suggestions) or instrumental (e.g., helpful assistance) for both mothers and fathers of children with ASD. The most frequent type of negative social exchange was informational (e.g., intrusive advice), and this was particularly true for social exchanges with one's spouse and family. Thus, it may be beneficial for interventions to encourage parents of children with ASD to direct their spouse, family, and friends to listen to concerns or provide aid, as opposed to offering advice, which is often experienced negatively. Moreover, parents of children with ASD may benefit from interventions that encourage them to communicate preferences for informational social exchanges (e.g., how to frame and when to provide) with spouse and family. (p. 476)

Parents themselves have positive hopes for the future of their children with ASD yet are concerned about issues like language development, eye contact, motor skills, normalcy, and social isolation (Poirier, Vallée-Ouimet, Stip, Caron, & Pelletier, 2015). Watson, Hayes, Radford-Paz, and Coons (2013) reported that parents may be uncertain, concerned, anxious—even fearful—but also might have high expectations for improvement. Parents also feel hope; a certainty that, "despite life potentially being harder for them, their children could live fully independently, hold meaningful employment, and have their own families in the future" (p. 89). However, while this may hold true for some contexts (e.g., the general community), other contexts and situations may prove to be more challenging or stressful (Ferguson, 2002). One example is raising children with ASD in rural, isolated, or northern settings, not uncommon experiences for Canadian families. Hoogsteen and Woodgate (2013), for example, examined the family experiences of parenting children with ASD in a rural setting within a Canadian mid-Western setting. The study found that, upon diagnosis, family dynamics changed significantly as the child with ASD became the focus of the whole family. All family decisions are made around concerns about and meeting the needs of the child, which results in parents taking on multiple roles, such as advocates, problem-solvers, and coaches: "Parents expressed that the majority of their energy was spent on their child with autism which often led to fatigue, exhaustion and burning out" (p. 137). Overall, parents indicated that they have had to put their needs aside to fulfill those of the child, but they also came to realize that striking a balance is significant in preserving the family structure.

> Overall, parents in this study parented without question and did whatever they could, whenever they could, with whatever they had. Parents believed in the "try everything" approach and learned through trial and error. Parents sought out

> different treatment options, diet changes and biomedical models. Although parents acquired multiple roles and faced many unmet needs, parents strived for balance while parenting a child with autism in a rural area. (p. 139)

Findings from this research also emerged within the role of professionals supporting rural healthcare, specifically nursing care:

> Increased training and further education in the area of childhood autism are warranted for rural nurses and physicians and other professionals residing in rural communities. Parents expressed the need for increased professional support as communities often went for months to years without providing specialized services and programs needed for children with autism. Also lacking were supportive and counselling services meant to help parents cope with parenting a child with autism. Rural nurses could take the lead in organizing and running support groups and information sessions for parents. With the appropriate training and knowledge, nurses could empower parents to learn how to cope and best support their child with autism. (p. 139)

Even within positive models of the current context, "parents, especially mothers, are held individually responsible and accountable for 'problems' that occur within the family," even when their children, perhaps those with a developmental disability, are adults (Saaltink & Ouellette-Kuntz, 2014). This is evident in gendered issues such as maternal employment when a child with ASD is involved. Alberta-based researchers Hodgetts, McConnell, Zwaigenbaum, and Nicholas (2014) found that 78% of surveyed mothers shared that "the professional supports and services for their child impacted their employment above and beyond the lived experience of parenting a child with autism" (p. 87).

Yet parents persist with hopes and dreams for their children, even when others are not as forgiving. In fact, it has been demonstrated that "the hopes and goals for the parents of children with ASD are very similar to what all parents wish for their children regardless of disability" (Starr & Foy, 2012, p. 212). And perhaps more systemic help and support is possible through calls for organized service provision, which are ongoing. Services for individuals with ASD—and their families—are included in a recent Government of Newfoundland and Labrador publication entitled *The Way Forward: Building for Our Future* (2018). Action 3.11.3 is entitled "Providing Better Services to Persons Living with and Treating Autism" (p. 46). It acknowledges the difficulties with accessing services in a piecemeal approach and notes a commitment to integrated service provision, improved assessment, resources, and decision-making protocols, as well as an upcoming formalized action plan.

More than a decade ago, an Alberta study suggested that "attention also needs to be directed toward the organization of services, and not only the service elements, given parents [sic] continued struggles navigating complex service systems" (McLennan,

Huculak, & Sheehan, 2008, p. 1196). Given the impact that an ASD diagnosis can have on the family unit, the study suggests that families and professionals work cohesively to balance out such impacts. *Family-centered care* (FCC) is one service delivery option described by Hodgetts, Nicholas, Zwaigenbaum, and McConnell (2013), where the services are tailored to suit the changing needs and priorities of families. Numerous researchers and specialists advocate for the implementation of FCC across all services. Despite the fact that supports for ASD usually occur in schools, it is less likely for them to practise FCC, especially as the child advances along different academic levels: "limited research available on FCC for families of children with ASD suggests that services are often not perceived to be family-centered which is surprising because FCC is particularly well suited to complex service needs, common with persons with ASD" (Hodgetts et al., 2013, p. 139).

> Family-centered "carers", but not a family-centered "care system", generally characterize services for families with children with ASD in Alberta. Our findings lend themselves to both specific practice recommendations, and broad policy implications. At the practice level, our findings reinforce the importance of teaching professionals, across disciplines, of the importance of therapeutic rapport. (Hodgetts et al., 2013, p. 145)

In addition, the authors found that varied systems of care, provided in a piecemeal, discrete manner, "appear to be especially exhausting for families due to the lack of coordination and continuity of care for families across sectors and the lifespan" (p. 145) and suggest that Alberta should adopt a "'key worker' model of service delivery, where one person acts as a single point of contact to help a family navigate supports and services across sectors, [which] could dramatically decrease [the] burden on families" (Hodgetts et al., 2013, p. 145).

Read about It. Think about It. Write about It.

- In your professional or personal experience, how does a lack of integrated services impact families?
- What benefits would the family-centred approach have for families?

Levels of Awareness

One unique model to support reconciliation of the differing interpretations of parents, families, and educators is *Levels of Awareness: A Closer Look at Communication between Parents and Professionals* (Ulrich & Bauer, 2003). These levels of awareness contrast with the accepted supposition of the grief cycle as the foundation experienced by parents in raising a child with exceptionalities (Anderegg, Vergason, & Smith, 1992). Anderegg

Table 9.2: Levels of Awareness

Level	Phase Name	Main Feature
1	The Ostrich Phase	Lack of awareness, knowledge, and/or understanding
2	Special Designation	Seeking services to meet special needs
3	Normalization	Minimizing differences; maximizing normality
4	Self-actualization	Reality, acceptance, and development of self-advocacy

Source: Ulrich & Bauer, 2003.

and colleagues (1992) adapted the classic Kubler-Ross grief sequence to the immediate and extended families of children with disabilities, with the development of a three-stage model framed by confronting, adjusting, and adapting and then matched practical educator interventions to each component. Although the grief cycle model moves past the view of the parent as dysfunctional (Anderegg et al., 1992), it maintains an assumption of parental *denial*—an all-too-common vocalization by professionals working with parents, which can be perceived as "condescending and patronizing" (p. 20). Alternatively, the levels-of-awareness approach suggests that parents move through four main levels of understanding, each with its own name and features (see Table 9.2).

In this model, it is thought that parents will progress through these stages in a fairly linear fashion, moving to the next one when they have a transformational experience that elicits a change in thinking. For example, the authors share an example of a parent in the special designation phase who suddenly realized that the constant, compensatory tutoring she was seeking and providing for her child (e.g., flash cards in the car) was negatively affecting her family's quality of life (an "Aha!" moment). This helped her to move on to the next phase—normalization—where seeking services was not such a focus. For professionals working with parents of children with special needs, understanding these levels can help foster empathy and communication. If parental responses change over time, such change is reasonable, acceptable, and even beneficial within this model—rather than being a negative rationale for a critical response—as it underlies not an inconsistency but a movement through the levels of awareness toward self-actualization.

***Accessible Canada Act*:** new legislation that enhances accessibility for Canadians with disabilities, focused on making Canada barrier-free from a federal perspective (Government of Canada, 2019).

RESOURCES

Information for Parents

While access to the Internet has exponentially increased the ease of gathering information on almost any topic, serious information seekers—including parents of children with ASD—now have a new challenge: struggling with filtering through masses of dubious information to find suitable sources of correct information (e.g., evidence-based interventions). Some jurisdictions provide information targeted specifically to parents, such as Yukon Education's (2015) parent handbook, provided by Student Support Services. Although this updated manual does not provide ASD-specific information like its 2006 counterpart, it does offer a comprehensive framework through which services for all students with special educational needs are provided—including parental partnerships.

Regional, provincial, and national organizations have also been formed, focusing on the needs of not only those with ASD but the families who support them. The Autism-Intellectual Disability National Resource and Exchange Network (AIDE): A Collaborative Initiative of the Pacific Autism Family Network and the Miriam Foundation is one example on Canada's west coast. The Pacific Autism Family Network, located in Richmond, British Columbia, is dedicated to providing services, supports, and resources to individuals of all ages with autism spectrum disorder and their families. Focused on cutting-edge research, innovative approaches, and multidisciplinary collaboration, the Pacific Autism Family Network seeks to help individuals with ASD and their families sort through the often-overwhelming amount of information and the sometimes-confusing systems they may encounter in their search for the right services and supports. The Goodlife Fitness Autism Family Hub, which serves as the centre of the Pacific Autism Family Network, is home to a range of partner organizations and services. The ABLE Developmental Clinic provides assessment and diagnostic services, intervention for young children with ASD, and support services for siblings. AutismBC is an organization created and directed by parents of individuals with ASD and dedicated to spreading awareness, providing education and training, and helping those affected by ASD achieve success. The provincial Autism Information Services British Columbia (AIS BC), along with many other organizations that provide resources and supports for individuals with ASD and their families, are also part of the Pacific Autism Family Network's "hub."

In February 2018, as part of the 2018–2019 federal budget, the Canadian Government announced an investment of $20 million over 5 years to support a collaborative initiative of the Pacific Autism Family Network and the Miriam Foundation. The Miriam Foundation is recognized throughout Canada as a leader in collaborative and multidisciplinary initiatives to provide information and resources to individuals with ASD and intellectual disabilities, their families, caregivers, and the professionals who support them. Collaborations with hospitals, schools, community services organizations, and many other partners characterize much of the work of the Miriam Foundation. The funding announced by the federal government will allow the Miriam Foundation and the Pacific Autism Family Partnership to develop a resource called the Autism-Intellectual Disability National Resource and Exchange Network (AIDE). The initiative will provide individuals with ASD and intellectual disabilities and their families access to a unique and comprehensive website, curated resource library, asset maps, and other valuable tools that target their unique individual needs. The goal is to provide equitable access for individuals and families across Canada and beyond to materials and supports that are specifically focused on individuals with ASD and intellectual disabilities and their families (Miriam Foundation, 2018; Pacific Autism Family Network, 2018; Stevens, 2018).

Clinicians themselves, individually or in teams, are also moving into advocacy and training for parents and families—historically difficult services to access. For example, CoField Inc. (n.d.a, b) in London, Ontario, not only offers applied behaviour analysis (ABA) interventions but also training and consultation focused on "empowerment, commitment, accessibility, and individualization."

CoField Inc.

Alyssa Davis

As advocates for children with autism spectrum disorder and developmental delays and their families, the CoField team is dedicated to developing programs that will positively impact the quality of life for every child and family they serve. CoField is "committed to never underestimating the potential of a child, or their capacity to learn" (CoField Inc., n.d.b). Its services are guided by the principles of empowerment, commitment, accessibility, and individualization. CoField provides several ABA-based services, including intensive behaviour intervention and program supervision, parent and community training, and community consultation.

The CoField team is committed to supporting each individual child and also the members of their family. They view families not as clients but as members of the team. By collaborating together, the team can create the ideal plan of action to achieve unique goals and overcome obstacles. For many children who are involved with CoField's services, a goal of intervention often involves the development of functional communication. Increasing communication skills may be one way to promote a child's independence and reduce frustration and challenging behaviour. Parent training is a critical component of this goal, as parents have an important role to play in helping their children use and practice functional communication skills across a variety of environments. Parents who are equipped with skills and knowledge to support their children's learning and intervention programs may become more confident and more successful in aiding with their child's progress.

The CoField team believes that everyone should have access to information and education about ASD and behavioural strategies. They are actively involved in educating their community on these topics through parent education and community training. Topics of training have included basic principles of ABA, understanding ASD, and using iPads to support communication. Training is tailored to the individual needs of each participating family or organization, and the CoField team uses a hands-on, practical approach to teaching, with an emphasis on applying the training in everyday life.

CoField was founded in 2012 by Lyndsay Collard and Alison Ditchfield and has grown to include a team of instructor-therapists. They provide services in London, Ontario, and surrounding communities. Lyndsay and Alison each have several years of experience working in the field of ABA. Lyndsay is a board-certified behavior analyst (BCBA) who completed her Master's degree in Applied Disability Studies. She is also a faculty member at Fanshawe College in the Autism and Behavioural Science Program. Alison has provided ABA services in a wide range of settings including in homes, schools, and daycares. Her pursuit of further education has earned her two university degrees and a diploma in Child and Youth Work. Together, Lyndsay and Alison are responsible for creating individualized skill acquisition programs, developing behaviour support plans, conducting assessments, and training parents and instructor-therapists. Both are members of Autism Ontario and the Ontario Association for Behaviour Analysis (ONTABA).

The CoField team also includes Dr. F. J. Barrera, a registered clinical psychologist and doctoral level board-certified behavior analyst (BCBA-D). He has extensive experience in the field of ABA, including serving as the Clinical Director of the Applied Behaviour Analysis program at the Southwestern Regional Centre in Blenheim, Ontario, where he oversaw research and treatment related to high-risk behaviours and severe self-injury. Dr. Barrera supervises the intensive behavioural intervention teams at CoField, and his passion and dedication help to make the CoField team even stronger. CoField staff work together as an effective team, providing quality ABA-based services for every family and child they serve.

How to Prepare for a Diagnostic Appointment

Before the appointment, it might be helpful to ...

- List all medications your child is taking (including vitamins, herbs or supplements, or any other over-the-counter medication).
- List any changes that you or anyone else has noticed in your child's behaviour. If your child has been evaluated by a pre-school or any other early childhood educator, bring their notes.

- Bring a video or photograph of behaviour, rituals, or routines displayed by your child. Many cell phones or digital cameras can be used to assist with this.
- If your child has siblings, try to make note of their siblings' major developmental milestones to help spot differences and signs of development, which may indicate an ASD (such as the age they began talking).
- Make some notes about and be prepared to discuss how your child plays with other children, siblings, and parents.

Source: Ontario Ministry of Children and Youth Services, 2011, para. 3.

Organization

A particularly practical recommendation is the creation of a child-specific binder or binders to easily compile and share printed documents, and to keep complex, important information readily available and organized. Contents should begin with a photo and a profile of the child with ASD, and include copies of government-issued identification (e.g., birth certificate), medical information (e.g., diagnosis, medications), education information (e.g., reports, IEP), contact information (e.g., therapy providers, physician), a related schedule of typical time commitments, and important financial and legal information (e.g., insurance policies). If parents are looking for a binder to use, rather than suggestions on its creation, McMaster University's CanChild Centre for Disability Research has created the KIT: Keeping It Together. While the KIT is not ASD-specific, it is intended for parents of children with disabilities (CanChild Centre for Disability Research, 2015). This inexpensive answer to day-to-day organization is self-described as

> a way to organize information for your child, and to assist you when interacting with different service systems, for example health, education, and recreation. Included is a User's Guide that will help you through the initial process of how to use the KIT. It is useful for parents of children with a wide variety of special needs and all developmental ages from birth to 21 years. (para. 1)

A self-directed kit is also available for transition to adulthood, called the Youth KIT.

Regionalized and Non-exclusive Resources

A French-language research project in Quebec (Cappe & Poirier, 2016) found that parents of children with ASD tend to seek professional advice (or online information) rather than soliciting help from other parents. Such region- and community-specific

KIT FORMS

Our Family Vision Statement

The family vision statement can help you make decisions for your child and family. It gives continuity and direction.

Use the following questions to get you started. Refer to pages 23–27 in the User's Guide.

1. What are your greatest dreams for your child?

2. What are your greatest fears for your child?

3. Think and talk about your basic family values (e.g., to have your child accepted for who he or she is)

4. What are your goals for your child? (e.g., playing with other children in the neighbourhood, going to summer camp, living on his or her own, having friends)

5. How do you like to be treated by one another in your family? (e.g., with respect, respect our privacy, etc.)

Figure 9.1: The "Keeping It Together" KIT

Source: CanChild Centre for Childhood Disability Research, 2015.

information that includes jurisdictional resources typically accessed by parents of children with ASD is available but not in a systematic or comprehensive manner. Many other information resources are easily accessible online to support the needs of parents in turn supporting children with ASD, which are not specific to regional or provincial information but are nonetheless helpful. One example is the 100-Day Kit: A Tool Kit to Assist Families in Getting the Critical Information They Need in the First 100 Days after an Autism Diagnosis (Autism Speaks, 2011a). The 100-Day Kit is made up of 10 main sections, with a lengthy focus on treatments for children with ASD. The 10 components include *About Autism*; *You, Your Family, and Autism*; *Getting Your Child Services*; *Treating Autism*; and *Making It Happen*. Parents will also find practical suggestions to managing this critical period, including a template for week-by-week planning, with embedded action plans appropriate to each phase. For example, in Week 1, initiating a phone log is suggested:

> Try to set aside some time each day to make the phone calls necessary to set up the evaluations and to start the process of getting services. There may be a waiting list for services and evaluations, so make the calls as soon as possible and follow up as needed—and don't hesitate to put your name on multiple lists so you can get the earliest appointment possible. Some of the professionals who provide services through Early Intervention or Special Education may take a specified number of days to complete evaluations or begin services. (Autism Speaks, 2011a, p. 43)

Lastly, this resource provides more practical planning support, such as ideas for community awareness and safety concerns, emergency situations, (e.g., creating a personalized information page), informing neighbours, option of medical identification bracelet, a service provider planner, templates for contact information, assessment tracking, goal tracking, and a comprehensive glossary.

Autism Speaks Canada

Sarah Ahmed, Director, Marketing & Communications, Autism Speaks Canada

Autism Speaks Canada is a Canadian charitable organization operating coast to coast to coast, working to enhance lives today and to build a spectrum of solutions for tomorrow.

We are dedicated to promoting solutions, across the spectrum and throughout the life span, for the needs of individuals with autism and their families by supporting and working with community partners; enhancing resources and services; increasing understanding, acceptance, and inclusion of people with autism spectrum disorder; and advancing research into causes and better interventions for autism spectrum disorder and related conditions.

Together with Autism Speaks, we have invested over $300 million to scientific research, $9.5 million directly to Canadian science grants. Since 2010, Autism Speaks Canada has granted over $5 million to service organizations across Canada promoting collaboration and building capacity to support individuals with autism spectrum disorder and their families.

Our Impact

- Increasing Global Understanding and Acceptance of People with Autism
- Increasing Early Childhood Screening and Timely Intervention
- Improving the Transition to Adulthood and Employment
- Being a Catalyst for Research Breakthroughs
- Ensuring Access to Reliable Information and Services Throughout the Life Span

We offer a variety of necessary resources and services to the autism community across a spectrum and along the lifespan. Listed below are some of our most popular resources and programs developed based on the highest needs of the community:

- Tool Kits: Navigating a complex system is preventing Canadians with autism from receiving vital services. For people who have been recently diagnosed with autism, we have over 40 tool kits available to download for free on our website. These tool kits range from the 100 Day Kit, which was created specifically for newly diagnosed families to make the best possible use out of the first 100 days following their child's diagnosis of autism, to the Advocacy Tool Kit, which aims to help both individuals on the spectrum and their families develop and use critical advocacy skills in order to achieve the best possible outcomes.
- Autism Speaks Canada CONNECT: Canada's first virtual, multifaceted platform supporting the autism community to get informed and engaged. CONNECT provides a platform for navigation support, access to resources, and community groups. Currently there are 15,500 members on CONNECT, 4,600 service listings, and 900 resources. Membership is free and CONNECT operates in English and French (connect.autismspeaks.ca).
- Family Service Community Grants (FSCG): Our FSCG program provides funding to other not-for-profit organizations serving the individuals with autism and their families. We have funded over $4 million to 280 organizations across Canada. Grants are collaborative and focus on the highest needs of the community, including aging with autism, culture and language diversity, sexual and gender diversity, dual diagnosis, and social inclusion.
- National Autism Strategy: We sit on the board of the Canadian Autism Spectrum Disorder Alliance (CASDA), working to develop a national autism

strategy in Canada. This strategy would mean federal leadership and action to improve quality of life of autistic Canadians so that they have full and equitable access to the resources they need.

- Awareness: We are committed to helping increase understanding and acceptance of ASD. We spread the message of inclusion and acceptance through campaigns such as Light It Up Blue throughout World Autism Month in April. We promote action and participation in building more inclusive communities throughout Canada. Our Walk events are the single-most important annual fundraising initiative for Autism Speaks Canada to support our mission. The walks across the country bring the community together while providing an opportunity to make connections and to celebrate. Since the first walk, they have raised more than $13.6 million.

> **World Autism Day:** takes place on April 2nd each year. It was developed by the United Nations, to raise awareness and acceptance of ASD (United Nations, 2019). April is considered World Autism Month.

- Employment: As a board member of the Canadian Autism Spectrum Disorder Alliance (CASDA), we continue to play a key role with the Ready Willing and Able Program aimed to promote hiring opportunities for people with ASD by working with employees to hire inclusively. As well, ASC and the Sinneave Family Foundation have been awarded a federal grant to enhance employment readiness and skills to reach successful employment outcomes through the Employment Works Program. ASC has facilitated five national employment conferences and co-hosted the first annual meeting of the national employment network with attendance from over 50 organizations representing a diverse stakeholder group including autistic adults. To date, ASC has 56 grants for $1.4 million specifically focused on young adult and adult programs.
- Autism Treatment Network (ATN): a network of 12 sites (hospitals and academic institutions) comprising the largest autism medical network and registry in the world. This network focuses on multidisciplinary medical care for individuals with autism. In Canada, we have three ATN sites in Toronto (Hospital for Sick Children/Holland Bloorview Kids Rehab Hospital/Surrey Place Centre) and Edmonton (Glenrose Rehabilitation Hospital/University of Alberta). Five hundred thousand families have been served through the ATN, with 130 publications developed through the ATN developing best practice standards of care.
- MSSNG: Google and Autism Speaks have created one of the world's largest genomic databases on autism. The goal is to sequence the DNA of 10,000 families affected by autism. MSSNG will help answer the many

questions we still have about the disorder. Already, MSSNG has led to new discoveries about autism and its associated health conditions. With 10,000 or more whole genomes and the help of the global science community, MSSNG will identify many subtypes of autism, leading us to better and more personalized and effective treatments.

For more information about Autism Speaks Canada, please visit:

- Company Website: www.AutismSpeaks.ca
- Walk Website: www.ASCWalk.ca
- Autism Speaks Canada CONNECT: connect.autismspeaks.ca
- Facebook, Instagram, LinkedIn: @AutismSpeaksCanada
- Twitter: @AutismSpeaksCan

genomic database: a database that has been developed to categorize conditions that have known genetic components (National Human Genome Research Institute, 2019).

Read about It. Think about It. Write about It.

- Reflect on the number of tasks families need to complete, information they need to gather, and information they need to provide about their child and family when receiving an ASD diagnosis. What parts do you imagine are the most cumbersome? If you were a service provider, how could you adapt for some of these barriers to make it easier for families?

ADVOCACY

Information leads to knowledge; thus, writing and accessing trustworthy information is essential in developing knowledgeable parents of children with ASD who can, in turn, make appropriate, informed choices (Matson & Williams, 2015; see Figure 9.3). However, parents also work diligently on developing new skills to support their children with ASD and other disabilities, and one of these skills is advocacy. In the disability field in Canada (and beyond) many advocacy groups exist, prompted by the political strength found in the parental groups of the 1960s (Bennett & Dworet, 2013). Many Canadian jurisdictions have regional advocacy groups, such as Autism Nova Scotia. Autism Nova Scotia is a "community-based organization that fosters understanding, acceptance, and collaborative approaches for those living with Autism Spectrum Disorders throughout Nova Scotia" (Autism Nova Scotia, n.d.). One important role played by this organization is to support individuals with ASD and their families by providing access to information and resources. Its *Parent Education Guide* provides valuable information about the rights, but also responsibilities, of parents of children with ASD in Nova Scotia schools (Autism Nova Scotia, n.d.). It highlights parental rights (e.g., involvement in the program planning process for their children, accessing their children's school records), as well as general information such as school procedures and routines, schedules, and classroom information. The guide also highlights parent responsibilities, including communicating and working with the school team, supporting school and classroom rules, participating in school functions, and serving as a positive role model for their children with respect to school situations and interactions with school personnel.

Advocacy also leads to change. Jordan's Principle is an important example. Jordan's Principle was named in memory of Jordan River Anderson, a First Nations child from Norway House Cree Nation in Manitoba. Jordan was born with complex medical needs and spent his first two years of life in hospital receiving medical treatment. However, when doctors declared that Jordan could go home and continue to have his medical needs met in that setting, he remained in hospital due to disagreements between the provincial and federal governments over who would be responsible for covering the costs associated with his medical needs if he were to return home (First Nations Child & Family Caring Society of Canada, 2014, 2016). Jordan died in hospital at the age of five without ever having returned to his family home.

In response to the tragic situation experienced by Jordan River Anderson, Jordan's Principle was created. A private member's bill in support of Jordan's Principle passed unanimously in the Canadian House of Commons in December 2007. Jordan's Principle is a child-first principle, based on the highest consideration for the needs of each child, to ensure that every First Nations child living on- or off-reserve can access all publicly funded services (First Nations Child & Family Caring Society of Canada, 2014). Canadian government policy now requires that the government department of first contact is responsible to pay, without delay, for costs associated with services that are deemed necessary for the child. Any questions or concerns between levels of government or departments about who should ultimately be responsible for costs, or how those costs should be divided, are to be worked out among the relevant government parties later. Required services and supports may be associated with medical, educational, mental health, early childhood, and language or cultural needs, among others.

advocacy: "advocacy refers to the process of supporting and enabling others to express their views, experiences and concerns ... it is important that your perspective is heard, respected, and taken into account" (Autism Speaks Canada, 2018a, p. 4). There are eight steps to advocacy: (1) figuring out goals; (2) planning a strategy; (3) paying attention to those you are advocating for (e.g., feelings, concerns); (4) attending to emotions; (5) knowing where you are advocating—and who you are advocating for; (6) being available to share information (e.g., meeting attendance); (7) thinking about various ways to resolve problems; and, (8) ensuring notes are taken (e.g., meetings).

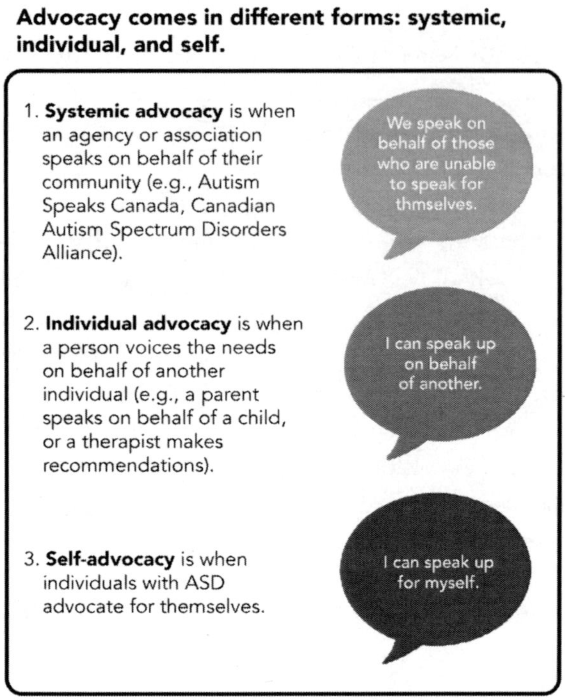

Figure 9.2: Types and Principles of Advocacy
Source: Holland Bloorview Kids Rehabilitation Hospital, 2018, p. 4.

While Jordan's Principle received support by the Canadian Government in 2007, changes did not happen immediately, and First Nations communities and advocacy groups found themselves engaged in ongoing litigation with the Canadian government to ensure that the spirit of Jordan's Principle was reflected in practice and fully implemented across Canada (David Asper Centre for Constitutional Rights, n.d.a, b; First Nations Child & Family Caring Society of Canada, 2016). Rulings by the Canadian Human Rights Tribunal (2018) have upheld the obligation of governments to comply with Jordan's Principle and to fully implement the policies and practices that would ensure that all First Nations children who may require government services and supports have equitable access to those opportunities in a timely manner.

In an Ontario-based study of parental experiences supporting adult children with intellectual and other disabilities, it is notable that even waiting takes effort; however, successful parental advocacy takes much more. Successful parents

> engaged intensively in the above described activities and benefitted from positive relationships with service providers who were able to advocate on their behalf, assist them in application processes, or provide them with flexible service options. These parents trusted that the services they had obtained or continued to seek would be able to meet their needs and their adult children's needs. (Saaltink & Ouellette-Kuntz, 2014)

Table 9.3: The Seven Principles of Advocacy

The principles listed below may seem overwhelming at first. You as a parent or a caregiver will develop the skills necessary for each of these over time—and at your own pace. At times, family members (spouse, siblings, parents and even close friends) can help reduce some of the load by sharing roles/tasks based on their strengths.

1. Take responsibility—Be a leader: Your child's future is in your hands. This is your chance to set goals and develop a plan of action. Decide what is best for your child.	**5. Document—Be prepared:** Keep your notes close at hand, and do your best to document everything. Documentation can also help you feel prepared and in control, and this information can then be shared with others as needed to support your child. Choosing a filing system is also critical, be it digital or paper, whichever suits you best.
2. Learn—Be an expert: Make a reading list. Include educational policies and protocols, and read them. Build a network of experts, who you might want to refer to or rely on for advice. Attend conferences, workshops and webinars. Educate yourself on translating Internet science resources.	**6. Collaborate—Be a team builder:** The aim is to achieve your goal/goals with everyone to whom you advocate. Contribute to their environment; volunteer where possible, and allow them to ask for your help or advice.
3. Think critically: Read and evaluate all the information you have before responding. Keep in mind your goal/goals, make a list of pros and cons, and be prepared to discuss and reach a compromise.	**7. Educate—Be a voice for you child:** Share your experiences, resources and sensitize others to the needs of your child and the community supporting him or her. Your lived experiences are important for other people to understand. This will in turn encourage or strengthen you in your role as an advocate.
4. Speak with authority—Be proactive: Take the first step. You know your child best. Some strategies include: asking for a meeting with those you are advocating to, and providing helpful resources and documentation. Bring the cookies, be confident in meetings, and take notes.	

Source: Holland Bloorview Kids Rehabilitation Hospital, 2018, p. 5.

Parental advocacy does make a difference, exemplified by parents of young children with ASD in Saskatchewan seeking change. In 2014, reporter Amber Rockliffe published an article in *Global News* highlighting Saskatchewan parents and their advocacy efforts to change provincial funding models. In 2016, the Saskatchewan Party announced such a funding change accompanied by future planning for widespread individualized funding: "Shannon Hill, President of Parent Advocates for Autism Treatment in Saskatchewan (PAATS) said this is a landmark day for autism treatment in Saskatchewan" (Saskatchewan Party, 2019, para. 4).

Large, well-known groups supporting parents of children with disabilities (including ASD) bring change, but so do small, relevant or emerging groups—or individuals—that specialize in a particular area. One very well-known and well-respected parental advocate was the late Lindsay Moir (1946–2012) of Comhnadh Consulting, well-known to struggling parents for not only his presentations and consultations but for his tireless will to teach others how to best support children with exceptionalities, especially in Ontario's publicly funded school system. As a former insider to that system—a retired employee of the Ontario Ministry of Education—Moir was "an extraordinary advocate for students with special needs" (Ontario Association of Children's Rehabilitation Services, 2012, para. 1) and was hailed by Autism Ontario as an advocacy hero, described as follows:

> As with any effective advocate, not everyone agreed with all his views, but no one questioned Lindsay Moir's commitment to keeping the learning needs of the children in the forefront, or his passion for the sustained work of advocacy. He made the process of navigating the special education system in Ontario more understandable and he empowered parents to be their child's most effective advocate. He helped parents to not be afraid to insist on the best possible education for their child, and much of his work involved students with ASD. Autism Ontario is grateful to Lindsay Moir for his dedication to the field of autism, his listening ear, his practical and helpful ideas along with his commitment to families and their children. Lindsay made a positive difference in the lives of many people. (Spoelstra, 2012, p. 35)

One of Moir's particularly well-loved initiatives was his readily accessed and responsive column, *Ask Lindsay*. Though this column is no longer active, it remains hosted online by the Ontario Association of Children's Rehabilitation Services (www.oacrs.com/en/asklindsay). Ask Lindsay responded to parent questions—oftentimes difficult, contentious ones. Some of the included, now-archived topics cover issues like school suspensions, school supports, and healthcare. These responses not only answered parental questions but taught important advocacy skills and provided encouragement for the challenging job of parenting a child with special needs through the ages and stages of life. Larger groups with a strong overall advocacy component specific to ASD include Autism Speaks Canada and the Canadian Autism Spectrum Disorder Alliance (CASDA).

CASDA is a national group focused on a national strategy with national attention for ASD. Their work is described as pan-Canadian, multi-level (provincial/territorial as well as federal), multi-ministerial, emphasizing knowledge gathering and dissemination for positive impact specific to the Canadian context. CASDA has a mission, vision, and a strategic plan intertwined with federal political action, widespread advocacy, and major project work.

Autism Speaks Canada, like its high-profile US-based counterpart, raises awareness about ASD for the Canadian population and takes advantage of regionally developed resources such as easily accessible online tool kits (e.g., Challenging Behaviours Tool Kit, Dental Tool Kit, etc.). Although these resources are not focused on Canadian legislation, they have many areas of knowledge and skills that are not limited by geopolitical boundaries. Some are translated and available online in French. Autism Speaks Canada provides a helpful summary of all their advocacy-focused Family Services Tool Kits (2015, 2018), including those highlighted in Table 9.4.

One of the prominent fundraising strategies utilized by Autism Speaks is its *Walk Now* for Autism Speaks Canada, which "support[s] Scientific Research, Services, Advocacy and Awareness. Yet, the Walks are more than a fundraiser, they provide an incredible opportunity for the ASD community to come together and make connections and feel the support" (para. 1). Its initiatives are recognized by its well-known bright

Table 9.4: Advocacy-focused Tool Kits

Kit*	Knowledge & Skills
Advocacy Tool Kit	• Advocacy skills (school, community) • Negotiation skills
A Parent's Guide to Autism	• ASD • Strategies, resources, support • Promoting positivity
A Sibling's Guide to Autism	• ASD • Feelings
A Grandparent's Guide to Autism	• ASD • Supporting self and others • Developing relationships
A Friend's Guide to Autism	• ASD • Empathy, support, and relationships

*All kits are available at autismspeaks.org.
Source: Autism Speaks Canada, 2015.

blue puzzle piece, which has led to growing demonstrations of community support for ASD such as Light It Up Blue, encouraging outdoor illumination with this signature colour for World Autism Awareness Day on April 2nd, recognized in Canada since 2012 (Autism Speaks, 2015; Parliament of Canada, 2012). Another important resource for developing understanding about ASD is the unique online *Video Glossary* (Florida State University, 2018). This one-of-a-kind tool allows open access to more than 100 video clips of both typically developing children and those with red flags for ASD, modelled by children diagnosed with ASD. The Autism Navigator describes it as follows:

> The ASD Video Glossary is a web-based tool built to help families and professionals learn more about the early signs of autism. This tool was developed by the Florida State University Autism Institute in collaboration with First Signs and Autism Speaks and has been available to the public free of charge since 2007. The Glossary contains more than 100 video clips illustrating the diagnostic features of ASD. Side-by-side video clips show behaviors that are typical in contrast with those that are red flags for autism. The Glossary also contains over 100 video clips to illustrate common treatments available for children with autism. The ASD Video Glossary has been brought into the Autism Navigator collection and updated to be in line with the new DSM-5 diagnostic framework. (Florida State University, 2018)

Videos are categorized by inclusion in categories such as Overview (e.g., developmental milestones), Social Interaction (e.g., social reciprocity), Communication (e.g., make believe play, preoccupation with parts of objects), and Regulatory and Sensory Systems (e.g., emotional regulation). A recently added subdivision is Treatments. Accessing this option allows viewing of multiple examples of each of the 11 treatment options (e.g., positive behaviour support, pivotal response training, picture exchange communication system, the Lovaas model of ABA, discrete trial training, etc.), as well as helpful overviews of each option.

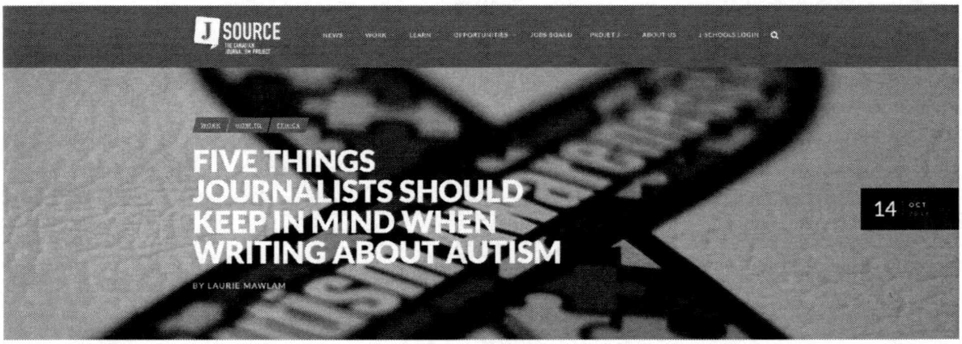

Figure 9.3: Five Things Journalists Should Keep in Mind When Writing about Autism

Source: Mawlam, 2016.

Autism Canada, an advocacy group with a Canada-wide reach, uses the tagline *See the Spectrum Differently* and is described as "the only autism advocacy organization with a national perspective on the issues currently facing those with ASD, their families and other stakeholders" (Autism Canada, 2019). They maintain an online presence providing information on ASD, living with ASD, resources, and more. Autism Canada hosts conferences, such as *See the Spectrum Differently* in 2017, co-hosted with Autism Yukon. They also share information on current calls for participation in relevant research studies related to ASD. Autism Canada also initiates unique advocacy and education programs such as Canadian national education initiatives for recipients like emergency responders, tax reforms advocacy to the Canadian senate—and even teaching media sources how to best represent ASD.

Autism Society of Newfoundland and Labrador

Scott Crocker, Chief Executive Officer, ASNL

Autism Society of Newfoundland and Labrador (ASNL) is a provincial, non-profit, charitable organization dedicated to fostering the development of individualized, lifelong, community-based supports and services for persons with autism spectrum disorder. ASNL is committed to the promotion of acceptance, independence, productivity, and opportunities for inclusion in all facets of life for persons with ASD and their families.

ASNL began as an advocacy and parent support group in 1984—a time when there were no supports or services available to individuals with ASD. It was incorporated in 1987. Thanks to the tireless efforts of families, professionals, and community advocates, the Elaine Dobbin Centre for Autism was opened in 2006 as a place where individuals living with autism, and their families, could access programs and supports following diagnosis and into adulthood. ASNL receives half its annual budget from grant funding from the provincial government and the remainder from self-generated revenues via fundaising initiatives.

The Elaine Dobbin Centre for Autism is the provincial headquarters for ASNL and sits on eight acres of historic farmland—Shamrock Farm—in the centre of St. John's, adjoining the Health Sciences Centre, Janeway Children's Hospital, and Memorial University of Newfoundland. It services the St. John's Metro Area and the Avalon Region. The property has two program buildings, including an extensive library and two greenhouses surrounded by a vegetable garden, flower bed, tree orchard, 11 berry garden beds and 36 community garden beds. ASNL operates two social enterprises from this location, The Pantry Café & Catering and Good Roots Gardening, both of which capitalize on the property to provide education, employment, work experience, and training opportunities for individuals on the spectrum. ASNL has regional offices in Clarenville, Grand Falls-Windsor, and Corner Brook. They

Figure 9.4: Autism Society Newfoundland and Labrador
Source: ASNL.

provide engagement and outreach services, advocacy, and navigational supports to all other areas of the province: Eastern Region, South Central Region, and Western/Labrador Region.

ASNL's staff delivers programs designed to be flexible to meet the unique needs of children, youth, and adults on the spectrum. It offers a Transitions pre-employment program; an Employment Works employment preparedness training program; a STEP (Students Transitioning into Employment and Post-Secondary) transitional and career development service for senior high school students; Sibling Workshops; and Family Events. It also offers Community-Based Leisure Exploration (i.e., swimming lessons, rock climbing, music therapy, individual art therapy, video game creation classes, coding clubs, and horse discovery programs) and Centre-Based Leisure Exploration (i.e., programs on special interests, such as LEGO and Dungeons & Dragons) to encourage socialization and the making of new friendships.

ASNL's programs fall under six areas of learning: Life Skills, Pre-Employment & Career Services, Family Supports, Engagement Offerings, Advocacy, and Navigational Support. Life Skills programming provides leisure and socialization opportunities for those facing barriers to community integration, in a safe and supported way for individuals living with autism of all ages. Pre-Employment and Career Services include provincially and nationally funded programs that target the barriers participants may face in their preparation for adulthood.

ASNL has a significant role advocating for appropriate supports and services to be made available by those affected by ASD at the local, provincial, and national levels. Building a community that is educated about ASD is a high priority, and ASNL staff are consistently engaged with community members to build capacity for inclusion. Outreach services are accessed by classrooms, community groups, businesses, health and education professionals, employers, police and other first responders, among many others. Addressing barriers and working toward a more knowledgeable community is a key component of increasing accessibility and acceptance.

This organization recognizes the need for research-informed practice and the importance of concerted research efforts in building better supports and services for this population. ASNL stays abreast of current research, engages in research activities itself in partnership with Memorial University, and partners with provincial and national organizations to establish and offer evidence-based programs and services for those it serves.

Table 9.5: Provincial and Territorial Advocacy and Resource Organizations

Jurisdiction	Organization	Website
AB	Autism Calgary	http://www.autismcalgary.com/
	Autism Edmonton	https://www.autismedmonton.org/
	Autism Society AB	https://www.autismalberta.ca/
	Centre for Autism Services AB	https://centreforautism.ab.ca/
	Children's Autism Services of Edmonton	https://www.childrensautism.ca/
	Disability Services, Government of AB	http://www.humanservices.alberta.ca/disability-services/15775.html
	Society for Treatment of Autism	https://sta-ab.com/

(continued)

Table 9.5: *Continued*

Jurisdiction	Organization	Website
BC	AutismBC	https://www.autismbc.ca/
	Autism Community Training	https://www.actcommunity.ca/information/autism-diagnosis-in-bc/
	Autism Funding in BC	https://asdfunding.com/
	Autism Support Network	https://autismsupportbc.ca/
	BC Autism Assessment Network	http://www.phsa.ca/our-services/programs-services/bc-autism-assessment-network
	Canucks Autism Network	https://www.canucksautism.ca/
	Families for Early Autism Treatment of BC	http://featbc.org/
	Pacific Autism Family Network	https://pacificautismfamily.com/
	PALS Autism School	http://palsautismschool.ca/site/school-program/
	Provincial Outreach Program for Autism and Related Disorders (POPARD)	https://www.autismoutreach.ca/
MB	Association for Developmental Autism Programs and Therapies (ADAPT) MB	http://www.adaptmanitoba.ca/
	Asperger MB	http://www.asperger-manitoba.ca/
	Autism Learning Centre	http://www.autismlearningcentre.ca/
	Autism Spectrum Disorders MB	http://asdmb.ca/
	Autism Society of MB	http://www.autismmanitoba.com/
	Thrive	http://www.gov.mb.ca/fs/thrive/

Jurisdiction	Organization	Website
NB	Autism Intervention Services	https://www.aisfredericton.ca/
	Autism Resource Centre	http://www.monctonarc.com/
	Autism Resources Miramichi	http://www.autismmiramichi.com/
	Dragonfly Centre for Autism, Inc.	http://www.dragonflyforautism.ca/home
NL	Autism Society—NL	http://www.autismnovascotia.ca/
	Health and Community Services, Government of NL	http://www.health.gov.nl.ca/health/personsdisabilities/fundingprograms_hcs.html
	Thrive Community Youth Network St. John's	http://www.thrivecyn.ca/
	Western Health—Autism Services	http://westernhealth.nl.ca/index.php/programs-and-services/services-a-z/autism-services
NS	Autism Nova Scotia	http://www.autismnovascotia.ca/
	IWK Health Centre	http://www.iwk.nshealth.ca/mental-health/parents/autism
NT	Autism Society NT	http://nwtautismsociety.org/
	On Thin Ice Emergency Planning NT	http://onthiniceproject.ca/nwt-resources-and-links/
	NT Disabilities Council	http://www.nwtdc.net/
NU	On Thin Ice Emergency Planning Nunavut	http://onthiniceproject.ca/nunavut-resources-and-links/
	Nunavummi Disabilities Makinnasuaqtiit Society	https://nuability.ca/
ON	Autism Ontario	https://www.autismontario.com/
	ON Autism Coalition	https://ontarioautismcoalition.com/
	ON Ministry of Children and Youth Services	http://www.children.gov.on.ca/htdocs/English/specialneeds/autism/index.aspx

(*continued*)

Table 9.5: *Continued*

Jurisdiction	Organization	Website
PE	Autism Services—Government of PE	http://www.gov.pe.ca/eecd/autismservices
	Autism Society of PE	www.autismsociety.pe.ca
	Education, Early Learning and Culture—Government of PE	https://www.princeedwardisland.ca/en/information/education-and-lifelong-learning/autism-services-children-and-youth
QC	Autisme Quebec	https://www.autisme.qc.ca/
	Centre of Excellence—Autism Spectrum Disorder	http://coeasd.lbpsb.qc.ca/
	SACCADE—Centre d'Experise en Autisme	http://saccade.ca/
SK	Autism Services of Saskatoon	http://www.autismservices.ca/
	Government of Saskatchewan Autism Services	https://www.saskatchewan.ca/residents/health/accessing-health-care-services/health-services-for-people-with-disabilities/autism-services
	Saskatchewan Families for Early Autism Treatment	www.saskfeat.com
YT	Autism YT	https://www.autismyukon.org/
	Child Development Centre Yukon	http://www.cdcyukon.ca/ourprograms/fasdservices.html
	Health and Social Services—YT	http://www.hss.gov.yk.ca/disabilites.php
Canada	Autism Awareness	https://autismawarenesscentre.com/resource-regions/canada/
	Autism Canada	https://autismcanada.org/
	Autism Speaks Canada	http://www.autismspeaks.ca/
	Canadian Autism Spectrum Disorders Alliance	http://www.casda.ca/

With varied types of service provision happening across the country, some clinicians are taking the reins of service provision for parents, caregivers, families, and children firmly in hand. Small business owners Karen Manuel and Emma Kenney in Niagara, Ontario, for example, joined together clinical and business skills to create GAIN Learning Centre, Inc.

Entrepreneurship Supporting Families

Karen Manuel

As board-certified behavior analysts (BCBAs), it is our duty to always ask: Will this action or decision be in the best interest of the client? When one is both the BCBA and the business owner, it is also necessary to ask the same question regarding the business, although for a BCBA, it most frequently takes the form of: Will this action or decision harm or put the business at risk? The thought being that if the business is at risk, the clients may be at risk of no longer having access to services. For myself and my business partner Emma Kenney since opening GAIN Learning Centre, Inc., in 2016, these questions have been asked daily, and the discussions that led to our answers were not always so straight forward.

The outlook for applied behaviour analysis in Ontario has shifted drastically since our opening. Even now in early 2020, the future continues to remain unclear for Direct Funding Service providers. Small businesses succeed when there is a strong business plan and clear goals. Timelines are of the essence to ensure one doesn't get too far in that the debt becomes too much to bear, nor one waits too long before taking a leap that will send the business into the next level of success. The recent uncertainty in Ontario had left business planning almost impossible, with unclear requirements for supervision, administration, documentation, as well as the dollar allotment available to cover these services. With families having to wait long periods for reconciliation of funds and therefore leaving large gaps in payment, the businesses were the ones to have to absorb those costs while in waiting. Looking just at determining the cost, the discussion of determining an appropriate fee for service included reviewing adequate coverage, supervision payment, room for increasing costs due to inflation and growth, as well as maintaining overhead and administrative costs, all while ensuring that our decisions are keeping our clients' interests at the forefront and in no way are families at risk of losing high quality and consistent service.

Holding both roles, BCBA and business owner, is a challenging position that is recognized in our Ethical Compliance Code (Behavior Analyst Certification Board, 2019). Specifically, for those of us that are clinician and business owner, we must reflect on Code 1.06: "Responsible Conduct of Behavior Analysts: Multiple

Relationships and Conflicts of Interest." This code describes that it is required to, whenever possible, not hold multiple relationships, and if necessary to identify all potential harmful effects to our clients as well as work to eliminate these risks or resolve the conflict as soon as possible. For this reason alone, I know we made the right choice in maintaining our roles, Emma as the Business Operations Director and myself as the Clinical Director, to ensure we find the balance that keeps GAIN moving not only forward but upward. To say I am not also a business owner would be false, as I am. Transparency is key. In being transparent, GAIN has grown from a 6-room centre, servicing fewer than 10 clients with a handful of staff to now having over 20 rooms, servicing over 50 clients, 6 days a week. Through uncertainty and lack of clarity, I held strong to my requirements to my clients, and Emma to our business requirements. It may not always be easy, although finally we see, that no matter what the government offers in regard to support, we are in a place that we can make a clear plan, for our families and for our business, that both will see success!

SPOTLIGHTS ACROSS CANADA

Research: British Columbia

The perspectives of home and family are important for many reasons, with an additional consideration and concern around inadequate support systems which may, in turn, force parents of children with ASD who need high levels of care to take on even more roles. It is important to qualify this statement, however.

> Many individuals are supported by parents, siblings and extended family out of love and respect, and these caregivers do not wish to hand over or "farm out" the care. Many do not consider the care to be a burden, and they are simply looking for the best possible quality of life for their loved one. Still, many families are burdened under the tremendous demands of lifelong caregiving to the point of exhaustion and ill health. (Dudley & Emery, 2014, p. 5)
>
> With that being said,
>
> across Canada, there are significant gaps in the publicly provided support system, leaving the cost burden to be picked up by families. In the case of those individuals requiring constant support, 24 hours a day, every day, the cost of hiring caregivers

> alone would require an annual income of $200,000—before a family even begins to pay for shelter, clothing, groceries and other basic necessities. Already families with severe high-needs children are more likely to experience lower income than they might otherwise, due to the extra care commitment their loved one requires. Only a very few families will have the means to afford to pay for total care. So, in most cases, the responsibility for care falls largely, if not entirely, on the family, or in a worst-case scenario, the autistic individual is left with inadequate care. (Dudley & Emery, 2014, p. 1)

The importance of early diagnosis and intervention in ASD is well-established, yet the diagnostic process, which provided the entryway to such services, can lag and can be highly problematic for parents advocating for diagnoses. In *Assessing the Diagnostic Experiences of Children with Autism Spectrum Disorders* researchers Siklos and Kerns (2007) examined the parental experiences of 56 formally diagnosed children (between 2 and 18 years of age) in what they describe as stressful and lengthy diagnostic processes (especially for older children). Utilizing three questionnaires with a total of 113 items, Silkos and Kerns found that, on average, families consulted with 4.46 professionals while some (5%) needed to consult 10 professionals during the diagnostic process—a process that took an average of close to three years. Since their diagnoses, most families (53%) were not satisfied with the help provided to their children and family, but the top three areas of help that were supported included the provision of resources/knowledge (25.3%), and the provision of speech-language, behaviour, or learning supports (20%). They also found a "significant negative correlation ... between the current age of the child and satisfaction with the diagnostic process" (2007, p. 16), as well as families of female children being diagnosed.

Greater behaviour problems were significantly related to more dissatisfaction, and greater communication problems were significantly related to more satisfaction as well as higher service satisfaction. The authors concluded, "communication impairments are likely to be less ambiguous to parents, and may be a clear indicator that something is significantly wrong with their child" (p. 19); thus, diagnoses were more evident and expected. Following these analyses, the authors made a number of suggestions:

- Parents need support services (e.g., counselling and support groups).
- Sensitivity toward parents and the provision of coping skills are also needed.
- Referrals from a family physician or pediatrician to a developmental specialist may decrease the wait time for diagnoses.

Initiative: Ontario

ASD Summer Movement Camp

Maureen Connolly, PhD, Professor of Physical Education and Kinesiology in the Faculty of Applied Health Sciences, and cross-appointed to the Department of Child and Youth Studies and the Centre for Applied Disability Studies, in the Faculty of Social Sciences at Brock University, Niagara, Ontario

Autism spectrum disorder summer movement camp has been in operation since the summer of 1996. The program offers a developmentally appropriate movement education–based embedded curriculum but it is more specifically focused on the needs of children, youth, teens, and young adults on the autism spectrum. The summer movement camp is also a community service learning pedagogy and attracts 30–50 undergraduate students, typically engaging in independent study and practicum course credit, and between 45 to 65 campers. Campers range in age from 3 years to teens and transition aged youth (18–25) and increasingly a young adult population (25–30). The past five years have also seen increasing numbers of master's and PhD students involved in various capacities. The ASD summer movement camp appreciates the ongoing foundation funding from Niagara Recycling, a non-profit organization who employs and actively supports and advocates for persons with disabilities.

SNAP (Supporting Neurodiversity through Adaptive Programming) is a developmentally appropriate movement education–based embedded curriculum offered to children and youth with disabilities in the Niagara region. SNAP is a community service-learning initiative that has been running since the 1994–95 academic year (it actually began as the independent study project of then-graduate student Jason Candy; Dr. Candy is now employed at Niagara College and his legacy lives on in the SNAP). In collaboration with all the school boards and a number of disability services organizations, SNAP offers 1:1 facilitated instruction in physical activity contexts one morning a week between October and April. Coordinated by a team of undergraduate students who fulfill an honours thesis credit, SNAP also relies on approximately 150–200 volunteers per session. Students from a number of degree programs, both grad and undergrad, also do independent study and practicum course credit at SNAP. Numbers of participants have increased over the two decades of SNAP's existence with approximately 1,600 school-aged children involved during a typical academic year.

Both SNAP and ASD movement camp operate as sites for research as well as service learning and pedagogy. The programs have won several awards, and research on the programs' development, implementation, and ongoing refinement has been and continues to be presented and published nationally and internationally.

Research: Ontario

Ontario researchers Weiss, Cappadocia, MacMullin, Viecili, and Lunsky (2012) carried out a survey-based evaluation of how problem behaviour of children with ASD affects parental mental health, utilizing statistical analyses of standardized questionnaires from 228 (largely) cross-Canada parents. They found items negatively associated with parental mental health problems and their severity (income levels, empowerment, psychological acceptance) and items positively associated with parental mental health problems and their severity (problem behaviour). Overall, parents of male children reported lower levels of mental health problems than parents of female children with ASD. An important outcome was that "child problem behavior was a significant predictor of parent mental health problems" (p. 267) and that "psychological acceptance [or challenging thoughts/emotions] was the only unique indirect pathway mediating the relationship between child problem behavior and parent mental health problems" (p. 268); a decrease in that psychological acceptance also predicts mental health difficulties in parents. Weiss and colleagues (2012) also pointed out that children with ASD may have fairly chronic or ongoing problem behaviour, which may explain the importance of psychological acceptance in this group of parents. In other words, the situation may be difficult to support, manage, or change, perhaps decreasing the potential effect of parental empowerment.

Research: Prince Edward Island

Timmons and Breitenbach (2004) researched helpful inclusionary practices for children with ASD in PEI, noting the importance of consistency between home and school for their effective implementation. Parents and educators from 15 rural and urban island schools in PEI took part in the study, and interview data from 36 parents and 60 educators were obtained. Parents reported information in these areas: the diagnostic process, health interventions, school, developmental and behavioural issues, home life, and provided suggestions for improvements needed, such as additional training, collaboration, and respite. In the area of home life, parents reported:

> The word challenges surfaced the most during the analysis of this category. The following areas were listed as challenges by parents: finances, lack of services, individuals not understanding autistic behaviors, maintaining a family while learning to cope with autism, knowing when to pick battles, family excursions, as well as emotional stress. Parents listed job issues (3/7) and paying for private help (4/7) as their two main concerns when finances were discussed.
>
> In general, parents are tired, frustrated, worried about the future, and stated that they often feel alone in their struggle. Some parents feel as though they have to fight continuously to make any progress. Parents were asked to describe the skills they felt were necessary to manage the challenges presented by their children.

> Patience (13/18) and being an advocate for their child (6/18) were the top two responses given by parents. They also said that having a positive attitude, being consistent, using clear instructions, and being flexible helped them to cope with daily stressors. Parents stated that they receive the most support from family members (5/18) and themselves (4/18). However, friends, the school, respite, and the Disability Support Program were also mentioned as being helpful supports for the family. (Timmons & Breitenbach, 2004)

A LOOK BACK

Chapter 9, "Parents and Families," focused on:

- A historical perspective of parents of children with ASD, with highlights on the negative stereotypes developed
- More recent positive models for assisting and understanding families that have children with ASD
- Jurisdictional resources available for families
- Advocacy and developing advocacy skills for families
- Regional highlights of family-centred models and supports

ADDITIONAL RESOURCES

Active Living Alliance for Canadians Living with a Disability

https://ala.ca

Active Living Alliance assists local, provincial, and national organizations to incorporate inclusive, active living opportunities for individuals with disabilities. This website includes resources on suggested terminology when discussing disabilities, tip sheets, and links to current research.

Advocacy Tool Kit for Parents of Children and Youth with ASD and Other Neurodevelopmental Disorders

https://hollandbloorview.ca/Assets/Research/ARC/AdvocacyToolKit-July24-LINKED-LOCKED.pdf

This tool kit provides a detailed description on advocacy. Parents, professionals, and service providers can access useful information on steps to advocate in education, health care, and the community.

Autism Physician Handbook: Autism Canada

https://autismcanada.org/wp-content/uploads/2018/01/PhyHandbook_EN_2018.pdf

This download provides a comprehensive profile of the behavioural, sensory, and medical issues often related to a diagnosis of ASD. This guide is presented with visuals and simple text.

Autism Junction: Canada's Online Autism Service Directory

http://www.autismjunction.ca

Autism Canada is compiling a wide-reaching online autism service directory. Parents can search available services in all provinces and territories. Professionals can add a service to this directory.

Easter Seals of Canada

https://easterseals.ca/english/

Easter Seals is Canada's largest provider of local programs and services for individuals with physical, intellectual, sensory, and learning disabilities. This website provides statistics on current prevalence of disabilities and information on the wide range of campaigns organized by Easter Seals.

Autism Awareness Centre, Inc.

https://autismawarenesscentre.com

Autism Awareness Centre organizes professional development opportunities for parents and professionals. This website links to books, blog posts, and an extensive list of resources.

Cineplex Canada Access2Entertainment

https://www.cineplex.com/Theatres/Access2Entertainment

The Access2Entertainment Program (organized by Easter Seals Canada) provides free or discounted admissions for an individual with a disability (or a support person) to parks, theatres, and attractions across Canada. This link provides details on Cineplex Entertainment's affiliation with this program.

Disability Travel Card

https://easterseals.ca/english/wp-content/uploads/2018/08/Disability-Travel-Card-NEW-EST-Application-Form-EN.pdf

The Disability Travel Card (organized by Easter Seals Canada) provides reduced fees on VIA Rail Canada, Greyhound Canada, and Coach Canada for a support person travelling with an individual with a permanent disability.

Autism Society Manitoba

http://www.autismmanitoba.com/about.php

Autism Society Manitoba provides information and resources for individuals with ASD, families, and professionals. This website links to services and supports available across Winnipeg and Manitoba.

Autism Spectrum Disorders Manitoba

http://asdmb.ca/

Autism Spectrum Disorders Manitoba provides information to families on ASD across the lifespan. Users can access a searchable database with links categorized by age, diagnosis, and geographic location.

Autism Speaks Canada

www.autismspeaks.ca/

Autism Speaks Canada is a large national charity. This website provides information on national fundraising walks, links to current research, and resources.

Autism Speaks Family Services Tool Kits

https://www.autismspeaks.ca/science-services-resources/resources/tool-kits/

Autism Speaks Canada provides several tool kits for parents, service providers, and educators. Family Support Tool Kits, tailored to parents, siblings, and grandparents, describe the impact of ASD on family members.

David Asper Centre for Constitutional Rights, University of Toronto

http://aspercentre.ca

The David Asper Centre is a legal clinic dedicated to advocacy initiatives. This website links to advocacy-related links, blog posts, and advocacy cases currently before the courts.

Autism Navigator

https://autismnavigator.com/asd-video-glossary/

This website links parents and professionals to several video clips demonstrating early red flags of ASD. Informational growth and milestone charts are provided to assist with informal assessment.

The KIT: Keeping It Together (CanChild Centre for Childhood Disability Research)

https://www.canchild.ca/en/research-in-practice/the-kit-keeping-it-together

This website provides parents with tips on compiling a binder/kit to organize forms, reports, and contact information related to a child's diagnosis. This website provides additional suggestions for parents to be involved and engaged in their child's services.

First Nations Child & Family Caring Society of Canada

https://fncaringsociety.com

First Nations Child & Family Caring Society of Canada supports education and equitable opportunities for First Nations children. This website links to an online journal, a research database, and current news events.

A Resource Guide for Families of Children Who Have Been Recently Diagnosed with an Autism Spectrum Disorder

https://www.autismontario.com/sites/default/files/2019-03/Simcoe%20Next%20Steps%20English.pdf

This resource provides an overview of the characteristics of autism spectrum disorders. It also provides a list of the financial resources available to families, as well as a list of publicly funded community agencies, recreation services, respite, and mental health services available in the Simcoe County region. A list of private agencies is included, such as occupational therapy, physiotherapy, psychology, social work, and speech, as well as a comprehensive list of websites available for families.

Shared Solutions (Ontario Ministry of Education)

www.edu.gov.on.ca/eng/general/elemsec/speced/shared.pdf

This guide provides preventative strategies to mitigate conflict when planning for the special education needs of students.

The Essentials of Advocacy: A Parents' Guide to Advocating for Their Child with Special Needs

https://www.actcommunity.ca/education/videos/the-essentials-of-advocacy-a-parents-guide#contents-part2thebigpicturewh

This website links to an information workshop on guiding principles of advocacy. Examples provided are taken from British Columbia's school system; however, the strategies for meaningful advocacy are relevant regardless of location.

The Special Needs Planning Group

www.specialneedsplanning.ca/

The Special Needs Planning Group is an organization comprised of parents of individuals with disabilities. This website provides information on available financial services, and frequently asked questions.

SECTION IV

A Critical Look at Autism Spectrum Disorder

This section is composed of one chapter that examines case studies, media coverage, reviews of current topics, and projects that are all focusing on current issues at the forefront of the autism spectrum disorder (ASD) discussion across Canada. Although many studies, programs, and policies have been developed to support persons with ASD across Canada in the last 20 years, debated areas still remain where people are not able to access services or experience states of well-being because of characteristics of ASD. This chapter allows for a critical look at these areas that are making headlines currently. The questions posed throughout the chapter then allow for the reader to reflect on the author's point of view and debate topics that often have many different important points to consider. The purpose of this section is not to provide a solution but to allow the reader an opportunity to see how approaches to assisting persons with ASD can vary and often be controversial.

CHAPTER 10

Additional Critical Issues

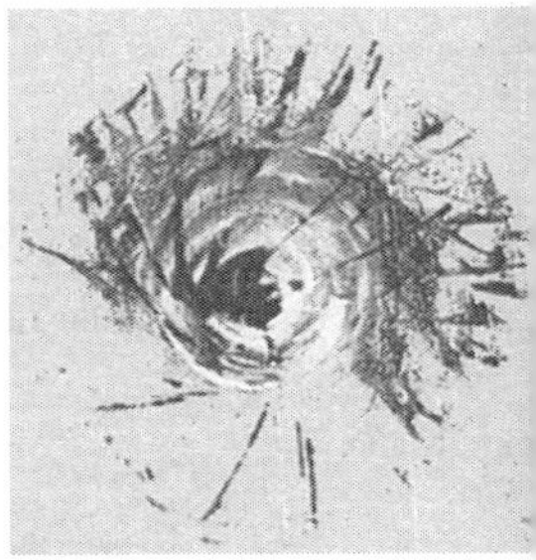

LEARNING OBJECTIVES

Discuss critical issues that are influencing the field of ASD, including:

- Media
- Human rights
- Sport
- Relaxation
- Sexuality
- Inclusion
- Peer relationships
- Acceptance
- School leadership
- Immigration

CRITICAL ISSUE #1: POPULAR MEDIA

Media Perspectives and ASD

Christina Belcher, Professor, Redeemer University, Hamilton, Ontario

As technological intervention in learning and the use of media becomes more evident, it is important to think about their messages. Has media technology gone too far in presenting its own perspectives (often inaccurate) regarding personhood, available every day on television and in the movies, to young minds? For example, I can remember that after seeing *Rain Man*, a movie about an autistic man starring Dustin Hoffman (Guber et al., 1988), I thought all persons with this disorder must be brilliant, savant, and need to be somewhat managed. We learn as much from what we see as from what informed people teach us, it seems. Since my youth, I have learned not to believe everything I see.

Clinical traits of ASD are of current interest to movie and sitcom producers. This is because media, predominantly television and the big screen, educates through stereotyping. Stereotyping provides a more interesting viewer perception than reality (Draaisma, 2009). Any social screen experience is a more appealing venue to explore the ASD personality than dry clinical diagnosis. This new mediated, albeit somewhat imaginary, Asperger's person is being very welcomed within media. Thus, media has assisted greatly in providing a different portrayal of ASD than what was previously understood. The academic paper "Autism Spectrum Disorder in Popular Media: Storied Reflections of Societal Views" (Belcher & Maich, 2014) further explores this topic.

In sitcoms and movies, the depiction of persons on the spectrum may be viewed as suspect—not because of what is stereotypical but rather because of what is frequently omitted from the *real life* of a person not represented on the big screen. While physiological and psychological profiling depicts people with ASD as having specific clinical and observable traits, the traits portrayed in popular media are largely on the savant end of the scale. And savants are rare. Media depicts ASD character types who often have multiple PhDs and brilliant decision-making skills in a crisis (e.g., TV characters such as Dr. Temperance Brennan, a socially literate yet comically inept personality in her social life, on *Bones* [Hanson, 2005]; Dr. Spencer Reid, an acclaimed profiler often unable to recognize social cues, on *Criminal Minds* [Davis, 2005]; and more recently, Dr. Shaun Murphy, a young surgeon with savant syndrome in *The Good Doctor* [Shore & Kim, 2017]). In the latter depiction, for the first time, some awkwardness and realistic breakdown moments are included in the depiction of the character of Dr. Shaun Murphy—however, he is depicted more like a piece of technology in some episodes than a surgeon. Such stereotyped characters are seen as brilliant and socially awkward in a lovable way (e.g., characters depicted with Asperger-"type" traits, such as Sheldon on *The Big Bang Theory* [Lorre, Prady, & Molero, 2007] and its 2017 spin-off, *Young Sheldon* [Lorre, Molero, & Parsons, 2017]), stars in their workplaces, incapable or comedic irritants in their home lives, and heroic leaders in their vocational fields. Few traumas are included; few problematic social situations are referred to; no medication is noted; no normal daily life is seen without either humour or a glimpse of the magnificent.

savant: a person defined by remarkable talents in one or more areas along with a comorbid disability such as a developmental disability or ASD. The skill or skills that they demonstrate (e.g., memory, music) are far above what their intellectual ability would seem to predict (Hughes et al., 2018).

psychological profiling: action toward a certain group of persons because of a stereotype about the group to which they belong. It usually results in a different treatment of the person or a more intense scrutiny (Ontario Human Rights Commission, 2019).

In the pursuit of a truthful representation, it is essential to present a balanced view—a view that realistically presents and prepares persons with ASD for life and also notes that life is a struggle at times. However, media frequently neglects to include the real-life pressures and accommodations necessary for persons on the spectrum struggling with social interactions and life skills.

Within the last two decades, *autistic fiction* has become a genre in its own right. In *The Boy on the Bridge* (2017) by M. R. Carey, the main character is represented as alien or superior, but in tandem as a poorly treated superhero. Is media, in its portrayals, creating not only a new venue for perception but also a new kind of person entirely, less human and more machine? Is our humanity being reformed in media's image?

Read about It. Think about It. Write about It.

- What was the first movie or television show you saw in which one of the characters had ASD or ASD-type traits? What were your perceptions? How did these perceptions change when you met people with ASD?
- Have you heard these perceptions of persons with ASD portrayed by others, either within or outside of the field? How are the general population's perceptions shaped by the media and what they saw versus a person they know who has ASD?
- Do you think the increased presence of ASD in TV and movies has helped or hindered the awareness, acceptance, and understanding of ASD?

CRITICAL ISSUE #2: HUMAN RIGHTS

Gloria Sparkes v. The Department of Health and Community Services

Newfoundland & Labrador Human Rights Commission Report (2002)

Ms. Sparkes filed a complaint with the Commission on behalf of her grandson, Brandon Sparkes, who had been diagnosed with autism. The attending physician referred him for the Applied Behavioural Analysis Program (ABAP), noting that this is the treatment of preference and that early intervention is critical. When Ms. Sparkes approached the respondent to have her grandson enrolled in the Autism Pilot Project, she was told the program was full and there were several people on the waitlist. The Human Rights Commission ordered the complaint to a Board of Inquiry. The respondent has since filed an application with the Court seeking to stop the Board of Inquiry from convening. Brandon has been placed in the ABAP and the respondent says the Board of Inquiry is moot. Adjudicator Valerie Marshall heard this matter in August 2002. A decision is pending.

Newfoundland & Labrador Human Rights Commission Report (2004/05)

The Department of Health and Community Services had appealed a decision of a Board of Inquiry which found that a waiting list for services for autistic children discriminated against those children on the basis of their mental disability. The Board of Inquiry had ordered, inter alia that funding be provided so as to eliminate those waitlists. On appeal, the Trial Division confirmed the factual and legal findings of the Board of Inquiry and declared the remedy imposed by the Board of Inquiry to be appropriate. The Department has not further appealed this decision.

Sources: Newfoundland & Labrador Human Rights Commission (2002); Newfoundland & Labrador Human Rights Commission (2005)

> **discrimination:** when a person does not have equal access to supports and suffers a disadvantage because of a personal characteristic (Government of Canada, 2018b).

Read about It. Think about It. Write about It.

- Waitlists for provincially funded early intervention and early intensive behaviour intervention (EIBI) are common across the country. How does the waitlist scenario portrayed here compare to the waitlist in your province or territory?
- Do you think waitlists in all areas of health and services for persons with disabilities are discriminatory?
- Looking at the *Convention on the Rights of Persons with Disabilities* (CRPD), created by the United Nations, do you think that waitlists for early intervention are discriminatory?

CRITICAL ISSUE #3: PHYSICAL FITNESS

Sport & ASD

Joyce Magat, Graduate Student, York University

JorDen Tyson is a figure skater and gold medal Special Olympian. Tommy Des Brisay, a long-distance runner, was a Paralympic Tokyo 2020 hopeful. Ron Canney has two medals in para-swimming from the 2017 Canada Games. Colin Rose has a black belt in Taekwondo. What these individuals have in common is that they are all accomplished athletes in their respective sport. But of critical relevance here is that Tyson, Des Brisay, Canney, and Rose were all diagnosed with ASD. From their stories, people may learn that sport and ASD are not mutually exclusive. This was certainly the case for these Canadian athletes. In Des Brisay's words,

> "I have been running for so long. Five years ago on August 2nd, 2006." (0:32)
> "I'm not nervous. I'm too excited." (0:57)
> "I would like to try … win the first place." (2:01; CTV News, 2012)

Des Brisay's story may have started with a discussion about his ASD diagnosis, but it does not end with one. He demonstrates a strong passion for his sport. Though these athletes are indeed exceptional cases, what we may learn is that accomplishment, high performance, and something "normal" like sports are possible for individuals with ASD.

> **paralympian**: an athlete who participates in the Paralympic games, where persons with disabilities compete. Eligibility differs across sports and disability group and is classified by functional ability to ensure fairness (Sportanddev.org, n.d.).

There is a growing intersection between sport and ASD in Canada. A large contributor has been the (positive) change in the autism community regarding sport. Over time, the shift has gone from viewing sport as impractical to seeing it as useful, feasible, and desirable. Individuals with ASD reap the benefits of sport as a therapeutic tool, as well as for fun and enjoyment. While ASD may create specific challenges to sport participation, there is a greater understanding of how sport may open up new possibilities for individuals with ASD.

There are several avenues for sport participation for individuals with ASD. Individuals on the autism spectrum can participate in "typical" sports (i.e., alongside "typically developed" peers), but there are also targeted sport opportunities. Many sport programs have been due to parents' personal experiences, which inspire them to take action and create adapted sport programs. Other times, new sport initiatives are led by citizens wanting to better support individuals with ASD in their community. Together with these programs, there is an increased awareness that individuals with ASD are more accepted—and successful—in sport.

One example of a targeted sport program is located in Toronto. In 1995, the Hockey Association for the Developmentally Challenged (HADC) Gladiators Hockey Club brought the game of hockey to individuals with developmental disabilities, including ASD. At present, there are 38 athletes and 18 coaches. With games and practices, the athletes gain the full hockey experience. This program is unique in that prior hockey or skating expertise is not a prerequisite. In their words, "all individuals have the right to play hockey" (HADC, 2017, para. 3), whether or not the athletes know they can. The HADC Gladiators' coaches, volunteers, and supporters have a strong belief in the program they deliver but even more belief in their athletes.

Northeast of Toronto is Ausome Ottawa, developed in 2015 by parents of a child with ASD. Ausome provides sport programming to children with ASD. Families may purchase a yearly membership ($25) in order to access various sports (e.g., basketball, tennis, water polo, soccer, gymnastics). Benefits of this multisport program include improved physical health, increased self-esteem, reduced anxiety, and making new friends (Rice, 2015). Ausome recognizes that playing sports may not be easy for children with ASD, but their vision is to give each child on the autism spectrum a chance or opportunity to try (Ausome Ottawa, 2019).

In the last two years, the inception of more sport programs has specifically targeted children and teens with autism. From New Brunswick, there is No Limits Soccer, with some of its own volunteer coaches diagnosed with ASD. Established in Montreal, but located also in Ottawa and Toronto, is Proset Autism, which uses tennis as a therapeutic tool. Autisme Karaté, also in Montreal, teaches karate basics. Though not exclusive to children or teens with ASD, in January 2019, Newfoundland launched a squash program for individuals in wheelchairs or living with ASD, with hopes of bringing squash to the Paralympics (CBC News, 2019).

Nationally, Special Olympics Canada provides sports for individuals with intellectual or developmental disabilities. Special Olympics Canada caters to all levels (i.e., local, regional, national, and global), with over 30 Olympic-style sports. Its program is both transformative and empowering for its athletes. For example, individuals with ASD can find "joy, confidence, and fulfillment" (Special Olympics, 2019, para. 3) that may originate in sport but extend to everyday life outside of sport. All types of programs, be it national or regional, show the potential of sport to provide not only physical benefits but also mental and psychosocial benefits. Altogether, the broad encompass of sport (recreational/competitive, non-adapted/adapted, individual/team) implies that there are multiple ways of imagining what sport looks like for individuals with ASD.

Though sport is a relatively new area within the autism community, so far it shows much promise. While sport is shown to have direct benefits to athletes with ASD, oftentimes there are benefits also for parents and families. Lorraine Whaley, president of the HADC Gladiators, shares that it is gratifying to see the athletes' growth and changes. She adds, "we really need to get the word out" (personal communication, January 30, 2020). It seems the conversations around sport and ASD have only just begun.

Read about It. Think about It. Write about It.

- How many individuals with ASD do you know that participate in sports? Do you find they are actively invited and participating in your community?
- There have been stereotypes that individuals with ASD are more suited for computers and other more science and math-based activities. Do you think this is true in your experience? How do you think this has influenced access to sport for persons with ASD?
- What is needed in your province or territory to change the perception of sport for persons with ASD and make it more accessible?

CRITICAL ISSUE #4: REFLECTION, RELAXATION, AND SELF-CALMING

Relaxation Station, Zen Zone, or Cozy Corner?

Today's inclusive classrooms feature many diverse groups of students who have a need for teaching and supporting effective self-regulation skills. One element of classroom design that can support this area of need that permeates everyday interactions—and classroom successes—is the creation of a classroom space where all students can head for reflection, relaxation, and self-calming. Although such spaces can be beneficial for many students, it can be essential for some students, such as a student with autism spectrum disorder who is beginning to learn strategies to self-regulate in group settings like classrooms. Because such spaces are not restricted by age or grade and can support students with or without exceptionalities, a range of students in varying classrooms and schools can use this approach for those moments of everyday disquiet, stress, or anxiety that occur throughout the school day.

Whatever students and teachers choose to name it, a relaxation station is a proactive way of setting up the classroom to give students a way to initiate and practice self-regulation—right in a classroom space. The below 10-step process can help.

> **self-regulation**: the intentional or automatic modification of one's own emotional state so one can work toward a goal-directed behaviour (Mazefsky et al., 2013).

Step 1: Choose Location Carefully

Consider which spaces are easily accessible and/or make use of nooks or spaces in the classroom while providing a balance of some privacy with supervision. Spaces can be created under reading lofts, utilizing play tents that sit on desks—depending on the grade level and needs of the classroom and its students, keeping safety foremost in mind.

Step 2: Set Physical Boundaries
Pseudo-barriers, such as translucent curtains, low furniture, or even tri-fold cardboard cubbies can be used to create boundaries around spaces set up in Step 1. These elements give a message to the classroom community that some privacy is needed, for now.

Step 3: Create Names & Labels
This space can be given a positive name like "The Nest" or "The Office," with inviting visuals promoting its use as an everyday classroom tool.

Step 4: Provide Expectations
Simple and concrete procedures and rules should be created and posted. Rules should be limited in number and be brief and explicit, such as "Use the relaxation station only when it is needed." A procedure might include "Set the timer for five minutes."

Step 5: Develop Entry Procedures
Choose how students will let teachers know that they need to use this classroom space. A verbal comment to the teacher is an option, or the use of a sign-up sheet or a break card that can be placed on students' desks.

> **Incredible Five-point Scale:** a tool developed by Kari Dunn Buron to teach and assist individuals with ASD with understanding and implementing social and emotional concepts and regulation (The Incredible 5-point Scale, 2015).

Step 6: Providing Relaxation Tools
Sensory and self-regulation tools are critical components of relaxation stations and may include manipulatives and/or visuals, such as stories or posters, that encourage students to utilize self-regulation strategies. One example is the Incredible Five-point Scale. Such tools should be taught and described to the whole class so that students are familiar with them once encountered within (or outside of) the relaxation station.

Step 7: Comfort Objects and Preferred Items
The relaxation station must be structured utilizing physically comfortable and pleasing materials, which could include family photos, comfort objects, drawings—or photos of some items if space is limited. For younger students, the station may include an *All About Me* book. For older students, it may include more in-depth materials, such as photos of favourite people, hobbies, or items. Students' interests, strengths, and passions should be considered when developing a relaxation station, as these items can be utilized to provide a comforting and calming effect.

Step 8: Sensory Items
Sensory items can provide benefits when utilized appropriately within relaxation stations. Such items may be tactile (like fidget items) or target other sensory systems, such as noise-cancelling headphones and/or calming music. These items encourage student direction and individualized choice around self-regulation when students experience and learn which strategies and/or tools help them best to self-regulate.

Step 9: Using Reflective Teaching Tools
Reflective tools may be open-ended (such as journals) or more structured, such as sentence completion exercises that focus on emotions and/or behaviours—as well as future self-regulation plans.

Step 10: Creating Exit Procedures
To establish relaxation stations that work smoothly and effectively, teachers can consider establishing guidelines and procedures which can be taught and displayed (e.g., the maximum number of breaks per day and the length of breaks). Additionally, timers and/or self-monitoring forms may be utilized to reinforce such criteria and allow for increased student independence.

It is important to remember that the set-up and use of a relaxation station depends on age, grade, and functioning level of students—but such stations can be utilized in a range of teaching and learning environments in a positive way. There are many possibilities and choices in setting up such a station, and there are many commercial kits and resources that can guide teachers in developing relaxation stations. Just search Pinterest or *Teachers Pay Teachers* to see examples of what others have accomplished.

Source: Maich, O'Keefe, van Rhijn, & Davies. (2018). *The Bulletin*, http://www.nlta.nl.ca/wp-content/uploads/2018/09/bultn_sept_oct18.pdf

---

In late 2019, Octagon Pond School in Paradise, Newfoundland and Labrador (part of the Newfoundland and Labrador English School District [NLESD]), received a grant from the Wellness Coalition-Avalon East. This funding, *Everyday Wellness Strategies at School*, helped to enhance mindfulness strategies, such as school-wide mindful Monday moments incorporated into the announcements by principal Kirk Smith. Educational psychologist Florence Strang and guidance counsellor Wanda Pelley utilized this funding to create a relaxation station and trained students and teachers in its use. This joint initiative between NLESD and Memorial University used a soft-sided play tent with sensory toys, children's literature, calming music, and soft furnishings to create a space for students to practise their self-regulation skills for "those moments of everyday disquiet, stress, or anxiety that occur throughout the school day." So far, the relaxation station has visited each classroom as a model set-up that teachers and students could create in their own classroom environments.

Figure 10.1: Florence Strang, Wanda Pelley, and Kimberly Maich with the Relaxation Station

Source: Authors.

Read about It. Think about It. Write about It.

- How do you think a relaxation station or similar area in a classroom could help with inclusion?
- Given the sensory profiles common in persons with ASD, as highlighted in Chapter 5, what additional considerations must be considered when creating a relaxation station for students with ASD?
- What are your experiences with sensory equipment, materials, and relaxation methods used for persons with ASD? Are they made solely for students with ASD, or do other children have access to them? Does the sensory equipment include children with ASD or separate them more from their peers?

CRITICAL ISSUE #5: ASD AND SEXUALITY

ASD and Sexuality—Starting the Conversation

Adam W. J. Davies, PhD Candidate, OISE/University of Toronto; Assistant Professor, University of Guelph

Everyday expressions of sexuality are within movies, television, media, and online; however, little discussion is had that connects conversations of autism spectrum disorder (ASD) with conversations of sexuality. Regardless of common misconceptions, individuals with ASD do have actively developing sexualities, yet are commonly considered without a sexuality, without sexual desires, or are desexualized (Bennett, Webster, Goodall, & Rowland, 2018). As well, misconceptions stereotype those with ASD as inherently asexual or without any sexual feelings or desires (Decker, 2015). Thus, it is important to engage with some issues regarding ASD and sexuality and how common notions of the sexualities of those with ASD impact their access to sexual health information, as well as their sexual and romantic lives.

sexual health: a state of well-being in the physical, mental, and social aspects as it relates to sexuality (World Health Organization, 2019).

ASD and Sexuality: An Introduction

Due to social and cultural misconceptions of those with ASD as "lacking" in social and cognitive capabilities, there is limited research regarding the sexualities of those with ASD. Sexuality, defined by the World Health Organization (WHO, 2006) as "a central aspect of being human that throughout life encompasses sex, gender identities and roles, sexual orientation, eroticism, pleasure, intimacy and reproduction" (para. 4), is an important part of one's developing self and humanity. However, for individuals with ASD, social interventions and skill development are important to ensure that those with ASD can provide basic consent and understand conceptions of bodily autonomy for themselves and others (Barnett & Maticka-Tyndale, 2015). Due to challenges with social cues and norms, individuals with ASD can experience frustrations when attempting to make romantic and sexual connections, which can harm their sense of self and self-esteem (Sullivan & Caterino, 2008). Individuals with ASD can experience social isolation in schools, and thus, might not experience the same processes of socialization and discussions of sexuality with peers that typically developing peers might (such as dating in school, or sexuality education; Brooks, 2018). Thus, interventions, such as social narratives and explicit conversations about "public" and "private" behaviours, can specifically assist individuals with ASD in learning social and relational cues in conjunction with their developing sexualities.

Social Narratives

Social narratives are descriptions of everyday social activities with the intent of assisting children with developmental delays and social cognitive impairments with learning social cues and common routines (Autism Canada, 2017b). Narratives can be utilized to assist individuals with ASD with understanding common social scripts and norms, such as asking for consent before hugging or touching someone, or with assisting in developing empathy and theory of mind (the ability to think of the mental states of self and others) in young children and adolescents. Tarnai and Wolfe (2008) suggest using narratives with children and adults with ASD to aid in understanding a variety of norms in relationship to self-pleasuring, romantic relationships and dating, and bodily development. Moreover, narratives can be effective for having explicit conversations about puberty and the development of one's body. Narratives can be developed by teachers and educators in relationship with a student or individual with ASD themselves, with follow-ups necessary to assess whether the intervention has been effective in developing their social understanding. Narratives can be important for assisting children with ASD in comprehending simple hygienic procedures regarding one's body, such as washing hands and toiletry procedures, as children with ASD, due to communication and sensory differences, might take a longer time to learn toileting skills, require extra assistance with day-to-day toileting and bodily habits, and need help understanding bodily cues for when it is time to use the washroom (MacAlister, 2014). These interventions can be utilized with individuals of varying ages.

Public versus *Private* Behaviours

Individuals with ASD are vulnerable in terms of experiences of sexual abuse and victimization during sexual interactions (Sevlever, Roth, & Gillis, 2013). Due to common difficulties in social interactions and engaging with peers, individuals with ASD might not pick up social and sexual norms, cues, and behaviours in the same manner as their nondisabled peers (Brown-Lavoie, Viecili, & Weiss, 2014). When responding to inappropriate or questionable behaviours, such as self-stimulating in public or inappropriate language, it is important to remain positive and be proactive. This can be done by having a conversation about "public versus private" behaviours and encouraging the understanding that certain behaviours are private and for within the home. Such conversations should be undertaken without shaming the child or individual to make sure they do not associate their developing sexuality with shame and negativity. Instead of merely telling a child or individual to "stop" an undesirable behaviour, it is best to provide a temporary behaviour as a replacement. Tuzikow (n.d.) suggests implementing a task for the child to do that would then temporarily replace the undesirable behavior (e.g., "Can you help me by holding this for me?"). Positive affirmation is important when an individual begins to learn social cues and feels comfortable asking questions regarding their sexuality. Thus, if the child or individual asks to go to the bathroom or resorts to the replacement behavior to distract themselves, positive affirmation is important (Tuzikow, n.d.).

Autism Spectrum Disorder and the LGBTQ+ Community

Gender and sexual diversity and identification with the LGBTQ+ (lesbian, gay, bisexual, transgender, and queer) community are common for individuals with ASD (Hillier et al., 2019). Mendes and Maroney (2019) describe how the voices of individuals with ASD who identify as a gender and/or sexual minority are not often heard; thus, their stories and experiences are commonly silenced in both autism and LGBTQ+ communities. As noted above, individuals with ASD are commonly thought of as asexual, which can disregard their developing sexual interests and curiosities (although some might be authentically and genuinely asexual and should be acknowledged as such if self-identified). As well, it is important to allow those with ASD to self-identify their own gender identity and/or sexual orientation, as many young adults with ASD have their ability to understand or identify their own sexual or gender identity questioned (McGuire & Zenner, 2019). Further conversations about the intersections of autism and LGBTQ+ communities are necessary to ensure that individuals with ASD see themselves represented within LGBTQ+ and autism communities and that stereotypes of individuals with ASD as always nonsexual are challenged.

asexual: a lack of sexual interest in other persons or not being interested in sex (Betchen, 2014).

So ... Let's Talk about Autism and Sexuality!

It is important to acknowledge and support the developing sexualities of individuals with ASD by providing direct and accurate information for any questions that might arise, while teaching social cues and norms in a manner that does not instill shame. Some evidence-based interventions, such as narratives and positive affirmations, are ways to aid in the development of social cues. Further understanding is important relating to the shame and lack of confidence that individuals with ASD might acquire regarding their respective sexualities. Through encouraging open conversations and questions regarding sexuality and the specific needs of children and individuals with ASD, healthy sexual development for all can be fostered.

Read about It. Think about It. Write about It.

- What has been your experience around individuals' acceptance and exploration of sexuality with persons with ASD? Do parents and/or professionals avoid the conversation or provide appropriate supports?

- How do you navigate the need to protect the person with ASD from being taken advantage of in relationships and sexual encounters but allow them to express themselves like anyone else?
- Are there appropriate services and expertise in your province or territory to support persons with ASD in exploring sexuality safely?

CRITICAL ISSUE #6: SCHOOL EXCLUSION

Educating Grayson: Are Inclusive Classrooms Failing Students?

For decades, educators have tried to welcome students with special needs in regular classrooms—but faced with behavioural problems and violence, some school boards resort to sending those pupils home. What will it take to make inclusive education work?

Lisa Kahn developed a daily routine this fall. She'd eat breakfast, feed her family and get her two children ready for school—Grayson, a seven-year-old boy with strawberry blond hair and blue eyes, and his older sister, Avery. After she dropped them off, she'd practise deep breathing with help from an app on her watch. And then she would brace herself for the phone call.

At some point during the day, she knew that Grayson's school was likely to call and ask her to pick him up because he was causing trouble. If she made it through the day without the phone ringing, she'd steel herself at pickup for a staff member to approach and tell her about something awful her son had done.

Ms. Kahn had hoped the school could accommodate Grayson's developmental disorder—he was diagnosed with autism in the summer of 2017, and while he's verbal and can impressively add figures in his head, he becomes aggressive if rules change or the work becomes too difficult.

But in September, he was suspended for part of the day after attempting to push an educational assistant down the stairs. A couple of weeks later, he picked up a chair and tossed it at another child. On other occasions, he punched, shoved, kicked and threatened staff and other students, school administrators say.

And then in late October, everything boiled over. After an incident when Grayson struck an educational assistant, leaving her with bruises, scrapes and a concussion, the seven-year-old was expelled from school.

Now Ms. Kahn and her husband Dave are scrambling to piece together a new plan for educating Grayson, who they firmly believe belongs in the public school system.

"Not only has he been stripped of all his peer connections," says Ms. Kahn, "but he's been stripped of his right to an education."

The Kahns have filed a complaint with the Human Rights Tribunal of Ontario and they've appealed the expulsion. For now, at least, they're keeping Grayson at home, and up until recently, the school district was providing him with home instruction. Ms. Kahn now works with him daily, doing lessons in reading, writing and math.

human rights tribunal: committees that are similar to courts of law, available provincially and through the Canadian Human Rights Tribunal to ensure each Canadian has access to fair treatment and equal opportunity. This tribunal only hears about cases with discrimination (Canadian Human Rights Tribunal, 2016).

It's an imperfect solution for their son, they say, and makes it difficult for both of them to work during the daytime.

The family's experience highlights the growing challenges that parents—and educators—face when it comes to accommodating special-needs children in the public school system. Over the past few decades, schools across Canada have moved toward a model of inclusive education, but many are struggling to find the best ways to include children with complex needs in regular classrooms.

The issue of inclusive classrooms has become a matter of fierce debate—and some educators wonder if inclusion has gone too far for students with very complex needs. Inclusiveness can't work, they say, without a thoughtful rethinking of how we teach children with diverse needs and how we structure the school day.

Teachers report an uptick in violent incidents disrupting classrooms, tensions arise among families who feel the safety and learning of their own children are at risk, and school districts struggle with embracing inclusion while providing a safe environment for staff and students. Meanwhile, families with children who have intellectual and developmental disabilities are increasingly being asked to pick up kids early, start the school day later or simply keep them home for the entire day. Complicating matters is the fact that apart from a few advocacy or parent group surveys, most school districts don't formally track these exclusions or shortened days.

Jacqueline Specht, director of the Canadian Research Centre on Inclusive Education and a professor at the University of Western Ontario's faculty of education, says the system is clearly broken when a seven-year-old is expelled and can't be properly accommodated. "What are we doing that we expel seven-year-olds instead of really looking at what's causing this behaviour, and how do we stop that behaviour?"

Research shows young people in inclusive classrooms tend to have more friends, and are better off academically and feel better about themselves than they do when they're educated in separate, segregated classrooms, Dr. Specht says. But administrators at Grayson's school, John McCrae Public School in Guelph, Ont., say that they can't safely accommodate Grayson.

So, as children across Canada head back to school this week, Ms. Kahn's son will be staying at home. As she and her family have discovered, the road to inclusion is paved with good intentions, but riddled with cracks.

Before the 1970s, it was not uncommon for children with special needs to be excluded from schooling. Too often, these children barely got an education; many were early dropouts.

The 1960s civil-rights movement in the United States, while it focused on race, also spurred awareness about the challenges facing students with complex needs, according to researcher Sheila Bennett, a professor at Brock University and co-author of *Special Education in Ontario Schools*. Riding that wave, organizations such as the Association for Community Living successfully pushed for changes that called for more inclusive education in several provinces, Dr. Bennett says.

In Ontario, Bill 82 in 1980 was a game-changer, requiring every school board to provide special-education programs and services for students with complex needs. Over time—and as a result of advances in thinking combined with lobbying from parents and advocacy groups—schools began including more of these children in regular classrooms full-time, rather than segregating them in separate classrooms. To support special-needs students, school boards often employ educational assistants to work collaboratively with teachers, although teachers' unions argue that most classrooms don't have enough of them.

Philosophically, the Kahns embrace the idea of inclusive education. They believe Grayson should learn alongside his neighbourhood peers, and they try to expose him to a range of activities, including swimming and hip-hop dance lessons.

They were proactive when Grayson started having trouble in senior kindergarten. For the most part, students aren't assessed for disabilities until Grade 3, but when they heard reports of behavioural issues, including pushing classmates, the Kahns did not want to wait. They wanted their son to thrive socially and academically, so they spent $2,800 to have him privately assessed and discovered he had autism.

With the help of an educational assistant, Grayson had a successful school year in Grade 1, with no suspensions or calls for early pickups. When he began Grade 2, Ms. Kahn met with school administrators. Grayson had shown more aggressive behaviour over the summer—he'd struck his mother for the first time, after becoming frustrated about not being able to express himself—and she wanted to ensure there was a plan in place at school to deal with the challenges.

Because the school team believed it would be too stressful for one person to work with him for the whole day, they assigned two educational assistants—one for the morning and another for the afternoon. The approach raised red flags with Ms. Kahn, who says her child does better with one person.

The plan fell apart almost instantly. Students and staff reported physical and verbal assaults. Grayson was spending large chunks of the school day in the office.

At first, administrators asked Ms. Kahn to pick up Grayson early or keep him home for several days. Later, they hatched a return-to-school plan: They would let Grayson come back, but only for 15 minutes a day, Ms. Kahn says. His return would be graduated over a period of time.

Ms. Kahn was exasperated: "Who's going to pay my bills?" she recalls saying. "Who's taking care of my child? We work. What about his education?"

A few years ago, Annie Kidder's organization, People for Education, an education advocacy group, began receiving calls from parents with similar questions: Are principals allowed to ask that I keep my child home for all or part of the day? Can my child be asked to come in later than his classmates?

The answer to these questions is yes. But nobody had documented the scope of the problem. So four years ago, in its annual survey, the group asked principals if they had ever requested that children stay home.

Ms. Kidder says she was "astounded" by the response: 48 per cent of elementary-school principals and 40 per cent of high-school principals reported asking that a student with special needs not attend school for the full day, citing insufficient classroom support. "We didn't expect that. We thought it was a rare occurrence," she says. In its latest report, released last year, the numbers have risen to 58 per cent and 48 per cent, respectively.

Similarly, a survey of parents of children with special needs released in November 2017 by the B.C. Confederation of Parent Advisory Councils found that children with special needs were missing anywhere from half an hour to three hours of school daily or being told to stay home because of staff shortages. A number of children, the survey found, were sent home because of behavioural incidents at school, and these exclusions, which were undocumented, would continue for days or weeks. Another survey, conducted by an advocacy group called BCEdAccess, found that a number of parents are being forced out of the public education system as a result.

Expulsions such as Grayson's are rare, but it's difficult to know how common other measures are. Most school districts or provinces don't formally track when a child's school day is shortened—a so-called undocumented suspension. Ms. Kidder says her survey results suggest it's a problem that should be tracked. (Ms. Kahn was asked to keep Grayson home for a number of days with no formal paperwork from the district.)

Luke Reid, a lawyer at ARCH Disability Law Centre, who practises primarily in the areas of education law and human rights for people with disabilities requiring accommodation, says school administrators see it as a "request" that a parent voluntarily withdraw their children for part of the school day.

"However, as you might guess, these often don't feel like requests to parents and they happen with surprising regularity in many cases, all of which can have a big impact on the family," Mr. Reid says. "There needs to be some sort of accountability mechanism in place to ensure that school boards are properly exercising these powers."

The issue has become so top-of-mind that two school districts—North Vancouver and Greater Victoria—passed motions this fall to record how many children with special needs are being asked to stay home, or are sent home early or dropped off late and being excluded from field trips.

Jordan Watters, chair of the Greater Victoria School Board, says school staff need to understand the challenges so supports can address them and children with special needs can be meaningfully included. "Our move to track incidents of exclusion is intended to help us do that," she says.

The head of Canada's largest school district, the Toronto District School Board, says it, too, has started tracking how many children are being excluded, and is asking principals to work with superintendents before requesting a child stay home.

John Malloy, the director of education, says many children are successfully included in schools, and there will always be a small number who need a special program, but the board is committed to including, "wherever possible," students in the neighbourhood school.

"We are really looking at how we can serve more of our students in their community school where it's appropriate," Dr. Malloy says. Still, he cautions, "there are only so many resources. There are only so many staff."

"What remains our challenge is that even though we want to serve each and every student in the most inclusive way possible, some students may have needs that exceed our level of experience and that is something we are sometimes challenged by," he says, adding that school districts often partner with community agencies and hospitals.

Part of the problem, some academics say, is that more students are being diagnosed with intellectual and developmental disabilities that were for a long time overlooked. People for Education found that the proportion of elementary kids receiving special-education support—anything from a little extra help in a regular class to the provision of one, or even two, dedicated staff—has doubled over the past two decades. At the TDSB, about 40,000 students, roughly 16 per cent of kids, are supported through individual education plans.

Integration, though, still makes some parents uneasy. In Grayson's classroom, parents were concerned for the safety of their children.

"I know that the Kahns are likely arguing his right to an education, but what about the rights of the rest of the kids?" one parent wrote in a letter that was included in the principal's expulsion investigation report. "In addition to the threat to safety, his actions are a near constant disruption to classroom activities. This is not acceptable."

Another parent said her daughter hasn't been physically harmed by Grayson, but she was "uncomfortable in class and worried for those around her" when Grayson was present.

There were reports that some of Grayson's classmates felt anxious and reported stomach aches. Some of the staff said they had trouble sleeping and felt worried and anxious being around the young boy.

Ms. Kahn is sympathetic, but wonders why her son should be punished for his condition. She says Grayson is the victim of a system that cannot properly handle children who have special needs that come with behavioural issues.

The Upper Grand District School Board, for its part, wouldn't comment on Grayson's case, but also said it is strongly committed to supporting students with special needs while balancing the safety of students and staff. In the principal's expulsion report, obtained by the *Globe and Mail*, the school said that Ms. Kahn's "extreme hostility" and "repeated verbal assaults" to staff had been stressful and caused emotional harm. She counters that she was only serving as an advocate for her son.

School staff suggested alternative programs, including a therapeutic school, as well as switching him to the English stream (Grayson was in French immersion), which has an intervention program that teaches self-regulation skills and frustration management. But Ms. Kahn says the therapeutic school, an hour's drive away, was too far from home, and the board hasn't spelled out to her what supports he would have at the English school.

Grayson wants to rejoin his classmates, she says. "There's a lot of little things the school could have been doing to help facilitate that but they didn't. So they just kind of let the behaviours get to the point where they're out of control, and they say, 'Sorry, this child is a threat to safety. He can't be here.'"

The principal, on the other hand, argues the school made "significant efforts" to accommodate Grayson's needs while keeping both him and his classmates safe, including drawing up support plans, providing him with full-time educational assistant support and having the board's mental-health clinician observe him.

Leslie Newman writes in her report that she is satisfied staff made all "reasonable efforts" to accommodate Grayson and "that some of them have suffered significant physical and emotional harm in the course of these accommodation efforts."

In Ontario, and across much of the country, school districts are responsible for determining how best to accommodate special-needs students and aim to include them in regular classrooms, wherever possible.

New Brunswick takes the policy of inclusive education the furthest—it calls for a "common learning environment" for all students. Segregated classrooms aren't an option, and instruction must be primarily provided by the classroom teacher.

The provincial government doesn't track how many students are attending for only part of the day, and the New Brunswick Teachers' Association president, George Daley, says while the model is important, it has been "difficult." He says teachers need more supports and there needs to be flexibility so students with behavioural issues can spend time outside the regular classroom learning different life skills.

Teachers' unions say that violent behaviour in classrooms is disrupting teaching and student learning. The Elementary Teachers' Federation of Ontario, for example, reports that 83 per cent of its members say violence in school is making teaching more difficult.

Paul Bennett, an education consultant based in Halifax, says a movement to make the classroom the be-all and end-all of inclusion is short-sighted.

"The system is not built to accommodate the range of diversity we now have in our school system," he says.

In the case of children such as Grayson, who have the most complex and acute needs, Mr. Bennett says the public education system should provide one-on-one intensive supports and only provide alternative school settings if integration doesn't work.

"I do not believe in segregation," Mr. Bennett says. "I believe in integration of everyone as far as they possibly can be integrated. But when they fall two, three, four grades behind everyone else, when they're not able to follow, when they're acting out, when they're extremely frustrated, parents are looking for alternatives."

Prof. Specht, of Western, has seen students who have struggled with aggressive behaviour moved to another school and do much better. Others, she says, may need time away for intense therapy, or to spend 15 minutes in the regular classroom and work on being there longer.

"There are still too many students who are in segregated classes who could be included. Cases like this one [Grayson's case] are used to say inclusion does not work rather than perhaps thinking it is a rare occurrence," she says. "There are many positive stories of inclusion that will say, inclusion is what we ought to move toward."

But some parents say the positive stories stem from efforts made by individual teachers, and not necessarily the public school system.

Tina McGee's nine-year-old daughter, Kherrigan, has severe autism, medical issues and a severe intellectual disability. In Grade 1 at a school in Abbotsford, B.C., Kherrigan had what Ms. McGee describes as a "phenomenal teacher," who was supported by a full-time educational assistant.

Before Valentine's Day, knowing that Kherrigan would not be able to chew the treats being brought to school, the teacher sent a note home asking kids to think of what they could give their classmate instead. Some brought cupcakes, others came in with stuffed animals and hair accessories, mostly red as they knew it was Kherrigan's favourite colour. "She would make plans around Kherrigan and include her in everything," Ms. McGee says.

But when the family moved to Chilliwack, B.C., and changed schools, she was asked almost weekly to keep Kherrigan home in her Grade 3 year due to staffing shortages—educational assistants were juggling as many as five children each. Ms. McGee responded by enrolling Kherrigan in a private school that could accommodate her daughter's needs.

Still, she says she believes that inclusion can work. "It can if the teachers and staff aren't so overworked."

Bruce Uditsky of Inclusion Alberta, a non-profit organization that advocates for children and adults with developmental disabilities, says inclusion is dependent on the leadership and mindset of those in charge. Two school districts could have equal funding, but one will successfully include children and the other won't, he says.

"Teachers or principals or districts should not be guardians to the classroom door as to which kid is valued and which isn't," he says. "Both government and the system are being allowed to escape [their] responsibility for ensuring that kids with disabilities have access to the same education as would be true for kids without disabilities." Some parents, he says, are tired of fighting.

Laurie Pett turned to home schooling as a last resort when her 10-year-old son, Connor, was deemed too burdensome for the regular school system. The family moved to Quesnel, B.C., in the middle of the last school year, and Ms. Pett met with the school principal to discuss how best to accommodate Connor, who has been diagnosed with autism, oppositional defiant disorder and apraxia. He has behavioural issues, including aggression and a tendency to run.

She was told that Connor could attend the school's breakfast club every morning for the first few months. When she said that wasn't acceptable, the principal increased the plan to one hour at school a day. There wasn't funding in the school's budget, he said, to support Connor more.

The family has four other children with behavioural issues, all of whom have been accommodated by the school. But Connor is "definitely not welcome," she says. "And I don't get the feeling that he's welcome in our district."

When Ms. Pett speaks about inclusion, she laughs. "It's not about cracks in the system," she says. "They're big gaping holes."

Ms. Kahn agrees, and has now pulled her daughter Avery, who is nine and has also been diagnosed with autism, out of their local school because she doesn't believe she'll get the support she needs.

"It's not just that I'm fighting for my kid," Ms. Kahn says. "I'm fighting for all those other kids who have left the system, all the ones who are coming behind us who are not going to have the financial means to hire a lawyer, or financial means to stay home with their children."

Source: Alphonso, C. (2019, 7 January). Educating Grayson: Are inclusive classrooms failing students? *The Globe and Mail*. Retrieved from https://www.theglobeandmail.com/canada/education/article-educating-grayson-are-inclusive-classrooms-failing-students/

Read about It. Think about It. Write about It.

- What is your first reaction to reading this article about students being expelled? Do you see both sides of the story? Are you more likely to side with the child with ASD or the educators/school system?
- What do public school systems need to do in order to really include children with higher support needs?
- What role does awareness and acceptance play in terms of individual educators to include children with more complex needs? The author mentioned that it is often more about the individual educator than the system as a whole. How do we make changes on this front?

CRITICAL ISSUE #7: AUTHENTIC PEER RELATIONSHIPS

Spreading Inclusion in Recreation through Camps on TRACKS

Ashley Parker, Camps on TRACKS Project Lead, Thames Valley Children's Centre (TVCC)

For all children, building and maintaining social relationships is highly important (Carter et al., 2013). Many authors suggest that the inclusion of people with disabilities must move beyond an educational setting and into other community settings that provide participation and social interaction with typically developing peers (Carr et al., 2002). A peer-mediated social skills approach meets these needs by training typical developing peers on how to prompt and teach skills to their peers with less developed social skills. It provides increased opportunities for social skills as compared to an adult-mediated approach where the adult teaches the child the skills. The adult-led approach can lead to age-inappropriate social skills and limit the number of skills taught. When placed with typically developing peers, children are likely to increase and generalize their peer-related interaction skills (Whalon, Conroy, Martinez, & Werch, 2015).

adult-mediated social skills instruction: social skills instruction directed and taught by the support staff to the person with social skills difficulties.

Although most of the literature has focused on peer-mediated social skills training in schools, many recreational opportunities occur outside of the school setting. When examining perceptions of children with disability in physical activity, gaining entry, being legitimate participants, and having friends were important factors as to whether children felt included (Spencer-Cavaliere & Watkinson, 2010). Children did refer to the roles of adults, but it was concluded that peers played the most significant role in inclusion (Spencer-Cavaliere & Watkinson, 2010).

Camps are great settings for peer-to-peer interactions as there are many social opportunities for practise. Also, camp settings have a more flexible schedule and focus on having fun and making friends. In addition, there are a large volume of peers in the same place, at the same time, and doing the same activity. Since video game and technology use is on the rise, opportunities may decrease for peer interaction. Therefore, it is important when these children are together to teach social skills, inclusion, and how to be a better friend to children with special needs or social challenges. Parents of children with autism spectrum disorder (ASD) and other disabilities have identified added stress in the summer months due to lack of services available for their children and disruption in routines (Brookman et al., 2003). Therefore, the camp setting is vitally important to foster and build social skills, as well as decrease stress for parents.

Camps are a great place to implement such programs as they typically run during times when parents are in need of services. There are many types of camps thus children's strengths and interests can be matched to an appropriate camp. Many camps are also aiming toward full inclusion and providing a peer-mediated approach ensures inclusion is successful and children with social skills challenges can learn skills and get the support they need.

Camps on TRACKS began in 2011 from the PEER Pals (Thames Valley Children's Centre [TVCC], 2008b) and Stay, Play & Talk (Thames Valley Children's Centre, Fanshawe College, & All Kids Belong, 2012) programs. Both Stay, Play & Talk and PEER Pals were originally school/preschool-focused, and although they had positive outcomes, there were no programs offered with this approach within the camp setting. Therefore, a pilot project began in 2011 at the City of London's day camps, as the camp leadership saw that although children were included, the social interaction piece was missing.

TRACKS stands for

Try Again (Persistence)
Right Thing (Correcting)
Assist (Prompting)
Congratulate (Reinforcement)
Keep Trying (Persistence)
Show (Modelling)

The proximity of the adults changed when the program was implemented at the City of London day camps. Rather than being beside the child with a disability, the camp counsellors were able to be standing at the sidelines and facilitate the interactions. Children were authentically learning social skills in the moment instead of being taught separately from their peers.

Using evidence-based, peer-mediated approaches, the Camps on TRACKS program supports adult camp counsellors to teach children the skills to include and assist children who have social skills difficulties. The Camps on TRACKS project involves five steps that are completed each week, beginning on the Monday campers start camp. As the summer continues and there are returning campers, often the training is led by those peers who have become TRACKS champions.

1. Introduction to Camps on TRACKS: First thing Monday morning when campers learn about camp rules, they are told that it is a TRACKS camp and that the focus is about being a good friend. Activities are included that highlight inclusion and being included.
2. Reward Systems: A group reward system is established Monday. As a group, the campers decide what they will work toward to receive at the end of the

week. They get rewarded each time they complete a TRACKS skill and be a good friend. Usually achieving 100–200 stickers throughout the week to throw water balloons at the camp counsellors is highly motivating.

3. Camper Awareness: Campers then proceed through a series of activities that focus on similarities and differences. Some may simulate a particular disability. The focus is on how we are similar and how everyone can overcome their challenges.
4. Teaching TRACKS: Campers are taught the particular skills to include everyone and be a good friend and prompted by the counsellors to use in natural situations throughout the week.
5. Prompting through Peers: The camp counsellors are taught to prompt through peers to use the TRACKS skills rather than prompt the child with social skills difficulties.

disability simulation activities: activities that people engage in that simulate a certain type of disability or difficulty to provide awareness about disability. Although controversy exists about whether attitudes change with these activities, it is vital that additional teaching and an appropriate debriefing is completed to safeguard against such issues.

The peer-mediated approach involves the adult approaching the peers to prompt the child with social challenges or disabilities to participate. This approach teaches the adult to reduce their proximity to the child to let those natural peer-to-peer interactions happen. TRACKS creates an inclusive place where all kids have fun, belong, and are meaningful participants. The peer-mediated approach is crucial and a core concept in the TRACKS program. People who have implemented Camps on TRACKS have noted many benefits. Some include: enhancing social interactions for ALL children, educating peers on how to interact with children with social challenge, and enhancing problem solving skills.

To learn more about being trained in TRACKS, check out the website (www.campsontracks.com). We provide in-person trainings of varying lengths available all across Ontario. In addition, TRACKS has two online training modules: Camps on TRACKS and TRACKS for Schools.

Read about It. Think about It. Write about It.

- When reading about an approach that teaches peers instead of teaching the person with ASD, what is your initial reaction? Is this needed in order to make more change and acceptance? Do you think individual social skill instruction to the person with ASD is needed concurrently?

- Do you think an approach like this puts too much pressure on the peers? Why or why not?
- How do peer-mediated social skills allow the person with ASD to move beyond just physical inclusion to true inclusion and the development of friendships?

CRITICAL ISSUE #8: AUTISM ACCEPTANCE

Autistic People Aren't Really Accepted—and It's Impacting Their Mental Health

Up to 70% of autistic people experience mental health conditions such as depression and anxiety, according to some research. Unfortunately, we still don't know why autistic people are at a higher risk for mental health problems than non-autistic people. But one important factor is whether an individual's autism is recognised and accepted by those around them. My colleagues and I recently published research that shows a lack of acceptance can significantly impact on the mental health of autistic adults.

> **mental health:** a state of emotional well-being that is essential for living a healthy life and is a core feature of overall health (Government of Canada, 2015).

While medical professionals have become much better at diagnosing autism, many people with the condition feel it is still not accepted as a potentially positive aspect of who they are. Autism is a lifelong neurodevelopmental condition, meaning that the brain develops differently. This results in differences in social communication and interactions, sensory experiences and restricted interests. For our research, we surveyed 111 cognitively able autistic adults about how their experiences of autism acceptance related to their mental health, and many commented on experiencing a negative reaction.

"Since being diagnosed I have found that mention of autism is met blankly or dismissed," said one participant. Another explained how searching for acceptance from others could be incredibly draining: "As the years pass, I suffer increasing anxiety for lack of even casual acceptance by my species."

Take a moment to think about a crucial part of who you are. For example, I am Scottish, and that is a very important part of me. Now think about whether other people accept that part of you. Perhaps you feel a disconnection between how much you accept yourself and how much others seem to accept you. If you feel like others don't accept you for that part of your identity, this could impact on your mental health. As human beings, we have a natural desire to be accepted and to belong.

For people who have a diagnosis of an autism spectrum condition, autism can be an integral part of who they are. This is why many prefer the term "autistic person" rather than "person with autism" (just as I prefer to be called a Scottish person rather than a person with Scottishness). But do other people accept autistic people for who they are? Recent research suggests not, and that first impressions of autistic people tend to be negative.

Our survey found that autistic people who felt less accepted by others were more likely to experience higher symptoms of depression and stress. Lower self-acceptance was also related to higher symptoms of depression. These findings suggest that simply feeling accepted plays a key role in a person's mental health.

Another important aspect of our research was that we also asked participants to share any thoughts they had on their experiences of autism acceptance. Their answers revealed that many thought that they "camouflaged" or "masked" the fact they were autistic. In other words, in certain situations they tried to act "neurotypical" (non-autistic). As one participant said, "I mask so well that I am accepted, but not for being autistic."

We found that the participants who said that they camouflaged also reported higher symptoms of depression. One participant explained that "[camouflaging] is incredibly exhausting and stressful and has ultimately led to mental and physical health problems." Hopefully you can imagine how draining it must be to feel like you have to constantly hide a major part of yourself from others. We are just starting to learn about camouflaging in autism, and more research needs to be done to understand the impact it could have on autistic people's lives.

camouflaging: disguising the signs of autism or other characteristics that are part of a diagnosis (Russo, 2018).

Celebrating Diversity

We need to accept autistic people for being who they are, and to enable them to feel like they can disclose the fact that they are autistic to others and be accepted for this. My past research with autistic adolescents found that many of these adolescents had a desire to fit in with their peers, but they also wanted to be accepted for who they were. In our societies, we should be celebrating diversity and enabling autistic people to be themselves.

Perhaps by creating a more accepting society, we might see fewer mental health difficulties in autism. But we need more work on autism acceptance to work out how we can actually do this. For example, research on online training for university students has shown that teaching them about autism and neurodiversity (the idea that autism is a part of human diversity) can improve attitudes.

Mental health research in autism is the number one research priority in this area, and autism acceptance is likely just one factor among many that could contribute to mental health difficulties in autism. But by being more accepting and positive when people are diagnosed with autism, we could make a real difference to their lives.

Source: Cage, E. (2017, November 7). Autistic people aren't really accepted—and it's impacting their mental health. *The Conversation*. Retrieved from https://theconversation.com/autistic-people-arent-really-accepted-and-its-impacting-their-mental-health-86817

Read about It. Think about It. Write about It.

- Many people say that people with ASD need to learn social skills to fit in—part of inclusion and normalization. They then have the same expectations as everyone else. How do you think we find a balance between camouflaging and diversity acceptance?
- When you read about the amount of mental health issues that result from camouflaging, what is your initial impression? Has this changed your impression on how we balance social skills teaching and diversity acceptance?
- What do you feel is the number one way that celebrating diversity has occurred in your province or territory?

CRITICAL ISSUE #9: SCHOOL LEADERSHIP

Every Child Matters: What Principals Need to Effectively Lead Inclusive Schools

Canadians continue to grapple with what it means to be an inclusive society. Despite a general trend to inclusive education in provinces across Canada, policies and services are inconsistent.

Inclusive education is quality education that aims at the full participation of all learners with a belief that all students can make valued contributions to classrooms and schools.

Recent education announcements by the Ontario government, for example, are emblematic of challenging contexts both for families and school communities.

Decisions such as increasing class size, changing the funding model for children with autism and potentially changing the full-day kindergarten framework could dramatically affect students with special education needs in inclusive schools. Reports of escalating classroom violence have drawn widespread media attention, as have accounts that students with special education needs are being asked to stay home from school.

In Newfoundland, the Advocate for Children and Youth released a January 2019 report on chronic student absenteeism within the province. The report found that factors such as learning disabilities, mental health issues, behavioural issues and developmental delays contributed to absenteeism.

In 2018, Inclusion Alberta reported that 53 per cent of children with disabilities had been secluded or restrained at school. The same year, Inclusion B.C. reported that many students with special education needs are still being negatively affected by inappropriate and outdated teaching practices.

Prior to this in British Columbia, two legal cases exemplified how contested and precarious inclusive education is in Canadian schools.

In 2016, the Supreme Court of Canada ruled in favour of the B.C. Teachers' Federation and against the province with regard to limiting class size and composition.

In 2012, the Court also affirmed the legal right of students with learning disabilities to receive adequate special education supports in schools in what became known as the Moore case. At the centre of this case was student Jeffrey Moore and his father.

New Brunswick has provided a model of inclusive education that has served as an example for other contexts, most recently Ireland.

As a former elementary and secondary school teacher and school administrator, I am aware of the lived realities of teaching students with special education needs in inclusive classrooms. Many teachers experience having classes with 25 or 30 students, sometimes with combined grades. Such a scenario could include teaching two grades of curricula, plus teaching multiple students with individual education plans, who may require accommodations, support staff and specialized equipment.

Leadership and Inclusion

The realistic challenges inherent in this worthy ideal in pursuit of human dignity and belonging are lived out every day in schools. Students, teachers, support staff and principals are in many ways at the forefront of inclusion in society at large.

Yet one area that has been lacking has been an informed understanding of what kinds of support principals need as they provide leadership for inclusive schools. Our research team, made up of members of the Canadian Research Centre on Inclusive Education, recently completed a study on this topic.

We collected data from 285 principals and vice-principals about their experiences in inclusive schools—that means schools practising the full participation of all learners, as defined by the Council of Ministers of Education Canada. We asked principals from British Columbia, Alberta, Ontario, Quebec, New Brunswick and Newfoundland to consider the ways in which they support students with special education needs in inclusive schools. The participants were from elementary and secondary schools, in both English and French language school systems, in urban and rural areas.

After this initial data collection, we interviewed 46 of these participants. We wanted to further examine the types of experiences principals described about leading inclusive schools and what kind of professional learning they felt would be helpful.

The results of the study point to some key lessons for school systems across Canada.

1. Invest in the Right Professional Development

School systems and professional associations responsible for the preparation of future school principals need to invest in professional development specifically about inclusive education. Professional learning needs to be extended beyond technical aspects related to special education such as legal requirements or staffing needs.

One principal said: "I say to staff right at the beginning, if you feel like running away, that's when you need to run into my office. When you find that you are withdrawing and you're feeling overwhelmed, that's when you need to run in, not out."

This principal had fostered a leadership competency that reflected empathy and a skill in supporting the mental health of staff.

> **professional development:** educational practices that professionals engage in to change practices, understanding, and beliefs toward a defined goal (Guskey, 2002).

Professional learning should develop leadership competencies in fostering a healthy school culture, including enhancing communication skills to support students, staff, parents and other caregivers.

2. Strong Professional Relationships Matter

Principals who developed strong professional relationships with students, parents and caregivers, and teaching and support staff were best equipped to support a wide variety of student needs.

One principal commented: "Relationships are the foundation of everything I do as a school administrator."

The feeling behind this statement was shared by many of the participants who identified relationships as core to their work in supporting inclusive school environments.

Another principal described a conversation with the father of a child with special education needs: "At the end of the conversation, the dad came around the table and gave me a hug and said 'I have never had someone want to include my kid in the school before.'"

Principals have complex and competing demands on their time. Those who prioritized spending time interacting with students, engaging with parents and caregivers and supporting staff reported high levels of effectiveness in supporting inclusive schools.

3. The Demands of the Job Take a Toll

Despite being surrounded by people, principals frequently reported that they often work in isolation and without a lot of support. There is a strong indication that the demands of the job, particularly with diverse and pronounced student needs, take a heavy toll on them.

Our society has become increasingly aware of the complex mental health needs of students in Canada and there needs to be a recognition of the similar mental health needs of teachers and principals.

Further research and knowledge mobilization is needed to build the capacity of principals to effectively lead inclusive schools.

> **knowledge mobilization:** actions and efforts to target gaps in education between policy, practice, and research (Cooper, 2010).

Source: Sider, S. (2019, April 1). Every child matters: What principals need to effectively lead inclusive schools. *The Conversation*. Retrieved from https://theconversation.com/every-child-matters-what-principals-need-to-effectively-lead-inclusive-schools-114249

Read about It. Think about It. Write about It.

- In your experience, what role(s) do the principal and school leaders play in the successful inclusion of children with ASD and other special needs?
- How do school leaders balance the right of every student to learn in their school with the right for an accommodated education for each child with special needs?
- What initiatives have you been involved with in your province or territory that train school leaders? Do you think this is something that has been occurring regularly, or is it lacking?

CRITICAL ISSUE #10: IMMIGRATION REFORMS

Immigration Reforms to Accept Persons with ASD

Father of Son with Autism Calls Canada's New Immigration Policy a "Blessing for All of Us"

After Canada's immigration minister, Ahmed Hussen, announced major reforms to Canada's immigration policy on Monday, making it easier for persons with disabilities and their family members to immigrate to Canada, advocates, lawyers and those affected by the law are speaking out.

Some have expressed caution—saying they're worried about who will pay for the changes or that the changes don't go far enough toward ensuring equality for persons with disabilities—while others say they're overjoyed Canada has taken a principled stand on protecting the rights of all people, especially children with disabilities.

"After getting the good news—I was driving so I had to be careful—I was pretty excited," said Samrat Saha, 38, whose family was denied permanent residency in Canada last May because his six-year-old son, Rajarshi, has autism.

"We've all been waiting for this change for a long time," he said. "Because disability is not by choice, it's by birth, right? And I don't think anybody should be discriminated against based on their disability."

The changes Saha is referring to were announced Monday by Hussen. They reverse many of the key components of a 40-year-old policy known as "medical inadmissibility" due to excessive demand.

As currently written, the law allows the government to deny residency to an entire family if even one person in the group has a disability or medical condition that could place "excessive demand" on Canada's publicly funded health and social service systems—meaning it will cost more than $6,655 a year to care for them, a figure the government says was the average, per-capita health and social service spending in Canada in 2016.

But after Monday's announcement, Canada will no longer consider certain costs when deciding if someone can come to Canada—such as special education costs for children with intellectual disabilities. The government said it will also triple the cost threshold for denying someone based on medical conditions to nearly $20,000 a year.

In making the announcement, Hussen said Canada will no longer consider people with a disability as a "burden" when they apply to immigrate.

For Saha, a software engineer with an advanced university degree, this announcement means he and his wife no longer need to worry about their future in Canada—or whether they might be forced to leave.

"It was a pretty exciting day," he said. "I can now reapply for permanent residency, which I am already in the process of doing. And, of course, now I will not be discriminated against and my son will not be rejected based on his disability."

Advocacy groups say changes don't go far enough.

Following Monday's announcement, advocacy groups representing those often affected by the law—such as migrant workers whose children have disabilities and people with HIV/AIDS—were quick to respond to the changes, saying the government didn't go far enough toward ending a "discriminatory" policy they say unfairly targets people with disabilities and their immediate family members.

In a joint statement released Monday, representatives from several groups—the HIV/AIDS Legal Network, Council of Canadians with Disabilities and the Migrant Workers Alliance—said the government failed to do the right thing by not eliminating the law altogether. They pointed to a parliamentary committee report from last December recommending the law be repealed as justification for their feelings.

"Organizations representing key groups of immigrants excluded from Canada due to medical inadmissibility are very disappointed," read the statement.

"While explicitly agreeing with the Standing Committee's recommendation [that the law should be repealed, the government] has failed to bring its policies in line with inclusivity for persons with disabilities and with Canada's domestic and international human rights obligations."

The government disagrees with this position. When directly challenged on whether keeping this law in place—albeit in a limited fashion—which only serves to perpetuate a system that discriminates against people with disabilities, Hussen said he believes it does not.

"It is vital that we ensure greater accessibility and opportunities for Canadians with disabilities," Hussen said on Monday. "Sadly, this has not been the reality for many newcomers to Canada over the last 40 years."

"The decision to deny applicants with low-cost health conditions or with dependent children who have special needs has profound consequence for these families, as well as the Canadian communities that welcome them," he said. "We must take the steps needed to promote the inclusion of persons with disabilities in Canada and highlight this as a core societal value."

Meanwhile, Adrienne Smith, an immigration lawyer from Toronto who's been an outspoken opponent of the law, says it remains to be seen how the government will implement these changes.

"Obviously, this is a very positive first step," she said. "For right now, the government has responded to some of the negative media attention they've received about the way they treat people with disabilities, but it remains to be seen how this actually plays out [in the future]."

Following the announcement Monday, officials from Immigration, Refugees and Citizenship Canada reached out to several of the families profiled by *Global News* in the series "Inadmissible," an eight-month investigation that revealed serious flaws with the way the government handles residency applications of persons with disabilities.

One of the families contacted by Immigration Canada was the Warkentins, who moved from Colorado to Waterhen, Man., in 2013 to fulfil their lifelong dream of owning a hunting and fishing lodge.

But their application for permanent residency was denied by Immigration Canada because their six-year-old daughter, Karalynn, had epilepsy and a mild intellectual disability. Their application was denied despite the fact they'd invested more than $600,000 into the Canadian economy and had become a fixture in their local church and community.

Jon Warkentin, Karalynn's father, said officials from Immigration Canada assured him during the phone call that, going forward, the government plans to take a more holistic approach when assessing permanent residency applications that include people with disabilities. This means looking at the benefits they bring to Canadian society, not just the cost.

"If you treat Canada as a business—meaning, are you going to hire these people or not hire these people by having them come to Canada—you've got to look at the whole picture," Warkentin said. "But if all you're looking at is the cost side of the equation, and you're not looking at the benefit side of the equation, then how can you possibly make a good decision?"

Warkentin said he believes the attention his family's story received was a key reason for the government to reach out to him and for making the ultimate decision to reverse key aspects of its policy.

"Our story really highlighted the shortfalls of the previous system," Warkentin said. "If there weren't personal stories that people could connect with that really showed the faults in the program, I don't think this would have changed. I think they would have just kept on going. I don't think anybody would have really knew about it."

A spokesperson for Hussen said the government contacted the Warkentins and other families because it was important to hear their experiences and share with them how things will be done differently in the future. He added that the government has been working toward greater inclusion of persons with disabilities since taking office in 2015.

Meanwhile, Warkentin believes the changes—rather than being viewed as a potential threat to Canada's health-care system—should be seen as an opportunity. He thinks hard-working, professional families like his whose children have disabilities may now see Canada as a viable option instead of automatically writing it off as a place to live because of an "antiquated" law that he says sees their children as having less value.

"We're all immigrants," he said. "If someone has a special needs child and is thinking about moving to Canada—whether they're lawyers, doctors, teachers, etc.—they now don't have to worry about this hurdle."

Source: Hill, B. (2018, April 17). Father of son with autism calls Canada's new immigration policy a "blessing for all of us." *Global News*. Retrieved from https://globalnews.ca/news/4150860/disability-immigration-law-a-blessing-says-father-autistic-child/.

Read about It. Think about It. Write about It.

- Given the focus on eliminating discrimination in the Canadian Constitution, do you think the previous policy of not allowing immigration for persons with disabilities such as ASD was discriminatory?
- How does this policy change align with other countries' immigration policies?
- Do you think that this policy change is fair or do you agree with people in opposition that feel the policy needs additional change? Why or why not?

A LOOK BACK

Chapter 10, "Additional Critical Issues," focused on critical issues that are currently highlighted in the field and the media, including:

- Media perspectives and ASD
- Newfoundland and Labrador Human Rights Commission Report
- Sport and ASD
- Reflection, relaxation, and self-calming
- ASD and sexuality
- School exclusion
- Authentic peer relationships
- Autism acceptance
- School leadership
- Immigration

References

Accardi, C., & Duhaime, S. (2013). Finding and keeping employment. *Autism Matters, 61,* 1–3. Retrieved from autismontario.novosolutions.net/default.asp?id=153

Acevedo, B., Aron, E., Pospos, S., & Jessen, D. (2018). The functional highly sensitive brain: A review of the brain circuits underlying sensory processing sensitivity and seemingly related disorders. *Philosophical Transactions of the Royal Society of London. Series B, Biological Sciences, 373*(1744), 20170161. doi:10.1098/rstb.2017.0161

Adelson, J. (1997). The creation of Dr. B by Richard Pollak. *Commentary, 6*, 67–68.

Adreon, D., & Durocher, J. (2007). Evaluating the college transition needs of individuals with high-functioning autism spectrum disorder. *Intervention in School and Clinic, 42*(5), 271–279.

Affiliated Services for Children and Youth. (2020). Home page. Retrieved from www.ascy.ca

Ahn, R. R., Miller, L. J., Milberger, S., & McIntosh, D. N. (2004). Prevalence of parents' perceptions of sensory processing disorders among kindergarten children. *American Journal of Occupational Therapy, 58*(3), 287–293.

Albert, K. M., Carbone, V. J., Murray, D. D., Hagerty, M., & Sweeney-Kerwin, E. J. (2012). Increasing the mand repertoire in children with autism through the use of an interrupted chain procedure. *Behaviour Analysis in Practice, 5*(2), 65–76. Retrieved from https://www.ncbi.nlm.nih.gov/pmc/articles/PMC3592491/

Alberta Learning. (2003). *Teaching students with autism spectrum disorders.* Edmonton, AB: Alberta Learning, Special Programs Branch.

Alberto, P., & Troutman, A. C. (2013). *Applied behavior analysis for teachers* (9th ed.). Toronto, ON: Pearson.

Alberto, P., & Troutman, A. C. (2017). *Applied behavior analysis for teachers* (10th ed.). Boston, MA: Pearson.

Alcorn MacKay, S. (2010). *Identifying trends and supports for students with autism spectrum disorder transitioning into postsecondary.* Toronto, ON: Higher Education Quality Council of Ontario.

Allen, K. (2014, August 7). Adults with autism focus of new Ontario working group. *The Toronto Star.* Retrieved from www.thestar.com/news/world/2014/08/07/adults_with_autism_focus_of_new_ontario_working_group.html

Allen, K. E., Cowdery, G. E., Paasche, C. L., Langford, R., Nolan, K., & Cipparrone, B. (2015). *Inclusion in early childhood programs: Children with exceptionalities* (6th ed.). Toronto, ON: Nelson.

Alphonso, C. (2019, 7 January). Educating Grayson: Are inclusive classrooms failing students? *The Globe and Mail*. Retrieved from https://www.theglobeandmail.com/canada/education/article-educating-grayson-are-inclusive-classrooms-failing-students/

Alves, K., & Maich, K. (2019). A parent's perspective is worth a thousand words: Parents of children with ASD and their perspectives on a community-based parent education program. *Canadian Journal for New Scholars in Education, 10*(1), 7–18. Retrieved from https://journalhosting.ucalgary.ca/index.php/cjnse/article/view/43470/pdf

American Psychiatric Association. (1980). *Diagnostic and statistical manual of mental disorders* (3rd ed.). Washington, DC: Author.

American Psychiatric Association. (1994). *Diagnostic and statistical manual of mental disorders* (4th ed.). Arlington, VA: American Psychiatric Publishing.

American Psychiatric Association. (2000). *Diagnostic and statistical manual of psychiatric disorders* (4th ed., text rev.). Washington, DC: Author.

American Psychiatric Association. (2013a). Autism spectrum disorder fact sheet. Retrieved from www.dsm5.org/Documents/Autism%20Spectrum%20Disorder%20Fact%20Sheet.pdf

American Psychiatric Association. (2013b). *Diagnostic and statistical manual: DSM-5* (5th ed.). Washington, DC: Author.

American Psychiatric Association. (2013c). *Highlights of changes from DSM-IV-TR to DSM-5*. Retrieved from http://www.dsm5.org/Documents/changes%20from%20dsm-iv-tr%20to%20dsm-5.pdf

American Psychiatric Association. (2018). What is mental illness? Retrieved from www.psychiatry.org/patients-families/what-is-mental-illness

Anagnostou, E., Jones, N., Huerta, M., Halladay, A. K., Wang, P., Scahill, L., … & Dawson, G. (2015). Measuring social communication behaviour as a treatment endpoint in individuals with autism spectrum disorder. *Autism, 19*(5), 622–636. doi:10.1177/1362361314542955

Anagnostou, E., Zwaigenbaum, L., Szatmari, P., Fombonne, E., Fernandez, B. A., Woodbury-Smith, M., … & Scherer, S. W. (2014). Autism spectrum disorder: Advances in evidence-based practice. *Canadian Medical Association Journal, 186*(7), 509–519.

Anderegg, M. L., Vergason, G. A., & Smith, M. C. (1992). A visual representation of the grief cycle for use by teachers with families of children with disabilities. *Remedial & Special Education, 13*(2), 17–23.

Arora, T. (2012). Understanding the perseveration displayed by students with an autism spectrum disorder. *Education, 132*(4), 799–808.

Ashwin, C., Chapman, E., Howells, J., Rhydderch, D., & Baron-Cohen, S. (2014). Enhanced olfactory sensitivity in autism spectrum conditions. *Molecular Autism, 5*, 53. doi:10.1186/2040-2392-5-53

Asperger, H. (1944). Die "autistischen psychopathen" im kindesalter. *Archiv fur Psychiatrie und Nervenkrankheiten, 117*, 76–136.

Atlantic Provinces Special Education Authority (APSEA). (2015). *Transition to school for learners with autism spectrum disorder: Information paper.* Retrieved from https://autismineducation.ca/assets/files/info-papers/transition-school-learners-asd.pdf

Atlantic Provinces Special Education Authority (APSEA). (2020). Home - Autism in Education. Retrieved from https://autismineducation.ca/

Audas, R., Ryan, D., Harris Walsh, K., Wells, S., & Murphy, P. (2015, October). *Report: Needs assessment of the autism spectrum community of Newfoundland and Labrador.* Submitted to Autism Society Newfoundland and Labrador. Retrieved from https://www.autism.nf.net/wp-content/uploads/2017/03/Needs-Assesment-2015.pdf

Ausome Ottawa. (2019). About us. Retrieved from https://ausomeottawa.com/about/

Autism Canada. (2017). Social stories. Retrieved from https://autismcanada.org/living-with-autism/treatments/non-medical/communication/social-stories/

Autism Canada. (2019). See the spectrum differently. Retrieved from www.autismcanada.org

Autism in Education Partnership. (2018). *Sorting through the science: Sensory differences and ASD.* Retrieved from https://autismineducation.ca/assets/files/info-papers/sensory-differences-asd-research-snapshot-2018.pdf

Autism Nova Scotia. (2019). *Choosing now: Investing in Nova Scotians living with autism.* Retrieved from http://autismnovascotia.ca/userfiles/1/Choosing_Now_final_new_cover.pdf

Autism Nova Scotia. (n.d.). Parent education guide. Halifax, NS: Author. Retrieved from http://www.autismnovascotia.ca/userfiles/1/test1ANS_ParentEducationGuide.pdf

Autism Ontario. (2008). *Forgotten: Ontario adults with autism and adults with Aspergers.* Retrieved from www.autismsocietycanada.ca/images/dox/KeyReports/ForgottenReportAutismOntario.pdf

Autism Society of Baltimore-Chesapeake. (2019). Social reciprocity. Retrieved from https://www.baltimoreautismsociety.org/glossary/term/social-reciprocity/

Autism Speaks. (2009). Autism speaks video glossary. Retrieved from www.autismspeaks.ca/community-services/resources/video-glossary/

Autism Speaks. (2011a). 100 day kit for newly diagnosed families of young children. Retrieved from https://www.autismspeaks.org/sites/default/files/100_Day_Tool_Kit_Young_Children.pdf

Autism Speaks. (2011b). Housing and residential supports tool kit. Retrieved from www.autismspeaks.org/sites/default/files/housing_tool_kit_web2.pdf

Autism Speaks Canada. (2015). Advocacy-focused tool kits. Retrieved from http://www.autismspeaks.ca/

Autism Speaks Canada. (2018). Learn the signs of autism. Retrieved from https://www.autismspeaks.ca/about/about-autism/learn-the-signs-of-autism/

Autism Speaks Canada. (2019). Know what to look for. Retrieved from https://autismcanada.org/about-autism/early-signs/

Ayres, A. J. (1972). Improving academic scores through sensory integration. *Journal of Learning Disabilities, 5*(6), 23–28.

Ayres, A. J. (1989). *(SIPT) The sensory integration and praxis test.* Los Angeles, CA: Western Psychological Services. Retrieved from https://www.wpspublish.com/store/p/2971/sipt-sensory-integration-and-praxis-tests

Ayres, A. J. (2005). *Sensory integration and the child.* Los Angeles: Western Psychological Services.

Ayres, A. J., Mailloux, Z. K., & Wendler, C. L. (1987). Developmental dyspraxia: Is it a unitary function? *Occupational Therapy Journal of Research, 7*(2), 93–110.

Baker, B. L., & Blacher, J. (2015). Disruptive behavior disorders in adolescents with ASD: Comparison to youth with intellectual disability or typical cognitive development. *Journal of Mental Health Research, 8*, 98–116. doi:10.1080/19315864.2015.1018395

Bandura, A. (1977). Self-efficacy: Toward a unifying theory of behavioral change. *Psychological Review, 84*(2), 191–215. doi:10.1037/0033-295X.84.2.191

Baranek, G. T. (2002). Efficacy of sensory and motor interventions for children with autism. *Journal of Autism and Developmental Disorders, 32*(5), 397–422.

Baranek, G. T., David, F. J., Poe, M. D., Stone, W., & Watson, L. R. (2006). Sensory experiences questionnaire: Discriminating sensory features in young children with autism, developmental delays, and atypical development. *Journal of Child Psychology and Psychiatry, 47*(6), 591–601.

Baranek, G. T., Little, L. M., Parham, L. D., Ausderau, K. K., & Sabatos-DeVito, M. G. (2014). Sensory features in autism spectrum disorder. In F. R. Volkmar, R. Paul, S. J. Rogers, & K. A. Pelphrey (Eds.), *Handbook of autism and pervasive developmental disorders* (vol. 1, 4th ed., pp. 378–407). Hoboken, NJ: John Wiley & Sons Publishing.

Barbera, M. L. (2010). The experiences of "autism mothers" who become behavior analysts: A qualitative study. *The Journal of Speech-Language Pathology and Applied Behavior Analysis, 4*, 56–73.

Barnett, J. P., & Maticka-Tyndale, E. (2015). Qualitative exploration of sexual experiences among adults on the autism spectrum: Implications for sex education. *Perspectives on Sexual and Reproductive Health, 47*(4), 171–179.

Baron-Cohen, S., Wheelwright, S., Skinner, R., Martin, J., & Clubley, E. (2001). The Autism-Spectrum Quotient (AQ): Evidence from Asperger syndrome/high-functioning autism, males and females, scientists and mathematicians. *Journal of Autism and Developmental Disorders, 31*, 5–17.

Barton, E. E., & Harn, B. (2012). *Educating young children with autism spectrum disorder.* Thousand Oaks, CA: Corwin.

Barton, E. E., Reichow, B., Schnitz, A., Smith, I. C., & Sherlock, D. (2015). A systematic review of sensory-based treatments for children with disabilities. *Research in Developmental Disabilities, 37*, 64–80. doi:10.1016/j.ridd.2014.11.006

Beck, A. T. (1979). *Cognitive therapy and the emotional disorders.* New York, NY: Penguin Press.

Behavior Analyst Certification Board (BACB). (2019). Professional and ethical compliance code for behavior analysts. Retrieved from https://www.bacb.com/ethics/ethics-code/

Belcher, E. C., & Maich, K. (2014). Autism spectrum disorder in popular media: Storied reflections of societal views. *Brock Education: A Journal of Educational Research and Practice, 23*(2), 1–19. doi:10.1177/1088357609356094

Bellini, S. (2016). *Building social relationships 2: A systematic approach to teaching social interaction skills to children and adolescents with autism spectrum disorders and other social difficulties.* Shawnee, KS: AAPC Publishing.

Bellows, G., Di Loreto, D., Edwards, A., Ferguson, S., Lister, P., Owen, A., Saines, E. G., Spence, G. (Producers), & Jackson, M. (Director). (2010). *Temple Grandin* (motion picture). United States: HBO.

Bennett, K., Brady, M. P., Scott, J., Dukes, C., & Frain, M. (2010). The effects of covert audio coaching on the job performance of supported employees. *Focus on Autism and Other Developmental Disabilities, 25*(3), 173–185.

Bennett, M., Webster, A. A., Goodall, E., & Rowland, S. (2018). Intimacy and romance across the autism spectrum: Unpacking the "not interested in sex" myth. In M. Bennett, A. A. Webster, E. Goodall, & S. Rowland (Eds.), *Life on the autism spectrum* (pp. 195–211). Singapore: Springer.

Bennett, S. (2009). Including students with exceptionalities. *What Works? Research into Practice Monograph Series #16.* Retrieved from www.edu.gov.on.ca/eng/literacynumeracy/inspire/research/Bennett.pdf

Bennett, S., & Dworet, D. (2013). *Special education in Ontario schools* (7th ed.). Niagara-on-the-Lake, ON: Highland Press.

Bennett, T. A., Szatmari, P., Georgiades, K., Hanna, S., Janus, M., Georgiades, S., … & Thompson, A. (2015). Do reciprocal associations exist between social and language pathways in preschoolers with autism spectrum disorders? *Journal of Child Psychology and Psychiatry, 56*(8), 874–883. doi:10.1111/jcpp.12356

Ben-Sasson, A., Cermak, S. A., Orsmond, G. I., Tager-Flusberg, H., Kadlec, M. B., & Carter, A. S. (2008). Sensory clusters of toddlers with autism spectrum disorders: Differences in affective symptoms. *Journal of Child Psychology and Psychiatry, 49*(8), 817–825. doi:10.111/j.1469-7610.2008.01899.x

Bertilsdotter Rosqvist, H. (2014). Becoming an "autistic couple": Narratives of sexuality and couplehood within the Swedish autistic self-advocacy movement. *Sexuality and Disability, 32*(3), 351–363. doi:10.1007/s11195-013-9336-2

Betchen, S. J. (2014, June 8). Asexuality: Movement towards a new sexual orientation. *Psychology Today.* Retrieved from https://www.psychologytoday.com/ca/blog/magnetic-partners/201406/asexuality

Bettelheim, B. (1959). Feral children and autistic children. *American Journal of Sociology, 64*(5), 455–467.

Bettelheim, B. (1967). *The empty fortress: Infantile autism and the birth of the self.* New York, NY: The Free Press.

Bhojne, U., & Chilnis, A. (2002). The vestibular dysfunction in children with pervasive developmental disorder. *The Indian Journal of Occupational Therapy, 35*(1). Retrieved from http://medind.nic.in/iba/t02/i1/ibat02i1p3.pdf

Bilaver, L. A., & Havlicek, J. (2013). Foster children with autism spectrum disorder: Prevalence, length of stay, and placement patterns. *Journal of Public Child Welfare, 7*(5), 496–519.

Blacher, J., & Christensen, L. (2011). Sowing the seeds of the autism field: Leo Kanner (1943). *Intellectual & Developmental Disabilities, 49*(3), 172–191. doi:10.1352/1934-9556-49.3.172

Black, K. R., Stevenson, R. A., Segers, M., Ncube, B. L., Sun, S. Z., Philipp-Muller, A., … & Ferber, S. (2017). Linking anxiety and insistence on sameness in autistic children: The role of hypersensitivity. *Journal of Autism and Developmental Disorders, 47*(8), 2459–2470. doi:10.1007/s10803-017-3161-x

Blanche, E. I., Reinoso, G., Chang, M. C., & Bodison, S. (2012). Proprioception processing difficulties among children with autism spectrum disorders and developmental disabilities. *The American Journal of Occupational Therapy, 66*(5), 621–624. doi:10.5014/ajot.2012.004234

Boer, A., Pijl, S., Minnaert, A., & Post, W. (2014). Evaluating the effectiveness of an intervention program to influence attitudes of students towards peers with disabilities. *Journal of Autism and Developmental Disorders, 44*(3), 572–583. doi:10.1007/s10803-013-1908-6

Bondy, A., & Frost, L. (2001). The picture exchange communication system. *Behavior Modification, 25*(5), 725–744. doi:10.1177/0145445501255004

Boudjarane, M. A., Grandgeorge, M., Marianowski, R., Misery, L., & Lemonnier, E. (2017). Perceptions of odors and tastes in autism spectrum disorders: A systematic review of assessment. *Autism Research, 10*(6), 1045–1059. doi:10.1002/aur.1760

Boudreau, E., & D'Entremont, B. (2010). Improving the pretend play skills of preschoolers with autism spectrum disorders: The effects of video modelling. *Journal of Developmental and Physical Disabilities, 22*(4), 415–431. doi:10.1007/s10882-010-9201-5

Brain, T., & Mirenda, P. (2019). Effectiveness of low-intensity peer-mediated intervention for middle school students with autism spectrum disorder. *Research in Autism Spectrum Disorders, 62*, 26–38. doi:10.1016/j.rasd.2019.02.003

Brereton, A. V., Tonge, B. J., & Einfeld, S. L. (2006). Psychopathology in children and adolescents with autism compared to young people with intellectual disability. *Journal of Autism and Developmental Disorders, 36*(7), 863–870. doi:10.1007/s10803-006-0125-y

Brewin, C. R. (2006). Understanding cognitive behaviour therapy: A retrieval competition account. *Behaviour Research and Therapy, 44*(6), 765–784. doi:10.1016/j.brat.2006.02.005

Brian, J. A., Zwaigenbaum, L., & Ip, A. (2019). Standards of diagnostic assessment for autism spectrum disorder. *Pediatrics and Child Health, 24*(7), 444–451. doi:10.1093/pch/pxz117

Brian, J., Smith, I. M., Zwaigenbaum, L., Roberts, W., & Bryson, S. E. (2016). The social ABCs: Caregiver-mediated intervention for toddlers with autism spectrum disorder: Feasibility, acceptability and evidence of promise from a multisite study. *Autism Research, 9*(8), 899–912. doi:10.1003/aur.1582

Brookman, L., Boettcher, M., Klein, E., Openden, D., Koegel, R. L., & Koegel, L. K. (2003). Facilitating social interactions in a community summer camp setting for children with autism. *Journal of Positive Behavior Interventions, 5*(4), 249–252.

Brooks, E. (2018). "Healthy sexuality": Opposing forces? Autism and dating, romance, and sexuality in the mainstream media. *Canadian Journal of Disability Studies, 7*(2), 161–186.

Brown, C., & Dunn, W. (2002). The adolescent/adult sensory profile. San Antonio, TX: Psychological Corporation.

Brown, C., Tollefson, N., Dunn, W., Cromwell, R., & Filion, D. (2001). The adult sensory profile: Measuring patterns of sensory processing. *American Journal of Occupational Therapy, 55*, 75–82.

Brown-Lavoie, S. M., Viecili, M. A., & Weiss, J. A. (2014). Sexual knowledge and victimization in adults with autism spectrum disorders. *Journal of Autism and Developmental Disorders, 44*(9), 2185–2196.

Buck, T. R., Viskochil, J., Farley, M., Coon, H., McMahon, W. M., Morgan, J., & Bilder, D. A. (2014). Psychiatric comorbidity and medication use in adults with autism spectrum disorder. *Journal of autism and developmental disorders, 44*(12), 3063–3071.

Bulmer, S., McLean, S., Breitenbach, M., Cowan, I., Fewer-Jackson, D., Jackman, P., … & Michaud, J. (2012/2016). Evidence-based practice for learners with autism spectrum disorder. *Autism in Education Partnership*. Halifax, NS: Atlantic Provinces Special Education Authority (APSEA). Retrieved from https://autismineducation.ca/information-papers.html

Burke, L. (2005). Psychological assessment of more able adults with autism spectrum disorder. In K. Stoddart (Ed.), *Children, youth, and adults with Asperger syndrome* (pp. 211–225). London, UK: Jessica Kingsley Publishers.

Cadogan, S., & McCrimmon, A. W. (2015). Pivotal response treatment for children with autism spectrum disorder: A systematic review of research quality. *Developmental Neurorehabilitation, 18*(2), 137–144. doi:10.3109/17518423.2013.845615

Cage, E. (2017, November 7). Autistic people aren't really accepted—and it's impacting their mental health. *The Conversation*. Retrieved from https://theconversation.com/autistic-people-arent-really-accepted-and-its-impacting-their-mental-health-86817

Canada Revenue Agency. (2019a). Disability tax credit. Retrieved from https://www.canada.ca/en/revenue-agency/services/tax/individuals/segments/tax-credits-deductions-persons-disabilities/disability-tax-credit.html

Canada Revenue Agency. (2019b). Tax credits and deductions for persons with disabilities. Retrieved from www.cra-arc.gc.ca/disability/

Canadian Association of Occupational Therapists. (2016). What is occupational therapy. Retrieved from https://www.caot.ca/site/aboutot/whatisot?nav=sidebar

Canadian Healthcare Technology. (2018, October 1). Newfoundland and Labrador extend use of remote patient monitoring. Retrieved from https://www.canhealth.com/2018/10/01/newfoundland-and-labrador-extend-use-of-remote-patient-monitoring/

Canadian Human Rights Tribunal. (2016). About the tribunal. Retrieved from https://www.chrt-tcdp.gc.ca/about/about-the-tribunal-en.html

Canadian Human Rights Tribunal. (2018). Information sheet: Jordan's Principle—Summary Orders from the Canadian Human Rights Tribunal. Retrieved from https://fncaringsociety.com/sites/default/files/Summary%20of%20Jordan%27s%20Principle%20Orders%20%282018%20update%29.pdf

Canadian Mortgage and Housing Association (CMHC). (2018). Rental Residential Rehabilitation Assistance Program. Retrieved from https://www.cmhc-schl.gc.ca/en/developing-and-renovating/funding-opportunities/on-reserve-renovation-programs/residential-rehabilitation-assistance-program/rental-residential-rehabilitation-assistance-program

Canadian Task Force on Preventative Health Care. (2016). Recommendations on screening for developmental delay. *Canadian Medical Association Journal, 188*(8), 579–587.

CanChild Centre for Childhood Disability Research. (2015). The KIT: Keeping it together. Retrieved from https://www.canchild.ca/en/research-in-practice/the-kit-keeping-it-together

Cannella-Malone, H. I., Sabielny, L. M., Jimenez, E. D., & Miller, M. M. (2013). Pick one! Conducting preference assessments with students with significant disabilities. *TEACHING Exceptional Children*, *45*(6), 16–23.

Cappe, É., & Poirier, N. (2016). Les besoins exprimés par les parents d'enfants ayant un TSA: Une étude exploratoire franco-québécoise. *Annales Médico-psychologiques*, *174*, 639–643. doi:10.1016/j.amp.2015.06.003

Carey, M. R. (2017). *The boy on the bridge*. New York, NY: Hachette Book Group.

CarlysVoice. (2013). Carly's voice: Changing the world of autism. Retrieved from carlysvoice.com/home/aboutcarly

Caron, V., Bérubé, A., & Paquet, A. (2017). Implementation evaluation of early intensive behavioural intervention programs for children with autism spectrum disorders: A systematic review of studies in the last decade. *Evaluation and Program Planning, 62*, 1–8. doi:10.10116/j.evalprogplan.2017.01.004

Carr, E. G., Dunlap, G., Horner, R. H., Koegel, R. L., Turnbull, A. P., Sailor, W., ... & Fox, L. (2002). Positive behavior support: Evolution of an applied science. *Journal of positive behavior interventions, 4*(1), 4–16.

Carter, E. W., Common, E. A., Sreckovic, M. A., Huber, H. B., Bottema-Beutel, K., Gustafson, J. R., ... & Hume, K. (2014). Promoting social competence and peer relationships for adolescents with autism spectrum disorders. *Remedial and Special Education, 35*(2), 91–101.

Case-Smith, J., Weaver, L. L., & Fristad, M. A. (2014). A systematic review of sensory processing interventions for children with autism spectrum disorders. *Autism, 19*(2), 133–148. doi:10.1177/13623

CBC News. (2013, May 1). The new definition of autism: Trying to make sense of a confusing world. Retrieved from www.cbc.ca/news/health/the-new-definition-of-autism-1.1366823

CBC News. (2019). New "inclusive squash" program in N.L. could be a global first. Retrieved from https://www.cbc.ca/ news/canada/newfoundland-labrador/inclusive-squash-cbs-1.4969103

Cengher, M., Shamoun, K., Moss, P., Roll, D., Feliciano, G., & Fienup, D. M. (2016). A comparison of the effects of two prompt-fading strategies on skill acquisition in children with autism spectrum disorders. *Behavior Analysis in Practice, 9*(2), 115–125. doi:10.1007/s40617-015-0096-6

Center for Applied Special Technology. (2013). What is universal design for learning? Retrieved from www.cast.org/udl/

Centers for Disease Control and Prevention (CDC). (2007). Prevalence of autism spectrum disorders—Autism and Developmental Disabilities Monitoring Network, six sites, United States, 2000. *MMWR Surveillance Summaries, 56*(SS01), 1–11.

Centers for Disease Control and Prevention (CDC). (2017). Identified prevalence of autism spectrum disorder. Retrieved from https://www.cdc.gov/ncbddd/autism/data.html

Centers for Disease Control and Prevention (CDC). (2018). Screening and diagnoses of autism spectrum disorder. Retrieved from https://www.cdc.gov/ncbddd/autism/screening.html

Centre for ADHD Awareness, Canada (CADDAC). (2017). The individual education plan. Retrieved from www.caddac.ca

Ceponiene, R., Lepisto, T., Shestakova, A., Vanhala, R., Alku, P., Naatanen, R., … & Yaguchi, K. (2003). Speech-sound-selective auditory impairment in children with autism: They can perceive but do not attend. *Proceedings of the National Academy of Sciences, 100*(9), 5567–5572.

Cermak, S. A., Curtin, C., & Bandini, L. G. (2010). Food selectivity and sensory sensitivity in children with autism spectrum disorder. *Journal of American Dietetic Association, 110*(2), 238–246. doi:10.10161/j.jada.2009.10.032

Chikazoe, J., Lee, D. H., Kriegestorte, N., & Anderson, A. K. (2019). Distinct representations of basic taste qualities in human gustatory cortex. *Nature Communication, 10*, 1048. doi:101038/s41467-019-08857-2

Choueiri, R., & Wagner, S. (2015). A new interactive screening test for autism spectrum disorders in toddlers. *The Journal of Pediatrics, 167*(2), 460–466. doi:10.1016/j.jpeds.2015.05.029

Chown, N. (2012). "History and first descriptions" of autism: A response to Michael Fitzgerald. *Journal of Autism & Developmental Disorders, 42*(10), 2263–2265. doi:10.1007/s10803-012-1529-5

CoField Inc. (n.d.a). The team. Retrieved from https://www.cofield-aba.com/about-1

CoField Inc. (n.d.b). Service principles. Retrieved from https://www.cofield-aba.com/service-principles

Colorado State University. (2012). Grandin, Temple. Retrieved from http://ansci.agsci.colostate.edu/grandin-temple/

Cook, J. L., Rapp, J. T., Mann, K. R., McHugh, C., Burji, C., & Nuta, R. (2017). A practitioner model for increasing eye contact in children with autism. *Behaviour Modification, 41*(3), 382–404. doi:10.1177/01454455196689323

Cooper, A. (2010). Knowledge mobilization intermediaries in education. Ontario Institute for Studies in Education (OISE), University of Toronto. Retrieved from oise.utoronto.ca

Cooper, J. O., Heron, T. E., & Heward, W. L. (2007). *Applied behavior analysis* (2nd ed.). Upper Saddle River, NJ: Pearson Education.

Cooper, J. O., Heron, T. E., & Heward, W. L. (2020). *Applied behavior analysis* (3rd ed.). Upper Saddle River, NJ: Pearson Education.

Coulter, R. A. (2009). Understanding the visual symptoms of individuals with autism spectrum disorder (ASD). *Optometry and Vision Development, 40*(3), 164–175.

Crane, L., Goddard, L., & Pring, L. (2009). Sensory processing in adults with autism spectrum disorders. *Autism, 13*(3), 215–228. doi:10.1177/1362361309103794

Crowther, I. (2010). *Inclusion in early childhood settings: Children with special needs in Canada* (2nd ed.). Toronto, ON: Pearson.

CTV News. (2012, January 25). Paralympian with autism—Tommy Des Brisay—CTV athlete of the week interview [Video file]. Retrieved from http://videoholder.com/video/IqGI0KiiFMw

Cullen, K. E. (2012). The vestibular system: Multimodal integration and encoding of self-motion for motor control. *Trends in Neuroscience, 35*(3), 185–196. doi:10.1016/j.tins.2011.12.001

Cullen, K. E., Brooks, J. X., & Sadeghi, S. G. (2009). How actions alter sensory processing: Reafference in the vestibular system. *Annals of the New York Academy of Sciences, 1164*, 29–36. doi:10.1111/j.1749-6632.2009.03866.x

Danial, J. T., & Wood, J. J. (2013). Cognitive behavioral therapy for children with autism. *Journal of Developmental & Behavioral Pediatrics, 34*(9), 702–715. doi:10.1097/dbp.0b013e31829f676c

David Asper Centre for Constitutional Rights, University of Toronto. (n.d.a). Advocacy projects. Retrieved from http://aspercentre.ca/clinic/advocacy-projects/

David Asper Centre for Constitutional Rights, University of Toronto. (n.d.b). Fact sheet: Jordan's Principle. Retrieved from http://aspercentre.ca/wp-content/uploads/2017/06/JORDAN.pdf

Davidson, L., Stayner, D. A., Nickou, C., Styron, T. H., Rowe, M., & Chinman, M. L. (2001). "Simply to be let in": Inclusion as a basis for recovery. *Psychiatric Rehabilitation Journal, 24*(4), 375–388.

Davis, J. (Producer). (2005, September 22). *Criminal Minds* [Television broadcast]. United States: CBS.

DeBoth, K. K., & Reynolds, S. (2017). A systematic review of sensory based autism subtypes. *Research in Autism Spectrum Disorders, 36*, 44–56. doi:10.1016/j.rasd.2017.01.05

Decker, J. S. (2015). *The invisible orientation: An introduction to asexuality*. New York, NY: Simon & Schuster.

Department of Community Services, Nova Scotia. (2009, July 11). Independent living support. Retrieved from https://novascotia.ca/coms/disabilities/IndependentLiving.html

de Rivera, C. (2008). The use of intensive behavioural intervention for children with autism. *Journal of Developmental Disabilities, 14*(2), 1–15.

Dimian, A. F., Botteron, K. N., Dager, S. R., Elison, J. T., Estes, A. M., Pruett Jr., J. R., … & Wolff, J. J. (2017). Potential risk factors for the development of self-injurious behavior among infants at risk for autism spectrum disorder. *Journal of Autism and Developmental Disabilities, 47*(5), 1403–1415. doi:10.1007/s10803-017-3057-9

Dionne, C., Paquet, A., Joly, J., & Rivard, M. (2011). L'intervention comportementale intensive (ICI) au Québec: Portrait de son implantation et mesure de ses effets chez l'enfant ayant un trouble envahissant du développement, sa famille et ses milieux. Trois-Rivières, QC: UQTR.

DisabilityAwards.ca. (n.d.). Government funding Ontario. Retrieved from disabilityawards.ca/gov.php?ID=ON&lang=EN

Division of Behavioral and Social Sciences and Education of the National Research Council. (2001). *Educating children with autism.* Washington, DC: National Academy Press.

Dixon, M. R. (2014). *The PEAK relational training system: Direct training module.* Carbondale, IL: Shawnee Scientific Press.

Dobson, K. S., & Dozois, D. J. A. (2001). Historical and philosophical bases of the cognitive-behavioral therapies. In K. Dobson (Ed.), *Handbook of Cognitive-Behavioral Therapies* (pp. 3–39). New York, NY: Guilford Press.

Donvan, J., & Zucker, C. (2010, October). Autism's first child. *The Atlantic.* Retrieved from https://www.theatlantic.com/magazine/archive/2010/10/autisms-first-child/308227/

Draaisma, D. (2009). Stereotypes of autism. *Philosophical Transactions of the Royal Society of Biological Sciences, 364*, 1475–1480. doi:10.1098/rstb.2008.0324

Dua, K. (2003). *Standards and guidelines for the assessment and diagnosis of young children with autism spectrum disorder in British Columbia: An evidence-based report prepared for the British Columbia Ministry of Health Planning.* Retrieved from http://www.health.gov.bc.ca/library/publications/year/2003/asd_standards_0318.pdf

Dudley, C., & Emery, J. H. (2014). The value of caregiver time: Costs of support and care for individuals living with autism spectrum disorder. *School of Public Policy Research Papers, 1*(7), 1–48.

Dudley, C., & Nankane, S. (2017). *Who will take care of our kids (when we no longer can)? The challenges facing adults with ASD and their aging parents: A discussion paper prepared for Autism Society Alberta.* Retrieved from https://autismalberta.ca/files/Who_Will_Take_Care_Report.pdf

Dudley, C., & Zwicker, J. D. (2016). Laying the foundation for policy: Measuring local prevalence for autism spectrum disorder. *The School of Public Policy Publications, 9.* doi:10.11575/sppp.v9i0.42563

Dugas, C., Simard, M. N., Fombonne, E., & Couture, M. (2018). Comparison of two tools to assess sensory features in children with autism spectrum disorders. *The American Journal of Occupational Therapy, 72*(1), 1–9. doi:105014/ajot.2018.024604

Dunkel-Jackson, S. M., Kenney, K., Borch, S., & Neely Neveu, C. (2018). Case report: Intervention, evaluation of trial-based functional analyses in school. *Journal on Developmental Disabilities, 23*(2), 55–65. Retrieved from http://oadd.org/page/142/

Dunlap, G., Carr, E. G., Horner, R. H., Koegel, R. L., Sailor, W., Clarke, S., … & Foxe, L. (2010). A descriptive, multiyear examination of Positive Behavior Support. *Behavioral Disorders, 35*(4), 259–279. doi:10.1177/019874291003500401

Dunn, D. S., & Andrews, E. E. (2015). Person-first and identity-first language: Developing psychologists' cultural competence using disability language. *American Psychologist, 70*(3), 255–264.

Dunn, S., & Zwicker, J. (2018). Policy brief: Why is uptake of the Disability Tax Credit low in Canada? Exploring possible barriers to access. Calgary, AB: University of Calgary. Retrieved from https://www.policyschool.ca/wp-content/uploads/2018/01/Disability-Tax-Credit-Dunn-Zwicker.pdf

Dunn, W. (1997). The impact of sensory processing abilities on the daily lives of young children and their families: A conceptual model. *Infants and Young Children, 9*(4), 23–35.

Dunn, W. (2001). The sensations of everyday life: Empirical, theoretical, and pragmatic considerations, 2001 Eleanor Clarke Slagle Lecture. *American Journal of Occupational Therapy, 55*, 608–620.

Dunn, W. (2002). *Infant toddler sensory profile: User's manual.* San Antonio, TX: Psychological Corporation.

Dunn, W. (2014). *The sensory profile second edition: User's manual.* New York, NY: Pearson.

EduGains. (2015). Sample individual education plans. Retrieved from http://www.beta.edugains.ca/newsite/SpecialEducation/transitions.html

Elfert, M., & Mirenda, P. (2015). Evaluation of a support group for fathers of children with autism spectrum disorder/L' évaluation d'un groupe de soutien pour des pères d'enfants ayant des troubles du spectre autistique. *Canadian Journal of Counselling and Psychotherapy, 49*(2), 115–138. Retrieved from https://cjc-rcc.ucalgary.ca/issue/archive

Eliot, S. (2002). *Not the thing I was: Thirteen years at Bruno Bettelheim's orthogenic school.* New York, NY: St. Martin's Press.

Ellement, J., Boris, A., Martin, G., & Fazzio, D. (2017). Teaching staff who work with children with autism spectrum disorders to evaluate the treatment integrity of discrete-trials teaching sessions. *Journal on Developmental Disabilities, 23*(1). Retrieved from https://oadd.org/page/142/

Ellis, A., & Harper, R. A. (1961). *A guide to rational living.* Oxford, UK: Prentice-Hall.

Factor, D. C., Perry, A., & Freeman, N. (1990). Brief report: Stress, social support, and respite care use in families with autistic children. *Journal of Autism & Developmental Disorders, 20*(1), 139–146.

Falkmer, T., Anderson, K., Falkmer, M., & Horlin, C. (2013). Diagnostic procedures in autism spectrum disorder: A systematic literature review. *European Child and Adolescent Psychiatry, 22*(6), 329–340. doi:10.1007/s00787-013-0375-0

Falvo, N. (2009). Toronto's housing first programme and implications for leadership. *Housing, Care and Support, 12*(2), 16–25.

Fennell, L., Hearsey, P., & Eckenrode, K. (2013). *Tasks galore.* Raleigh, NC: Tasks Galore Publishing.

Ferguson, P. M. (2002). A place in the family: An historical interpretation of research on parental reactions to having a child with a disability. *Journal of Special Education, 36*(3), 124–130, 147. https://doi.org/10.1177/00224669020360030201

Fernández-Andrés, M. I., Pastor-Cerezuela, G., Sanz-Cervera, P., & Tárraga-Minguez, R. (2015). A comparative study of sensory processing in children with and without autism spectrum disorder in the home and classroom environments. *Research in Developmental Disabilities, 38*, 202–212. doi:10.1016/j.ridd.2014.12.034

Fernell, E., Eriksson, M. A., & Gillberg, C. (2012). Early diagnosis of autism and impact on prognosis: A narrative review. *Clinical Epidemiology, 5*, 33–43.

First Nations Child & Family Caring Society of Canada. (2014). Jordan's Principle: A brief history. Retrieved from https://fncaringsociety.com/sites/default/files/Jordan%27s%20 Principle%20Information%20Sheet.pdf

First Nations Child & Family Caring Society of Canada. (2016). Jordan's Principle. Retrieved from https://fncaringsociety.com/jordans-principle

Fleck, C., & Müller, A. (1997). Bruno Bettelheim and the concentration camps. *Journal of the History of the Behavioural Sciences, 33*(1), 1–37.

Fleischmann, A., & Fleischmann, C. (2012). *Carly's voice: Breaking through autism*. Toronto, ON: Simon & Schuster.

Florida State University. (2018). Autism navigator. Retrieved from www.autismnavigator.com

Freedman, B. H., Kalb, L. G., Zablotsky, B., & Stuart, E. A. (2012). Relationship status among parents of children with autism spectrum disorders: A population-based study. *Journal of Autism & Developmental Disorders, 42*, 539–548. doi:10.1007/s10803-011-1269-y

Frenette, P., Dodds, L., MacPherson, K., Flowerdew, G., Hennen, B., & Bryson, S. (2011). Factors affecting the age at diagnosis of autism spectrum disorders in Nova Scotia, Canada. *Autism, 17*(2), 184–195.

Friendly, M., Larsen, E., Feltham, L. E., Grady, B., Forer, B., & Jones, M. (2018). *Early childhood education and care in Canada 2016*. Toronto, ON: Childcare Resource and Research Unit.

Fuentes, C. T., Mostofsky, S. H., & Bastian, A. J. (2011). No proprioceptive deficits in autism despite movement-related sensory and execution impairments. *Journal of Autism and Developmental Disorders, 41*(10), 1352–1361.

Fung, L. K., & Hardan, A. Y. (2014). Autism in DSM-5 under the microscope: Implications to patients, families, clinicians, and researchers. *Asian Journal of Psychiatry, 11*, 93–97. doi:10.1016/j.ajp.2014.08.010

Furlong, M. (2013, July 10). The latest trend on TV: Characters with Asperger's. *The Huffington Post*. Retrieved from www.huffingtonpost.com/maggie-furlong/aspergers-on-tv_b_3574366.html

García-Villamisar, D. A., & Dattilo, J. (2010). Effects of a leisure programme on quality of life and stress of individuals with ASD. *Journal of Intellectual Disability Research, 54*(7), 611–619.

Geneva Centre for Autism. (2006). What is IBI and is it the same as ABA? Retrieved from https://www.autism.net/faqs/595-what-is-ibi-and-is-it-the-same-as-aba.html

Germani, T., Zwaigenbaum, L., Bryson, S., Brian, J., Smith, I., Roberts, W., … & Vaillancourt, T. (2014). Brief report: Assessment of early sensory processing in infant at high risk of autism spectrum disorder. *Journal of Autism and Developmental Disorders*, 44, 3264–3270. doi:10.1007/s10803-014-2175-x

Ghaziuddin, M. (2010). Brief report: Should the DSM V drop Asperger syndrome? *Journal of Autism and Developmental Disorders, 40*, 1146–1148.

Gibbs, L., & Gambrill, E. (2002). Evidence-based practice: Counterarguments to objections. *Research on Social Work Practice, 12*(3), 452–476.

Glennon, T., Miller-Kuhaneck, H., Henry, D. A., Parham, L. D., & Ecker, C. (2007). Sensory Processing Measure manual. Los Angeles, CA: Western Psychological Services.

Glennon, T., Miller-Kuhaneck, H., Henry, D. A., Parham, L. D., & Ecker, C. (2010). Sensory Processing Measure – Preschool manual. Los Angeles, CA: Western Psychological Services.

Godin, J., Freeman, A., & Rigby, P. (2017). Interventions to promote the playful engagement in social interaction of preschool-aged children with autism spectrum disorder (ASD): A scoping study. *Early Childhood Development and Care,* 3–17. doi:10.180/030004430.2017.1404999

Goldstein, H., Schneider, N., & Thiemann, K. (2007). Peer-mediated social communication intervention: When clinical expertise informs treatment development and evaluation. *Topics in Language Disorders, 27*(2), 182–199. doi:10.1097/01.TLD.0000269932.26504.a8

Government of British Columbia, Ministry of Education. (2000). *Teaching students with Autism: A resource guide.* Retrieved from https://www2.gov.bc.ca/assets/gov/education/kindergarten-to-grade-12/teach/teaching-tools/inclusive/autism.pdf

Government of Canada. (1996). *Overview of the employment equity act (1996) from a public service perspective.* Retrieved from http://www.tbssct.gc.ca/pubs_pol/hrpubs/tb_852/overpr-eng.asp

Government of Canada. (2014). Evaluation of the action plan to protect human health from environmental contaminants 2008–2009 to 2012–2013. Retrieved from https://www.canada.ca/en/health-canada/corporate/about-health-canada/accountability-performance-financial-reporting/evaluation-reports/evaluation-action-plan-protect-human-health-environmental-contaminants-2008-2009-2012-2013.html#a2.1

Government of Canada. (2015). About mental health. Retrieved from https://www.canada.ca/en/public-health/services/about-mental-health.html

Government of Canada. (2017). Registered disability savings plan. Retrieved from https://www.canada.ca/en/employment-social-development/programs/disability/savings.html

Government of Canada. (2018a). Guide to the Canadian Charter of Rights and Freedoms. Retrieved from https://www.canada.ca/en/canadian-heritage/services/how-rights-protected/guide-canadian-charter-rights-freedoms.html

Government of Canada. (2018b). The new Canadian caregiver credit. Retrieved from https://www.canada.ca/en/revenue-agency/services/tax/individuals/topics/about- your-tax-return/tax-return/completing-a-tax-return/deductions-credits-expenses/family-caregiver-amount.

html?utm_campaign=not-applicable&utm_medium=vanity-url&utm_source=canada-ca_caregiver-credit

Government of Canada. (2018c). Signs and symptoms of autism spectrum disorder. Retrieved from https://www.canada.ca/en/public-health/services/diseases/autism-spectrum-disorder-asd/signs-symptoms-autism-spectrum-disorder-asd.html

Government of Canada. (2019). Canada's first federal accessibility legislation received Royal Assent. Retrieved from https://www.canada.ca/en/employment-social-development/news/2019/06/canadas-first-federal-accessibility-legislation-receives-royal-assent.html

Government of Manitoba. (2013). *Thrive: A five-year plan for helping Manitobans with autism spectrum disorders and their families*. Retrieved from http://www.gov.mb.ca/fs/thrive/

Government of Newfoundland and Labrador. (2018). *The way forward: Building our future*. Retrieved from https://www.gov.nl.ca/thewayforward/files/TWF-Building-for-Our-Future-III-Web.pdf

Government of Newfoundland and Labrador. (2019). *Autism action plan*. Retrieved from https://www.releases.gov.nl.ca/releases/2019/health/0417n01.aspx

Government of Nova Scotia. (2016). Individual program plan (IPP) review: Themes and recommendations. Retrieved from https://www.ednet.ns.ca/docs/individualprogramplanreview.pdf

Grandy, S. (2018, August 2). JASPER: Therapy through play for children with autism. Retrieved from https://storyline.easternhealth.ca/2018/08/02/jasper-therapy-through-play-for-children-with-autism/

Gray, C. (2010). *The new social story book* (10th ed.). Arlington, TX: Future Horizons.

Gray, C. (2019). *What is a social story?* Retrieved from carolgraysocialstories.com/social-stories/what-is-it/

Green, D., Chandler, S., Charman, T., Simonoff, E., & Baird, G. (2016). Brief report: DSM-5 sensory behaviours in children with and without an autism spectrum disorder. *Journal of Autism and Developmental Disorders, 46*(11), 3597–3606. doi:10.1007/s10803-016-2881-7

Green, G. (2010). Training practitioners to evaluate evidence about interventions. *European Journal of Behavior Analysis, 11*(2), 223–228.

Green, G., & Perry, L. (1999). Science, pseudoscience and antiscience. *Science in Autism Treatment, 1*(1), 5–6. Retrieved from https://asatonline.org/research-treatment/making-sense-of-autism-treatments-weighing-the-evidence/science-pseudoscience-and-antiscience/

Grzadzinski, R., Huerta, M., & Lord, C. (2013). DSM-5 and autism spectrum disorders (ASDs): An opportunity for identifying ASD subtypes. *Molecular Autism, 4*, 12. doi:10.1186/2040-2392-4-12

Guber, P., Johnson, M., McGiffert, D., Molen, G. R., Mutrux, G., Peters, J. (Producers), & Levinson, B. (1988). *Rain man* [motion picture]. United States: United Artists.

Gugliolmo, A., & Tourville, J. (2018). *How to build a hug: Temple Grandin and her amazing squeeze machine*. New York, NY: Simon & Schuster.

Guskey, T. R. (2002). Professional development and teacher change. *Teaching and Teaching: Theory and Practice, 8*(3/4), 381–391.

Haesen, B., Boets, B., & Wagemans, J. (2011). A review of behavioural and electrophysiological studies on auditory processing and speech perception in autism spectrum disorders. *Research in Autism Spectrum Disorders, 5*(2), 701–714. doi:101016/j.rasd.2010.11.006

Hall, B. (2015). *Reaching and teaching all students—A model to guide the practice of inclusive education in Nunavut: Final report of the external review of inclusive education.* Retrieved from http://assembly.nu.ca/library/GNedocs/2015/002137-e.pdf

Hall, L. J. (2013). *Autism spectrum disorder: From theory to practi*ce (2nd ed.). Upper Saddle River, NJ: Pearson.

Hansen, B. D., & Wadsworth, J. P. (2015). Effects of an antecedent intervention on repetitive behaviors of a child with autism. *Child and Family Behavior Therapy, 37*(1), 51–62. doi:10.1080/07317107.2015.1000235

Hanson, H. (Producer). (2005, September 13). *Bones* [Television broadcast]. Los Angeles, CA: 20th Century Fox.

Harper, R. A. (1975). *A new guide to rational living.* Chatsworth, CA: Wilshire Book Company.

Hartley, S. L., & Sikora, D. M. (2010). Detecting autism spectrum disorder in children with intellectual disability: Which DSM-IV-TR criteria are most useful? *Focus on Autism and Other Developmental Disabilities, 25*(2), 85–97.

Hassan, M., Thomson, K. M., Khan, M., Riosa, P. B., & Weiss, J. (2017). Behavioral skills training for graduate students providing cognitive behavior therapy to children with autism spectrum disorder. *Behavior Analysis: Research and Practice, 17*(2), 155–165. doi:10.1037/bar0000078

Hebert, J. (2014, June 12). Lorna Wing: Psychiatrist whose work did much to improve the understanding of autism after her only child had the condition diagnosed. *The Times*, p. 58. Retrieved from www.thetimes.co.uk/tto/opinion/obituaries/article4116049.ece

Heflin, L. J., & Alaimo, D. F. (2007). *Students with autism spectrum disorders: Effective instructional practices.* Upper Saddle River, NJ: Pearson.

Henry, K. A. (2005). *How do I teach this kid? Visual work tasks for beginning learners on the autism spectrum.* Arlington, TX: Future Horizons.

Herlihy, L., Knoch, K., Vibert, B., & Fein, D. (2013). Parents' first concerns about toddlers with autism spectrum disorder: Effect of sibling status. *Autism: The International Journal of Research and Practice, 19*(1), 20–28. doi:10.1177/1362361313509731

Hickey, E. J., Dubois, L., & Hartley, S. L. (2018). Positive and negative social exchanges experienced by fathers and mothers of children with autism. *Autism: The International Journal of Research & Practice, 22*(4), 469–478.

Hill, B. (2018, April 17). Father of son with autism calls Canada's new immigration policy a "blessing for all of us." *Global News.* Retrieved from https://globalnews.ca/news/4150860/disability-immigration-law-a-blessing-says-father-autistic-child/

Hillier, A., Gallop, N., Mendes, E., Tellez, D., Buckingham, A., Nizami, A., & OToole, D. (2019). LGBTQ+ and autism spectrum disorder: Experiences and challenges. *International Journal of Transgenderism*, 1–13.

Hippler, K., & Klicpera, C. (2003). A retrospective analysis of the clinical case records of "autistic psychopaths" diagnosed by Hans Asperger and his team at the University Children's Hospital, Vienna. *Philosophical Transactions of the Royal Society B: Biological Sciences, 358*(1430), 291–301.

Ho, H., Fergus, K., & Perry, A. (2018). Looking back and moving forward: The experiences of Canadian parents raising an adolescent with autism spectrum disorder. *Research in Autism Spectrum Disorders, 52*(1), 12–22. doi:10.1016/j.rasd.2018.05.004

Hobbs, N. (1978). Families, schools, and communities: An ecosystem for children. *Teachers College Record, 79*(4), 756–766.

Hockey Association for the Developmentally Challenged (HADC). (2017). Welcome! Retrieved from https://hadc-gladiators.org/

Hodgetts, S., McConnell, D., Zwaigenbaum, L., & Nicholas, D. (2014). The impact of autism services on mothers' occupational balance and participation. *The Occupational Therapy Journal of Research: Occupation, Participation, and Health, 34*(2), 81–93.

Hodgetts, S., Nicholas, D., Zwaigenbaum, L., & McConnell, D. (2013). Parents' and professionals' perceptions of family-centered care for children with autism spectrum disorder across service sectors. *Social Science & Medicine, 96*, 138–146. doi:10.1016/j.socscimed.2013.07.012

Hodgetts, S., Zwaigenbaum, L., & Nicholas, D. (2015). Profile and predictors of service needs for families of children with autism spectrum disorders. *Autism, 19*(6), 673–683. doi:10.1177/1362361314543531

Hofmann, S. G., Asnaani, A., Vonk, I. J., Sawyer, A. T., & Fang, A. (2012). The efficacy of cognitive behavioral therapy: A review of meta-analyses. *Cognitive Therapy and Research, 36*(5), 427–440. doi: 10.1007és10608-012-9476-1

Holland Bloorview Kids Rehabilitation Hospital. (2018). Advocacy tool kit for parents of children and youth with autism spectrum disorder (ASD) and other neurodevelopmental disorders (NDDs), pp. 4–5. Retrieved from https://hollandbloorview.ca/Assets/Research/ARC/AdvocacyToolKit-July24-LINKED-LOCKED.pdf

Homme, L., Csanyi, A. P., Gonzales, M. A., & Rechs, J. R. (1970). *How to use contingency contracting in the classroom* (rev. ed.). Champaign, IL: Research Press Co.

Hoogsteen, L., & Woodgate, R. (2013). Centering autism within the family: A qualitative approach to autism and the family. *Journal of Pediatric Nursing, 28*, 135–140.

Horner, R. H., Carr, E. G., Halle, J., McGee, G., Odom, S., & Wolery, M. (2005). The use of single-subject research to identify evidence-based practice in special education. *Exceptional Children, 71*(2), 165–179. doi:10.1177/001440290507100203

Housing Study Group. (2013). Ending the wait: An action agenda to address the housing crisis confronting adults with developmental disabilities. Retrieved from www.autismontario.com/Client/ASO/AO.nsf/object/Sep13ENews/$file/Ending+the+Wait+final+sep6.pdf

Hudson, C. C., Hall, L., & Harkness, K. L. (2019). Prevalence of depressive disorders in individuals with autism spectrum disorder: A meta-analysis. *Journal of Abnormal Child Psychology, 47*(1), 165–175. doi:10.1007/s10802-018-0402-1

Hughes, J. E. A., Ward, J., Gruffydd, E., Baron-Cohen, S., Smith, P., Allison, C., & Simner, J. (2018). Savant syndrome has a distinct psychological profile in autism. *Molecular Autism, 9*(53), 1–18.

Hundert, J., Rowe, S., & Harrison, E. (2014). The combined effects of social script training and peer buddies on generalized peer interaction of children with ASD in inclusive classrooms. *Focus on Autism and Other Developmental Disorders, 29*(4), 206–215. doi:10.1177/1088357614522288

Hyche, K., & Maertz, V. (2014). *Classroom strategies for children with ADHD, autism, & sensory processing disorders: Solutions for behavior, attention and emotional regulation*. Eau Claire, WI: PESI Publishing & Media.

Ide, M., Yaguchi, A., Sano, M., Fukatsu, R., & Wada, M. (2019). Higher tactile temporal resolution as a basis of hypersensitivity in individuals with autism spectrum disorder. *Journal of Autism and Developmental Disorders, 49*(1), 44–53. doi:10.1007/s10803-018-3677-8

Inclusive Education Canada. (2017). What is inclusive education? Retrieved from www.inclusiveeducation.ca

Independent Living Canada. (n.d.). What is independent living? Retrieved from ilcanada.ca

Ingersoll, B., & Dvortcsak, A. (2010). *Teaching social communication to children with autism.* New York, NY: Guilford.

Ingvarsson, E. T. (2017). Tutorial: Teaching verbal behaviour to children with ASD. *International Electronic Journal of Elementary Education, 2*, 433–450. Retrieved from https://www.iejee.com/index.php/IEJEE/article/view/168

Iwata, B. A., DeLeon, I. G., & Roscoe, E. M. (2013). Reliability and validity of the Functional Analysis Screening Tool. *Journal of Applied Behavior Analysis, 46*, 271–284.

Jackman, P. (2016). Online course: ASD and behavioural interventions: An introduction for school personnel. *Newfoundland and Labrador Teachers' Association: The Bulletin*, 25.

Jacobsen, K. (2010). Diagnostic politics: The curious case of Kanner's syndrome. *History of Psychiatry, 21*(4), 436–454. doi:10.1177/0957154X09341438

Jiujas, M., Kelley, E., & Hall, L. (2017). Restricted, repetitive behaviors in autism spectrum disorder and obsessive-compulsive disorder: A comparative review. *Child Psychiatry and Human Development, 48*(6), 944–959. doi:10.1007/s10578-017-0717-0

Johnson, C. P. (2004). Early clinical characteristics of children with autism. In V. B. Gupta (Ed.), *Autistic spectrum disorders in children* (pp. 96–134). New York, NY: Marcel Dekker.

Joosten, A. V., & Bundy, A. C. (2010). Sensory processing and stereotypical and repetitive behaviour in children with autism and intellectual disabilities. *Australian Occupational Therapy Journal, 57*(6), 366–372. doi:10.1111/j.1440-1630.2009.00835.x

Jull, S., & Mirenda, P. (2016). Effects of staff training program on community instructors' ability to teach swimming skills to children with autism. *Journal of Positive Behavior Interventions, 18*(1), 29–40. doi: 10.1177/1098300715576797

Jung, L. A. (2007). Writing SMART objectives and strategies that fit the ROUTINE. *Teaching Exceptional Children, 39*(4), 54–58.

Kanner, L. (1943). Autistic disturbances of affective contact. *Nervous Child, 2*, 217–250. Retrieved from http://simonsfoundation.s3.amazonaws.com/share/071207-leo-kanner-autistic-affective-contact.pdf

Kanner, L. (1968). Autistic disturbances of affective contact. *Acta Paedopsychiatrica: International Journal of Child & Adolescent Psychiatry, 35*(4–8), 98–136.

Kasari, C., Freeman, S., & Paparella, T. (2006). Joint attention and symbolic play in young children with autism: A randomized control intervention study. *Journal of Child Psychology and Psychiatry, 47*(6), 611–620. doi:10.1111/j.1469-7610.2005.01567.x

Kearney, A. J. (2008). *Understanding applied behavior analysis.* Philadelphia, PA: Jessica Kingsley Publishers.

Kern, J. K., Trivedi, M. H., Garver, C. R., Grannemann, B. D., Andrews, A. A., Savla, J. S., ... & Schroeder, J. L. (2006). The pattern of sensory processing abnormalities in autism. *Autism, 10*(5), 480–494. doi:10.1177/1362361307075702

Kern, L., & Clemens, N. H. (2007). Antecedent strategies to promote appropriate classroom behavior. *Psychology in the Schools, 44*(1), 65–75. doi:10.1002/pits.20206

Killoran, I., Tymon, D., & Frempong, G. (2007). Disabilities and inclusive practices within Toronto preschools. *International Journal of Inclusive Education, 11*(1), 81–95. doi:10.1080/13603110500375473

Killoran, I., Zaretsky, H., Jordan, A., Smith, D., Allard, C., & Moloney, J. (2013). Supporting teachers to work with children with exceptionalities. *Canadian Journal of Education, 36*(1), 240–270.

Kirby, A. W., White, T. J., & Baranek, G. T. (2015). Caregiver strain and sensory features in children with autism spectrum disorders and other developmental disabilities. *American Journal on Intellectual and Developmental Disabilities, 120*(1), 32–45. doi:10.1352/1944-7558-120.1.32

Kleeberger, V., & Mirenda, P. (2010). Teaching generalized imitation skills to a preschooler with autism using video modelling. *Journal of Positive Behaviour Interventions, 12*(2), 116–127. doi:10.1177/1098300708329279

Koegel, R. L., & Koegel, L. K. (2006). *Pivotal response treatment for autism: Communication, social and academic development.* Baltimore, MD: Paul H. Brookes.

Koegel, R. L., Koegel, L. K., & Brookman, L. I. (2003). Empirically supported pivotal response interventions for children with autism. In A. E. Kazdin & J. R. Weisz (Eds.), *Evidence-based psychotherapies for children and adolescents* (pp. 341–357). New York, NY: Guilford Press.

Konst, M. J., & Matson, J. L. (2014). Comorbid psychopathology symptom rates in infants and toddlers with autism spectrum disorders. *Research in Autism Spectrum Disorders, 8*(2), 147–155. doi:10.1016/j.rasd.2013.10.011

Kurtz, A., & Jordan, M. (2008). Institute brief: Supporting individuals with autism spectrum disorders: Quality employment practices. *The Institute Brief,* 25. Retrieved from https://www.communityinclusion.org/article.php?article_id=266

Lamb, H. R., & Bachrach, L. L. (2001). Some perspectives on deinstitutionalization. *Psychiatric Services, 52*(8), 1039–1045.

Lane, A. E., Young, R. L., Baker, A. E. Z., & Angley, M. T. (2010). Sensory processing subtypes in autism: Association with adaptive behaviour. *Journal of Autism and Developmental Disorders, 40*(1), 112–122. doi:10.1007/s10803-009-0840-2

Lane, K. (2016, March/April). Supporting students with ASD. *Newfoundland and Labrador Teachers' Association: The Bulletin,* 26–27.

Laugeson, E. A., & Frankel, F. (2010). *The PEERS treatment manual.* New York, NY: Taylor and Francis.

Laugeson, E. A., Frankel, F., Gantman, A., Dillon, A. R., & Mogil, C. (2012). Evidence-based social skills training for adolescents with autism spectrum disorder: The UCLA PEERS program. *Journal of Autism and Developmental Disorders, 42*(6), 1025–1036.

Lauritsen, M. (2013). Autism spectrum disorder. *European Child and Adolescent Psychiatry, 22*(Suppl. 1), S37–S42. doi:10.1007/s00787-012-0359-5

Laushey, K., & Heflin, L. (2000). Enhancing social skills of kindergarten children with autism through the training of multiple peers as tutors. *Journal of Autism and Developmental Disabilities, 30*(3), 183–193. doi:10.1023/A:1005558101038

Law, M. (2006). Autism spectrum disorders and occupational therapy. Briefing to the Senate Standing Committee on Social Affairs, Science and Technology. *Canadian Association of Occupational Therapists.* Retrieved from https://www.canchild.ca/system/tenon/assets/attachments/000/000/618/original/Autism_Brief_Nov_06.pdf

Leaf, J. B., Cihon, J. H., Townley-Cochran, D., Miller, K., Leaf, R., McEachin, J., … & Taubman, M. (2016). An evaluation of positional prompts for teaching receptive identification to individuals diagnosed with autism spectrum disorder. *Behavior Analysis in Practice, 9*(4), 349–363. doi:10.1007/s40617-016-0146-8

Leekam, S. (2014, August). Lorna Wing (1928–2014). *Psychologist*, 564.

Letto, A., & Bornstein, S. (2018). Rapid Evidence Reports: Preschool screening. Newfoundland & Labrador Centre for Applied Health Research. Retrieved from https://www.nlcahr.mun.ca/CHRSP/Preschool_Screening_RER_Oct_2018.pdf

Li, A. (2009). Identification and intervention for students who are visually impaired and who have autism spectrum disorder. *Teaching Exceptional Children*, *41*(4), 22–32.

Lindblom, A. (2014). Under-detection of autism among First Nations children in British Columbia, Canada. *Disability & Society, 29*(8), 1248–1259. doi:10.1080/09687599.2014.923750

Liss, M., Harel, B., Fein, D., Allen, D., Dunn, M., Feinstein, I., ... & Rapin, I. (2001). Predictors and correlates of adaptive functioning in children with developmental disorders. *Journal of Autism and Developmental Disorders, 31*(2), 219–230.

Liss, M., Saulnier, C., Fein, D., & Kinsbourne, M. (2006). Sensory and attention abnormalities in autistic spectrum disorders. *Autism, 10*(2), 155–172.

Lombardo, M. V., & Baron-Cohen, S. (2011). The role of the self in mindblindness in autism. *Consciousness and cognition*, *20*(1), 130–140.

Lorah, E. R., Parnell, A., Whitby, P. S., & Hantula, D. (2015). A systematic review of tablet computers and portable media players as speech generating devices for individuals with autism spectrum disorder. *Journal of Autism and Developmental Disorders, 45*(12), 3792–3804. doi:10.1007/s10803-014-2314-4

Lord, C., & Jones, R. M. (2012). Re-thinking the classification of autism spectrum disorders. *Journal of Child Psychology and Psychiatry, 53*(5), 490–509.

Lord, C., Petkova, E., Hus, V., Gan, W., Lu, F., Martin, D. M., … & Risi, S. (2012). A multisite study of the clinical diagnosis of different autism spectrum disorder. *Archives of General Psychiatry, 3*, 306.

Lord, C., Rutter, M., & Le Couteur, A. (1994). Autism Diagnostic Interview–Revised: A revised version of a diagnostic interview for caregivers of individuals with possible pervasive developmental disorders. *Journal of Autism and Developmental Disorders, 24*(5), 659–685. doi:10.1007/bf02172145

Lorre, C., & Molero, S. (Producers), & Parsons, J. (Director). (2017, September 25). *Young Sheldon*. [Television broadcast]. Los Angeles, CA: CBS.

Lorre, C., Prady, B., & Molero, S. (Producers). (2007, September 24). *The big bang theory*. [Television broadcast]. Los Angeles, CA: Warner Brothers Television & Chuck Lorre Productions.

Lovaas, O. I. (1987). Behavioral treatment and normal educational and intellectual functioning in young autistic children. *Journal of Consulting and Clinical Psychology, 55*(1), 3–9.

Lunsky, Y., Garcin, N., Morin, D., Cobigo, V., & Bradley, E. (2007). Mental health services for individuals with intellectual disabilities in Canada: Findings from a national survey. *Journal of Applied Research in Intellectual Disabilities, 20*(5), 439–447.

Lyons, V., & Fitzgerald, M. (2007). Asperger (1906–1980) and Kanner (1894–1981), the two pioneers of autism. *Journal of Autism and Developmental Disorders, 37*, 2022–2023. doi:10.1007/s10803-007-0383-3

MacAlister, L. (2014). Toileting problems in children with autism. *Nursing Times, 110*(43), 18–20. Retrieved from https://www.nursingtimes.net/Journals/2014/10/17/a/m/u/141022Toileting-problems-in-children-with-autism.pdf

Maich, K. (2010). *Opening a can of worms: Perceptions and practices of teachers in Newfoundland and Labrador incorporating the role of a therapist.* Saarbrücken, Germany: Lambert Academic Publishing.

Maich, K. (2012). Celebrating another housing option for adults with disabilities. *Autism Matters,* (Fall 2010). Retrieved from https://www.autismontario.com/node/563

Maich, K., Davies, A., & Sohrabi, T. (2019). Autism spectrum disorder and maternal employment barriers: A comprehensive gender-based inquiry. *Canadian Journal of Family & Youth, 11*(1), 104–153. Retrieved from https://journals.library.ualberta.ca/cjfy/index.php/cjfy/article/view/29407/21401

Maich, K., Hall, C., & Sider, S. (2013). Learning people skills: Social literacy for students with autism spectrum disorder. *Education Canada, 53*(2). Retrieved from https://www.edcan.ca/articles/learning-people-skills/

Maich, K., Hill, R., & Somma, M. (2018). Canadian school programs for students with emotional/behavioral disorders: A decade of programs, policy, and practice. *Emotional &*

Behavioural Difficulties, 23(4), 441–456. Retrieved from https://www.tandfonline.com/doi/full/10.1080/13632752.2018.1497006

Maich, K., O'Keefe, C., van Rhijn, T., & Davies, A. W. J. (2018, September/October). Relaxation station, zen zone, or cozy corner? *The Bulletin 62*(1), 26–27. Retrieved from http://www.nlta.nl.ca/wp-content/uploads/2018/09/bultn_sept_oct18.pdf

Maich, K., & Sider, S. (2019a). Canada secondary education of special educational needs and disabilities. *Bloomsbury Encyclopedia of Special Education.*

Maich, K., & Sider, S. (2019b). Special education needs and disabilities in secondary education (Canada). *Bloomsbury Education and Childhood Studies.* London: Bloomsbury Academic. doi:10.5040/9781474209441.0054

Malkin, A., Dixon, M. R., Speelman, R. C., & Luke, N. (2017). Evaluating the relationships between the PEAK relational training system—direct training module, Assessment of Basic Language and Learning Skills–Revised, and the Vineland Adaptive Behaviour Scales–II. *Journal of Developmental and Physical Disabilities, 29*(2), 341–351. doi:10.1007/s10882-016-9527-8

Malott, R. W., & Shane, J. T. (2014). *Principles of behavior* (7th ed.). Upper Saddle River, NJ: Pearson Education.

Manett, J., & Stoddart, K. (2012). Facing the challenges of post-secondary education: Strategies for individuals with autism spectrum disorder (ASD). *Autism Matters, 46*, 1–3. Retrieved from www.autismontario.com/client/aso/ao.nsf/docs/149395542949b52a85257bc10060dbc6/$file/facing+the+challenges+of+post+secondary+education.pdf

Manitoba Education, Citizenship and Youth. (2005). *Supporting inclusive schools: A handbook for developing and implementing programming for students with autism spectrum disorder.* Retrieved from https://www.edu.gov.mb.ca/k12/specedu/aut/pdf/ASD_Document.pdf

Mansell, W., & Morris, K. (2004). A survey of parents' reactions to the diagnosis of an autistic spectrum disorder by a local service: Access to information and use of services. *Autism, 8*(4), 387–407.

Mansour, R., Dovi, A. T., Lane, D. M., Loveland, K. A., & Pearson, D. A. (2017). ADHD severity as it relates to comorbid psychiatric symptomatology in children with autism spectrum disorders (ASD). *Research in Developmental Disabilities, 60*, 52–64.

Marchica, L., & D'Amico, M. (2016). Examining the efficacy of an adapted version of the UCLA PEERS® program with Canadian adolescents. *Journal of Education & Social Policy, 3*(4), 54–65. Retrieved from https://www.semel.ucla.edu/peers/research

Martin, G., & Pear, J. (2015). *Behavior modification* (10th ed.). Upper Saddle River, NJ: Pearson Education.

Masataka, N. (2017). Implications of the idea of neurodiversity for understanding the origins of developmental disorders. *Physics of Life Review, 20*, 85–108. doi:10.1016/j.plrev.2016.11.02

Matson, J. L., & Williams, J. L. (2015). The curious selection process of treatments for autism spectrum disorder. *Research in Autism Spectrum Disorder, 9*, 21–25.

Matson, M. L., Mahan, S., & Matson, J. L. (2009). Parent training: A review of methods for children with autism spectrum disorders, *Research in Autism Spectrum Disorders, 3*(4), 868–875. doi:10.1016/j.rasd.2009.02.003

Mawlam, L. (2016). Five things journalists should keep in mind when writing about autism. *JSource*. Retrieved from https://j-source.ca/article/five-things-journalists-should-keep-in-mind-when-writing-about-autism/

May-Benson, T. A., & Koomar, J. A. (2010). Systematic review of the research evidence examining the effectiveness of interventions using a sensory integrative approach for children. *The American Journal of Occupational Therapy, 64*(3), 403–412.

Mayer, G. R., Sulzer-Azaroff, B., & Wallace, M. (2018). *Behavior analysis for lasting change* (4th ed.). Cornwall-on-Houston, NY: Sloan Publishing.

Mayer, J. L. (2017). The relationship between autistic traits and atypical sensory functioning in neurotypical and ASD adults: A spectrum approach. *Journal of Autism and Developmental Disorders, 47*(2), 316–327. doi:10.1007/s10803-016-2948-5

Mazefsky, C. A., Herrington, J., Siegel, M., Scarpa, A., Maddox, B. B., Scahill, L., & White, S. W. (2013). The role of emotion regulation in autism spectrum disorder. *Journal of the American Academy of Child & Adolescent Psychiatry, 52*(7), 679–688.

McClannahan, L. E., & Krantz, P. J. (1999). *Activity schedules for children with autism: Teaching independent behavior.* Bethesda, MD: Woodbine House.

McColl, M. A., Jaiswal, A., Jones, S., Roberts, L., & Murphy, C. (2017). *A review of disability policy in Canada.* Canadian Disability Policy Alliance. Retrieved from http://www.disabilitypolicyalliance.ca/wp-content/uploads/2018/01/A-Review-of-Disability-Policy-in-Canada-3rd-edition-Final-1-1.pdf

McColl, M. A., & Jones, S. (2020). *Government offices most responsible for disability issues across Canada.* Canadian Disability Policy Alliance. Retrieved from http://www.disabilitypolicyalliance.ca/wp-content/uploads/2020/03/CDPA-Government-Offices-Most-Responsible-for-Disability-Issues.pdf

McCrimmon, A. W. (2015). Inclusive education in Canada: Issues in teacher preparation. *Intervention in School and Clinic, 50*(4), 234–237.

McCrimmon, A. W., Altomore, A. A., Matchullis, R. L., & Jitlina, K. (2012). School-based practices for Asperger syndrome: A Canadian perspective. *Canadian Journal of School Psychology, 27*(4), 319–336. doi:10.1177/0829573512454991

McGuire, W., & Zenner, D. (2019). When autistic students are LGBTQ2+. *Education Canada, 59*(2). Retrieved from https://www.edcan.ca/articles/lgbtq2-autistic-students/

McKinnon, K., & Krempa, J. L. (2002). *Social skills solutions: A hands-on manual for teaching social skills to children with autism.* New York, NY: DRL Books.

McLaughlin, J., & Schneider, M. (2019). *Autism services in Ontario: Impacts on family and child well-being.* Laurier Autism Research Consortium. Retrieved from https://www.wlu.ca/academics/faculties/faculty-of-human-and-social-sciences/faculty-profiles/janet-mclaughlin/larc/assets/documents/larc-report.pdf

McLean, S., Breitenbach, M., Cowan, I., Jackman, P., Jozsa, S., & Michaud, J. (2016). *Teaching essential skills to prevent the development of challenging behaviour in learners with autism spectrum disorder.* Halifax, NS: Autism in Education Partnership, Atlantic Provinces Special Education Authority (APSEA). Retrieved from https://autismineducation.ca/assets/files/info-papers/teach-skills-prevent-challenging-behaviour.pdf

McLennan, J. D., Huculak, S., & Sheehan, D. (2008). Brief report: Pilot investigation of service receipt by young children with autistic spectrum disorders. *Journal of Autism and Developmental Disorders, 38*(6), 1192–1196.

McNaughton, D., & Light, J. (2015). What we write about when we write about AAC: The past 30 years of research and future directions. *Augmentative and Alternative Communication, 31*(4), 261–270. doi:10.3109/07434618.2015.1099736

McVey, A. J., Schiltz, H., Haendel, A., Dolan, B. K., Willar, K. S., Pleiss, S., … & van Hecke, A. V. (2017). Brief report: Does gender matter in interventions for ASD? Examining the impact of PEERS® social skills intervention on social behaviour among females with ASD. *Journal of Autism and Developmental Disorders, 47*(7), 2282–2289. doi:10.1007/s10803-017-3121-5

Memorial University of Newfoundland Health Research Unit. (2003). *A constant struggle.* Retrieved from https://www.med.mun.ca/getdoc/0ff13c8c-28cf-4ad8-ae0f-af59caefe571/autism_report_full-pdf.aspx

Mendes, E. A., & Maroney, M. R. (2019). *Gender identity, sexuality and autism: Voices from across the spectrum.* London, UK: Jessica Kingsley Publishers.

Miklos, M., & Dipuglia, A. (2010). Mand training with the PaTTAN autism initiative. Retrieved from https://www.mand.framewelder.com

Miller, L. J. (2012, December 3). *Final decision for DSM-V.* Retrieved from https://web.archive.org/web/20131004214132/http://spdfoundation.net/sensory-processing-blog/2012/12/05/final-decision-for-dsm-v/

Miller, L. J., Anzalone, M., Cermak, S. A., Lane, S. J., Osten, E., Wieder, S., & Greenspan, S. I. (2005). *The Interdisciplinary Council on Developmental and Learning Disorders: Diagnostic Manual for Infancy and Early Childhood (ICDL-DMIC).* Bethesda, MD: The Interdisciplinary Council on Developmental and Learning Disorders.

Miller-Kuhaneck, H., & Kelleher, J. (2018). The classroom environment assessment as an educational tool for teachers. *Journal of Occupational Therapy, Schools and Early Intervention, 11*(2), 161–171. doi:10.1080/19411243.2018.1432442

Miltenberger, R. G. (2016). *Behavior modification: Principles and procedures* (6th ed.). Boston, MA: Cengage Learning.

Ministry of Children, Community and Social Services. (2018). Introduction to the Ontario autism program. Retrieved from https://www.ontario.ca/document/ontario-autism-program-guidelines#section-1

Mirenda, P. (2003). Toward functional augmentative and alternative communication for students with autism: Manual signs, graphic symbols, and voice output communication aids. *Language, Speech, and Hearing Services in Schools, 34*(3), 203–216. Retrieved from http://web.a.ebscohost.com.libaccess.senecacollege.ca

Miriam Foundation. (2008). Canadian best practice guidelines: Screening, assessment of young children with ASD. Retrieved from https://www.goldlearningcentre.com/handbook_english_web-final.pdf

Miriam Foundation. (2018). About us: Past, present, and future. Retrieved from http://www.miriamfoundation.ca/en/the-foundation/61-about-us.html

Mosca, J. (2017). *The girl who thought in pictures: The story of Dr. Temple Grandin.* New York, NY: The Innovation Press.

Musset, P. (2010). Initial teaching education and continuing training policies in a comparative perspective: Current practices in OECD countries and a literature review on potential effects. *OECD Education Working Papers, No. 48.* doi:10.1787/5kmbphn7s47h-en

Myles, B. S., & Simpson, R. L. (2001). Understanding the hidden curriculum: An essential social skill for children and youth with Asperger syndrome. *Intervention in School and Clinic, 36*(5), 279.

Nadon, G., Ehrmann Feldman, D., Dunn, W., & Gisel, E. (2011). Association of sensory processing and eating problems in children with autism spectrum disorders. *Autism Research and Treatment, 2011*, 1–8. doi:10.1155/2011/541926

National Autism Center (NAC). (2009). *Historical perspective: National standards project—Phase 1.* Retrieved from https://www.nationalautismcenter.org/national-standards-project/history/

National Autism Center (NAC). (2015). *Findings and conclusions: National standards project—Phase 2.* Retrieved from https://www.nationalautismcenter.org/national-standards-project/phase-2/significant-findings/

National Human Genome Research Institute. (2019). Clinical genomic database. Retrieved from https://research.nhgri.nih.gov/CGD/

National Institutes of Health & National Institute on Deafness and Other Communication Disorders. (2010). NIH workshop on nonverbal school-aged children with autism. April 13–14, 2010. Retrieved from https://www.nidcd.nih.gov

Neely, L., Rispoli, M., Gerow, S., & Hong, R. E. (2016). Preparing interventionists via telepractice in incidental teaching for children with autism. *Journal of Behavioural Education, 25*(4), 393–416. doi:10.1007/s10864-016-9250-7

Neil, N., Vause, T., Jaksic, H., & Feldman, M. (2017). Effects of group functional behavior-based cognitive-behavioral therapy for obsessive compulsive behavior in a youth with autism spectrum disorder. *Child and Family Behavior Therapy, 39*(3), 179–190. doi:10.1080/07317107.2017.1338448

Neumärker, K. (2003). Leo Kanner: His years in Berlin, 1906–24. The roots of autistic disorder. *History of Psychiatry, 14*(54), 205–218.

New Brunswick Department of Education and Early Childhood Development. (2016). *Preschool autism program standards.* Retrieved from http://www2.gnb.ca/content/dam/gnb/Departments/ed/pdf/ELCC/ECHDPE/PreschoolAutismStandards.pdf

Newfoundland & Labrador Department of Health & Community Services. (2019). *Autism action plan, 2019–2022.* Retrieved https://www.health.gov.nl.ca/health/from publications/pdf/autism_action_plan_2019-22.pdf

Newfoundland & Labrador Human Rights Commission. (2002). *Report for 2002*. Retrieved from https://thinkhumanrights.ca/wp-content/uploads/hrc_annrep_2002.pdf

Newfoundland & Labrador Human Rights Commission. (2005). *Report for 2004/05*. Retrieved from https://thinkhumanrights.ca/wp-content/uploads/hrc_annrep_2004_05.pdf

Nicholas, D. B., Zwaigenbaum, L., Zwicker, J., Clarke, M. E., Lamsal, R., Stoddart, K. P., … & Lowe, K. (2018). Evaluation of employment-support services for adults with autism spectrum disorder. *Autism: The International Journal of Research and Practice, 22*(6), 693–702.

Njie, A., Shea, S., & Williams, M. (2018). *Students first: Report of the Commission on Inclusive Education*. Retrieved from https://inclusiveedns.ca/wp-content/uploads/2018/03/CIE-Students-First-WEBreport-2.pdf

Normore, A. (2015). Honoring the cultural integrity of Canada's First Nations. In G. Jean-Marie, S. Sider, & C. Desir (Eds.), *Comparative international perspectives on education and social change in developing countries and Indigenous Peoples in developed countries* (pp. 103–122). Charlotte, NC: Information Age Publishing.

Nova Scotia Department of Education. (2010). *Autism management advisory team report on lifespan needs for persons with autism spectrum disorder* (DesLibris. Documents collection). Halifax, NS: Author.

Nova Scotia Department of Education. (2016). *Individual program plan (IPP) review: Themes and recommendations*. Halifax, NS: Author. Retrieved from https://www.ednet.ns.ca/docs/individualprogramplanreview.pdf

Nova Scotia, Student Services Division. (2012). *Developing and implementing programming for students with autism spectrum disorder*. Halifax, NS: Author.

Odle, T. G., Barstow, D. G., & Cataldo, L. J. (2011). *Pervasive developmental disorders*. Independence, KY: Gale, Cengage Learning.

Ollendick, T. H., King, N. J., & Chorpita, B. F. (2006). Empirically supported treatments for children and adolescents. In P. C. Kendall (Ed.), *Child and adolescent therapy: Cognitive-behavioral procedures* (3rd ed., pp. 492–520). doi:10.1097/00004703-199204000-00013

Ombudsman Ontario. (2012). Ontario ombudsman to investigate province's services for adults with developmental disabilities in crisis. Retrieved from www.ombudsman.on.ca/Newsroom/Press-Release/2012/Ontario-Ombudsman-to-investigate-provinces-servic.aspx?lang=en-CA

Ontario Association for Behaviour Analysis (ONTABA). (2017). *Evidence-based practices for individuals with autism spectrum disorder: Recommendations for caregivers, practitioners, and policy makers*. Retrieved from https://www.ontaba.org/pdf/ONTABA%20OSETT-ASD%20REPORT%20WEB.pdf

Ontario Association of Children's Rehabilitation Service. (2012). Ask Lindsay. Retrieved from www.oacrs.com/en/asklindsay

Ontario College of Early Childhood Educators. (n.d.). Becoming an RECE in Ontario. Retrieved from www.college-ece.ca/en/Documents/Become_an_RECE.pdf

Ontario College of Teachers. (2019). Ontario College of Teachers. Retrieved from www.oct.ca

Ontario Human Rights Commission. (2019). *Eliminating racial profiling in law enforcement*. Retrieved from http://www.ohrc.on.ca/sites/default/files/RACIAL%20PROFILING%20Policy%20FINAL%20for%20Remediation.pdf

Ontario Ministry of Children and Youth Services. (2011). ASD diagnosis and treatment. Retrieved from www.children.gov.on.ca/htdocs/English/topics/specialneeds/autism/aprk/asd-diagnosis-and-treatment/diagnosis.aspx

Ontario Ministry of Community and Social Services. (2018). Ontario disability support program: Employment supports. Retrieved from https://www.mcss.gov.on.ca/en/mcss/programs/social/directives/odsp/es/1_1_ODSP_ESDirectives.aspx

Ontario Ministry of Community and Social Services. (2018). Ontario autism program. Retrieved from https://www.ontario.ca/page/ontario-autism-program

Ontario Ministry of Education. (2004). The individual education plan: A resource guide. Retrieved from http://www.edu.gov.on.ca/eng/general/elemsec/speced/guide/resource/iepresguid.pdf

Ontario Ministry of Education. (2007). *Program/policy memorandum no. 140: Incorporating methods of applied behaviour analysis (ABA), into programs for students with autism spectrum disorder (ASD).* Retrieved from www.edu.gov.on.ca/extra/eng/ppm/140.html

Ontario Ministry of Education. (2013). *Program/policy memorandum no. 156: Supporting transitions for students with special educational needs.* Retrieved from www.edu.gov.on.ca/extra/eng/ppm/ppm156.pdf

Oriane, L., & Philippe A. C. (2016). Why we should study the broader autism phenotype in typically developing populations. *Journal of Cognition and Development, 17*(4), 584–595. doi:10.1080/15248372.2016.1200046

Ouellette-Kuntz, H., Coo, H., Lam, M., Breitenbach, M. M., Hennessey, P. E., Jackman, P. D., … & Chung, A. M. (2014). The changing prevalence of autism in three regions of Canada. *Journal of Autism and Developmental Disorders, 44*(1), 120–136. doi:10.1007/s10803-013-1856-1

Owen, J. P., Marco, E. J., Desai, S., Fourie, E., Harris, J., Hill, S. S., … & Mukherjee, P. (2013). Abnormal white matter microstructure in children with sensory processing disorders. *NeuroImage: Clinical, 2*, 844–853. Retrieved from doi:10.1016/j.nicl.2013.06.009

Owren, T. (2013). Neurodiversity: Accepting autistic difference. *Learning Disability Practice, 16*(4), 32–37.

Ozonoff, S., Iosif, A. M., Baguio, F., Cook, I. C., Hill, M. M., Hutman, T., … & Young, G. S. (2010). A prospective study of the emergence of early behavioural signs of autism. *Journal of the American Academy of Child and Adolescent Psychiatry, 49*(3), 256–266. doi:10.1016/j.jaac.2009.11.009

Pacific Autism Family Network. (2018). PAFN overview. Retrieved from http://pacificautismfamily.com/overview/

Pahnke, J., Lundgren, T., Hursti, T., & Hirvikoski, T. (2014). Outcomes of an acceptance and commitment therapy-based skills training group for students with high-functioning autism spectrum disorder: A quasi-experimental pilot study. *Autism, 18*(8), 953–964. doi:10.1177/1362361313501091

Panju, S., Brian, J., Dupuis, A., Anagnostou, E., & Kushki, A. (2015). Atypical sympathetic arousal in children with autism spectrum disorder and its association with anxiety symptomatology. *Molecular Autism, 6*(1), 64.

Parliament of Canada. (2012). Senate public bill S-206: An Act respecting World Autism Day. Retrieved from www.parl.gc.ca/LegisInfo/BillDetails.aspx?Language=E&Mode=1&Bill=S206&Parl=41&Ses=1

Parten, M. B. (1932). Social participation among preschool children. *Journal of Abnormal and Social Psychology, 27*(3), 243–269. doi:10.1037/h0074524

Partington, J. W. (2010). *The assessment of basic language and learning skills—revised (the ABLLS-R).* Pleasant Hill, CA: Partington Behavior Analysts.

Pearce, J. M. S. (2005). Kanner's infantile autism and Asperger's syndrome. *Journal of Neurology, Neurosurgery, & Psychiatry, 76*, 200–205. doi:1136/jnnp.2004.041012

Pearce, L. (2008, Winter). Ministry of Education ASD initiatives and what they mean for you. *Autism Matters, 5*(1), 5–7.

Pelly, L., Vardy, C., Fernandez, B., Newhook, L., & Chafe, R. (2015). Incidence and cohort prevalence for autism spectrum disorders in the Avalon Peninsula, Newfoundland and Labrador. *Canadian Medical Association Journal (CMAJ) OPEN, 3*(3), E276–80. doi:10.9778/cmajo.20140056

Penner, M., Anagnostou, E., & Ungar, W. (2018). Practice patterns and determinants of wait time for autism spectrum disorder diagnosis in Canada (report). *Molecular Autism, 9*(1), 16. doi:10.1186/s13229-018-0201-0

Penney, S. C. (2013). Qualitative investigation of school-related issues affecting individuals diagnosed with autism spectrum disorder and co-occurring anxiety and/or depression. *Autism Insights, 5*, 75–91. doi:10.4137/AUI.S10746

Perez Repetto, L., Jasmin, E., Fombonne, E., Gisel, E., & Couture, M. (2017). Longitudinal study of sensory features in children with autism spectrum disorder. *Autism Research and Treatment, 2017.* doi:10.1155/2017/1934701

Perry, A., & Condillac, R. A. (2003). Evidence-based practices for children and adolescents with autism spectrum disorders: Review of the literature and practice guide. Toronto, ON: Children's Mental Health Ontario. Retrieved from https://perry.lab.yorku.ca/members/dr-adrienne-perry

Peters, L. C., & Thompson, R. H. (2018). How teaching perspective taking to individuals with autism spectrum disorders affects social skills: Findings from research and suggestions for practitioners. *Behavior Analysis in Practice, 11*(4), 467–478.

Peverill, S., Smith, I. M., Duku, E., Szatmari, P., Mirenda, P., Villiancourt, T., … & Unger, W. J. (2019). Developmental trajectories of feeding problems in children with autism spectrum disorders. *Journal of Pediatric Psychology, 44*(8), 988–998. doi:10.1093/jpepsy/jsz033

Pfeiffer, B., May-Benson, T. A., & Bodison, S. C. (2018). State of science of sensory integration research with children and youth. *The American Journal of Occupational Therapy, 72*(1), 7201170010p1–7201170010p4. doi:10.5014/ajot.2018.721003

Philpott, D., Young, G., Maich, K., Penney, S., & Butler, E. (2019). *The preemptive nature of quality early child education on special educational needs in children*. St. John's, NL: Memorial University of Newfoundland. Retrieved from https://research.library.mun.ca/13571/1/The%20Preemptive%20Nature%20of%20ECE%2C%20Feb%2012.pdf

Poirier, N., Vallée-Ouimet, J., Stip, E., Caron, J., & Pelletier, J. (2015). Le parcours des parents et des enfants présentant un TSA. *Santé mentale au Québec, 40*, 203–226. doi:10.7202/1032391ar

Pollark, N. (2009). Sensory integration: A review of the current state of the evidence. *Occupational Therapy Now, 11*(5), 6–10. Retrieved from https://autismodiario.org/wp-content/uploads/2011/05/Sensory-Integration.pdf

Porter, J. (2016, March 14). First Nations students get 30 per cent less funding than other children, economist says. *CBC News*. Retrieved September 13, 2018, from www.cbc.ca/news/canada/thunder-bay/first-nations-education-funding-gap-1.3487822

Poverty Free Ontario. (2015). Social assistance recipients. Retrieved from www.povertyfreeontario.ca/poverty-in-ontario/status-of-poverty-in-ontario/#_ftn1

Preece, D., & Trajkovski, V. (2017). Parent education in autism spectrum disorder: A review of the literature. *Croatian Review of Rehabilitation Research, 53*(1), 128–138. Retrieved from http://go.galegroup.com.libaccess.senecacollege.ca

Preschl, B., Maercker, A., & Wagner, B. (2011). The working alliance in a randomized controlled trial comparing online with face-to-face cognitive-behavioral therapy for depression. *BMC Psychiatry, 11*, 189. doi:10.1186/1471-244X-11-189

Province of British Columbia. (2019). Intellectual disabilities. Retrieved from https://www2.gov.bc.ca/gov/content/health/managing-your-health/healthy-women-children/child-behaviour-development/special-needs/intellectual-disabilities

Province of Manitoba. (n.d.). Developmental centre. Retrieved from https://www.gov.mb.ca/fs/mdc/index.html

Public Broadcasting System (PBS). (2013). "Neurotypical" in context: Neurodiversity. Retrieved from www.pbs.org

Public Health Agency of Canada. (2018a). The autism spectrum disorder strategic fund. Retrieved from https://www.canada.ca/en/public-health/services/funding-opportunities/autism-spectrum-disorder-strategic-fund.html

Public Health Agency of Canada. (2018b). Autism prevalence among children and youth across Canada. Retrieved from https://www.canada.ca/en/public-health/services/publications/diseases-conditions/infographic-autism-spectrum-disorder-children-youth-canada-2018.html

Public Health Agency of Canada. (2018c). *Autism spectrum disorder among children and youth in Canada 2018: A Report of the National Autism Spectrum Disorder Surveillance System*. Retrieved from https://www.canada.ca/en/public-health/services/publications/diseases-conditions/autism-spectrum-disorder-children-youth-canada-2018.html

Public Service Alliance of Canada. (2015). Defining disability: From a medical model to a social model of disability. Retrieved from http://psac-ncr.com/defining-disability-medical-model-social-model-disability

Rabiee, P. (2012). Exploring the relationships between choice and independence: experiences of disabled and older people. *British Journal of Social Work, 43*(5), 872–888.

Raines, T. (2002). *Rising to the light: A portrait of Bruno Bettelheim*. New York, NY: Knopf.

Randell, M., Egberts, K., Samtani, A., Scholten, R., Hooft, L., Livingstone, N., … & Williams, K. (2018). Diagnostic tests for autism spectrum disorder (ASD) in preschool children. *Cochrane Database of Systematic Reviews, 2018, 7*, CD009044. doi:10.1002/14651858.CD009044.pub2

Rapoport, J., Chavez, A., Greenstein, D., Addington, A., & Gogtay, N. (2009). Autism spectrum disorder and childhood-onset schizophrenia: Clinical and biological contributions to a relation revisited. *Journal of the American Academy of Child & Adolescent Psychiatry, 48*(1), 10–18.

Rapp, J. T., & Gunby, K. (2016). Task interspersal for individuals with autism and other neurodevelopmental disorders. *Journal of Applied Behavior Analysis, 49*(3), 730–734. doi:10.1002/jaba.319

Rashid, R. (Creator). (2017). *Atypical.* Netflix.

RDSP Plan Institute. (2020). About the Registered Disability Savings Plan. Retrieved from https://www.rdsp.com/about/

Reaven, J. (2011). The treatment of anxiety symptoms in youth with high-functioning autism spectrum disorders: Developmental considerations for parents. *Brain Research, 1380*, 255–263. doi:10.1016/j.brainres.2010.09.075

Reebye, P., & Stalker, A. (2008). *Understanding regulation disorders of sensory processing in children: Management strategies for parents and professionals.* London, UK: Jessica Kingsley Publishers.

Reichow, B., Hume, K., Barton, E. E., & Boyd, B. A. (2018). Early intensive behavioural intervention (EIBI) for young children with autism spectrum disorders (ASD). *Cochrane Database of Systematic Reviews, 5*, CD009260. doi:10.1002/14651858.CD009260.pub3

Remington, B., Hastings, R. P., Kovshoff, H., degli Espinosa, F., Jahr, E., Brown, T., … & Ward, N. (2007). Early intensive behavioral intervention: Outcomes for children with autism and their parents after two years. *American Journal on Mental Retardation, 112*(6), 418–438.

Reynolds, K. E. (2017). *What to do about smearing: A practical guide for parents and caregivers of people with autism, developmental and intellectual disabilities.* London, UK: Jessica Kingsley Publishers.

Rice, W. (2015). Ottawa couple launches new sports initiative for kids with autism. *CBC News.* Retrieved from https://www.cbc.ca/news/canada/ottawa/ottawa-couple-launches-new-sports-initiative-for-kids-with-autism-1.3284294

Robb, A. S. (2010). Managing irritability and aggression in autism spectrum disorders in children and adolescents. *Developmental Disabilities Research Reviews, 16*(3), 258–264. doi:10.1002/ddrr.11

Robertson, A. E., & Simmons, D. R. (2013). The relationships between sensory sensitivity and autistic traits in the general population. *Journal of Autism and Developmental Disorders, 43*, 775–784. doi:1007/s10803-012-1608-7

Robins, D. L., Fein, D., & Barton, M. (2009a). Modified checklist for autism in toddlers, revised (M-CHAT-R). Retrieved from www.m-chat.org

Robins, D. L., Fein, D., & Barton, M. (2009b). Modified checklist for autism in toddlers, revised, with follow-up (M-CHAT-R/F). Retrieved from www.m-chat.org

Robins, D. L., Fein, D., Barton, M., & Green, J. A. (2001). The modified checklist for autism in toddlers (M-CHAT): An initial investigation in the early detection of autism and pervasive developmental disorders. *Journal of Autism and Developmental Disorders, 31*(2), 131–144.

Rockliffe, A. (2016, April 6). Saskatchewan families moving due to lack of autism funding. *Global News.* Retrieved from https://globalnews.ca/news/1251877/lack-of-autism-funding-sending-families-out-of-province/

Rogers, S. J., & Dawson, G. (2010). *Early Start Denver Model for young children with autism.* New York, NY: Guilford.

Rogers, S. J., Dawson, G., & Vismara, L. A. (2012). *An early start for your child with autism.* New York, NY: Guilford.

Rose, E. A., Porcerelli, J. H., & Neale, A. V. (2000). Pica: Common but commonly missed. *Journal of the American Board of Family Practice, 13*(5), 353–358.

Rudy, L. (2019, January 4). What does it mean to be neurotypical? *Verywell Health.* Retrieved from https://www.verywellhealth.com/what-does-it-mean-to-be-neurotypical-260047

Russell, A. J., Jassi, A., Fullana, M. A., Mack, H., Johnston, K., Heyman, I., … & Mataix-Cols, D. (2013). Cognitive behavior therapy for comorbid obsessive-compulsive disorder in high-functioning autism spectrum disorders: A randomized controlled trial. *Depression and Anxiety, 30*(8), 697–708. doi:10.1002/da.22053

Russo, F. (2018, February 21). The costs of camouflaging autism. *Spectrum.* Retrieved from https://www.spectrumnews.org/features/deep-dive/costs-camouflaging-autism/

Rutherford, M. D., Walsh, J. A., & Lee, V. (2015). Brief report: Infants developing ASD show a unique developmental pattern of facial feature scanning. *Journal of Autism and Developmental Disorders, 45*(8), 2618–2623. doi:10. 1007/s10803-015-2396-7

Ryan, T. G. (2009). Inclusive attitudes: A pre-service analysis. *Journal of Research in Special Educational Needs, 9*(3), 180–187. doi:10.1111/j.1471-3802.2009.01134.x

Saaltink, R., & Ouellette-Kuntz, H. (2014). "You did everything": Effort, motherhood, and disability in parents' narratives of their attempts to obtain services. *Journal on Developmental Disabilities, 20*(2), 44–54.

Sanz-Cervera, P., Pastor-Cerezuela, G., González-Sala, F., Tárraga-Minguez, R., & Fernández-Andrés, M. I. (2017). Sensory processing in children with autism spectrum disorder and/or attention deficit hyperactivity disorder in the home and school. *Frontiers in Psychology, 8*, 1772. doi:10.3389/fpsyg.2017.01772

Saskatchewan Education, Special Education Unit. (1999). Teaching students with autism. *Special Education Unit, A Guide for Educators.* Retrieved from http://sitotapsy.com/wp-content/uploads/2016/07/ASD.pdf

Saskatchewan Party. (2016, March 15). Individualized funding for autism spectrum disorder. Retrieved from http://www.saskparty.com/funding_for_autism_spectrum_disorder

Saskatchewan Party. (2019). Individualized funding for ASD. Retrieved from https://www.saskparty.com/funding_for_autism_spectrum_disorder

Scahill, L., Aman, M. G., Lecavalier, L., Halladay, A. K., Bishop, S. L., Bodfish, J. W., … & Dawson, G. (2015). Measuring repetitive behaviors as a treatment endpoint in youth with autism spectrum disorder. *Autism, 19*(1), 38–52. doi:10.1177/1362361313510069

Schaaf, R. C., & Blanche, E. I. (2011). Comparison of behavioral interventions and sensory integration therapy in the treatment of challenging behavior. *Journal of Autism and Developmental Disorders, 41*(10), 1436–1438. doi:10.1007/s10803-011-1303-0

Schaaf, R. C., & Lane, A. E. (2015). Toward a best-practice protocol for assessment of sensory features in ASD. *Journal of Autism and Developmental Disorders, 45*(5), 1380–1395. doi:10.1007/s10803-014-2299-z

Schauder, K. B., & Bennetto, L. (2016). Towards an interdisciplinary understanding of sensory dysfunction in autism spectrum disorder: A integration of the neural and symptom literatures. *Frontiers in Neuroscience, 10.* doi:10.3389/fnins.2016.00268

Schiltz, H. K., McVey, A. J., Dolan, B. K., Willar, K. S., Pleiss, S., Karst, J. S., … & van Hecke, A. V. (2018). Changes in depressive symptoms among adolescents with ASD completing PEERS® social skills intervention. *Journal of Autism and Developmental Disorders, 48*(3), 834–843. doi:10.1007/s10803-017-3396-6

Schoen, S. A., Miller, L. J., Brett-Green, K. E., & Neilson, D. M. (2009). Psychological and behavioural differences in sensory processing: A comparison of children with autism spectrum disorders and sensory modulation disorder. *Frontiers in Neuroscience, 3*(29). doi:10.3389/neuro.07.029.2009

Schoen, S. A., Miller, L. J., & Sullivan, J. C. (2014). Measurement in Sensory Modulation: The Sensory Processing Scale Assessment. *American Journal of Occupational Therapy, 68*(5), 522–530. doi:10.5014/ajot.2014.012377

Schopler, E., Van Bourgondien, M. E., Wellman, G. J., & Love, S. R. (2010). *Childhood Autism Rating Scale* (2nd ed.). Los Angeles, CA: Western Psychological Services.

Semel Institute for Neuroscience and Human Behavior. (2020). UCLA PEERS® clinic. Retrieved from https://www.semel.ucla.edu/peers/research

Sevlever, M., Roth, M. E., & Gillis, J. M. (2013). Sexual abuse and offending in autism spectrum disorders. *Sexuality and Disability, 31*(2), 189–200.

Shea, B., & Mesibov, G. (2009). Age-related issues in the assessment of autism spectrum disorders. In S. Goldstein, J. Naglieri, & S. Ozonoff (Eds.), *Assessment of autism spectrum disorder* (pp. 117–137). New York, NY: Guilford.

Shepherd, C. A., & Waddell, C. (2015). A qualitative study of autism policy in Canada: Seeking consensus on children's services. *Journal of Autism and Developmental Disabilities, 45*(11), 3550–3564. doi:10.1007/s10803-015-2502-x

Shore, D. D. (Producer), & Kim, D. D. (Director). (2017, May). *The good doctor* [Television broadcast]. Vancouver, BC: ABC Studios & Shore Z Productions.

Sider, S. (2019, April 1). Every child matters: What principals need to effectively lead inclusive schools. *The Conversation.* Retrieved from https://theconversation.com/every-child-matters-what-principals-need-to-effectively-lead-inclusive-schools-114249

Siklos, S., & Kerns, K. A. (2007). Assessing the diagnostic experiences of a small sample of parents of children with autism spectrum disorder. *Research in Developmental Disabilities, 28*, 9–22.

Simmons, A. (2006). *The story factor.* New York, NY: Basic Books

Skinner, B. F. (1957). *Verbal behavior.* New York, NY: Appleton-Century-Crofts.

Skuse, D., Warrington, R., Bishop, D., Chowdhury, U., Lau, J., Mandy, W., & Place, M. (2004). The developmental, dimensional and diagnostic interview (3di): A novel computerized assessment for autism spectrum disorders. *Journal of the American Academy of Child and Adolescent Psychiatry, 43*(5), 548–558.

Slocum, T. A., Detrich, R., Wilczynski, S. M., Spencer, T. D., Lewis, T., & Wolfe, K. (2014). The evidence-based practice of applied behavior analysis. *The Behavior Analyst, 37*(1). doi:10.1007/s40614-014-0005-2

Smith, I. M., Flanagan, H. E., Garon, N., & Bryson, S. E. (2015). Effectiveness of community-based early intervention based on pivotal response treatment. *Journal of Autism and Developmental Disorders, 45*(6), 1858–1872. doi:10.100/s10803-014-2345-x

Smith, I. M., Flanagan, H. E., Ungar, W. J., D'Entremont, B., Caron, N., den Otter, J., … & Murray, P. (2019). Comparing the 1-year impact of preschool autism intervention programs in two Canadian provinces. *Autism Research, 12*, 667–681. doi:10.1002/aur.2072

Smith, I. M., & MacDonald, N. E. (2017). Countering evidence denial and the promotion of pseudoscience in autism spectrum disorder. *Autism Research, 10*(8), 1334–1337. doi:10.1002/aur.1810

Smith, T. (2001). Discrete trial training in the treatment of autism. *Focus on Autism and Other Developmental Disorders, 16*(2), 86–92. doi:10.1177/108835760101600204

Smith, T., & Eikeseth, S. (2011). O. Ivar Lovaas: Pioneer of applied behavior analysis and intervention for children with autism. *Journal of Autism and Developmental Disorders, 41*(3), 375–378. doi:10.1007/s10803-010-1162-0

Smith Roley, S., Mailloux, Z., Miller-Kuhaneck, H., & Glennon, T. J. (2007). Understanding Ayres' sensory integration. *Occupational Therapy Practice, 12*(7). Retrieved from https://digitalcommons.sacredheart.edu/cgi/viewcontent.cgi?referer=https://www.google.com/&httpsredir=1&article=1017&context=ot_fac

Snoezelen. (2019). Sensory rooms and therapy explained. Retrieved from https://www.snoezelen.info

SpeciaLink: The National Centre for Child Care Inclusion. (2009). *The SpeciaLink early childhood inclusion quality scale.* Sydney, NS: Author.

Spencer-Cavaliere, N., & Watkinson, E. J. (2010). Inclusion understood from the perspectives of children with disability. *Adapted Physical Activity Quarterly, 27*(4), 275–293.

Spoelstra, M. (2012). Ontario loses a hero: Lindsay Moir (1946–2012). *Autism Matters, 19*(1), 1–40. Retrieved from www.autismontario.com/Client/ASO/AO.nsf/object/AMWinter2012/$file/AM+Winter+2012.pdf

Sportanddev. (n.d.). Eligibility and classification. Retrieved from https://www.sportanddev.org/en/learn-more/disability/technical-considerations/eligibility-and-classification

Starr, E. M., & Foy, J. B. (2012). In parents' voices: The education of children with autism spectrum disorder. *Remedial & Special Education, 33*(4), 207–216. doi:10.1177/0741932510383161

Statistics Canada. (2017). *Aboriginal Peoples in Canada: Key results from the 2016 Census.* Retrieved from http://www.statcan.gc.ca/daily-quotidien/171025/dq171025a-eng.htm

Steinhausen, H. C., & Metzke, C. W. (2004). Differentiating the behavioural profile in autism and mental retardation and testing of a screener. *European Child and Adolescent Psychiatry, 13*(4), 214–220. doi:10.1007/s00787-004-0400-4

Stevens, K. (2018, February 27). PAFN & Miriam Foundation receive federal funding to help Canadians impacted by autism. *Pacific Autism Family Network.* Retrieved from http://pacificautismfamily.com/2018/03/pafn-miriam-foundation-receive-federal-funding-to-help-canadians-impacted-by-autism/

Stoddart, K. P., Burke, L., Muskat, B., Manett, J., Duhaime, S., Accardi, C., … & Bradley, E. (2013). *Diversity in Ontario's youth and adults with ASD: Complex needs in unprepared systems.* Retrieved from http://www.community-networks.ca/wp-content/uploads/2015/11/march-14-2013-final-diversity-in-ontarios-youth-and-adults-with-asds-february-2013.pdf

Strain, P. S., & Shores, R. E. (1977). Social reciprocity: A review of research and educational implications. *Exceptional Children, 43*(8), 526–530.

Straus, J. N. (2013). Autism as culture. In L. J. Davis (Ed.), *The disability studies reader* (pp. 460–484). New York, NY: Routledge.

Strauss, K., Mancini, F., & Fava, L. (2013). Parent inclusion in early intensive behavior interventions for young children with ASD: A synthesis of meta-analyses from 2009 to 2011. *Research in Developmental Disabilities, 34*(9), 2967–2985.

Sullivan, A., & Caterino, L. C. (2008). Addressing the sexuality and sex education of individuals with autism spectrum disorders. *Education and Treatment of Children, 31*(3), 381–394.

Sundberg, M. L. (2008). *Verbal behavior milestones assessment and placement program.* Concord, CA: AVB.

Suppo, J., & Floyd, K. (2012). Parent training for families who have children with autism: A review of the literature. *Rural Special Education Quarterly, 31*(2), 12–26. doi:10.1177/875687051203100203

Sussman, F. (1999). *More than words.* Austin, TX: Pro-Ed.

Szatmari P., Mérette, C., Bryson, S., Thivierge, J., Roy, M. A., Cayer, M., & Maziade, M. (2002). Quantifying dimensions in autism: A factor-analytic study. *Journal of the American Academy of Child & Adolescent Psychiatry, 41*, 467–474. doi:10.1097/00004583-200204000-00020

Taheri, A., & Perry, A. (2012). Exploring the proposed DSM-5 criteria in a clinical sample. *Journal of Autism and Developmental Disorders, 42*(9), 1810–1817. doi:10.1007/s10803-012-1599-4

Taheri, A., Perry, A., & Factor, D. C. (2014). Brief report: A further examination of the DSM-5 autism spectrum disorder criteria in practice. *Journal on Developmental Disabilities, 20*(1), 116–121.

Tanaka, J. W., & Sung, A. (2016). The eye avoidance hypothesis of autism face processing. *Journal of Autism and Developmental Disorders, 46*(5), 1538–1552. doi:10.1007/s10803-013-1976-7

Tankersley, M., Harjusola-Webb, S., & Landrum, T. J. (2008). Using single-subject research to establish the evidence base of special education. *Intervention in School and Clinic, 44*(2). doi:10.1177/1053451208321600

Tanner, A., & Andreone, B. E. (2015). Using graduated exposure and differential reinforcement to increase food repertoire in a child with autism. *Behavior Analysis in Practice, 8*(2), 233–240. doi:10.1007/s40617-015-0077-9

Tarnai, B., & Wolfe, P. S. (2008). Social stories for sexuality education for persons with autism/pervasive developmental disorder. *Sexuality and Disability, 26*(1), 29–36.

Ten Eycke, K. D., & Müller, U. (2015). Brief report: New evidence for a social-specific imagination deficit in children with autism spectrum disorder. *Journal of Autism and Developmental Disorders, 45*(1), 213–220. doi:10.1007/s10803-014-2206-7

Thames Valley Children's Centre (TVCC). (2008a). *Paving the way for success: A supplementary guide for educators of students with autism spectrum disorder.* London, ON: Author.

Thames Valley Children's Centre (TVCC). (2008b). *PEER Pals.* London, ON: Author.

Thames Valley Children's Centre, Fanshawe College, All Kids Belong. (2012). *Stay, play, & talk.* London, ON: Author.

The Atkinson Centre for Society and Child Development. (2017). *Early childhood education report.* Retrieved from http://ecereport.ca/media/uploads/2017-report-pdfs/ece-report2017-en-feb6.pdf

The Incredible 5-point Scale. (2015). Home Page. Retrieved from www.5pointscale.com

Thilinie, R., & Tamara, P. (2010). Pharmacotherapeutics of Tourette syndrome and stereotypies in autism. *Seminars in Pediatric Neurology, 17,* 254–260. doi:10.1016/j.spen.2010.10.008

Thompson, T. (2013). Autism research and services for young children: History, progress and challenges. *Journal of Applied Research in Intellectual Disabilities, 26*(2), 81–107. doi:10.1111/jar.12021

TIME. (2010). The 2010 TIME 100. Retrieved from http://content.time.com/time/specials/packages/completelist/0,29569,1984685,00.html

Timmons, V., & Breitenbach, M. (2004). *Inclusionary practices for children with autism spectrum disorders.* Collaborative report from the University of Prince Edward Island and the Department of Education of Prince Edward Island, PEI.

Tomchek, S. D., & Dunn, W. (2007). Sensory processing in children with and without autism: A comparative study using the short sensory profile. *The American Journal of Occupational Therapy, 61*(2), 190–200.

Tomlinson, C. A. (1999). Mapping a route toward differentiated instruction. *Educational Leadership, 57*(1), 12–16.

Tomlinson, C. A. (2000). Differentiated instruction: Can it work? *Education Digest*, (5), 25.

Tonacci, A., Billeci, L., Tartarisco, G., Ruta, L., Muratori, F., Pioppia, G., & Gangemi, S. (2017). Olfaction in autism spectrum disorders: A systematic review. *Child Neuropsychology, 23*(1), 1–25. doi:10.1080/09297049.2015.1081678

Totsika, V., Hastings, R. P., Emerson, E., Berridge, D. M., & Lancaster, G. A. (2011). Behavior problems at 5 years of age and maternal mental health in autism and intellectual disability. *Journal of Abnormal Child Psychology, 39*(8), 1137–1147. doi:10.1007/s10802-011-9534-2

Tsai, L., & Ghaziuddin, M. (2013). DSM-5 ASD moves forward into the past. *Journal of Autism and Developmental Disorders, 44*(2), 321–330.

Tuzikow, J. (n.d.). Responding to inappropriate behaviors displayed by adolescents with autism spectrum disorders. Office for People with Developmental Disabilities. Retrieved from https://opwdd.ny.gov/opwdd_community_connections/autism_platform/parents_corner/responding_to_inappropriate_sexual_behaviors

Tyldum, M. (Director). (2014). *The imitation game* [Motion picture]. New York, NY: The Weinstein Company.

UCLA Jane & Terry Semel Institute for Neuroscience & Human Behavior. (2019). *Naturalistic developmental behavioral interventions (NDBI).* Retrieved from https://www.semel.ucla.edu/cap/service/naturalistic-developmental-behavioral-interventions-ndbi

Ulrich, M. E., & Bauer, A. E. (2003). Levels of awareness: A closer look at communication between parents and professionals. *TEACHING Exceptional Children, 35*(6), 20–23.

Underwood, K. (2013). Everyone is welcome: Inclusive early childhood education and care. Retrieved from www.edu.gov.on.ca/childcare/Underwood.pdf

United Nations. (2019). World Autism Day. Retrieved from https://www.un.org/en/events/autismday/

University of Calgary School of Public Policy. (2016). Laying the foundation for policy: Measuring local prevalence for autism spectrum disorder. *SSP Communiques, 8*(5). Retrieved from https://www.policyschool.ca/wp-content/uploads/2016/08/Prevalence-Brief.pdf

University of Calgary, Werklund School of Education. (n.d.). Educating children with an autism spectrum disorder. Retrieved March 2019 from https://werklund.ucalgary.ca/educating-children-with-an-autism-spectrum-disorder

Valderas, J. M., Starfield, B., Sibbald, B., Salisbury, C., & Roland, M. (2009). Defining comorbidity: Implications for understanding health and health services. *The Annals of Family Medicine, 7*(4), 357–363.

Veatch, O. J., Veenstra-VanderWeele, J., Potter, M., Pericak-Vance, M. A., & Haines, J. L. (2014). Genetically meaningful phenotypic subgroups in autism spectrum disorder. *Genes, Brain & Behavior, 13*(3), 276–285. doi:10.1111/gbb.12117

Vismara, L. A., McCormick, C. E. B., & Wagner, A. L. (2016). Telehealth parent training in the Early Start Denver Model: Results from a randomized controlled study. *Focus on Autism and Other Developmental Disabilities, 33*(2), 67–79. doi:10.1177/1099357616651064

Volden, J., Duku, E., Shepherd, C., Georgiades, S., Bennett, T., Di Rezze, B., … & Pathways in ASD Study Team. (2015). Service utilization in a sample of preschool children with autism spectrum disorder: A Canadian snapshot. *Paediatrics & Child Health, 20*(8), e43–e47. doi:10.1093/pch/20.8.e43

Waddington, H., van der Meer, L., & Sigafoos, J. (2016). Effectiveness of the early start Denver model: A systematic review. *Review Journal of Autism and Developmental Disorders, 3*(2), 93–106. doi:10.1007/s40489-015-0068-3

Wallace, M. D. (2007). A comprehensive analysis of mand training. *The Journal of Speech and Language Pathology—Applied Behaviour Analysis, 2*(3), 278–286. doi:10.1037/h0100225

Watkins, S. (n.d.). The causes of autism: A historical perspective. Wordpress. Retrieved from bdkmsw.umwblogs.org

Watson, S., Hayes, S., Radford-Paz, E., & Coons, K. (2013). "I'm hoping, I'm hoping …": Thoughts about the future from families of children with autism or fetal alcohol spectrum disorder in Ontario. *Journal on Developmental Disabilities, 19*(3), 76–93.

Watts, S. J., Rodgers, S., & Riby, D. (2016). A systematic review of the evidence for hyposensitivity in ASD. *Journal of Autism and Developmental Disorders*, 3, 286–301. doi:10.1007/s40489-016-0084-y

Waugh, C., & Peskin, J. (2015). Improving social skills of children with HFASD: An intervention study. *Journal of Autism and Developmental Disorders, 45*(9), 2961–2980. doi:10.1007/s10803-015-2459-9

Weiss, J., Cappadocia, C. M., MacMullin, J. A., Viecili, M., & Lunsky, Y. (2012). The impact of child problem behaviours of children with ASD on parent mental health: The mediating role of acceptance and empowerment. *Autism, 16*(3), 261–274.

Weiss, J., & Lunsky, Y. (2011). The brief family distress scale: A measure of crisis in caregivers of individuals with autism spectrum disorder. *Journal of Child & Family Studies, 20*(4), 521–528. doi:10.1007/s10826-010-9419-y

Weiss, J., White, S., & Spoelstra, M. (2008). *PPM-140 parent survey: An analysis on the implementation of PPM-140.* Toronto, ON: Autism Ontario.

Weiss, J. A., Thomson, K., Burnham Riosa, P., Albaum, C., Chan, V., Maughan, A., … & Black, K. (2018). A randomized waitlist-controlled trial of cognitive behavior therapy to improve emotion regulation in children with autism. *Journal of Child Psychology and Psychiatry and Allied Disciplines, 59*(11), 1180–1191. doi:10.1111/jcpp.12915

Weiss, J. A., Whelan, M., McMorris, C., Carroll, C., & Canadian Autism Spectrum Disorders Alliance (CASDA). (2014). Autism in Canada: National needs assessment survey for families, individuals with ASD and professionals. Retrieved from https://www.casda.ca/wp-content/uploads/2019/02/NationalNeedsAssessmentSurvey_July-30.pdf

Weiss, M. J. (2005). Comprehensive ABA programs: Integrating and evaluating the implementation of varied instructional approaches. *The Behaviour Analyst Today, 6*(4), 249–256. doi:10.1037/h0100077

Werner, S., & Stawski, M. (2012). Mental health: Knowledge, attitudes and training of professionals on dual diagnosis of intellectual disability and psychiatric disorder. *Journal of Intellectual Disability Research, 56*(3), 291–304.

Whalon, K. J., Conroy, M. A., Martinez, J. R., & Werch, B. L. (2015). School-based peer-related social competence interventions for children with autism spectrum disorder: A meta-analysis and descriptive review of single case research design studies. *Journal of Autism and Developmental Disorders, 45*(6), 1513–1531.

White, S. E., & Weiss, J. E. (2010). Brief report: Services for adults and adolescents with ASD in Ontario—Parent and professional perspectives. *Journal on Developmental Disabilities, 16*(1), 34–39.

Whittaker, J. K. (1976). Causes of childhood disorders: New findings. *Social Work, 21*(2), 91–96.

Wilczynski, S. M., Menousek, K., Hunter, M., & Mudgal, D. (2007). Individualized education programs for youth with autism spectrum disorders. *Psychology in the Schools, 44*(7), 653–666.

Wing, L. (1972). *Autistic children: A guide for parents and professionals.* Don Mills, ON: Musson Book Company.

Wing, L. (1981). Asperger's syndrome: A clinical account. *Psychological Medicine, 11*, 115–129.

Wing, L. (1993). The definition and prevalence of autism: A review. *European Child and Adolescent Psychiatry, 2*(1), 61. doi:10.1007/BF02098832

Wing, L., & Gould, J. (1979). Severe impairments of social interaction and associated abnormalities in children: Epidemiology and classification. *Journal of Autism and Developmental Disorders, 9*(1), 11–29.

Wing, L., Leekam, S., Libby, S., Gould, J., & Larcombe, M. (2002). The Diagnostic Interview for Social and Communication Disorders: Background, inter-rater reliability and clinical use. *Journal of Child Psychology and Psychiatry, 43*, 307–325.

Wing, L., & Potter, D. (2002). The epidemiology of autistic spectrum disorders: Is the prevalence rising? *Mental Retardation and Developmental Disabilities Research Reviews, 8*(3), 151–161.

Wong, C., Odom, S. L., Hume, K., Cox, A. W., Fettig, A., Kucharczyk, S., … & Schultz, T. R. (2014). *Evidence-based practices for children, youth, and young adults with autism spectrum disorder.* Chapel Hill, NC: University of North Carolina, Frank Porter Graham Child Development Institute, Autism Evidence-Based Practice Review Group.

Wood, J. J., Drahota, A., Sze, K., Har, K., Chiu, A., & Langer, D. A. (2009). Cognitive behavioral therapy for anxiety in children with autism spectrum disorders: A randomized, controlled trial. *Journal of Child Psychology and Psychiatry and Allied Disciplines, 50*(3), 224–234. doi:10.1111/j.1469-7610.2008.01948.x

Woods, A. G., Mahdavi, E., & Ryan, J. P. (2013). Treating clients with Asperger's syndrome and autism. *Child and Adolescent Psychiatry and Mental Health,* 7(1), 1–8. doi:10.1186/1753-2000-7-32

World Health Organization (WHO). (2006). Defining sexual health. Retrieved from https://www.who.int/reproductivehealth/topics/sexual_health/sh_definitions/en

World Health Organization (WHO). (2018). International classification of diseases (11th ed.). Retrieved from https://icd.who.int/browse11/lm/en#/http://id.who.int/icd/entity/1207960454

World Health Organization (WHO). (2019). Sexual health. Retrieved from https://www.who.int/topics/sexual_health/en/

Yanofsky, J. (2018). Does my child have autism? 10 red flags to watch out for. *Today's Parent*. Retrieved from https://www.todaysparent.com/family/special-needs/does-my-child-have-autism-10-red-flags-to-watch-out-for/

York Region. (2019). Red flags 2019: A quick reference guide for early years and health care professionals in York Region. Retrieved from https://www.york.ca/wps/wcm/connect/yorkpublic/054ca0a9-0027-46a3-b817-452890b3038b/red+flags+guide_web.pdf?MOD=AJPERES

Yukon Education. (2015). *Student support services: Parent handbook*. Retrieved from http://www.education.gov.yk.ca/pdf/schools/Parent_Handbook_2015.pdf

Zagona, A. L., & Mastergeorge, A. M. (2018). An empirical review of peer-mediated interventions: Implications for young children with autism spectrum disorders. *Focus on Autism and Other Developmental Disorders, 33*(3), 131–141. doi:10.1177/1088351616671295

Zaidman-Zait, A., Mirenda, P., Duku, E., Szatmari, P., Georgiades, S., Volden, J., … & the Pathways in ASD Study Team. (2014). Examination of bidirectional relationships between parent stress and two types of problem behavior in children with autism spectrum disorder. *Journal of Autism and Developmental Disabilities, 44*(8), 1908–1917. doi:10.1007/s10803-014-2064-3

Zlomislic, D. (2016, January 12). York university student wins mental-health fight. *The Toronto Star*. Retrieved from https://www.thestar.com/news/gta/2016/01/12/york-university-student-wins-mental-health-fight.html

Zwaigenbaum, L., & Penner, M. (2018). Autism spectrum disorder: Advances in diagnosis and evaluation. *British Medical Journal, 361*, k1674. doi:10.1136/bmj.k1674

Copyright Acknowledgements

CHAPTER 1

Figure 1.3: Thompson, T. (2013). Autism research and services for young children: History, progress and challenges. *Journal of Applied Research in Intellectual Disabilities, 26*, 81–107. Used by permission of John Wiley & Sons.

Figures 1.5 and 1.6: Thames Valley Children's Centre (TVCC). (2008). *Paving the way for success: A supplementary guide for educators of students with autism spectrum disorder.* London, ON: Author. Used by permission of the Thames Valley Children's Centre.

Figure 1.7: Lord, C., & Jones, R. M. (2012). Re-thinking the classification of autism spectrum disorders. *Journal of Child Psychology and Psychiatry, 53*(5), 490–509. Used by permission of John Wiley & Sons.

Pages 20–23: Reprinted with permission from the *Diagnostic and Statistical Manual of Mental Disorders, Fifth Edition*, (Copyright ©2013). American Psychiatric Association. All Rights Reserved.

Figure 1.8: Grzadzinski, R., Huerta, M., & Lord, C. (2013). DSM-5 and autism spectrum disorders (ASDs): An opportunity for identifying ASD subtypes. *Molecular Autism, 4*(1), 1–6. doi:10.1186/2040-2392-4-12. Published by BioMed Central. Used by permission of the authors.

Pages 43–46: © All rights reserved. *2018 Report of the National Autism Spectrum Disorder (ASD) Surveillance System in Canada among Children and Youth 5–17 years of age.* Public Health Agency of Canada. Reproduced with permission from the Minister of Health, 2020.

Figures 1.13, 1.14, and 1.15: © All rights reserved. *Autism Spectrum Disorder among Children and Youth in Canada – 2018.* Public Health Agency of Canada. Reproduced with permission from the Minister of Health, 2020.

CHAPTER 4

Figure 4.2: Iwata, B. A., DeLeon, I. G., & Roscoe, E. M. (2013). Reliability and validity of the Functional Analysis Screening Tool. *Journal of Applied Behavior Analysis, 46*, 271–284. (reproduced with permission by author)

CHAPTER 5

Figure 5.1: Selected items from *Sensory Integration and the Child* copyright © 2005 by Western Psychological Services. Reprinted for restricted use by Canadian Scholars, by permission of the publisher, WPS. Not to be reprinted in whole or in part for any other purpose without the prior, written authorization of WPS (rights@wpspublish.com).

Figure 5.3: Dunn, W. (1997). The impact of sensory processing abilities on the daily lives of young children and their families: A conceptual model. Philadelphia, PA: Wolters Kluwer Health, Inc.

CHAPTER 8

Figure 8.1: Reprinted from *The Value of Caregiver Time: Costs of Support and Care for Individuals Living with Autism Spectrum Disorder* (p. 21), by C. Dudley and H. Emery, 2014, School of Public Policy Publications. Copyright 2014 by the School of Public Policy. Reprinted with permission.

Figure 8.3: Reprinted from *The Value of Caregiver Time: Costs of Support and Care for Individuals Living with Autism Spectrum Disorder* (pp. 33–36), by C. Dudley and H. Emery, 2014, School of Public Policy Publications. Copyright 2014 by the School of Public Policy. Reprinted with permission.

Index